GENDER AND ELECTIONS, THIRD EDITION

The third edition of *Gender and Elections* offers a systematic, lively, and multi-faceted account of the role of gender in the electoral process through the 2012 elections. This timely yet enduring volume strikes a balance between highlighting the most important developments for women as voters and candidates in the 2012 elections and providing a more long-term, in-depth analysis of the ways that gender has helped shape the contours and outcomes of electoral politics in the United States. Individual chapters demonstrate the importance of gender in understanding and interpreting presidential elections, presidential and vice presidential candidacies, voter participation and turnout, voting choices, congressional elections, the political involvement of Latinas, the participation of African-American women, the support of political parties and women's organizations, candidate communications with voters, and state elections. Without question, *Gender and Elections* is the most comprehensive, reliable, and trustworthy resource on the role of gender in U.S. electoral politics.

Susan J. Carroll is a professor of political science and women's and gender studies at Rutgers University and Senior Scholar at the Center for American Women and Politics of the Eagleton Institute of Politics. She is the author of *Women as Candidates in American Politics* (second edition, 1994), coauthor (with Kira Sanbonmatsu) of *More Women Can Run: Gender and Pathways to the State Legislatures* (2013), and editor of *The Impact of Women in Public Office* (2001) and *Women and American Politics: New Questions, New Directions* (2003).

Richard L. Fox is a professor of political science at Loyola Marymount University. His research examines how gender affects voting behavior, state executive elections, congressional elections, and political ambition. He is the author of *Gender Dynamics in Congressional Elections* (1997) and coauthor of *Tabloid Justice: The Criminal Justice System in the Age of Media Frenzy* (second edition, 2007). He is also a coauthor, with Jennifer Lawless, of *It Still Takes a Candidate: Why Women Don't Run for Office* (second edition, 2010).

Gender and Elections

SHAPING THE FUTURE OF AMERICAN POLITICS

Third Edition

Edited by

Susan J. Carroll
Rutgers University

Richard L. Fox
Loyola Marymount University

CAMBRIDGE
UNIVERSITY PRESS

32 Avenue of the Americas, New York, NY 10013–2473, USA

Cambridge University Press is part of the University of Cambridge.

It furthers the University's mission by disseminating knowledge in the pursuit of education, learning, and research at the highest international levels of excellence.

www.cambridge.org
Information on this title: www.cambridge.org/9781107611610

First published 2014

Printed in the United States of America

A catalog record for this publication is available from the British Library.

Library of Congress Cataloging in Publication data
Gender and elections : shaping the future of American politics / edited by Susan J. Carroll and Richard L. Fox. – 3rd edition.
  pages cm
Includes bibliographical references and index.
ISBN 978-1-107-02604-9 (hardback)
ISBN 978-1-107-61161-0 (paperback)
1. Women – Political activity – United States. 2. Elections – United States. 3. Voting – United States. 4. Women political candidates – United States. 5. Sex role – Political aspects – United States. I. Carroll, Susan J., 1950– author, editor of compilation. II. Fox, Richard Logan, author, editor of compilation.
HQ1236.5.U6G444 2014
320.082–dc23   2013030372

ISBN 978-1-107-02604-9 Hardback
ISBN 978-1-107-61161-0 Paperback

Contents

List of Figures, Text Boxes, and Photos

Figures

Text Boxes

Photos

List of Tables

Contributors

Barbara Burrell is a professor emerita in the political science department at Northern Illinois University and former director of graduate studies for the political science department. She is the author of *A Woman's Place Is in the House: Campaigning for Congress in the Feminist Era* (1994) and *Public Opinion, the First Ladyship and Hillary Rodham Clinton* (2001). Burrell also has published numerous articles on how gender interacts with the electoral process.

Dianne Bystrom is the director of the Carrie Chapman Catt Center for Women and Politics at Iowa State University. A frequent commentator on political and women's issues for state and national media, she is a contributor to eighteen books – most recently *Women & Executive Office: Pathways and Performance* (2013); *Communication in the 2008 U.S. Election: Digital Natives Elect a President* (2011); *Cracking the Highest Glass Ceiling: A Global Comparison of Women's Campaigns for Executive Office* (2010); and *Legislative Women: Getting Elected, Getting Ahead* (2008) – and has written several journal articles. Her current research focuses on the styles and strategies that female and male political candidates use in their television advertising and their news coverage by the media.

Susan J. Carroll is a professor of political science and women's and gender studies at Rutgers University and senior scholar at the Center for American Women and Politics (CAWP) of the Eagleton Institute of Politics. She is the author of *Women as Candidates in American Politics* (second edition, 1994) and editor of *The Impact of Women in Public Office* (2001) and *Women and American Politics: New Questions, New Directions* (2003). Carroll has published numerous journal articles and book chapters focusing on women candidates, voters, elected officials, and political appointees.

Kelly Dittmar is assistant research professor at the CAWP at Rutgers University, where she manages national research projects; helps develop and implement CAWP's research agenda; and contributes to CAWP reports, publications, and analyses. Her research focuses on the role of gender within political institutions, the gender dynamics of U.S. campaigns and elections, and the influence of political professionals in strategy development and execution. She has published book chapters on gender stereotypes in campaigns and elections for executive candidates and their spouses.

Georgia Duerst-Lahti is a professor of political science and chair of the health and society program at Beloit College. She regularly provides analysis and commentary for state and national news coverage of U.S. politics, especially on gender and elections. She also works as a senior specialist on women's leadership and entrepreneurship for USAID projects. Her most recent coauthored book, *Creating Gender: The Sexual Politics of Welfare Policy* (2007), develops a theory of gender ideology in policy making. Her articles have appeared in journals such as *PS*, *Sex Roles*, and *Public Administration Review*. She currently researches fair trade and sustainability as a means to women's empowerment.

Richard L. Fox is a professor of political science at Loyola Marymount University in Los Angeles. He is the author of *Gender Dynamics in Congressional Elections* (1997) and coauthor of *Tabloid Justice: The Criminal Justice System in the Age of Media Frenzy* (second edition, 2007). More recently, he coauthored, with Jennifer Lawless, *It Takes a Candidate: Why Women Don't Run for Office* (second edition, 2001). His articles have appeared in *Journal of Politics*, *American Journal of Political Science*, *Political Psychology*, *PS*, *Women & Politics*, *Political Research Quarterly*, and *Public Administration Review*. His research focuses on the manner in which gender affects voting behavior, state executive elections, congressional elections, and political ambition.

Susan A. MacManus is Distinguished University Professor of Public Administration and Political Science in the Department of Government and International Affairs at the University of South Florida. She is the author of *Young v. Old: Generational Combat in the 21st Century* (1996) and *Targeting Senior Voters: Campaign Outreach to Elders and Others with Special Needs* (2000); editor of *Reapportionment and Representation in Florida: A Historical Collection* (1991) and *Mapping Florida's Political Landscape: The Changing Art and Politics of Reapportionment and Redistricting* (2002); coeditor, with

Kevin Hill and Dario Moreno, of *Florida's Politics: Ten Media Markets, One Powerful State* (2004); coauthor, with Aubrey Jewett, Thomas R. Dye, and David J. Bonanza, of *Politics in Florida* (third edition, 2011) and, with Thomas R. Dye, of *Politics in States and Communities* (fifteenth edition, 2014). Her research on women candidates, officeholders, activists, and voters has been published in *Social Science Quarterly, Public Administration Review, Journal of Politics, Women & Politics, Urban Affairs Quarterly, National Civic Review*, and *The Municipal Year Book*, among others. MacManus has been the political analyst for WFLA-TV (Tampa's NBC affiliate) since 1992.

Anna Sampaio is an associate professor of ethnic studies and political science at Santa Clara University, where she teaches and researches in the areas of Latina/o politics, race and gender politics, intersectionality, and immigration. She is a coeditor of *Transnational Latino/a Communities: Politics, Processes, and Cultures* (2002). Sampaio has published numerous journal articles and book chapters on Latina/o politics, immigration, and gender politics. Her current research examines the history of Latina political participation in the United States.

Kira Sanbonmatsu is professor of political science and senior scholar at the CAWP at Rutgers University. She is the coauthor, with Susan J. Carroll, of *More Women Can Run: Gender and Pathways to the State Legislatures* (2013). She is also the author of *Where Women Run: Gender and Party in the American States* (2006) and *Democrats, Republicans, and the Politics of Women's Place* (2002). Sanbonmatsu studies gender, race, parties, elections, public opinion, and state politics. Her research has appeared in journals such as *Politics & Gender, American Politics Research*, and *Journal of Politics*.

Wendy G. Smooth is an associate professor in the departments of women's gender and sexuality studies and political science at The Ohio State University and a senior faculty affiliate with the Kirwan Institute for the Study of Race and Ethnicity. Before joining the faculty at Ohio State, she served as an assistant professor of political science at the University of Nebraska–Lincoln. Her research focuses on the impact of gender and race in state legislatures. Smooth's research on women of color in U.S. politics has appeared in journals such as *Politics & Gender* and *Journal of Women, Politics and Policy*. Currently, she is completing a manuscript titled *Perceptions of Power and Influence: The Impact of Race and Gender in American State Legislatures*. Smooth is president of the National Conference of Black Political Scientists.

Acknowledgments

This volume had its origins in a series of three roundtable panels at professional meetings in 2002 and 2003 focusing on how women fared in the 2002 elections. Most of the contributors to this book were participants at those roundtables. As we gathered at these meetings, we began to talk among ourselves about a major frustration we faced in teaching courses on women and politics, campaigns and elections, and U.S. politics. We all had difficulty finding suitable, up-to-date materials on women candidates, the gender gap, and other facets of women's involvement in elections, and certainly none of us had been able to find a text focused specifically on gender and elections that we could use. We felt the literature was in great need of a recurring and reliable source that would first be published immediately following a presidential election and then updated every four years so that it remained current.

At some point in our discussions we all looked at one another and collectively asked: As the academic experts in this field, aren't we the ones to take on this project? Why don't we produce a volume suitable for classroom use that would also be a resource for scholars, journalists, and practitioners? In that moment *Gender and Elections* was born. We are enormously grateful to Barbara Burrell for organizing the first of our roundtable panels and thus identifying and pulling together the initial core of contributors to this volume.

We produced the first volume of *Gender and Elections* in the immediate aftermath of the 2004 presidential election, and an updated and expanded second edition came out following the elections of 2008. Gratified by the positive response, we are pleased to provide this third edition of the volume, which updates it to include information on the 2012 elections. We hope to continue to revise and publish new editions following future presidential elections.

The third edition of this book would not have been possible without the assistance of the Center for American Women and Politics (CAWP) at Rutgers University. Debbie Walsh, director of CAWP, has embraced and encouraged this project and been supportive in numerous ways, especially in making CAWP staff available to assist on the project. Gilda Morales, who is in charge of information services at CAWP, continues to be an invaluable source of knowledge about women and politics, and several contributors relied on her expertise as well as the data she has compiled over the years for CAWP.

While everyone at CAWP was helpful, we want to single out Kathy Kleeman, senior communications officer at CAWP, for assistance above and beyond what we ever could have expected. Kathy, for all three editions, has spent numerous hours making each volume much better than it otherwise would have been. She brought an additional set of critical eyes to the reading of every chapter and, as an extremely skilled writer, helped make all of our chapters more readable, accessible, and polished. We are especially indebted to her.

Finally, we would like to thank Cambridge University Press and our editor, Robert Dreesen, for their continued support for this project. We also thank Ed Parsons, our editor on previous editions, for helping us bring the initial idea of this volume to fruition.

Introduction

Gender and Electoral Politics in the Twenty-First Century

With unemployment hovering above 8 percent and a burgeoning national debt, the economy was the central policy issue of the 2012 presidential election. But the battle for female voters, attention to "women's issues," and the question of which party better understood the needs, values, and experiences of women also garnered substantial attention. Never before had women voters received so much media attention in a general election. A Lexis-Nexis search of major news publications found about three times more mentions of "women voters" in the context of the 2012 presidential election than in any prior election.[1] The attention placed on women voters and "women's issues" appeared to have a significant influence on the outcome in 2012, an election that featured one of the largest gender gaps ever in presidential voting. Women favored President Obama by a margin of 55 percent to 44 percent, whereas men favored former Massachusetts governor Mitt Romney by a margin of 52 percent to 45 percent. The 10-point difference in the proportions of women and men voting for Obama represents the second-largest gender gap in U.S. history, just slightly smaller than the 11 point gender gap in voting for Bill Clinton in 1996.[2]

Gender began to play an important role in the 2012 election long before the final votes were counted. In fact, the Democrats started to characterize the Republicans as engaging in a "war on women" months before Mitt Romney became the official GOP nominee. The "war on women"

---

[1] The LexisNexis search of "major publications" examined coverage from September 1 through November 15 for every presidential election since 1988. The search terms were "women voters," "female voters," and "presidential election."

[2] Center for American Women and Politics, "Women's Votes Decisive in 2012 Presidential Race." Press Release. November 7, 2012. http://www.cawp.rutgers.edu/press_room/news/documents/PressRelease_11-07-12-gendergap.pdf. Accessed March 25, 2013.

narrative came about and caught hold because of a series of remarks made by prominent Republicans. A prolonged and hotly contested Republican presidential primary race among several strongly conservative candidates who sometimes expressed extreme views provided initial material for the Democrats to exploit, and a series of comments by Republican U.S. Senate and House candidates fueled the "war on women" narrative throughout the fall of 2012.

Perhaps the candidate who posed the strongest primary challenge to Romney was former U.S. senator Rick Santorum. Some of Santorum's extreme views attracted considerable media attention. Most notably, in an October 2011 interview, Santorum claimed that contraception was "not okay." Rather, he suggested, "It's a license to do things in a sexual realm that is counter to how things are supposed to be."[3] Santorum also criticized "radical feminists" for encouraging women to work outside the home, objected to women serving in combat, and expressed his opposition to abortion in all circumstances – all views that provided Democrats with evidence to support their claim that Republicans were hopelessly out of touch with the needs of women.

Another critical event occurred when talk radio host and conservative icon Rush Limbaugh attacked Georgetown law student Sandra Fluke after she testified at a U.S. House hearing on whether employers should be required to include contraception in their health care coverage. Fluke had argued that employers must cover contraception because its use extends well beyond birth control.[4] Limbaugh's comments, however, veered from the substance of Fluke's testimony. On his national radio broadcast, Limbaugh asked:

> What does it say about the college co-ed Susan [sic] Fluke, who goes before a congressional committee and essentially says that she must be paid for sex? What does that make her? It makes her a slut, right? It makes her a prostitute.[5]

[3] Shane Vander Hart, Interview with Rick Santorum: A Champion for the Family, Manufacturing Jobs. Caffeinatedthoughts.com. http://caffeinatedthoughts.com/2011/10/interview-with-rick-santorum-a-champion-for-the-family-manufacturing-jobs/. Accessed October 19, 2011.

[4] Amanda Peterson Beadle, The Testimony About Birth Control Republicans Did Not Want You To Hear. ThinkProgress.org. http://thinkprogress.org/health/2012/02/16/427417/sandra-fluke-contraception-testimony/. Accessed February 16, 2012.

[5] Jack Mirkinson, Rush Limbaugh: Sandra Fluke, Woman Denied Right To Speak At Contraception Hearing, A "Slut." HuffingtonPost.com. http://www.huffingtonpost.com/2012/02/29/rush-limbaugh-sandra-fluke-slut_n_1311640.html. Accessed February 29, 2012.

Limbaugh was roundly criticized by women's organizations and Democratic politicians for thrusting a mild-mannered student into the national spotlight. And Fluke became a national hero of the left for being singled out by, and then standing up to, Rush Limbaugh. She was even invited to give a prime-time address at the Democratic National Convention.

The final incident more directly involved the eventual Republican nominee for president, Mitt Romney. Throughout the primary season, Romney had worked to shore up the socially conservative base of the Republican Party. He supported the Blunt Amendment, an initiative in the Senate to allow employers to opt out of providing health care coverage for contraception. He favored the Life Amendment, a proposed constitutional amendment that would establish that life begins at conception. Those positions, however, did not receive as much attention as an interview clip that would be played over and over in campaign commercials across the summer and fall. In response to a question about how he would cut the deficit, Romney stated, "Planned Parenthood, we're gonna get rid of that."[6] With this, Romney handed the Democrats a weapon to use against him in the battle for women's votes; he, too, could be portrayed as a candidate with a radical, socially conservative agenda when it came to women's reproductive rights.

As the fall presidential campaign took shape, several Republican congressional candidates helped further the narrative that Republicans were waging a "war on women." The first of these was Missouri Congressman Todd Akin, the Republican challenger to Democratic Senator Claire McCaskill. In a local television interview, Akin expressed his opposition to abortion even in the case of rape, claiming, "If it's a legitimate rape, the female body has ways to try to shut that whole thing down."[7] The video of Akin's comments immediately went viral and was played repeatedly on broadcast media outlets. Although the Republican National Committee and Mitt Romney immediately denounced Akin, he refused to step down as a candidate, and his continuing presence reinforced the "war on women" narrative advanced by Democrats, serving as a constant reminder of a segment of the Republican Party's "extreme anti-woman" positions.

[6] Laura Bassett, Planned Parenthood Makes Largest Single Ad Buy. HuffingtonPost.com. http://www.huffingtonpost.com/2012/09/10/planned-parenthood-ad-campaign_n_1870438.html. Accessed September 10, 2012.
[7] Charles Jaco, Jaco Report: Full Interview with Todd Akin. Fox2now.com. http://fox2now.com/2012/08/19/the-jaco-report-august-19-2012/. Accessed August 20, 2012.

Two months later, another Republican candidate made national head-lines for a similar reason. In a debate between candidates for the U.S. Senate seat in Indiana, Richard Mourdock, the Republican candidate, was asked whether there were circumstances under which he thought abortion should be legal. Like Akin, Mourdock said no, and followed up with this explanation: "I have thought long and hard about this and have concluded that even in the horrible situation of rape, that life is a gift from God and that God intended that to happen."[8] Again, pundits and reporters pounced, and liberal bloggers, reproductive rights groups, and Democrats went to work portraying Mourdock and Republicans as supporting draconian restrictions on women's autonomy and rights. The Mourdock comments, in particular, put Romney in a difficult spot, as he had just filmed a television ad endorsing Mourdock's candidacy.[9]

The Obama campaign took advantage of the extreme statements and missteps by Republicans and made Obama's support of women's rights one of the themes of his campaign. When Romney pledged to defund Planned Parenthood, Obama expressed support, mentioning Planned Parenthood five times in the second debate. The president made clear that he was pro-choice on abortion. He also stressed his support for equal pay, whereas Romney refused to take a position on the Lilly Ledbetter Fair Pay Act that Obama had signed into law.

Although economic issues, especially unemployment, were clearly most important issues in voters' minds as they went to the polls in 2012, voters were also offered a far clearer choice than usual on women's issues. The "Republican war on women" narrative, advanced by Democrats and fueled repeatedly by the statements of visible Republican candidates, seemed to hit its mark, offering an additional incentive beyond economic concerns for many women to turn out and cast their votes for Obama. In the end, Obama won a sizable majority of women voters.

All of these developments in the 2012 election came on the heels of the 2008 race, in which gender played a more direct and prominent role than at any previous time in history, albeit more on the candidate

[8] Lucy Madison, Richard Mourdock: Even pregnancy from rape something "God intended." CBSNews.com. http://www.cbsnews.com/8301-250_162-57538757/richard-mourdock-even-pregnancy-from-rape-something-god-intended/. Accessed October 23, 2012.
[9] Both Akin and Mourdock had significant leads prior to making their controversial comments. Both went on to lose the general election by roughly 16 percent and 6 percent, respectively.

side than among voters. In one election cycle the country experienced perhaps the two highest-profile candidacies of women in U.S. history. Senator Hillary Clinton emerged as the early front-runner for the Democratic nomination for president, ultimately winning twenty-three state primaries and caucuses in the longest and most competitive presidential nomination process in the modern era. After nominee Barack Obama chose Senator Joe Biden rather than Hillary Clinton as his running mate, Republican John McCain surprised the country and chose a woman, Alaska Governor Sarah Palin, as his vice presidential nominee. As the first Republican female candidate for vice president, Palin joined Democrat Geraldine Ferraro, who was Walter Mondale's vice presidential running mate in 1984, as the only women to have ever run on national tickets.

Women have clearly been making great strides in the political life of our nation, and gender has played an increasingly visible and important role in elections. This volume analyzes various aspects of electoral politics, showing how underlying gender dynamics are critical to shaping the contours and outcomes of elections in the United States. No interpretation of U.S. elections can be complete without an understanding of the growing role of women as political actors and the multiple ways that gender enters into and affects contemporary electoral politics.

THE GENDERED NATURE OF ELECTIONS

Elections in the United States are deeply gendered in several ways. Most obviously, men dominate the electoral playing field. Ten of the eleven major candidates who vied for the Democratic and Republican nominations for president in 2012 were men. Similarly, men constituted the vast majority of candidates for governor and Congress in 2012. Most behind-the-scenes campaign strategists and consultants – the pollsters, media experts, fund-raising advisers, and those who develop campaign messages – are also men. Further, most of the best-known network news reporters and anchors charged with telling the story of the 2012 election and previous elections (e.g., Scott Pelley, Brian Williams, Bill O'Reilly, Anderson Cooper) were men. The most visible exception was Diane Sawyer, anchor of ABC *World News Tonight*. A 2013 study from the Women's Media Center found that in the coverage of the 2012 election, male front-page bylines at top newspapers (such as *The New York Times* and *The Wall Street Journal*) outnumbered female bylines three to one, and that in television punditry surrounding the election, more than three-quarters of voices were men.[10] The leading voices in political talk radio, to whom millions of Americans listen every week, are men such as Rush Limbaugh, Sean Hannity, and Michael Savage. And the majority of those contributing the largest sums of money to candidates and parties – perhaps the most essential ingredient in American politics – are men.[11]

Beyond the continued dominance of men in politics, gendered language permeates our political landscape. Politics and elections are most often described in terms of analogies and metaphors drawn from the traditionally masculine domains of war and sports. Contests for office are often referred to by reporters and political pundits as battles requiring the necessary strategy to harm, damage, or even destroy the opponent. The inner sanctums of presidential campaigns where core strategic advisers convene are called war rooms. Candidates attack their opponents. They raise money for their war chests. The most attention in presidential races is focused on critical battleground states. In the post–9/11 election environment, candidates across the country have touted their toughness in wanting to hunt down and kill terrorists.

Along with the language of war, sports language is also prevalent in campaigns and in media coverage of campaigns. Considerable attention is devoted to which candidate is ahead or behind in the race. Similarly, commentators talk about how campaigns are rounding the bend, entering the stretch drive, or heading into the final lap – all horseracing analogies. Although language drawn from the racetrack is common, so, too, is language drawn from boxing, baseball, football, and other sports. Coverage of political debates often focuses on whether one of the candidates has scored a knockout punch. When a candidate becomes aggressive, he or she is described as taking the gloves off. A popular political cable television talk show is named *Hardball with Chris Matthews*. Candidates running for elective office frequently talk about making a comeback, scoring a victory, or being in the early innings of a campaign. When a campaign is in trouble, the candidate may need to throw a Hail Mary pass. An unexpected occurrence is labeled a curveball.

So prevalent is the language of war and sports in our political discourse that even those who wish to increase women's political involvement employ it. For example, to provide more opportunities for women

[10] Women's Media Center, The Status of Women in the U.S. Media 2013. http://www.womensmediacenter.com. Accessed April 16, 2013.
[11] Center for Responsive Politics, Donor Demographics: Gender. 2012. http://www.opensecrets.org/overview/donordemographics.php?cycle=2012&filter=G.   Accessed April 16, 2013.

to enter politics, advocates frequently argue that we need to level the playing field.

As the language used to analyze politics suggests, our expectations about the qualities, appearance, and behavior of candidates are also highly gendered. We want our leaders to be tough, dominant, and assertive – qualities much more associated with masculinity than femininity in American culture. In the post–9/11 environment, a military background, especially with combat experience, is considered desirable for a candidate, but military credentials remain largely the domain of male candidates. A military background is particularly prized for a presidential candidate who, if elected, will become commander in chief. However, because the American public has seen very few women among generals or top military officials, the idea of a female commander in chief remains an oxymoron to many.

Americans even have gendered expectations about how candidates and political leaders should dress. While women politicians are no longer expected to wear only neutral-colored, tailored business suits, jogging attire or blue jeans still are not nearly as acceptable for women as they are for men. Americans have grown accustomed to seeing their male political leaders in casual attire. During the 1990s, we frequently saw pictures of President Bill Clinton jogging in shorts, accompanied by members of the Secret Service. More recently, we saw images of President George W. Bush in jeans and cowboy boots and Barack Obama in swim trunks and basketball sweats. To counter criticisms that the McCain campaign had spent an extravagant amount on designer clothes for her and her family, Sarah Palin made a few campaign appearances in 2008 in her blue jeans – a first for a high-profile woman candidate! However, she was careful to pair her jeans with professional-looking jackets and nice jewelry, thus appearing casually dressed only from the waist down. Although Palin broke new ground in 2008 by wearing jeans in public, she is still the exception to the rule. We have yet to see a picture of House Majority Leader Nancy Pelosi or former Secretary of State Hillary Clinton outfitted in blue jeans and cowboy boots, a swimsuit, or sweatpants.

Finally, elections in the United States are gendered in the strategies that candidates employ in reaching out to the general public. Candidates, both men and women, strategize about how to present themselves to voters of the same and opposite sexes. Pollsters and campaign consultants routinely try to figure out what issues or themes will appeal specifically to women or to men. Increasingly, candidates and their strategists are segmenting voters on the basis of their gender and other demographics.

Specially devised appeals are directed at young women, working-class men, senior women, single women, married women, suburban women, white men, and women of color, to name only some of the targeted groups.

In short, when we look at the people, the language, the expectations, and the strategies of contemporary politics, we see that gender plays an important role in elections in the United States. Even when gender is not explicitly acknowledged, it often operates in the background, affecting our assumptions about who legitimate political actors are and how they should behave.

This is not to say, however, that the role of gender has been constant over time. Rather, we regard gender as malleable, manifesting itself differently at various times and in different contexts in the electoral process. In women's candidacies for elective office, for example, there has been obvious change. As recently as twenty years ago, a woman seeking high-level office almost anywhere in the United States was an anomaly and might have faced overt hostility. Clearly, the electoral environment is more hospitable now. Over the years, slowly but steadily, more and more women have entered the electoral arena at all levels. In 2008, Hillary Clinton was for many months the front-runner to become the Democratic Party's presidential nominee. Sarah Palin was frequently mentioned as a leading contender for the 2012 Republican presidential nomination until she opted not to run. And as we begin to look forward to the 2016 presidential elections, a Quinnipiac poll conducted in early 2013 shows that Hillary Clinton would be the favorite against any of the most prominent Republican contenders.[12]

POLITICAL REPRESENTATION AND SIMPLE JUSTICE: WHY GENDER MATTERS IN ELECTORAL POLITICS

Beyond the reality that gender is an underlying factor that shapes the contours of contemporary elections, it is important to examine and monitor the role of gender in the electoral process because of concerns about justice and the quality of political representation. The United States lags far behind many other nations in the number of women serving in its national legislature. Following the 2012 elections, the United States

[12] Quinnipiac University National Poll, Clinton, Christie Lead the Pack in Early Look at 2016. Press Release. March 7, 2013. http://www.quinnipiac.edu/institutes-centers/polling-institute/national/release-detail?ReleaseID=1861. Accessed April 30, 2013.

ranked ninety-first among countries throughout the world in the proportion of women serving in their national parliaments or legislatures; only 18.1 percent of all members of Congress were women. In early 2013, women served as governors in only five of the fifty states, and only 24.1 percent of all state legislators across the country were women, according to the Center for American Women and Politics.[13]

Despite the relatively low proportion of women in positions of political leadership, women constitute a majority of the voters who elect these leaders. In the 2012 elections, for example, 71.4 million women reported voting, compared with 61.6 million men, according to U.S. Census figures. Thus, 9.8 million more women than men voted in those elections.[14] As a matter of simple justice, something seems fundamentally wrong with a democratic system with a majority of women voters in which women remain dramatically underrepresented among elected political leaders. As Sue Thomas has explained, "A government that is democratically organized cannot be truly legitimate if all its citizens from...both sexes do not have a potential interest in and opportunity for serving their community and nation."[15] The fact that women constitute a majority of the electorate but only a small minority of public officials is a sufficient reason, in and of itself, to pay attention to the underlying gender dynamics of U.S. politics.

Beyond the issue of simple justice, however, are significant concerns over the quality of political representation in the United States. Beginning with a series of studies commissioned by the Center for American Women and Politics in the 1980s, a great deal of empirical research indicates that women and men support and devote attention to somewhat different issues as public officials.[16] At both the national and state levels, male and female legislators have been shown to have different policy priorities and preferences. Studies of members of the U.S. House of Representatives, for example, have found that women are more likely than men to support policies favoring gender equity, day-care programs, flextime in the workplace, legal and accessible abortion, minimum wage increases, and the

---

[13] Center for American Women and Politics. 2013. *Women in Elective Office. Fact Sheet.* New Brunswick, NJ: Center for American Women and Politics.

[14] Center for American Women and Politics. 2013. *Gender Differences in Voter Turnout.* New Brunswick, NJ: Center for American Women and Politics.

[15] Sue Thomas. 1998. Introduction: Women and Elective Office: Past, Present, and Future. In *Women and Elective Office: Past, Present, and Future,* eds. Sue Thomas and Clyde Wilcox. New York: Oxford University Press, 1–14, quote at 1.

[16] Debra Dodson, ed. 1991. *Gender and Policymaking: Studies of Women in Office.* New Brunswick, NJ: Center for American Women and Politics.

extension of the food stamp program.[17] Further, both Democratic and
moderate Republican women in Congress are more likely than men to
use their bill sponsorship and cosponsorship activity to focus on issues of
particular concern to women.[18] Similarly, several studies have found that
women serving in legislatures at the state level give priority to, introduce,
and work on legislation related to women's rights, health care, education,
and the welfare of families and children more often than men do.[19] When
women are not present in sufficient numbers among public officials, their
distinctive perspectives are underrepresented.

In addition to having priorities and voting records that differ from
those of men, women public officials exhibit leadership styles and ways
of conducting business different from those of their male colleagues. A
study of mayors found that women tend to adopt an approach to governing that emphasizes congeniality and cooperation, whereas men tend
to emphasize hierarchy.[20] Research on state legislators has also uncovered significant differences in the manner in which female and male committee chairs conduct themselves at hearings; women are more likely to
act as facilitators, whereas men tend to use their power to control the
direction of the hearings.[21] Other research has found that majorities of
female legislators and somewhat smaller majorities or sizable minorities
of male legislators believe that the increased presence of women has made
a difference in the access that the economically disadvantaged have to
the legislature, the extent to which the legislature is sympathetic to the
concerns of racial and ethnic minorities, and the degree to which legislative business is conducted in public view rather than behind closed
doors.[22] Women officials' propensity to conduct business in a manner

---

[17] For example, Michele Swers. 2002. *The Difference Women Make: The Policy Impact of Women in Congress*. Chicago: University of Chicago Press.

[18] Swers, The Difference Women Make, 2002.

[19] For examples, see Susan J. Carroll. 2001. Representing Women: Women State Legis-
lators as Agents of Policy-Related Change. In *The Impact of Women in Public Office*, ed.
Susan J. Carroll. Bloomington: Indiana University Press, 3–21; Sue Thomas. 1994. *How
Women Legislate*. New York: Oxford University Press; Michael B. Berkman and Robert E.
O'Connor. 1993. Women State Legislators Matter: Female Legislators and State Abortion
Policy. *American Politics Quarterly* 21(1): 102–24; and Lyn Kathlene. 1989. Uncovering the
Political Impacts of Gender: An Exploratory Study. *Western Political Quarterly* 42: 397–421.

[20] Sue Tolleson Rinehart. 2001. Do Women Leaders Make a Difference? Substance, Style,
and Perceptions. In *The Impact of Women in Public Office*, ed. Susan J. Carroll. Bloomington:
Indiana University Press, 149–65.

[21] Lyn Kathlene. 1995. Alternative Views of Crime: Legislative Policy-Making in Gendered
Terms. *Journal of Politics* 57: 696–723.

[22] Impact on the Legislative Process. 2001. In *Women in State Legislatures: Past, Present, Future*.
Fact Sheet Kit. New Brunswick, NJ: Center for American Women and Politics.

that is more cooperative, communicative, inclusive, public, and based on coalition building may well lead to policy outcomes that represent the input of a wider range of people and a greater diversity of perspectives.[23]

The presence of women among elected officials also helps empower other women. Barbara Burrell captures this idea well:

> Women in public office stand as symbols for other women, both enhancing their identification with the system and their ability to have influence within it. This subjective sense of being involved and heard for women, in general, alone makes the election of women to public office important.[24]

Women officials are committed to ensuring that other women follow in their footsteps, and large majorities mentor other women and encourage them to run for office.[25]

Thus, attention to the role of gender in the electoral process, and more specifically to the presence of women among elected officials, is critically important because it has implications for improving the quality of political representation. The election of more women to office would likely lead to more legislation and policies that reflect the greater priority women give to women's rights, the welfare of children and families, health care, and education. Further, the election of more women might lead to policies based on the input of a wider range of people and a greater diversity of perspectives. Finally, electing more women would most likely lead to enhanced political empowerment for other women.

ORGANIZATION OF THE BOOK

This volume utilizes a gendered lens to aid in the interpretation and understanding of contemporary elections in the United States. Contributors examine the ways that gender enters into, helps shape, and affects elections for offices ranging from president to state legislatures across the United States. As several chapters in this volume demonstrate, gender dynamics are important to the conduct and outcomes of presidential elections, even though, to date, a woman has not won a major party's

[23] For example, Cindy Simon Rosenthal. 1998. *How Women Lead*. New York: Oxford University Press.
[24] Barbara Burrell. 1996. *A Woman's Place Is in the House*. Ann Arbor: University of Michigan Press, 151.
[25] Debra L. Dodson and Susan J. Carroll. 1991. *Reshaping the Agenda: Women in State Legislatures*. New Brunswick, NJ: Center for the American Woman and Politics.

nomination for president. Gender also shapes both the ways candidates
appeal to voters and the ways voters respond to candidates. Many women
have run for Congress and for state offices; this volume analyzes the support they have received, the problems they have confronted, and the reasons that there are not more women candidates. Women of color face
additional and distinctive challenges in electoral politics because of the
interaction of their race or ethnicity and gender; this volume also contributes to an understanding of the status of women of color, particularly
African-American women and Latinas, and the electoral circumstances
they encounter.

In Chapter 1, Georgia Duerst-Lahti discusses the gender dynamics of
the presidential election process. She examines the meaning of the phrase
"presidential timber" to demonstrate how masculinity has shaped ideas
of suitable presidential candidates. Duerst-Lahti argues that embedded in
presidential elections and the traditions that accompany them are implicit
assumptions that make presidential elections masculine space, including
the test of executive toughness, a preference for military heroes, and
the sports-related metaphors employed in describing presidential debates.
Americans have carefully sought the right *man* for the job of single great
leader and commander in chief of "the greatest nation on earth." She
demonstrates how this construction of the presidency leads to struggles
over different forms of masculinity and has implications for women as
candidates and citizens.

In Chapter 2, Kelly Dittmar and Susan J. Carroll examine women
presidential and vice presidential candidates. They begin with the history
of the pioneering women who have dared to step forward to seek the
presidency or vice presidency. They then turn to the 2008 campaigns of
Hillary Clinton and Sarah Palin, analyzing the ways that gender stereotypes influenced the strategies they employed, media coverage of their
campaigns, and public reactions to their candidacies. Dittmar and Carroll
also examine Michele Bachmann's 2012 primary campaign in an effort
to assess whether the pioneering candidacies of Clinton and Palin altered
the path in any way for women who follow them as presidential and vice
presidential candidates.

In Chapter 3, Susan A. MacManus focuses on the changing dynamics
of gender and political participation, examining shifts within the female
electorate and the efforts that both presidential campaigns made in 2012
to win women's votes. She chronicles the historic fight for women's suffrage and reviews changes over time in registration and turnout rates.
MacManus describes mobilization efforts aimed at women voters at every

stage of the 2012 presidential campaign, concluding with a brief summary of how and why young voters, particularly women of color, played a
major role in 2012. As this chapter documents, the get-out-the-vote game
has become much more sophisticated over the years, and the women's
vote is increasingly split along generational lines.

In Chapter 4, Susan J. Carroll examines voting differences between
women and men in recent elections. A gender gap in voting, with women
usually more likely than men to support the Democratic candidate, has
been evident in every presidential election since 1980 and in majorities
of races at other levels of office. Carroll traces the history of the gender gap and documents its breadth and persistence. She examines the
complicated question of what happens to the gender gap when one of
the candidates in a race is a woman. Carroll reviews different explanations for gender gaps and identifies what we do and do not know about
why women and men in the aggregate differ in their voting choices.
She also analyzes the different strategies that candidates and campaigns
have employed for dealing with the gender gap and appealing to women
voters.

In Chapter 5, Anna Sampaio focuses on the role of Latinas in U.S.
politics. She assesses the evolving nature of the Latino electorate and
describes the political and voting behavior of Latinas, with particular
attention to their role in the 2012 presidential election. Sampaio analyzes the increasing electoral strength of Latinas as voters, the emergence of a significant Latina/o gender gap, and the roles Latinas played
as candidates, advisors, and surrogates in the 2012 elections. Comparing
and contrasting the role of Latinas/os in the 2008 and 2012 elections,
Sampaio concludes that 2012 was a pivotal year for Latinas/os generally
and Latinas in particular.

In Chapter 6, Wendy G. Smooth traces African-American women's
participation in electoral politics, from Democrat Shirley Chisholm's historic 1972 campaign for president of the United States, to former senator
Carol Moseley Braun's 2004 campaign for the Democratic nomination, to
the lower-profile, third-party presidential bid of former Congresswoman
Cynthia McKinney in 2008. The chapter provides a historical overview
of African-American women's political participation as candidates in U.S.
politics. Following the passage of the Voting Rights Act of 1965, African
Americans made unprecedented strides in electoral politics. Since the passage of that legislation, the number of African-American elected officials
serving at every level of government has soared. Smooth chronicles the
successes of African-American women in politics, the continued barriers

they face as they seek greater inclusion in the U.S. political system, and their activism in overcoming those barriers.

In Chapter 7, Richard L. Fox analyzes the historical evolution of women running for seats in the U.S. Congress. The fundamental question he addresses is why women continue to be so underrepresented in the congressional ranks. Fox examines the experiences of female and male candidates for Congress by comparing fund-raising totals and vote totals. His analysis also explores the subtler ways that gender dynamics manifest in the electoral arena, examining regional variation in the performance of women and men running for Congress, the difficulty of change in light of the incumbency advantage, and gender differences in political ambition to serve in the House or Senate. The chapter concludes with an assessment of the degree to which gender still plays an important role in congressional elections and the prospects for gender parity in the future.

In Chapter 8, Barbara Burrell examines the roles played by political parties and women's organizations in promoting and facilitating the election of women to public office. The conventional view has been that parties primarily have recruited women in "hopeless" races and as sacrificial candidates in contests in which the party had little prospect of winning. Over time, political parties have become somewhat more supportive of women's candidacies, even as the role of parties in campaigns has been challenged by other groups such as women's political action committees. Burrell describes the increasing involvement of women in the party organizations and the evolving focus on electing women to public office as a means to achieve equality. She examines the role of national party organizations and women's groups in increasing the numbers of women running for and elected to Congress, with particular attention to the financial support such organizations have provided for women candidates.

In Chapter 9, Dianne Bystrom examines the impact of the media on candidates' campaigns for political office. Studies have shown that newspapers often cover women less than their male opponents, focus on image attributes over issue stances, and raise questions about the women's viability. Consequently, candidate-mediated messages – television advertising and websites – are particularly important to women candidates as they attempt to present their issues and images directly to voters during a political campaign. The chapter reviews the state of knowledge about women candidates, their media coverage, television commercials, and websites, and it provides examples of how women candidates may be able to capitalize on their controlled communication channels to influence their media coverage and create a positive, integrated message that connects with voters.

Finally, in Chapter 10, Kira Sanbonmatsu turns to the often over-looked subject of gender in state elections. She addresses two central questions: How many women ran for state legislative and statewide offices in 2012? How did the performance of women candidates in 2012 compare with previous elections? Sanbonmatsu analyzes the cross-state variation in the presence of women candidates, including the role of political parties in shaping women's candidacies. She also considers the reasons for the variation across states in women's presence in statewide executive office. Understanding why women are more likely to run for and hold office in some states and not in others is critical to understanding women's status in electoral politics today, as well as their prospects for achieving higher office in the future.

Collectively, the chapters provide an overview of the major ways in which gender affects the contours and outcomes of contemporary elections. Our hope is that this volume will leave its readers with a better understanding of how underlying gender dynamics help shape the electoral process in the United States.

1 Presidential Elections

Gendered Space and the Case of 2012

The election of 2012 began November 5, 2008, the day after the 2008 election. While certain features, such as the presence of an incumbent, may make elections seem similar, every presidential campaign is a product of current circumstances, the prior election cycle, the party in power, and other variables. While the presence of Republican incumbent George W. Bush focused attention on the Democratic field in 2004, the presence of Democratic incumbent Barack Obama in 2012 placed the spotlight on the Republican field of candidates. Also and importantly, the Republican sweep in the 2010 congressional elections, driven by the Tea Party phenomenon, set the stage for 2012. In contrast, the 9/11 attacks figured prominently in the 2004 election. In both election cycles, gender – particularly masculinity – was central, and it remains an unspoken assumption in presidential elections.

In fact, shortly after the 2004 election, a tongue-in-cheek Associated Press (AP) article led with the following: "Wanted: a former altar boy from the Southwest who speaks Spanish, married into a rich Republican family from Ohio and revolutionized the Internet after working as a volunteer firefighter in Florida. Position: president of the United States."[1] Using findings from exit polls to construct the profile of the perfect presidential candidate for 2008, the article went on to propose that he:

- "[is] a Medal of Honor winner" with combat experience, who helped normalize relations with Vietnam
- loves outdoor sports and drops his "'g's' when talkin' about huntin' and fishin' and car racin'"
- is a former quarterback for the University of Michigan Rose Bowl team

---

[1] Ron Fournier. November 6, 2004. Exit Polls Can Lead the Way in Finding Mr. or Mrs. Right for a Run in 2008. *Wisconsin State Journal*.

- is a "trained economist who taught in Minnesota, where he met his wife, a nurse," whose father is a former governor
- "was a volunteer fireman" who "drove his pickup truck to help out the World Trade Center site"
- and is "a billionaire in his own right who developed software . . . "

Although not fitting this profile, five prominent men and Hillary Rodham Clinton were mentioned in this article as potential candidates. The article closed with, "Mr. Perfect might be a Mrs. – the first woman to head a majority party ticket. But it would be a lonely job, what with her husband fighting in Iraq."

For presidential candidacies, the press serves as the great mentioner, without whose attention no candidate can be seen as viable. The power of mentioning – or not – has implications beyond individual candidates. What the press assumes, and the way it frames its coverage of presidential elections and candidacies, has consequences for what readers think about and, to a lesser extent, how they think about it.

The AP article described here focuses on the candidate characteristics needed to win in the next election. Distributed on November 6, 2004, it was among the first articles to frame elements of the 2008 presidential election. Importantly, its framing is highly gendered (see Text Box 1.1), but one suspects that neither the author nor the readers thought much about it. As a result, its assumptions about masculinity as an implicit criterion for the presidency – combat experience, huntin', quarterback, and fireman – go unexamined.

Yet the article's headline, " . . . finding Mr. or Mrs. Right for a run in 2008," and closing paragraph both assume that a woman can be president. In other words, they cue the reader to think about a woman as potentially the right or perfect presidential candidate in 2008. This cuing is no small matter. Because only men have ever been president, and because certain functions of the presidency, such as commander in chief, are particularly associated with masculinity, the assumption that a woman could be "Mrs. Right candidate" represents a major shift in cultural understandings of both women and the institution of the presidency. The fact that Hillary Clinton was the Democratic frontrunner even at that early stage may have contributed to this assumption of a Mrs. Right candidate. Yet so potent is the association between masculinity and the presidency that an organization called the White House Project was established with a core purpose of making this cultural shift.[2] One of its

---

[2] The White House Project closed in early 2013 because of financial difficulties.

TEXT BOX 1.1: A gender primer: Basic concepts for gender analysis

To do gender analysis of presidential elections, some basic concepts and definitions are needed.

Gender can be defined as the culturally constructed meaning of biological sex differences. Males and females share far more physiologically than they differ, yet in culture we largely divide gender roles and expectations into masculine and feminine even though biologically and culturally more than two genders exist. Importantly, in contrast to sex, gender is not necessarily tied to a human body.

Gender is assigned as:

- An attribute or property of an individual, entity, institution, and the like.

    She's a wise woman.
    Men dominate physics.

- Ways of doing things – practices or performance.

    He throws like a girl.
    She fights like a man.

- Normative stances toward appropriate and proper ways of behaving, allocating resources, exercising power, and so on.

    Men shouldn't cry.
    Fathers must provide and mothers give care.
    A woman's place is in the home.

The process of assigning gender is "to gender" or "gendering."

- To gender or gendering is to establish a gender association.

    Metrosexuality describes yuppie urban men with a softer side.
    The highly feminized field of nursing.

- To regender or regendering is to change from one gender to another gender.

    Before typewriters, secretaries were men.
    Girls now outperform boys in school.

- To transgender or transgendering is to cross gender boundaries, weakening gender norms and associations, and is open to both men and women.

    Half of medical students now are women, so medicine is changing.

- Gender ethos is defined as the characteristic spirit or essential and ideal attributes that correspond to gender expectations.

    Football is among the most manly of all U.S. sports.
    A Madonna with child quintessentially expresses femininity.
    The military is imbued with masculinity.

Source: Compiled by author.

primary strategies, in fact, was to have the media treat a woman in the presidency as normal, much as the AP article seems to do.

However, most of the characteristics ascribed to the ideal candidate in this AP article suggest a profile consistent with men rather than women in U.S. society. Taking note of this fact helps to reveal how presidential elections are gendered space.

- Although a woman could easily be from the Southwest, speak Spanish, and have married into a rich Republican family, the Catholic Church only allowed altar boys, not altar girls, at the time current presidential candidates were growing up.
- Firefighters remain overwhelmingly men, especially in volunteer corps.
- Until very recently, women have been barred from combat duty, so few have been positioned to win the Medal of Honor. However, a woman might well have negotiated with the Vietnamese: women have long been associated with peace, more are in the diplomatic corps, and three of the recent secretaries of state have been women.
- No woman has yet played quarterback for a Big Ten or any major college team. In 1999 to 2000, a female place kicker on the Colorado State University football team encountered extreme sexual harassment. (Interestingly, Condoleezza Rice may have benefitted from an association with football simply because she claims that her dream job is some day to be National Football League commissioner.)
- While economics has the smallest proportion of female Ph.D.s in the social sciences, women have entered the field in growing numbers, so a woman might have strong economic credentials. However, only about 10 percent of nurses are male, so she probably would not have one as her husband.
- Finally, if a woman became president, she might well be lonely, as is the first woman to serve in any position. However, no commander in chief has ever faced the challenge of leading a nation in war with a spouse on the battlefront because the wives of presidents have always functioned as helpmates, regardless of their other career interests and professional credentials. Many in 2008 expressed concerns about the role Bill Clinton might play if Hillary Clinton won, but not because he would either be a helpmate or on the battlefront. Similarly, Sarah Palin's son went to Iraq, but not her husband, Todd. Michele Bachmann, too, has been criticized for relying upon her husband Marcus for advice.

In other words, although a widely distributed AP article mentioning that a woman could be a viable candidate may have helped to normalize the idea of a woman as president, much more still needs to happen. Hillary Clinton's 2008 candidacy certainly extended that normalizing, although the ongoing frame that she is an exceptional woman lessens the impact for all women. In 2012, only Michele Bachman emerged as a female candidate, although a second woman, Sarah Palin, received considerable early attention. Nonetheless, even with Hillary Clinton's success in 2008 and high popularity as we look to 2016, we cannot simply "add and stir in" a woman without changing the elements associated with masculinity. Such "equal treatment" ignores important differences and (dis)advantages. Because so much that is perceived as contributing to presidential capacity is strongly associated with men and masculinity, presidential capacity is gendered to the masculine; as such, women who dream of a presidency must negotiate masculinity, a feat that Hillary Clinton ultimately failed to achieve in 2008. Drawing attention to this dynamic, Michele Bachman highlighted this gendering in a humorous reference to the "this or that" questions posed by CNN's John King in the New Hampshire debate of June 13, 2011, saying, "I have to tell you I was a little nervous. I didn't know if they were going to ask boxers or briefs – a girl never knows."

Text Box 1.2 rewrites the AP article to approximate a perfect candidate based on culturally feminine roles and associations in order to illustrate the central claim of this chapter: that presidential elections are gendered space, that much of what happens in a presidential election becomes a contest about masculinity that is integrally intertwined with understandings of what makes a candidate suited for this masculinized office and institution. Neither Hillary Clinton nor Sarah Palin in 2008 nor Michele Bachmann in 2012 approximated this profile of Mrs. President. The woman within the presidential pool (governor, senator, vice president, military leader) who most closely fit the profile was arguably former Kansas Governor Kathleen Sebelius, whose name was floated in 2008 as a potential Democratic vice presidential pick and who was later appointed by Obama as Secretary of the Department of Health and Human Services. Sebelius is the daughter of former Ohio Governor John Gilligan. She has chaired the Democratic Governors Association but has spent her life in public service, not the private sector making millions. Her husband, K. Gary Sebelius, is a federal magistrate judge and the son of former Republican member of Congress. They have two grown sons. Rather than huntin' and fishin' – hobbies Sarah Palin claimed to great fanfare – Sebelius

TEXT BOX 1.2: Finding Mrs. Right for a run in 2012: Not the same as Mr. Right

A November 6, 2004, AP article used exit polls to "build a perfect candidate for 2008."* Despite suggesting that Mrs. Right could fit the bill equally well as Mr. Right, the article concentrated on aspects consistent with masculinity. Given the considerable difference in life experiences between women and men, what factors known from exit polls and other sources in 2004 could be used to create an ideal female candidate for 2008?

- A fifth-generation Latina American from Arizona, she comes from a long line of Democrats, including political office holders from New Mexico.

- As a child she considered becoming a nun, which endeared her to a favorite uncle, a Catholic bishop in Florida who has close ties to the Cuban community. They share a love of the outdoors, gardening, camping, and fly fishing.

- She took first place in the individual medley on the U.S. national swim team, missing the Olympics only because of an injury.

- As an Army nurse, she served in the waning days of the Vietnam War. She received a medal of commendation for helping evacuate mixed-race children.

- She married an Anglo Army officer who specialized in military intelligence. He retired as a general in 1992. He speaks Arabic fluently, and President George H. W. Bush recognized him for outstanding service during the Persian Gulf War.

- She founded a company that placed temporary nurses, becoming a multimillionaire when she franchised the business. She has helped many women start their own businesses as a result.

- Throughout this time, she raised four children and transformed the public education system in her city as a volunteer activist. She interrupted her career to care for her son for three months when he suffered life-threatening injuries caused by a drunk driver. She sits on the national board of Mothers Against Drunk Driving.

- Her company created software, now used nationwide, that digitized and standardized patient medical records and enabled patients to access them 24–7. She made even more money from the software than the nursing business.

- She became governor of Michigan and is in her second term. Her husband intends to campaign hard on her behalf, as he has done in the past.

* Ron Fournier. November 6, 2004. Exit Polls Can Lead the Way in Finding Mr. & Mrs. Right for a Run in 2008. *Wisconsin State Journal.*

has been active in many environmental causes. As governor, she worked closely with first responders, but she herself was not one. She is a Catholic, but her archbishop imposed a "pastoral action" on her, demanding she no longer receive the Eucharist because she is pro-choice. Although she was a governor, many consider her state of Kansas insignificant in presidential politics. Indeed she has connections to Michigan, but only through her vacation homes. In sum, the 2008 female candidate with the best profile came up short of the masculinized characteristics highlighted in polls.

This chapter's primary purpose is to show ways gender and especially masculinity manifests in campaigns. I attempt to raise awareness of this implicit dynamic and to counteract some of the potency masculinity gains from simply being invisibly "ordinary." This chapter also touches on the process of opening, or regendering, presidential election space for women, a process that moved some distance in 2008 with the strong primary race of Hillary Clinton and the Republican vice presidential pick of Sarah Palin, whose presence lingered into 2011. The process was carried forward by Michele Bachman during the 2012 cycle.

As Chapter 2 by Dittmar and Carroll in this volume shows clearly, women find a contest about masculinity a distinct hurdle compared to male candidates, but men who run for the presidency must also negotiate masculinity. Masculinity takes many forms, each competing to be considered hegemonic – that is, the controlling, best, and most valued version.[3] Drawing on work by R. W. Connell, this chapter looks into masculinity more carefully and explores the gendering of presidential timber – an ill-defined but commonly employed concept about suitability for the presidency that proved particularly salient for 2012. I examine overt references to masculinity as well as the ongoing struggle for hegemony between two forms of masculinity in the United States, "dominance" masculinity and "technical expert" masculinity. I do so in order to make explicit the implicit masculine qualities of the presidency deemed essential in a successful presidential candidate.

This chapter explores presidential elections through the concept of gendered space rather than just discussing elections. While elections – with their aspects of candidate recruitment and winnowing, formal primary and general elections, caucuses, conventions, debates, and the like – certainly are part of election space, so is much more. For example, the

---

[3] R. W. Connell. 1995. *Masculinities*. Berkeley: University of California Press.

presidency as an institution occupies a place in history, inside the U.S. government system, in relationship to Congress, other national institutions, and political parties. Each of these places is part of presidential election space. So is the entire environment of those elections, with their places in the public mind, the news and opinion media, American culture, and all the people – present and past – who help create and sustain presidential elections. These people include the candidates, the elite political gatekeepers, media pundits, pollsters, campaign consultants, campaign workers, voters, even apathetic citizens. Each of them occupies a place in presidential election space. This large and somewhat amorphous space that includes everything related to presidential elections is the locus of analysis.

Ironically, the 2008 "space invaders" Hillary Clinton and Sarah Palin, along with Michele Bachman in 2012, did not so much highlight masculinity as shift the gaze away from it, making the masculine nature of the presidency even harder to see. In 2008, and for some Republicans in 2012, racialization of the campaign also shifted the gaze from masculinity even though, of course, Barack Obama is a man. Hence, I focus on presidential selection processes to demonstrate ways that they are themselves implicitly imbued with masculinity and therefore foster (non)conscious beliefs that masculine persons should be president. To do so, the chapter tackles what David Collinson and Jeff Hearn have described as "a recurring paradox. The categories of men and masculinity are frequently central to analyses, yet they remain taken for granted, hidden and unexamined . . . [They are] both talked about and ignored, rendered simultaneously explicit and implicit . . . at the centre of the discourse but they are rarely the focus of the interrogation."[4] As will become clear, some media coverage – especially from op-ed pages and increasingly blogs – explicitly deals with men and masculinity in the presidential election. In 2012, embedded within the search for "presidential timber," masculinity proved central. Yet, as in the AP article examined at the beginning of this chapter, coverage generally treats masculinity paradoxically by ignoring its central place in presidential elections even while highlighting it. In the process, it ignores ways in which presidential elections are gendered, thereby perpetuating men's greater potential to be seen as presidential to the detriment of female candidates.

[4] David Collinson and Jeff Hearn. 2001. Naming Men as Men: Implications for Work, Organization, and Management. In *The Masculinities Reader*, ed. Stephen M. Whitehead and Frank J. Barrett. Cambridge, MA: Polity Press, 144–169.

STAGES OF PRESIDENTIAL ELECTIONS: PARTS
OF GENDERED SPACE

The early stages of any presidential election are an insider's game, with party elites and elected officials talking to the press about potential candidates and the press reporting on them. Year one begins the day after the previous campaign, or November 5, 2008, for the 2012 election. For the press to mention a candidate regularly is exceptionally important: no press mention, no candidacy. The press covers candidates who "test the water" and creates potential candidates simply by mentioning individuals in that context.

Years one and two of any election cycle focus on factors that provide candidates strategic advantages to win the next election. Chief among these factors is whether the race includes an incumbent president or is an open seat. In 2012, as was the case in 2004 for George W. Bush, Barack Obama ran as an incumbent president, and he was assumed to be running for re-election the moment he was declared the winner in 2008; hence, all the action surrounded the Republicans. Further, the 2012 election was tame compared to the 2008 election, which proved unusual because, for the first time since 1928, no incumbent or former president or vice president stepped forward as a candidate.

Another relevant factor is the influence of recent elections, reflected in such elements as the margin of victory, big mistakes made by a candidate or a campaign, and strategies that worked particularly well. The 2004 election taught Democrats to employ a fifty-state strategy, which they used effectively in both 2008 and 2012. The Democrats swept both houses of Congress in 2006 but became victims of a shellacking by Tea Party Republicans in 2010, shifting the momentum to the GOP. Since 2000, Republicans have accelerated tactics at polls to reduce voter fraud (or, according to the Democrats, suppress votes), such as challenging registrations and promoting legislation to require voters to show picture identification, while Democrats have prepared for Election Day by anticipating legal battles and implementing major get-out-the-vote efforts. Democrats, in turn, have developed highly sophisticated data mining and management strategies that carried Obama to the presidency in 2008 and that they extended in 2012. Further, since the 2004 elections, presidential campaigns have learned to anticipate action early in the summer, such as attacks by an outside group like Swift Boat Veterans. In 2012, Democrats went on the attack, spending $64 million to define Romney in advance of the general election campaign as rich and out of touch.

Finally, the economy is always important to elections. It stalled in part because the Tea Party members of Congress resisted the president at every turn, contributing to gridlock.

All of these factors combined to produce an incumbent president on the defensive in 2012 and to inspire a long list of Republican candidates who hoped to limit Obama to a single term.

The Press as the Great Mentioner

News coverage during the first year of any election cycle focuses on "aspirants" or individuals doing things that would clearly help them with a presidential bid. Aspirants might be traveling the country giving speeches, meeting with an unusual assortment of interest group leaders, forming exploratory committees, visiting states important to early selection processes such as New Hampshire and Iowa, and otherwise getting more positive press coverage than usual. Sarah Palin received enormous press attention immediately after the 2008 election. She often was mentioned as a potential candidate for 2012 and tested the waters in many ways until the Republican primary debates in 2011. Mitt Romney began to run immediately following the 2008 election. Press mentions of Mitt Romney, from the beginning of 2009 onward, helped make him the heir apparent.

A second set of individuals might better be thought of as "potential aspirants;" they do a few things that bring them press coverage but prove not to be serious candidates for that election cycle. However, such coverage in one cycle can become a resource for future cycles. Mike Huckabee, for example, started a PAC and endorsed and stumped for many conservative candidates. His Fox News show ran four times weekly, and polls showed he had a small but intensely loyal following, often leading the splintered Republican pack. His activity in the 2010 election also kept him high in press mentions, and his candidacy seemed inevitable until he declared in May 2011, "All the factors say go, but my heart says no."

A third set of potential candidates is spotlighted because they have characteristics consistent with presidential candidates, although they may not have given serious consideration to a presidential bid. These individuals can be thought of as "recruits;" the mere fact that the press mentions them as potential candidates begins to build the perception of their viability. The press plays an influential role in this process. When the media mention an individual as a presidential candidate, they create the perception that he or she could be one. With no mention in the press, regardless of aspirations and credentials, an individual will not be seen as a potential or actual candidate. Barack Obama was frequently mentioned in this way after his well-received speech at the 2004 Democratic convention. Rudy Giuliani and Jeb Bush fell into this category for 2012.

Table 1.1 shows the names of individuals mentioned by the *New York Times* or the *Washington Post* as possible candidates during the first three years of the cycle leading up to the 2012 election, the date each was first mentioned, and whether each proved to be an aspirant, a potential aspirant, or a recruit. Compared to recent cycles, the speculation was slow to emerge, perhaps in part because excitement over the first black president occupied news space or because the country faced economic emergencies.

An open presidential election without a sitting president, such as 2008, should offer more opportunities to identify prospective candidates, including women. In fact, a total of thirty-seven possible candidates were mentioned between the two parties in 2008. In contrast, the 2004 and 2012 cycles, with incumbents on the ballot, offered mentions of twenty-three and twenty-four total candidates respectively. Among these candidates, the press mentioned very few women; three were named in 2004 and 2008, and only two, Sarah Palin and Michele Bachmann, during the 2012 cycle.

During the third year of a presidential election cycle, the pace quickens. Candidates become active in early states, strive for viability by raising considerable campaign funds, and use the opportunity of an official announcement of their candidacy to garner press coverage. The aspirants become separated from others during this time. Since 2001, former first lady and Secretary of State Hillary Rodham Clinton has been particularly subject to speculation, with the third year of a cycle serving as make or break. Despite repeated claims that she was not running in 2004, the speculations persisted until 2003. They picked up again immediately after the 2004 election, opening her 2008 run as the undisputed Democratic frontrunner. Mentions of her as a 2016 candidate began even before the 2012 election was over. Just as Sarah Palin did in 2011, Clinton will likely wait until the year before the election to say whether she is actually running. By speculating often and well into a campaign cycle that a woman might become a candidate, the press helps to change the gendering of presidential election space simply because the idea is kept in front of the attentive public.

The 2012 election began to take shape during 2011 as the last of the candidate pool emerged, recruits and potentials withdrew, and aspirants tested the water, trying to tap top campaign talent, line up endorsements, and raise money. Meanwhile, a sitting president may receive very little coverage explicitly related to his role as a candidate, although everything

TABLE 1.1: Only two women were among the long list of candidates mentioned early for the 2012 election

Candidate	Party	Previous position	Date of first mention	Type of candidate
Sarah Palin	R	Former Governor, Alaska	Nov. 6, 2008	Aspirant
Mitt Romney	**R**	**Former Governor, Massachusetts**	**Nov. 8, 2008**	**Aspirant**
Mike Huckabee	R	Former Governor, Arkansas	Nov. 21, 2008	Potential
Jon Huntsman	**R**	**Former Governor, Utah; Ambassador to China**	**Dec. 9, 2008**	**Aspirant**
Jeb Bush	R	Former Governor, Florida	Jan. 4, 2009	Potential
Rick Perry	**R**	**Governor, Texas**	**Feb. 4, 2009**	**Aspirant**
Ron Paul	R	U.S. House of Representatives, Texas	Feb. 12, 2009	Aspirant
Newt Gingrich	**R**	**Former U.S. House of Representatives, Georgia**	**March 6, 2009**	**Aspirant**
Haley Barbour	R	Governor, Mississippi	Apr. 26, 2009	Potential
Mitch Daniels	**R**	**Former Governor, Indiana**	**June 5, 2009**	**Potential**
Rick Santorum	R	Former U.S. Senator, Pennsylvania	August 11, 2009	Aspirant
Herman Cain	**R**	**Chairman of the Federal Reserve Bank of Kansas City; businessman**	**August 12, 2009**	**Aspirant**
Michele Bachmann	R	U.S. Representative from Minnesota	Sept. 5, 2009	Aspirant
Tim Pawlenty	**R**	**Former Governor, Minnesota**	**Oct. 1, 2009**	**Aspirant**
Rudy Giuliani	R	Former Mayor, New York City	Nov. 19, 2009	Recruit
John Thune	**R**	**U.S. Senator, South Dakota**	**Oct. 4, 2010**	**Recruit**
John Bolton	R	Former Ambassador to the UN	Dec. 21, 2010	Recruit
Chris Christie	**R**	**Governor, New Jersey**	**April 4, 2011**	**Recruit**
Buddy Roemer	R	Former Governor, Louisiana	April 26, 2011	Aspirant
Donald Trump	**R**	**Chairman and President of the Trump Organization**	**April 28, 2011**	**Aspirant**
Mike Pence	R	Governor, Indiana; Former U.S. Representative	May 23, 2011	Recruit
Paul Ryan	**R**	**U.S. House of Representatives, Wisconsin**	**May 23, 2011**	**Recruit**
Gary Johnson	L	Former Governor, New Mexico	May 23, 2011	Aspirant
Thad McCotter	**R**	**U.S. House of Representatives, Michigan**	**July 2, 2011**	**Recruit**

Names mentioned in the *New York Times* and *Washington Post* articles searched with presiden! and 2012. Compiled by author.

he does as president reflects on his candidacy; this was true for President
Bush in 2004 and for President Obama in 2012. Also, just as Democrats
in 2004 fielded a large cast of contenders with an impassioned desire
to retake the White House, the Republicans held a series of twenty-five
debates leading up to Super Tuesday among their large field of aspiring
candidates. These began with a widely televised debate in South Carolina
on May 5, 2011. After Labor Day, the pace of debates and polls conducted by news outlets and polling organizations, as well as campaigns,
quickened, and the polls themselves provided candidates with frequent
press coverage, often in relationship to the many debates. Polls and press
coverage of these visits become critical. Do poorly in either, and a candidate loses the "press election" in which the media vet candidates for
their presidential viability and presidential timber. However, such coverage tends to be limited and can become detrimental if a candidate is not
polling well. In fact, a candidate's viability is shaped by the strength of his
or her fund-raising and press coverage. Many withdraw before October
during year three as a result.

Activity has tended to kick into high gear during year four of an election cycle, starting in early November and intensifying after January 1.
During the last ten months of any campaign season, press coverage esca-
lates greatly and presidential election space becomes highly visible and
national, drawing interest from a much broader audience. The Iowa caucuses and New Hampshire primary, which always come first, hold substantially more sway than others, but Nevada and, especially for Republicans, South Carolina have been added to the early contests. These are
followed by a series of state primaries and caucuses whose rules are
determined by states and political parties. For 2012, Republicans decided
to divide the states into three sections: the early states, whose rules
remained largely the same as in 2008; middle primaries from March 6
(Super Tuesday) through March 31, in which states could allocate delegates proportionally; and the late primaries, all of which would become
winner-take-all. The debates continued with each primary and caucus,
providing a circus of media coverage as one candidate after another
peaked and fell. Seven candidates remained heading into Iowa, six into
New Hampshire, and five into the important South Carolina primary on
January 21, 2012.

For the past several presidential elections, "Super Tuesday," a collection of many states' primaries taking place the first week of March, has
determined the presumptive nominees, even though primaries continue
until June. In 2012, Super Tuesday took place on March 6, but with only

ten states holding primaries or caucuses. Ohio received top billing by far in the press. The race between Romney and Santorum proved fierce, with Romney squeaking out a one-point victory. Santorum called for Gingrich, who came in third everywhere but his home state of Georgia, to withdraw from the race.

Following the pattern of Democrats in 2008, primaries played a heightened role for Republicans in 2012. Three different candidates won the first three contests – Santorum in Iowa, Romney in New Hampshire, and Gingrich in South Carolina – although Romney proved strong from the onset despite a decided enthusiasm gap from the conservative base. As a result, the campaign carried on longer, with Santorum dropping out on April 10 and Gingrich on May 2. As a result, press attention stayed on the race. In contrast to 2008, when Republican nominee John McCain struggled to capture any media attention during the exciting Democratic race, President Obama was able to take advantage of his presidency, garnering regular attention. Also taking a cue from the Bush campaign of 2004, the Obama campaign moved $65 million from general election coffers into June, focusing on defining Romney as rich and out of touch. The strategy worked, and Obama's pattern of vigorous campaigning continued, even during the summer doldrums prior to the conventions.

During late summer of presidential election years, press coverage shifts to each party as it approaches its nominating convention. In 2012, the Republican convention took place August 25 through 28 and the Democratic convention ran September 1 through 4. Conventions officially nominate a party's candidate, but they also showcase the candidate and other party notables, including potential future nominees. In contrast to 2004 when the separation between the two conventions was an unusually long full month, in 2012 they were separated by less than a week. And, unlike 2008 when John McCain selected Sarah Palin to be his vice presidential running mate during the Democratic convention and stole the media limelight, Mitt Romney opted for an August bounce in media attention and the polls, selecting Congressman Paul Ryan as his running mate weeks before either party's convention.

The final throes of the general campaign begin in earnest after the conventions, becoming ever more frenzied as Election Day nears. For the 2012 election, presidential debates between the nominees of the two parties, which always attract considerable press coverage, were compressed into October, taking place on October 3, 11, and 22, with the vice presidential debate on October 16. Romney's dominating performance and Obama's lackluster showing in the first debate gave Romney's campaign a bounce. By most accounts, Obama came back in the second debate, and the momentum carried him to victory on November 6, 2012. Because television networks faced severe criticism for "calling" the election too early on election night in 2000, they have given greater care since, and they generally consider waiting until the polls close on the West Coast before declaring a winner. However, because counting electoral college votes is easy, when Barack Obama was named the winner in Ohio at 8:15 p.m., all the major channels declared him the victor.

The next election cycle began on November 7, 2012, as the top political blogs mentioned six 2016 candidates: for the Democrats, Secretary of State Hillary Clinton, Vice President Joe Biden, and Governor Andrew Cuomo; for the Republicans, Congressman Paul Ryan, Governor Chris Christie, and Senator Marco Rubio. The 2016 presidential campaign space had opened, with only one woman mentioned.

THE GENDERED PRESIDENCY AND PRESIDENTIAL TIMBER

The term "presidential timber" implies the building products used to construct a president. So far, the human material that makes presidents has been male. Masculinity has been embedded through the traditions that dominate the presidency, but inside those traditions lie more implicit assumptions that make presidential elections masculine space: the test of executive toughness, a preference for military heroes, the sports and war metaphors of debates, and more. Implicit in the gendering of presidential election space is the common belief that the election picks a single leader and commander in chief of "the greatest nation on earth." This belief stands in a post–World War II context that includes the Cold War, the fall of communism, the emergence of the United States as the world's sole hyper-power, and the rise of terrorism.

In these conditions, Americans have carefully, albeit not necessarily systematically or rationally, sought the right man for the job. As judged from the number of candidates and the reaction to candidacies thus far, women had not yet been seriously considered as suitable to serve as president until Hillary Clinton's campaign of 2008, and even then, she did not win. Although many reasons can be proffered to explain the dearth of serious female attempts for the post, observations about the heavily masculinized character of the office, and hence masculinized selection process, remain among the strongest yet most difficult explanations to establish. In essence, because the institution is itself perceived as masculine, contests for the presidency are, among other things, struggles over dominant or hegemonic masculinity. Presidential elections also present real challenges for women, who must exhibit masculine characteristics (probably better than males) while retaining their femininity if they want to succeed: they must find the perfect blend of pantsuits and pearls.

Evidence that institutions have been gendered toward masculinity became obvious when women entered them; their novel presence made visible the ways masculinity is "normal." Thinking of men as having gender instead of "naturally" coinciding with a universal standard has occurred only quite recently. An institution becomes gendered because it takes on characteristics or preferences of the founders, incumbents, and important external actors who influence it over time. In doing so, these founders and influential incumbents create the institution's formal and informal structures, rules, and practices, reflecting their preferred mode of organizing. If men have played an overwhelming role in an institution's creation and evolution, it is only "natural" that masculine preferences become embedded in its ideal nature and it takes on a masculine gender ethos. This is what has happened to the U.S. presidency.

But gender is not static, and neither is the gendering of an institution that operates inside a social context. One can expect continual gender transformations as a result of women's activism, equal employment opportunity policies in education and the workplace, generational change, and cultural experiences of Americans' daily lives. Various types of masculinity vie for a hegemonic standing as well, including ideas about black and Mormon masculinity, central features of the Republican race in 2012. Similarly, campaigns and elections evolve from a particular history, influenced by key people and processes that have gendered aspects. This evolutionary process favors those whose preferences become reflected in presidential election campaigns, but those preferences can change over time. Although men have clearly had the advantage in shaping the presidency and presidential elections over time, gender has been in considerable flux over the past forty years. Even if only men have been seen as possessing presidential timber thus far, these assumptions may change in the future. The strong support for Hillary Clinton in 2013 suggests such a change. Similarly, an April 2013 poll showed positive and nuanced changes in views toward women as political leaders, although 14 percent still are not ready for a woman as president and a quarter think a man would perform better on the world stage.[5]

So how might presidential timber be gendered? Informal use would suggest that it combines a blend of overlapping elements of charisma,

---

[5] Lauren Fox. May 2, 2013. Poll: Voters Ready for a Woman President. *U.S. News.* http://www.usnews.com/news/articles/2013/05/02/poll-voters-ready-for-a-woman-president.

stature, experience, and viability in a particular election. It also has included ideas of proper manliness. Presidential historian Forrest McDonald provides insights into presidential timber through his description of presidential image:

> [T]he presidential office ... inherently had the ceremonial, ritualistic, and symbolic duties of a king-surrogate. Whether as warrior-leader, father of his people, or protector, the president is during his tenure the living embodiment of the nation. Hence, it is not enough to govern well; the president must also seem presidential. He must inspire confidence in his integrity, compassion, competence, and capacity to take charge in any conceivable situation. . . . The image thus determines the reality.[6]

The "king-surrogate, . . . warrior-leader, father . . . , protector" roles and images indisputably evoke men and masculinity.

One could imagine a queen, mother, and protector with Joan of Arc warrior qualities; former British Prime Minister Margaret Thatcher is often cited as having evoked these images. But British comedy often showed her baring a muscular, manly chest. Many argue that Britain's experience with highly successful queens opened the way for Thatcher.

In contrast, the United States has no such historical experience, so voters have a harder time seeing women as capable of fulfilling traditionally masculine leadership roles of the institution. This cultural (in)capacity to understand women as able public leaders likely is exaggerated because, according to Michael Kimmel, an expert on masculinity, the gendered public and private divide was much stronger in the United States than in Europe.[7]

Even more challenging, and perhaps most important for electing presidents, presidential timber derives from the perception of others. That is, others must see a potential candidate as possessing it. Forrest McDonald declares that a president must "seem presidential" and inspire confidence in his "capacity to take charge in *any* [emphasis added] conceivable situation . . . with image determining reality."[8]

If only men have been president, then having a presidential image presents a significant challenge for women who need political elites, party activists, and ultimately voters to perceive them as presidential. Further,

---

[6] Forrest McDonald. 1994. *The American Presidency: An Intellectual History.* Lawrence: University of Kansas Press.
[7] Michael Kimmel. 1996. *Manhood in American.* New York: The Free Press.
[8] McDonald, *The American Presidency: An Intellectual History,* 2004.

TABLE 1.2: Concerns about "presidential timber" were twice as prominent in the 2012 election as they were in 2008

Year	2008 Campaign			2012 Campaign		
	2006	2007	2008	2010	2011	2012
N =	13	10	73	46	69	86
Three-year totals			96			201

Note: Using the advance search for the North American LexisNexis database, I searched all U.S. newspapers for "presiden! AND candida! AND 2012 AND Presidential Timber."

men have more often been culturally been imbued with a "take charge" capacity, although women certainly do and can take charge, so this aspect of timber might be open for cross-gendering – that is, being understood as suitable for either women or men. However, because of stereotypes, the requirement that one be perceived as able to take charge in any conceivable situation undermines women, particularly during war or security threats such as 9/11. Jennifer Lawless found that considerable gender stereotyping re-emerged in post–9/11 America, with willingness to support a qualified female candidate falling to its lowest point in decades.[9] For these reasons, the ordinary usage of the term "presidential timber" and potential gendering of it deserve scrutiny, because its use is simultaneously the center of analysis and invisible.[10]

By examining how the term "presidential timber" is used in press accounts, we can better establish its meaning and its explicit and implicit gendering. To do so, I searched the North American Nexus database for all articles including the term, for the years 2010 (*N* = 46), 2011 (*N* = 69), and 2012 (*N* = 86) or 201 total mentions. As Table 1.2 shows, news references to presidential timber more than doubled from the 2008 cycle.

In the 2004 election, which offers the most recent comparison with an incumbent presidential candidate, George W. Bush's campaign repeatedly pointed to his post–9/11 performance and approval ratings whenever questions were raised about his credentials for the job. In essence, news accounts positioned him as possessing timber by virtue of serving as president, although this has not always worked for other recent presidents. Jimmy Carter purportedly lost because he anguished too much in public, and many commentators – and arguably voters – perceived George

[9] Jennifer L. Lawless. 2004. Women, War, and Winning Elections: Gender Stereotyping in the Post-September 11th Era. *Political Research Quarterly* 57: 479–490.

[10] Collinson and Hearn, 144–169.

H. W. Bush as lacking sufficient timber. Often, this perceived lack of timber has been linked to a "wimp factor" or other failure to fulfill the requisite image of presidential masculinity.[11] In an apparent response to this danger, George W. Bush positioned himself as exceptionally masculine, a steadfast cowboy willing to stand firm while taking on the world. In contrast, Barack Obama had avoided any suggestion of an "angry black man," instead cultivating an image of "no-drama Obama." He faced absolutely vitriolic Republican opposition from the onset and encountered particularly difficult economic challenges and fierce attacks on health care reform, all of which called into question his capacity as president – his presidential timber. The questions continued with the self-described Democratic "shellacking" in the 2010 election. In 2010, news accounts mentioned presidential timber forty-five times for Obama, thirteen times for Romney, and four times each for Gingrich and Perry. Except for Rick Perry, who was said to look presidential, these mentions overwhelmingly called into question the presidential timber of the candidates.

The importance of the idea of timber resides in "impressions," which are still largely unformed. Media coverage early on "is considered an important chance to form opinions that could help shape later aspects of the campaign."[12] Key to the impression and the opinions are "passion" and "appeal" that would help party activists "gauge which candidate could mount the strongest challenge." In other words, presidential timber involves a candidate's passion, appeal, and competitiveness as conveyed through early impressions reported by the press. None of these aspects appears to be particularly gendered, although a woman might be eliminated if she is not perceived – for reasons of sexism or feminine personal characteristics – as competitive against the other party's candidate. Appeal is a tricky thing, especially early on. The frequent references to Clinton as being too contentious to win suggested reasons to eliminate her without scrutinizing the gender dimensions of why she elicited that response. With Michele Bachmann rather than Hillary Clinton as the sole female candidate and conservative Republicans in the driver's seat, the election of 2012 saw very different gendering around the concept of presidential timber than in the 2008 election.

The nature of the impressions involved in presidential timber is magnified in individual coverage of candidates, for better or ill depending

---

[11] Stephen J. Ducat. 2004. *The Wimp Factor*. Boston: Beacon Press.
[12] James Gerstenzang and Mark Z. Barabak. May 3, 2003. Democrats Gather for a Debate in Deep South; Nine contenders for the presidential nomination assemble tonight in South Carolina in a bid to form opinions and capture voter interest. *Los Angeles Times*. All of the quotations in the remaining 2004 analysis of timber are from this article.

on the nature of that coverage. Michele Bachmann was treated to sexist remarks by Chris Wallace, who called her "a flake" and was dragged down by a wild-eyed cover photo in *Newsweek* and extensive coverage of her propensity to get migraine headaches. In contrast, much like Fred Thompson in 2007 who was featured in a lengthy *Washington Post* article entitled "Bigger Than Life," Rick Perry was heavily recruited to run as part of the anybody-but-Romney enthusiasm gap among the conservative base. Although in theory a woman could be deemed presidential, one must wonder how masculinity and manliness allowed Thompson and Perry to be so readily deemed to "look" presidential. Perry, in fact, embodies many of the features of the tongue-in-cheek article about the next president. He is from the Southwest, drives a pickup truck, and drops his g's talkin' about huntin' and fishin' and the like.

Gendering need not be bad, but it should be recognized. For example, in 2008 Clinton received a glowing column about her presidential timber in *Newsweek* that did just that. Why Clinton rubbed people the wrong way has seemed integrally linked to her sex from the start, as has casting Bachmann aside as crazy. Among other reasons often cited is the fact Bachmann did not demur about her own power. A successful tax attorney with a strong history in state political office, Bachmann said she was "insulted" by Chris Wallace's question asking if she was a "flake." Regardless, this treatment energized conservative women in particular and even some Democrats who oppose sexist treatment. Among other things, Bachmann's run provided the opportunity to learn what "conservative women need to be prepared for if they're going to enter the national spotlight."[13] In fact, invidious questioning about a female president is itself a gendered challenge to all women who would be president. This stands in stark contrast to Rick Perry, who looked presidential and so was cajoled into running.

Gendering can occur in many subtle ways. For example, Hillary Clinton's presidential timber was mentioned in a book review titled "Lionesses" about 100 years of "journalistas" and the best writing by female journalists. Such placement suggests that Clinton, too, is a lioness, a clearly gendered term, and that she is somehow insurgent as an "ista." More importantly, though, the text itself sets up judging her presidential timber and touts an Erica Jong piece in *The Nation* for capturing "her unquestionable smarts but also her penchant for striking bargains to acquire power. No one reading this piece could be surprised by Senator

---

[13] Martina Steward. July 19, 2011. From Clinton to Palin to Bachmann: Why some Dems now support GOP women. *CNNPolitics*.

Clinton's multisided utterances on Iraq policy or the steely discipline that helped get her elected."[14] Her timber is negated because she strikes bargains to acquire power. While male presidential candidates have likely done the same, her conduct made her suspect because of cultural norms for men, women, and political power.

No place is the paradoxical presence and invisibility of gender more visible than with "commander in chief." In a 2006 article on presidential timber that mentions several candidates, Clinton is said to need to "show her potential as commander in chief" and "regain her stature" as frontrunner in an area considered to be her strength – national security – in the face of "Democratic darling-of-the-moment" Barack Obama.[15] Again, none of this may appear gendered if all candidates must pass muster to win. However, a female heading the military would break gender norms of one of the most masculine of all undertakings. Clinton had no choice but to demonstrate her prowess in national security. Her time and success as Secretary of State have certainly contributed to calls for her to run in 2016 and assumptions about her credentials to do so.

Importantly, in an analysis of the term "commander in chief" in articles from eight major newspapers in the 2008 cycle, this gendering becomes obvious. The analysis searched for McCain, Clinton, or Obama with the term in the same sentence and found a total of six, nineteen, and twenty mentions respectively. McCain simply received less coverage, and no one doubted his capacity as commander in chief; all references were positive. The Clinton search produced a total of nineteen hits, seventeen of which were positive and two negative about her capacity. This finding is remarkable in that for the first time a woman was treated by the press as capable of commanding the world's greatest military. Obama received a total of twenty hits. Even more remarkably considering that he won, all twenty spoke negatively about his qualifications and capacity to be commander in chief, given his short time in Washington, DC, and limited exposure to the military. Yet they did not disqualify him for the office. It is not possible to discern whether the economy so overshadowed everything else that his weakness as commander in chief did not matter or whether assumptions about aggressiveness in black masculinity meant he was simply assumed to be able to function in the military realm.

Another dynamic also tends to introduce gender, not about women but about different kinds of men and masculinity. A comparison to a

[14] Jill Abramsom. January 8, 2006. The Lionesses. *The New York Times Book Review*, 17.
[15] Michael McAuliffe. December 5, 2006. Iraq Hearing a Test for Three Prez Rivals. *The New York Daily News*, 6.

former male president introduces masculinity without needing to do so explicitly. We "naturally" tend to compare a woman to other women and a man to men. In doing so for the presidency, we inadvertently and invisibly introduce gender. For example, both Romney and Gingrich were compared to Ronald Reagan, and both were found wanting. According to Jackson Katz, writing for the *Huffington Post*, Romney matched Reagan as an "older white man with movie star looks who could sell sunny optimism and project a can-do spirit to Americans."[16] However, Romney proved "totally unbelievable" as the aggressive cold warrior who could project anger so attractive to his supporters on the far right. Gingrich, who stayed in the race until May 2012, sensed his opportunity to "out-man Romney" by evoking Reagan and "throwing red meat" to the conservative base. However, he is far less attractive than Reagan and was readily deemed a flip-flopper, something Reagan was not considered with his "old school authoritarian masculinity."[17]

Unlike Rick Perry, women are less likely to be seen as having adequate timber because Americans do not yet know how a woman president looks, a catch-22. Further, because masculinity is so normal, we do not readily recognize when masculinity is being cued and women stigmatized. Masculine presidents are ordinary and hence masculinity is simply assumed. The question then becomes whether the masculinity is the right kind or good enough.

CONTESTING MASCULINITY: TWO EXPERTS IN A WORLD OF MASCULINE DOMINANCE

Masculinity is neither fixed nor uniform. Just as there are several versions of a "proper" woman – often varying by class, cultural subgroup, and gender ideology – men and masculinity are not singular. In the minds of presidential candidates, the political gatekeepers, and voters, certain expectations of masculinity exist for a president. Nonetheless, within broader ranges of gender expectations, analysis suggests that much of the heat around gender performances, or the way individuals "do gender," derives from contests to make one version of gender the hegemonic form, the form that is recognized as right, just, proper, and good and the form that is afforded the most value. It is the form most able to control all other forms, and therefore it becomes most "normal."

---

[16] Jackson Katz. December 16, 2011. Romney, Gingrich and the Two Versions of Ronald Reagan. http://www.huffingtonpost.com/jackson-katz/romney-gingrich-and-the-t_b_1152570.html. Accessed January 23, 2012.

[17] Ibid.

R. W. Connell has analyzed contemporary masculinity, finding ongoing contests between two major forms: dominance and technical expertise.[18] Dominance masculinity is preoccupied with dominating, controlling, commanding, and otherwise bending others to one's will. Often rooted in physical prowess and athleticism, this competitive and hierarchical masculinity can also be rooted in financial prowess in the corporate world or elsewhere. Michael Jordan and Arnold Schwarzenegger serve as archetypal examples.

Expertise masculinity emerges from capacity with technology or other intellectualized pursuits. Such masculinity also values wealth, a key marker of masculine status, but the hegemony arises from mastery of and capacity to deal with complex technology or ideas. Bill Gates and Carl Sagan are exemplars of technical expertise masculinity.

Connell says that these modes of masculinity "sometimes stand in opposition and sometimes coexist," because neither has succeeded in displacing the other.[19] Connell further argues that these modes of hegemonic masculinity always stand in relationship to other subordinated masculinities and to femininity.

If this struggle for hegemonic masculinity plays out in presidential elections, then it also has consequences for female candidates, because expertise has been a prime base of power for women in leadership roles. Whereas women gain credibility in leadership situations when they are perceived as possessing expertise, they face a considerably greater challenge in being perceived as leaders if they try to dominate. In fact, women are often punished for seeming too dominating. Therefore, the nature of the contest for hegemonic masculinity has implications for women, too. A strong showing of expertise masculinity would allow women easier access; a strong showing of dominance masculinity would cause women to face greater difficulty in the contest or even in being seen as suited to participate in the contest.

The past gives clues to the present. In 1992, George H. W. Bush had won the Persian Gulf War but had also been labeled a "wimp" who could not project a vision for the nation. Bush had the possibility of employing dominance masculinity as commander in chief but failed. Bill Clinton portrayed himself as intelligent, as a Rhodes Scholar, and as a policy wonk. He projected expertise masculinity and won by being smart about the economy. Once in office, however, he backed down from a disagreement

---

[18] Connell, 1995.
[19] Connell 1995, 194.

with the Joint Chiefs of Staff over gays in the military and let his wife lead his major health care initiative. He was portrayed as weak until a showdown over the budget with House Speaker Newt Gingrich and the Republican majority in the 104th Congress, when he dominated and won. Strangely, when he was again attacked, this time over sexual misconduct, his popularity rose. While reactions to Clinton are far too complicated to suggest a single cause, the manly vitality at stake – perhaps proof that he was not controlled by his strong wife, Hillary – figures as an aspect of dominance masculinity. Clinton did best as president when he projected dominance masculinity, not expertise masculinity.

The 2000 election might seem the perfect contest between expertise and dominance masculinity with Al Gore, the smart and technically savvy vice president, against George W. Bush, a former professional baseball team owner whose intelligence was regularly questioned. In the 2004 election, Bush entered the contest from an explicit position of dominance masculinity. He could not and likely would not choose to project expertise masculinity. Although ironic, when Bush called on his "expertise" with the office of the presidency, he did so from a dominance masculinity stance, claiming that expertise mostly in terms of a war presidency. Kerry tried to project both expertise and dominance masculinity. He was both smart and heroic. Kerry certainly had plenty of resources for expertise masculinity, from foreign policy to nineteenth-century British poetry. However, his primary election victory derived from his war hero status, firmly rooted in dominance masculinity. He also projected his athleticism at every available opportunity. Apparently his campaign recognized the potential liability of expertise masculinity. Kerry tried to have both and failed at dominance.

The 2008 cycle posed the professor against the war hero, but it also introduced black masculinity, which is very dominating to white Americans. Concerns were also raised about whether McCain's age and years of torture undermined confidence in his manly vigor.

In order to test the prevalence of each broad category of masculinity, I identified words that could be associated with each. I searched short but critical election stages (April and October 2000; January 2004; March and October 2008; March and October 2012) and looked for words that suggested either dominance or expertise in candidates.[20] Quite simply, for

[20] For the 2000 election, I looked at news accounts in the *Washington Post* and the *St. Louis Post-Dispatch* for the months of April and October; Peter Bartanen assisted with the research. For 2004, I looked in all seven papers for the month of January, a key time for winnowing Democratic candidates; Sarah Bryner and Sara Hyler provided excellent

TABLE 1.3: Dominance words were more than three times more common than expertise words in articles about presidential candidates during the 2012 campaign

Expertise masculinity		Dominance masculinity	
Words	# of times used	Words	# of times used
Technical	108	Dominate	263
Intelligent	147	Strong	778
Smart	153	Aggressive	280
Advocate	235	Attack	774
Wonk	39	Blast	58
Total	682	Total	2,153

Note: Articles analyzed from March and October 2012 in the *Washington Post, Atlanta Journal Constitution,* and *New York Times* in articles that contained presiden!, candida! and 2012. Compiled by author.

all time periods, consistent with Table 1.3, words common to dominance masculinity outnumbered expertise masculinity words greatly: roughly two to one for 2000 and four to one for 2004 and 2008, and three to one for 2012. This pattern strongly suggests that dominance rather than expertise drives the ethos of presidential campaigns. Women therefore face particular gendered challenges in their bid for the masculinized presidency.

The pattern also suggests that expertise matters far less than dominance, posing particular challenges for women. A closer look at the 2000 race shows that Bush and Gore received about the same amount of dominance coverage. Nonetheless, Gore did not "do" dominance masculinity well, with many references to his aggressiveness and attacks being cast negatively, "a kind of sanctimonious aggressiveness" ... "his principal weakness."[21] Romney suffered a similar fate in 2012 in that his attempts at dominance were often seen as unconvincing, perhaps because of the masculinity sought by Mormon men of "loving restraint" and "long-suffering gentleness and meekness."[22]

research assistance. For 2008, I added *The Seattle Times.* Laura Sunstrom and Kevin Symanietz proved outstanding research assistants. For 2012, I only used the *Washington Post* and *New York Times.* I thank Janelle Perez for her fine work as research assistant.

[21] The Associated Press. October 2, 2000. In Gore-Bush Debates, Voters Will See Personal As Well As Political Differences, TV Setting May Magnify Strengths and Weaknesses. *St. Louis Post-Dispatch.*

[22] Naomi Zeveloff. February 5, 2012. The ultimate Mormon male: Mitt Romney doesn't want to talk specifics about his Mormon faith, but it has defined his image, style and campaign. Salon. www.salon.com/2012/02/05/the_ultimate_mormon_male/.

But, for the gendered space of presidential elections, the fact that women and men do not "do" dominance in the same way, nor are women culturally "allowed" to dominate in the public world like men, matters greatly. Hence, a gender double bind results. Any show of dominance by Hillary Clinton risked a similar claim of ill-performed aggressiveness, even though some aggressiveness is expected for a president. Clinton inspired now legendary nutcrackers made in her likeness, cable news men likened her to the "first wife," and a nationally syndicated radio commentator called her a "testicle lockbox." No male candidate has faced such personal and sexualized derision. Female candidates must tread very lightly on dominance, and yet they must meet the demands of presidential timber. Michele Bachmann was not recognized for the expertise she has, nor did she get far enough to actually attempt to dominate. For all but Tea Party activists, she was portrayed as a crazy joke.

Expertise has been central to women's advancement in the public realm. In fact, since the 1970s when women began to enter the public realm, they have relied on expertise as a rational response to sexism, often having higher and better credentials than their male counterparts. In 2008, Clinton staked out her credentials through expertise gained in her experience as first lady and in the Senate, a traditional route to the presidency. Because women tend to be punished for dominance displays, a strong showing of expertise becomes rational. In fact, both Clinton and McCain evoked expertise through experience, in large part because Obama lacked experience. McCain already had masculine dominance, although in comparison to Obama, age and vitality became issues. Clinton faced different challenges: she sought to transform expertise into dominance. Obama, in contrast, played on change and the dominance required to change the system. Indisputably, he dominated the big campaign rally and, through his speeches, demonstrated a capacity to inspire committed followers. One suspects, however, that as president, Obama also felt constraints in displaying dominance as a black man in majority white America.

The 2012 cycle placed Obama in a very different position in terms of the level of enthusiasm of his followers, having disappointed many on the left especially and being perceived as having failed at bringing change to the system as promised. Because congressional Republicans had resisted him at every turn, even though he had achieved major legislation, the sputtering economy and his inability to move Congress made charges of his weakness believable. He nonetheless was a sitting president and could still dominate the big campaign rally. Romney was plagued throughout

TABLE 1.4: Manliness and wimp were mentioned more in 2004, but masculinity and testosterone were equally or more common topics in 2012

	Manly	Masculine	Wimp	Testosterone
2004	101	26	69	22
2008	6	12	5	6
2012	10	17	21	19

Note: Numbers indicate the number of times the word appeared in article set on the presidential election. Articles analyzed from January 1, 2003, to November 16, 2004, in the *Washington Post, New York Times, Atlanta Journal Constitution, Los Angeles Times, St. Louis Post-Dispatch, Houston Chronicle,* and *Boston Globe.* For 2008, words gathered from January 1, 2007, to October 31, 2008, from same newspapers and *Seattle Times* in addition. The 2012 search used only the first three newspapers in articles from January 1, 2011, to November 7, 2012.
Source: Compiled by author.

the campaign by a major enthusiasm gap from the Republican conservative base.

Importantly, because the 2012 election for the first time in recent history featured two candidates whose strengths rested on technical expertise masculinity, I searched articles related to candida!, presiden! and 2012 for expert! or domina! in three leading newspapers, the *New York Times, Washington Post,* and *Atlanta Journal Constitution.* The findings were surprising. On these terms only, rather than words that could be seen as characterizing each, expertise ($N = 205$) was about twice as likely to appear as dominate ($N = 141$). If dominance is becoming less important than technical expertise, perhaps more space for women is opening in presidential elections.

MAKING MASCULINITY VISIBLE: WHAT KIND OF MAN?

The use of particular words related to masculinity became the subject of explicit analysis and explicit campaign strategy during the 2004 elections. Table 1.4 shows such words as they appeared in newspaper coverage of the election; the counts include all forms of the word, such as manly and manliness or masculine and masculinity. The contrast is dramatic. The election of 2004 used masculinity as an overt tactic in ways 2008 and 2012 seem not to have, at least for explicit coverage of manliness and a wimp factor. The latter is true despite a July 29, 2011, *Newsweek* article focusing on Romney's wimp factor and claiming he was just too insecure to be president. Among other stated problems, he purportedly failed to "Man up, double down, take his lumps."[23] He also was photographed riding a Jet Ski with his wife driving, clearly an unmanly pose for president. Nonetheless, Romney did not suffer the charges of weakness that successfully stuck to Kerry in 2004, such as flip-flopper or "French," despite the fact he shared many of the same behaviors.

The 2012 election grew out of prior elections, and awareness of masculinity is no exception. The 2004 campaigns overtly projected hegemonic masculinity. By 2003, conservatives were "draping George W. Bush in a masculine mystique.... [T]he president is hailed as a symbol of virility – a manly man in contrast to the allegedly effeminate Bill Clinton."[24] But not only Republicans were concerned. One extended headline read, "Who's the Man? They Are; George Bush and John Kerry stand shoulder to shoulder in one respect: Macho is good. Very good. It's been that way since Jefferson's day."[25] Many experts claimed, "a good portion of the presidential image-making in 2004 will center on masculinity... Both candidates appear to come by their macho naturally." Both candidates also took every chance to overtly cultivate machismo images, whether through images of Bush powering his father's cigarette boat in Maine or Kerry taking shots and checks on the hockey rink. Despite use of explicit terms, most manly themes will be "cast in more subtle and euphemistic terms, as pundits talk about the candidates' 'authenticity,' 'decisiveness,' and 'toughness.'"[26]

Toughness has had masculine associations, and discourse throughout the space of presidential elections drips with evocations of it. Despite women making tough decisions all the time, decisiveness has generally been associated with men. Therefore, the extensive Republican effort to paint John Kerry as indecisive, a "flip-flopper," was also a way to cast him as like a stereotypical woman who keeps changing her mind. Such fears boxed Clinton in so that she risked charges of flip-flopping if she changed her mind, particularly on Iraq. Interestingly, despite considerable evidence of flip-flopping on many issues, Romney escaped such charges.

[23] Michael Tomansky. July 29, 2011. Mitt Romney's Wimp Factor. The Daily Beast, in *Newsweek*.
[24] Cathy Young. September 8, 2003. We're Still Playing the Gender Card. *Boston Globe*.
[25] James Rainey. March 18, 2004. Who's the Man? They are; George Bush and John Kerry stand shoulder to shoulder in one respect: Macho is good. Very good. It's been that way since Jefferson's day. *Los Angeles Times*.
[26] Ibid.

Associating authenticity with masculinity presents a puzzle. The answer, however, emerged in perceptions of authentic masculinity itself. Authenticity was linked to masculinity because the Republicans particularly displayed a strategy of:

> ...portraying opponents as less than fully masculine. Republicans retooled a Nixon plan from the 1972 campaign, and designed a plan to enable Bush to "capture the hearts and votes of the nation's white working men ... Nixon's plan was to build an image as 'a tough, courageous, masculine leader.'"[27]

George W. Bush's advisors intended to do the same. A key component of such masculinity is dominance. To be the manly leader who can rally other men requires the enemy to "be feminized."[28] But this is not new." American politicians have not been above feminizing their opponents dating back to the era of powdered wigs, playing on the stereotypical notion that only the "manly" can lead. Bush supporters called John Edwards the "Breck girl"[29] and mocked John Kerry. They also succeeded in raising questions about Kerry's status as a hero. Such attacks pushed Kerry into ever more explicit displays of his own dominance masculinity. His advisors began to declare it. "Different voters ... were really struck by John's presidentialness. He's big, he's masculine, he's a serious man for a serious time."[30] Kerry moved away from his expertise because it highlighted his "patrician airs" and did not play well with audiences, and the Bush camp systematically undermined Kerry's key weapon for the presidency, his heroic manliness. Similarly, the Romney campaign's relentless effort to show him as a successful businessman worthy of conservative support also fell short in the face of Democrats' framing of him as rich and out of touch.

But all campaigns evolve from previous ones. Hillary Clinton's 2008 campaign came after the hyper-masculinity of 2004, forcing her to demonstrate sufficient masculinity to be seen as presidential. The failures of 2008 hyper-masculinity may also have changed the terms of what would be valued in 2012. For example, the concept of "tough" has been important word for presidential politics and has become integral to the

---

[27] Arlie Hochschild. October 5, 2003. NASCAR Dads Fuel Strategies for Bush in '04. *Los Angeles Times.*

[28] Ducat, *The Wimp Factor*, 2004.

[29] Maureen Dowd. March 11, 2004. Whence the Wince? *New York Times.*

[30] Todd S. Purdum and David M. Halbfinger. February 1, 2004. With Cry of "Bring It On," Kerry Shifted Tack to Regain Footing. *The New York Times.*

discourse of the election. In fact, the most pronounced finding from word analysis is the extent to which presidential election space is infused with the concept of toughness; hence, one can predict that its regendering will hinge on the extent to which women can be seen as tough enough.

As a woman, Hillary Clinton faced a challenge of proving toughness to a standard beyond any of the men. Using the eight-newspaper dataset, I searched for the term "tough" and a candidate's name in the same paragraph from January 2007 through May 2009. During that time Clinton definitely became associated with toughness more than Obama. Clinton received 542 mentions with tough, compared to Obama's 498. McCain, who simply struggled for press coverage during the later primary season, was mentioned with tough 364 times. In other words, Clinton won the "tough" battle but may have lost the election in the process, in part because our culture does not necessarily reward tough women, even though we want a tough president.

If overt appeals to masculinity proved so common in 2004 and 2008, where were they in 2012? As a referent point, tough! appeared 2,039 times in articles related directly to the campaign in the three newspapers in 2012. Rather than framed as a contest of masculinity, 2008 was framed as a "historic election." The question was whether a woman or a black would receive the Democratic nomination. Of course the woman, Clinton, faced the challenges of masculinity associated with the presidency. As a *white* woman, she did not face the racial barrier because all presidents heretofore have been white. The black, Obama, faced challenges as a black *man*. He faced the usual questions about his masculinity discussed throughout this piece – could he dominate, would he inspire a large enough following to win, would he be judged as possessing sufficient presidential timber, and the like. However, he also needed to negotiate many obstacles of his blackness, such as whether white Americans would agree to a black man leading a national institution and how he could avoid fitting the stereotype of an angry black man.

In fact, Obama's need to stay calm may have contributed to his vulnerability in 2012, when he could be characterized as not tough enough to control Congress. His clear intellect and career as a law professor endowed him with sufficient expertise masculinity. In terms of dominance, white culture tends to assign hyper-masculinity to black men. So, despite the uniformly negative coverage of his qualifications to be commander in chief, he faced a far different need to prove his warrior credentials than Clinton in 2008 because whites tend to fear the martial capacities of black men and associate them with violence. By 2012, as commander in chief he had ended the war in Iraq, killed Osama bin Laden, and was working to end the war in Afghanistan. Obama therefore began on a strong basis of masculinity based on his presidency as well as such things as his basketball prowess. In 2008, gender was not about masculinity; gender was equated with the first woman candidate. Coverage of race was not about a black *man* but rather the first black presidential candidate.

By 2012, awareness of masculinity and testosterone seem to have come into public view, with more regular discussion of how men behave and awareness of men as gendered beings rather than simple reliance on masculine assumptions as the universal norm. News reports including references to masculinity and testosterone in 2012 were roughly equivalent to those found in the 2004 analysis.[31] The widespread discussion about masculinity and dominance after the first and second debates serves as a focal point for such analysis, particularly because of the importance of female voters to this election. Television coverage of the debates dripped with comments about masculinity through discussions of testosterone and dominance.

The kind of *man* each candidate was proved so important that the candidates' wives both spoke directly to this topic in their convention speeches, as did the vice presidential candidates. These speeches are carefully vetted by the campaigns in order to present the image the campaign wants, although the wives and vice presidential candidates must also agree and so have some influence over the message they deliver. Important for the gendering of the 2012 election, two very different kinds of men and masculinity emerge from what was said and not said.

Table 1.5 is based on content analysis of the convention addresses by Ann Romney, Michele Obama, Joe Biden, and Paul Ryan, simply counting the number of times a word was used *in relation to their candidate*. The terms are listed first, followed by key words from the main quote taken from each speech.

Clearly, both camps were talking about their candidate *as a man* in these important convention speeches, given the number of references to that word. TV commentators remarked loudly that the speeches dripped

---

[31] Analysis of 2004 and 2008 drew upon seven and eight newspapers respectively, while the 2012 analysis uses only three, albeit the two largest. As a result, masculinity and testosterone may actually have been covered more in 2012 than in earlier cycles. The fact remains that we now see steady coverage of masculinity in presidential elections, with a clear awareness that testosterone plays a role. This explicit coverage of male candidates as men is relatively new.

TABLE 1.5: The 2012 campaigns portrayed very different men and masculinities

Word spoken about their candidate	Michelle Obama	Joe Biden	Total for Obama	Ann Romney	Paul Ryan	Total for Romney
Man	8	6	14	11	4	15
Husband	8	0	8	2	0	2
Father, Dad	0	2	2	0	0	0
Son	4	2	6	2	1	3
Guy	2	0	2	1	0	1
Family	7	0	7	4	0	4
Faith	0	2	2	1	3	4
Love/Loving	15	2	17	15	0	15
Help	4	0	4	10	0	10
Tough	1	7	8	0	0	0
Leader	0	4	4	0	4	4
Main Quote Descriptors	Character, Conviction, Rebuild, Make difference	Tested, Strength, Command, Faith, Confidence		Decent, Loving, Family, Faith, Helping	Prayerful, Faithful, Honorable, Worthy, Businessman	

Note: Using a transcript of the speeches by Michelle Obama, Ann Romney, and the vice presidential candidates, I counted words used *in relation* to their respective candidate. Words were selected to capture dimensions of masculinity and to illustrate the particular emphasis by the wives. I then sought the most direct characterization of each candidate as a person, as who he is, and extracted descriptors.
http://www.npr.org/2012/08/28/160216442/transcript-ann-romneys-convention-speech
http://www.npr.org/2012/09/04/160578836/transcript-michelle-obamas-convention-speech

with "love," perhaps the most important theme highlighted by both wives as indicated by its status as the most often-used word I tested.

By looking at the number of times particular words – and silences – are used, particular themes emerge. Michelle Obama's speech conveys a loving husband, family man, and son; a good guy who helps. Ann Romney stresses how helpful her husband is to the family and beyond, through his church. That is, both candidates' wives emphasize love a great deal; Obama makes more family and family-roles references, while Romney returns repeatedly to helpfulness. The vice presidential candidates, in contrast to the wives, focus on their running mates as leaders. In sharp contrast, Biden references Obama's toughness (mostly in regard to decisions) while Ryan never refers to Romney in these terms. He instead highlights Romney as a leader with faith. Terms drawn from the main quotation of each speech further highlight the differences in the overall type of man each is portrayed to be. Obama is painted as a man of character, confidence, and conviction who is strong and commanding as he works to make a difference, rebuilding the country and people's lives. Romney, in comparison, is cast as a decent, helpful, worthy man of faith and an honorable businessman. While this characterization may be consistent with ideal Mormon masculinity and might have been meant to attract the conservative evangelical Republican base, it misses the mark of a dominant, tough masculinity commonly associated with the presidency. The Obama campaign seemed to understand the message needed for the presidency. In all likelihood, Michelle Obama stressed her husband's role as a good family man as much because it counters white Americans' stereotypes about black husbands and fathers as because she believes it is true. That is, both candidates were dealing with other aspects of masculinity more finely tuned to their particular identities.

By bringing implicit masculinity into awareness, people can think more clearly about masculinity as an assumed qualifier for office. Ideas about leadership, which have been adjusting to women leaders' successes in other realms, can inform judgments in presidential elections, too. To think explicitly about masculinity in presidential elections is to open the door wider for women. It is also to bring greater awareness to different types of masculinity and their relationship to how Americans understand the presidency and presidential timber. The 2012 election space and Michele Bachmann offered the opportunity to think about the continuing sexism in coverage of female candidates. More importantly, the 2012 election offered alternative views of masculinity. Questions remain about whether and how masculinity and sexism will shape the 2016 presidential space in a campaign that is already underway.

2 Cracking the "Highest, Hardest Glass Ceiling"

Women as Presidential and Vice Presidential Contenders

On Election Night 2008, defeated Republican vice presidential candidate Sarah Palin left the stage in Phoenix, Arizona, without being given a chance to speak the words she had prepared to deliver: "Now it is time for us go our way, neither bitter nor vanquished, but instead confident in the knowledge that there will be another day, we may gather once more and find new strength and rise to fight again."[1] Many believed that the 2012 presidential election would present that opportunity for Palin to fight again, this time at the top of the ticket.

Heightening speculation that she would run in 2012, Palin launched her own political action committee – SarahPAC – in February 2009. Five months later, she resigned as governor of Alaska, citing family needs and numerous ethics probes that she claimed were impeding her from doing her job. In November 2009, Palin released her autobiography, *Going Rogue;* just more than one month later, she signed a multiyear deal with Fox News. In 2010, Palin continued to make news as a pundit, reality-TV star, and top endorser for Republican candidates in the midterm elections. Her intentions with regard to the presidential race were unclear through much of 2011, despite her strength in some Republican primary polls. In May 2011, Palin launched her One Nation bus tour with a stop in New Hampshire. In August, she took the bus to Iowa one day before the Ames Straw Poll but continued to hedge on when or whether she was going to announce her candidacy. It was not until October 5, 2011, that Palin officially announced that she would not run for president in 2012.

---

[1] Sushannah Walshe and Scott Conroy, Sarah Palin's Lost Speeches. *The Daily Beast.* November 3, 2009. http://www.thedailybeast.com/articles/2009/11/03/sarah-palins-lost-victory-speech.html. Accessed March 15, 2013.

By that time, another woman, Congresswoman Michele Bachmann (R-MN), had entered the Republican primary race, making history as the first woman to ever win the Ames Straw Poll. However, Bachmann was unable to shatter the highest, hardest glass ceiling in American politics in 2012. And while she benefitted from the cracks made in it by Hillary Clinton as a candidate for the Democratic nomination and Sarah Palin as Republican vice presidential candidate in 2008, all three women's candidacies reveal the gender-based challenges that confront women who seek the most powerful executive offices in the United States and quite possibly the world.

Research by political scientists and pollsters has shown that voters have clear and specific stereotypes about women candidates and potential women political leaders.[2] Some of these stereotypes can work to the advantage of women seeking office, especially in elections in which voters want change and in which domestic – as opposed to international – issues are at the forefront of voters' concerns. For example, when compared with male candidates, women candidates are commonly viewed as more honest, more caring, more inclusive and collaborative, more likely to bring about change, and more likely to have expertise on domestic issues such as education and health care.

However, just as there are positive stereotypes that can work to the advantage of women candidates, strong negative stereotypes held by voters can seriously disadvantage women, especially when they run for national and/or executive offices. Voters are less confident that women can handle the emotional demands of high-level office, and they worry about whether women are tough enough and can act decisively. While voters readily assume that men have the necessary qualifications, they are concerned about whether women are qualified to hold top executive positions. Voters worry about whether women have the financial expertise to deal with big budgets, and they view women as less likely than men to be able to manage the military and to handle international

---

[2] For example, see Leonie Huddy and Nayda Terkildsen. 1993. Gender Stereotypes and the Perception of Male and Female Candidates. *American Journal of Political Science* 37(1): 119–47; Leonie Huddy and Nayda Terkildsen. 1993. The Consequences of Gender Stereotypes for Women Candidates at Different Levels and Types of Office. *Political Research Quarterly* 46(3): 503–25; Kim Fridkin Kahn. 1996. *The Political Consequences of Being a Woman: How Stereotypes Influence the Conduct and Consequences of Campaigns*. New York: Columbia University Press; and Barbara Lee Family Foundation. 2001. *Keys to the Governor's Office*. Brookline, MA: Barbara Lee Family Foundation.

crises. Finally, voters are more likely to scrutinize a woman candidate's family situation – expressing concern, for example, that the demands of running for office may lead her to neglect her family. When a man runs for office, his family is generally viewed as an important source of emotional and personal support. When a woman runs, her spouse and children are more often perceived as additional responsibilities that the candidate must shoulder.

Confronting these negative gender stereotypes, Hillary Clinton and Sarah Palin faced challenges in their 2008 campaigns that male contenders for president and vice president did not. Because they are very different women with distinct life experiences and situations, the specific nature of the gender-related challenges Clinton and Palin faced differed, as did their responses. Nevertheless, in each case gender helped significantly shape the candidate's campaign and the way the media and the public responded to her candidacy. Despite hopes that 2008 had made it easier, or at least "unremarkable," for other women to run for the nation's highest offices,[3] Michele Bachmann also faced unique challenges and treatment tied to her gender as a contender for the Republican nomination in 2012.

This chapter focuses on the history and treatment of women as presidential and vice presidential candidates. We begin with an overview of the pioneering women who have dared to step forward as presidential or vice presidential candidates throughout American history. We then turn to the 2008 campaigns of Hillary Clinton and Sarah Palin, analyzing the ways that gender stereotypes influenced the strategies they employed, the media's coverage of their campaigns, and public reactions to their candidacies. We also examine Michele Bachmann's 2012 primary campaign, asking whether the pioneering candidacies of Clinton and Palin altered the path in any way for the women who will follow them as presidential and vice presidential candidates.

[3] A June 2008 CBS poll showed that 69 percent of voters felt that Hillary Clinton's candidacy made it easier for other women to run for president, and a postelection survey of women ages 18 to 25 showed that at least one-third of respondents were encouraged by Hillary Clinton and Sarah Palin's candidacies to believe that they would live to see a woman president. CBS News. February 27, 2009. Poll: Clinton's Run Opens Door for Women. http://www.cbsnews.com/2100-500160_162-4151029.html. Accessed January 6, 2013; Linton Weeks. June 9, 2011. The Feminine Effect on Presidential Politics. *NPR News.* http://www.npr.org/2011/06/09/137056376/the-feminine-effect-on-presidential-politics. Accessed January 6, 2013.

HISTORY OF WOMEN CANDIDATES FOR PRESIDENT AND VICE PRESIDENT

While the nation's topmost executive posts – the presidency and the vice presidency – remain male preserves, a handful of women prior to Hillary Clinton, Sarah Palin, and Michele Bachmann have dared to put themselves forward as candidates for these offices. These women trailblazers slowly chipped away at the gender role expectations that have traditionally relegated women to the East Wing instead of the West Wing of the White House.

Two women became candidates for the presidency in the nineteenth century, even before they could cast ballots themselves. Victoria Woodhull in 1872 and Belva Lockwood in 1884 were both nominated as presidential candidates by a group of reformers identifying themselves as the Equal Rights Party. Woodhull, a newspaper publisher and the first woman stockbroker, was only thirty-three years old when she was nominated, too young to meet the constitutionally mandated age requirement of thirty-five for the presidency, and as an advocate of free love, Woodhull spent Election Day in jail on charges that she had sent obscene materials through the mail.[4] Unlike Woodhull, who made no real effort to convince voters to support her, Lockwood actively campaigned for the presidency despite public mockery and even criticism from her fellow suffragists. As the first woman to practice law in front of the U.S. Supreme Court, Lockwood knew what it felt like to stand alone and did so again in her second presidential bid in 1888.

Before the next female candidate claimed a space on the presidential ballot, three women had been considered for vice presidential slots. Nellie Tayloe Ross of Wyoming, a true pioneer as the nation's first female governor, won thirty-one votes for the vice presidency on the first ballot at the Democratic convention in 1928. Twenty-four years later, in 1952, two Democratic women – India Edwards and Sarah B. Hughes – were considered for the vice presidency, but both withdrew their names before convention balloting began.

In 1964, Republican Senator Margaret Chase Smith of Maine became the first female candidate to have her name placed in nomination for president at a major party convention, winning twenty-seven delegate

---

[4] Jo Freeman. 2008. We Will Be Heard: Women's Struggles for Political Power in the United States. Lanham, MD: Rowman and Littlefield.

votes from three states. Eight years later, in 1972, Congresswoman Shirley Chisholm of New York, the first African-American woman elected to Congress, became the first woman and the first African American to have her name placed in nomination for the presidency at a Democratic National Convention, winning 151.95 delegate votes. At the same convention, Frances (Sissy) Farenthold won more than 400 votes for the vice presidential slot, finishing second.[5]

Smith and Chisholm, like their predecessors Woodhull and Lockwood a century earlier, recognized the improbability of their nominations, measuring success in other terms. Smith prioritized normalizing the image of a woman running for executive office, and Chisholm sought to pave the way for women after her, proving that "it can be done."[6]

Despite the presence of women on some minor party ballots, no woman was nominated to a major party's presidential ticket until 1984, when New York Congresswoman Geraldine Ferraro was chosen as former Vice President Walter Mondale's Democratic running mate. Her candidacy was shaded with questions surrounding her gender, from whether she was schooled enough in military and foreign policy to how she should dress and interact with presidential nominee Mondale. Much attention, too, was paid to her husband, a trend that continued with female candidates who came after her, from Elizabeth Dole to Hillary Clinton.

While the defeat of the Mondale-Ferraro ticket in 1984 disappointed voters looking to make history, many supporters of women in politics had their hopes renewed in 1987 as they watched Congresswoman Patricia Schroeder of Colorado prepare to make a presidential bid. Despite the fact that Schroeder raised more money than any other woman candidate in U.S. history, she was not able to raise enough. Her decision, long before the first primary, not to become an official candidate resulted in tears from her supporters and Schroeder herself. Those tears, considered unacceptable for a woman candidate, made national news and provoked public debate about gender traits and presidential politics.

In 1999, two-time presidential cabinet member Elizabeth Dole established an exploratory committee and mounted a six-month campaign for the Republican nomination for president, taking the next step toward

---

[5] Center for American Women and Politics. January 2012. Women Presidential and Vice Presidential Candidates. http://www.cawp.rutgers.edu/fast_facts/levels_of_office/documents/prescand.pdf. Accessed March 18, 2013.

[6] Shirley Chisholm. 1973. *The Good Fight.* New York: Harper Collins.

putting a woman in the White House. Although Dole consistently came in second in public opinion polls, behind only George W. Bush, and benefited from name recognition, popularity, and political connections, many people doubted that she could win. Even her husband, Senator Bob Dole, who had been the Republican nominee for president in the previous election, expressed reservations about her campaign, telling a *New York Times* reporter:

> [that] he wanted to give money to a rival candidate [McCain] who was fighting for much of her support. He conceded that Mrs. Dole's operation had had growing pains, was slow to raise money early and was only beginning to hit its stride. And while Mr. Dole was hopeful, he allowed that he was by no means certain she would even stay in the race.[7]

In mid-October, five months after Bob Dole's comments and a few months before the first primary, Elizabeth Dole withdrew from the race for the Republican nomination.

In 2003, Carol Moseley Braun, the first African-American woman to serve in the U.S. Senate and a former ambassador to New Zealand, was the only woman among ten candidates who contended for the Democratic presidential nomination. Her appearance in six televised debates among the Democratic hopefuls helped disrupt the white, masculine image of presidential contenders so strongly embedded in the American psyche. Although major women's groups endorsed her, Moseley Braun dropped out of the race in January 2004, shortly before the first primaries and caucuses.

Ruth B. Mandel has described the legacy of the women who ran for the office of president prior to the 2008 elections this way: "They made a claim on public awareness by attaching voices and living images of accomplished woman leaders to the idea that one day a woman could conceivably be president. Their actions made the idea less outrageous to conceive."[8] These women blazed paths, opened doors, and challenged established gender stereotypes and gender role expectations.

---

[7] Richard L. Berke. May 17, 1999. As Political Spouse, Bob Dole Strays from Campaign Script. *New York Times.* http://www.nytimes.com/1999/05/17/us/as-political-spouse-bob-dole-strays-from-campaign-script.html?pagewanted=all&src=pm. Accessed March 18, 2013.

[8] Ruth Mandel. 2007. She's the Candidate! A Woman for President. In *Women and Leadership: The State of Play and Strategies for Change,* ed. Barbara Kellerman and Deborah L. Rhode. San Francisco: Jossey-Bass, 283–311.

2008 ELECTION

Hillary Clinton's claim that she was "in to win" the 2008 presidential election moved women candidates from novelty to viability. Standing on the shoulders of the pioneering women who came before her, Clinton took a major step forward in normalizing the idea of a female American president. Her candidacy, popularity, and challenge to gender norms had a near-immediate impact on American politics, as Republican John McCain noted the excitement over a woman candidate and chose Alaska Governor Sarah Palin as his running mate, only the second woman – and the first Republican woman – to win a spot on a major party's presidential ticket.

Accustomed to making news and, more important, to making history, Hillary Clinton built on a lifetime of leadership and trailblazing in her bid as the first serious female contender for the U.S. presidency. Clinton's political activism began early on as a "Goldwater girl" in the early 1960s and later as a college student supporting the Democratic antiwar candidate, Senator Eugene McCarthy, in 1968. As president of her college government association, she became the first student to speak at a Wellesley College commencement. After graduation, Clinton earned a law degree from Yale University, married Bill Clinton, and as a practicing attorney was twice named to the list of the 100 most influential lawyers in America.

Hillary Clinton's political and professional credentials became the subject of debate and discussion as she moved into the role of a political wife – albeit one who was far from traditional and at many times controversial. Clinton defied established expectations for a first lady, most notably by moving the first lady's office from the East Wing to the West Wing of the White House. Within five days of becoming first lady, she was named by her husband to head the President's Task Force on Health Care Reform, drawing criticism of her unrestrained ambition. The failure of the Clinton health care plan only fueled greater vilification of her by many political foes, but Hillary Clinton restored her political capital internationally with her 1995 address to the United Nations in Beijing on the importance of women's rights and her successful advocacy for the federal Children's Health Insurance Program in 1997. Despite these successes, Clinton's reputation was tarred by her rejection of a traditional role as first lady, her deep involvement in White House policy, repeated allegations about her possible involvement in political scandals, and her decision to stay with a cheating husband. Clinton left the White House as a controversial and polarizing figure, deeply admired by some and intensely disliked by others.

Unsurprisingly to most of her closest friends and political peers, Hillary Clinton began her own political campaign for the U.S. Senate from New York even before exiting the White House. After a tough campaign in which her motives and loyalty to the Empire State were questioned, Hillary Clinton became the first former first lady ever elected to public office in 2001. Clinton built her political credentials through her membership on the Senate Armed Services Committee and focused work for the people of New York, resulting in strong in-state popularity and a landslide victory in her 2006 reelection race.

However, speculation that she would seek the presidency began even before she was elected to the Senate and, in polls from as early as 2004 to 2007, Clinton emerged as the top contender in trial heats of Democratic candidates for the 2008 nomination.[9] After years of denying any ambition to run, Hillary Clinton announced that she would form an exploratory committee for a presidential bid on January 20, 2007, exactly two years before a new president would be sworn into the White House.

Holding the front-runner position throughout her first year of campaigning for the Democratic nomination, Hillary Clinton blazed a new trail, crossing the country with a motto of "making history" and exciting voters – especially women of all ages, for whom the prospect of a female president became real. Many observers thought her background, political clout, and wide coalition of supporters made her nomination inevitable. Historians and analysts will, for decades, look back at her campaign to see what shifted the narrative from almost-certain winner to underdog. Poor campaign management and strategy, perceptions of her status as a Washington insider, her vote in favor of the Iraq War, the role of her husband Bill Clinton, the altered primary season calendar, and the phenomenon of her major opponent, Senator Barack Obama, were among the many possible reasons for Clinton's downslide in polls and, later, in the Democratic primaries. After Clinton's initial defeat in the nation's first contest, the Iowa caucuses, the real battles stretched from the snowy terrain of New Hampshire – where Clinton, like her husband before her, became the state's "comeback kid" – to the deserts of Nevada. The historic primary season of 2008 was unprecedented, not only in length but also in

---

[9] Gallup. November 16, 2004. Hillary Clinton, Giuliani Early Favorites for 2008. http://www.gallup.com/poll/14053/Hillary-Clinton-Giuliani-Early-Favorites-2008.aspx. Accessed March 18, 2013.

the frequency with which front-runner status shifted. Over the course of six months, Hillary Clinton and Barack Obama competed in state primaries and caucuses from coast to coast and faced each other in seventeen debates.

After winning nine of the last sixteen primaries and caucuses and nearly 18 million votes nationwide, Hillary Clinton conceded the Democratic nomination on June 7, 2008. As she bowed out of the race, Clinton, who had downplayed her gender throughout most of the campaign, acknowledged that gender "barriers and biases" remain for women at the highest levels of power. She told a crowd of supporters:

> If we can blast 50 women into space, we will someday launch a woman into the White House. Although we weren't able to shatter that highest, hardest glass ceiling this time, thanks to you, it's got about 18 million cracks in it and the light is shining through like never before, filling us all with the hope and the sure knowledge that the path will be a little easier next time.[10]

Despite calls for her to contest the nomination at her party's convention in Denver, Clinton's preference for unity and loyalty to her party prevailed when she took to the convention floor to stop the roll-call vote and move that her primary rival, Barack Obama, be nominated by acclamation. Although she made history as only the second woman to have her name formally placed into nomination for president at the Democratic National Convention, Clinton took the opportunity to heal primary wounds, telling the crowd, "Whether you voted for me, or voted for Barack, the time is now to unite as a single party with a single purpose. We are on the same team, and none of us can sit on the sidelines."[11] With those words, the general election campaign season began, and Hillary Clinton shifted her role from history-making candidate to strong supporter and campaign surrogate for Obama. That shift was made complete when she accepted President Obama's appointment to serve as his Secretary of State, a position that brought her unprecedented popularity and an opportunity to further develop her image as a highly experienced stateswoman with a special commitment to women's equality worldwide.

[10] Washingtonpost.com. Transcript: Hillary Rodham Clinton Suspends Her Presidential Campaign. http://www.washingtonpost.com/wp-dyn/content/article/2008/06/07/AR 2008060701029.html. Accessed March 18, 2013.

[11] National Public Radio. August 26, 2008. Transcript: Hillary Clinton's Prime-Time Speech. http://www.npr.org/templates/story/story.php?storyId=94003143. Accessed March 18, 2013.

While the Democratic convention in Denver marked the end of Clinton's history-making campaign, it signaled the start of the 2008 campaign for another prominent woman. John McCain announced his choice of Alaska Governor Sarah Palin as the Republican candidate for vice president on the morning after Barack Obama's media-spectacle acceptance speech at Invesco Field. Motivated by hopes of curbing Obama's momentum, McCain's strategy proved successful, as Palin quickly became the focus of news media and water-cooler conversation. Palin was an unexpected candidate, novel for her outsider identity, her colloquial candor, and – for many – her gender. While nearly everyone in the country had an (often strong) opinion of Hillary Clinton after her nearly two decades in the national spotlight, Sarah Palin's route to celebrity was condensed into a two-and-a-half-month period between her selection by McCain and Election Day of 2008. By Election Day, Palin and Clinton were almost equally well known, according to public opinion polls.[12]

Palin was not politically active as an adolescent or young adult. She began her political career in 1992 when, at the age of twenty-eight, she was elected to the city council of the small Alaskan town of Wasilla. Palin unseated a three-term incumbent to become mayor of Wasilla in 1996, and she later served as president of the Alaska Conference of Mayors. It was not long before her political ambitions grew. In 2002, she sought the Republican nomination for lieutenant governor but was defeated. She was soon appointed to the Alaska Oil and Conservation Commission, gaining knowledge and experience that she used in later races, but she resigned from the board in 2004 citing ethics violations by its members, thereby helping shape her image as a pro-reform candidate for governor in 2006.

After defeating the incumbent governor to win the Republican nomination, Palin entered the 2006 general election race for governor as the clear front-runner. She campaigned as an outsider on an ethics reform platform, turning criticisms of her inexperience into evidence that she was not tied to established interests and would be a fresh face for Alaskan government. Her political skills were evident. Profiling herself as an antiestablishment underdog and agent of change, she became the first woman, and the youngest person, ever to serve as governor of Alaska.

Faced with an energized Democratic electorate and the wide appeal of Barack Obama's historic nomination, the McCain campaign needed a

[12] Gallup. Favorability: People in the News. http://www.gallup.com/poll/1618/Favorability-People-News.aspx. Accessed March 18, 2013.

vice presidential candidate who could bring attention and excitement to the Republican ticket. Palin not only was a popular governor, a rousing speaker, and a crowd pleaser but also had a reputation as a reformer and a maverick with strong ties to the social conservative base of the party. Moreover, her gender was viewed as a potential lure for any Clinton supporters harboring resentment over Clinton's loss. In fact, in Palin's first speech as the vice presidential candidate, she praised Clinton and drew from her concession remarks:

> It was rightly noted [at the Democratic Party convention] in Denver this week that Hillary left 18 million cracks in the highest, hardest glass ceiling in America. But it turns out the women of America aren't finished yet. And we can shatter that glass ceiling once and for all.[13]

As Palin took to the campaign trail, she did bring considerable energy and attention to the Republican ticket, attracting strong reactions, both positive and negative, from voters – particularly women, social conservatives, and working-class Republicans. She took the Republican National Convention by storm, demonstrating that she would gladly be John McCain's loyal surrogate and an attack dog when necessary. In the week following the convention, Palin received more media attention than either John McCain or Barack Obama, with more than half of the campaign news stories focused on her.[14] Throughout the remaining weeks of the campaign, Palin remained the subject of much media analysis and commentary, although the economic crisis chipped away at the Republican ticket's hope for a general election victory.

The McCain campaign's early attempts to keep Palin away from the press made news outlets only more eager for interviews with her, and when Palin stumbled in her first major interviews with news anchors Charlie Gibson of ABC and Katie Couric of CBS, the public impression grew that she was unprepared to be one heartbeat away from the presidency. Nevertheless, Palin continued to draw large and enthusiastic crowds at her campaign events. By the end of the 2008 presidential campaign, few voters seemed indifferent toward Palin; her supporters were as passionate in their enthusiasm for her as her detractors were in their criticism. Sarah Palin emerged from the 2008 election as one of the most

[13] Clips and Comment: News, Politics, and Society: Ohio and the World. http://www .clipsandcomment.com/2008/08/29/transcript-sarah-palin-speech-in-dayton-ohio/. Accessed March 18, 2013.

[14] Pew Project for Excellence in Journalism. October 22, 2009. Winning the Media Campaign: Sarah Palin. http://www.journalism.org/node/13310. Accessed March 18, 2013.

fascinating women on the political scene and a likely contender for the Republican presidential nomination in 2012.

2012 ELECTION

Few women other than Sarah Palin were touted as potential 2012 contenders; Barack Obama faced no opposition in the Democratic primaries, and Republicans seemed to make no special effort to field women candidates. Entering the race with little establishment backing and much ideological overlap with Palin, Michele Bachmann officially announced her candidacy for president on June 27, 2011. Her campaign began and ended in Iowa and hit a number of road-bumps along the way. Amid a crowded field of ten Republican contenders, Bachmann gained popularity in the summer of 2011 but struggled to maintain that momentum as the primary elections began. As the field of candidates narrowed by half by January 2012, Bachmann was among the candidates edged out because of waning popularity, campaign missteps and/or disorganization, and insufficient resources.

Michele Bachmann entered the 2012 Republican primary with Iowa roots, Christian principles, and a background in tax law and state politics. After leaving her job at the IRS to stay at home with her five children, Bachmann's path toward politics began with advocacy for issues that mattered to her personally. In the early 1990s, she protested abortion clinics, and in 1993, her opposition to statewide education reforms led her and six others to found New Heights Charter School in Stillwater, Minnesota. She continued her education advocacy throughout the 1990s, culminating with an unsuccessful bid for the Stillwater school board in 1999.

A year later, Bachmann made an unexpected run for the Minnesota State Senate and won her first elective office at the age of forty-four. During her six-year tenure, she championed a taxpayers' bill of rights and pushed strongly for a constitutional amendment to ban same-sex marriage. Bachmann's senate experience helped her in 2006 to become the first Republican woman elected to represent Minnesota in the United States House of Representatives, where she continued her push for tax reform and became a stalwart opponent of President Obama and his health care law. Describing herself as a "constitutional conservative," Bachmann established the Tea Party Caucus in 2010.

It was those Tea Party credentials that brought her before Iowans for Tax Relief in January 2011, increasing the speculation that she would toss her hat into the Republican presidential primary. At the June 13 Republican debate at which Bachmann announced her candidacy, pundits noted her strong performance and even touted her as a "breakout star."[15] She formally announced her presidential run in the Iowa town of her birth two weeks later, claiming, "My voice is a part of a movement to take back our country."[16]

Despite a jump in some polls, Bachmann's support fell from June through August, with insiders claiming a lack of campaign infrastructure and more detailed message. Still, on August 13, 2011, Bachmann became the first woman to win the Ames Straw Poll, drawing 29 percent of the vote. Her ability to capitalize on this success was curtailed by Texas Governor Rick Perry's entry into the Republican primary race on the same day. His appeal to Bachmann's conservative constituency and overall surge in the polls took much of the air out of her campaign, and she was never able to recover. By early September, Bachmann's top strategists left the campaign, and by late October her New Hampshire campaign staff resigned. Bachmann entered the Iowa Caucuses on January 3, 2012, with little expectation of success. She finished sixth in the polls, with only 5 percent of the vote, and suspended her campaign the next day.

As the general election began, women's presence among potential vice presidential candidates was also limited. There were occasional rumors that Hillary Clinton would replace Vice President Joe Biden as Obama's running mate, but they were never taken seriously, most importantly by Clinton herself. On the Republican side, neither Palin nor Bachmann was rumored to be on Mitt Romney's short list. In fact, some insiders argued that Palin's missteps in 2008 would deter Romney from selecting any woman as his running mate. The most serious female contender appeared to be former Secretary of State Condoleezza Rice, despite her own insistence to the contrary, and Romney ultimately chose Congressman Paul Ryan (WI) to join him on the Republican ticket. Thus, while many hoped that 2008 had altered the gendered landscape of presidential elections, 2012 demonstrated that much work remains to level the playing field for women at the highest level of American politics.

[15] Luisita Lopez Torregrosa. June 21, 2011. Bachmann Will Have a Fight to Stay at the Top Tier. *New York Times*. http://www.nytimes.com/2011/06/22/us/22iht-letter22.html?_r=0. Accessed January 6, 2013.

[16] Michele Bachmann. June 27, 2011. Full Transcript: Announcement of Presidential Run. *New Statesman*. http://www.newstatesman.com/blogs/star-spangled-staggers/2011/06/government-waterloo-america. Accessed January 6, 2013.

GENDER STEREOTYPES AND WOMEN'S CANDIDACIES FOR PRESIDENT AND VICE PRESIDENT

Despite women's political advancement over the past three decades from local to national office, the executive offices of the president and vice president remain political spaces defined by masculinity and men. Expectations of national executive officeholders are grounded in strong gender stereotypes that present hurdles to the women who run. Those stereotypes were most evident in Hillary Clinton's and Sarah Palin's 2008 candidacies, and they reemerged as Michele Bachmann campaigned in 2012. We continue this chapter with a more in-depth look at the gender stereotypes that these women confronted, noting how they informed both campaign strategies and perceptions of their campaigns.

EXPERIENCE AND QUALIFICATIONS

Women are assumed to be less qualified than men to hold public office, even when they have more experience and stronger credentials. This stereotype is evident not only in research on voters but also in studies of women officeholders. For example, research on women state legislators conducted by the Center for American Women and Politics has found that women legislators tend to be more qualified than their male counterparts on every measure of political experience except for holding previous elective office – an indication that women who run for office know that they need to accumulate more experience to be perceived as equal to male candidates in qualifications.[17]

To counter this stereotype, Hillary Clinton made experience the centerpiece of her campaign for the Democratic nomination in 2008. Her campaign advisors knew they still needed to convince voters that Clinton was qualified to be president, even though her credentials included seven years in the U.S. Senate, eight years as first lady, and many years of advocacy work on public policy. On the campaign trail, Clinton proclaimed that she would be "ready to lead on day 1," and she made frequent references to her more than thirty-five years of experience. While Barack Obama spoke in broad strokes with appealing rhetoric, Hillary Clinton emphasized her mastery of the details of public policy, demonstrating the knowledge she had gained through her years of experience in public life.

---

[17] Susan J. Carroll and Wendy S. Strimling. 1983. *Women's Routes to Elective Office: A Comparison with Men's*. New Brunswick, NJ: Center for the American Woman and Politics.

Of course, by emphasizing experience as the major theme of her campaign, Clinton ceded the idea of change to Obama, who made it the centerpiece of his campaign with the theme "Change We Can Believe In." The literature on women candidates shows that women, as traditional outsiders in politics, are viewed by voters as the embodiment of change and do particularly well in elections in which voters are dissatisfied with the status quo. However, this gender-based benefit likely expected by the Clinton campaign was unexpectedly lost to Obama. Although he did not have a lengthy record of political experience at the beginning of his campaign, having served for only two years in the U.S. Senate and for seven years as a state senator in Illinois, his campaign did not have to worry, as Clinton's did, that its candidate's gender would make him appear less qualified. Consequently, Obama chose to emphasize, as well as to embody, change. Thus, in one of the great ironies of the 2008 campaign, the first woman to make a serious run for the White House came to be seen as the representative of the status quo.

Hillary Clinton's campaign was very successful in countering the stereotype of women as unqualified for office. A *USA Today*/Gallup Poll, taken February 21–24, 2008, found that 65 percent of Americans agreed that Hillary Clinton had the necessary experience to be a good president.[18] In contrast, Sarah Palin was never able to overcome perceptions of inexperience. According to the national exit poll conducted on Election Day, only 38 percent of voters thought Palin was qualified to be president if necessary.[19]

The McCain-Palin campaign did make some attempts to address the issue of Palin's experience. For example, the campaign ran a thirty-second ad arguing that Palin's record as a reformer was stronger than Obama's. The McCain-Palin campaign also argued, both in an ad and through campaign spokespeople, that Palin's experience as a governor "who oversees 24,000 state employees, 14 statewide cabinet agencies and a $10 billion budget" exceeded that of "Barack Obama's experience as a one-term junior senator from Illinois."[20] But none of this seemed to work. Perhaps the campaign's attempts to compare Palin with Obama to counter the perception of Palin as inexperienced were not very compelling. Perhaps

[18] Gallup. March 4, 2008. The Experience Paradox. http://www.gallup.com/video/104737/ Experience-Necessary.aspx. Accessed March 18, 2013.

[19] CNN. Election Center 2008. President: National Exit Poll. http://www.cnn.com/ ELECTION/2008/results/polls/#val=USP00p4. Accessed March 18, 2013.

[20] Politico. Mike Allen. Ad: Palin More Qualified Than Obama. http://www.politico.com/ news/stories/0908/13111.html. Accessed March 18, 2013.

the short amount of time Palin was a candidate – only two months as opposed to two years for Hillary Clinton – was simply insufficient to combat such a strong gender stereotype. Or perhaps the fact that Palin was propelled onto the national stage before accumulating more experience made the problem insurmountable.

Regardless, one factor that clearly contributed to Palin's problem with the experience issue was her treatment by the press. She was repeatedly characterized by the media as lacking the experience necessary to be vice president or, if need be, president. Her first major interview after being selected as a vice presidential nominee was with Charlie Gibson, the anchor of the evening news on ABC. Gibson's very first question was, "Governor, let me start by asking you a question that I asked John McCain about you, and it is really the central question. Can you look the country in the eye and say 'I have the experience and I have the ability to be not just vice president, but perhaps president of the United States of America?'" Gibson continued to pursue the experience issue in his next question, "And you didn't say to yourself, 'Am I experienced enough? Am I ready? Do I know enough about international affairs? Do I – will I feel comfortable enough on the national stage to do this?'" When Palin answered that she "didn't hesitate, no," Gibson responded, "Didn't that take some hubris?"[21]

One wonders whether Gibson would have asked an equally inexperienced man, "Didn't that take some hubris?" Interestingly, Gibson never asked this question of Barack Obama or George W. Bush, although neither had impressive political or international experience before becoming a presidential candidate and president. No presidential or vice presidential candidates were ever asked about what newspapers and magazines they read, either. But when CBS News anchor Katie Couric posed the question to Palin in 2008, Palin's less than satisfying answer fueled further criticism of her qualifications for office.[22]

The media continually reinforced the impression of Palin as inexperienced and unqualified in the minds of their audiences. Unfortunately for Palin, so did the McCain campaign itself. The campaign tried to keep

[21] ABC News. September 11, 2008. EXCERPTS: Charlie Gibson Interviews Sarah Palin. http://abcnews.go.com/Politics/Vote2008/story?id=5782924&page=1. Accessed March 18, 2013.
[22] CBS News. CBS Evening News with Katie Couric. Palin Opens Up on Controversial Issues. http://www.cbsnews.com/stories/2008/09/30/eveningnews/main4490618.shtml. Accessed March 18, 2013.

Palin away from reporters for several weeks after she was nominated, playing into and reinforcing the stereotype of the inexperienced, unqualified woman instead of giving Palin an opportunity to try in some way to overcome this stereotype.

Like Palin, Michele Bachmann faced a high hurdle in combating claims of inexperience, because of both her relatively short tenure in the U.S. House and the unlikely route of jumping from the House to the U.S. presidency. It did not help that some of these claims came from her own staff; her former chief of staff said that Bachmann was neither electable nor ready for the highest office, and her own campaign manager decried her bid, remarking, "There's no substance" on stepping down from his post in the fall of 2011.[23] His critique was not entirely unfounded, as the Bachmann campaign did little to emphasize the candidate's credentials for office and instead relied more heavily on anti–Obama rhetoric and Tea Party principles than outlining Bachmann's own plan for American progress.

Doubts over Bachmann's qualifications were also raised by a number of gaffes made on the campaign trail, from her inaccurate historical references to multiple policy claims that were quickly fact-checked and found erroneous by experts and organizations.[24] Bachmann's missteps, and a lack of strategic attempts to counter them, were amplified by the press. In addition to highlighting her errors, pundits directly questioned her seriousness as an executive candidate. Most overtly, in June 2011, Fox News anchor Chris Wallace asked Bachmann, "Are you a flake?"[25] While he later apologized for the question, Wallace's characterization of Bachmann evidenced a gender stereotype of women's frivolous and/or fragile nature in a high-stakes political world. Like Charlie Gibson questioning Sarah Palin, Chris Wallace did not pose the same question to male candidates, not even to Rick Perry, who committed similar gaffes throughout his 2012 presidential campaign.

---

[23] Russell Goldman. October 31, 2011. Bachmann "Out of Money and Ideas" in Iowa, Says Former Campaign Manager. *ABC News*. http://abcnews.go.com/blogs/politics/2011/10/bachmann-out-of-money-and-ideas-in-iowa-says-former-campaign-manager/. Accessed January 6, 2013.

[24] Shannon Travis. October 5, 2011. Bachmann's Latest Gaffe Adds to a Long String of Them. *CNN*. http://politicalticker.blogs.cnn.com/2011/10/05/bachmanns-latest-gaffe-adds-to-a-long-string-of-them/. Accessed January 6, 2013.

[25] Sam Stein. June 26, 2011. Chris Wallace Asks Michele Bachmann "Are You a Flake?" *Huffington Post*. http://www.huffingtonpost.com/2011/06/26/michele-bachmann-chris-wallace_n_884686.html. Accessed January 6, 2013.

TOUGHNESS

Voters are concerned not only about whether women candidates are qualified and have sufficient experience to serve in high-level political office but also about whether they are tough enough to take command and handle the emotional demands of the job. This stereotype is especially problematic for women running for executive positions such as governor or president, held by only one person at a time. As a Barbara Lee Foundation study of voters' attitudes toward women governors reported, "Even when voters assume a woman is qualified for the job in terms of prior experience, they question whether she would be tough enough to be a good executive."[26]

What makes this toughness stereotype particularly difficult and tricky for women candidates is that those who come across as assertive and dominant are often labeled "aggressive" or "bitchy." Acceptable behavior for men is not necessarily acceptable for women. Voters also expect women candidates to be feminine – compassionate, nurturing, nice, womanly. As the Barbara Lee Foundation study explained, "Voters want women who are as tough and decisive as men, but voters do not want to elect 'manly' women.... Female candidates walk a tightrope in attempting to present a persona that's neither too strong and aggressive – too 'male' – nor too soft."[27] Women who aspire to the highest levels of political leadership must somehow find a way to strike a balance between masculine and feminine behavior, between toughness and niceness.

As the first woman to make a serious run for the presidency, Hillary Clinton faced great challenges, both in establishing her toughness and in walking the line between masculinity and femininity. Her campaign clearly recognized the need to portray her as strong and decisive, and they succeeded in doing so. She was rarely, if ever, described as weak. From the very beginning of her campaign, Clinton presented herself as a tough-as-nails fighter who would never give up. Campaigning in Ohio, she told a crowd of supporters, "I'm here today because I want to let you know, I'm a fighter, a doer and a champion, and I will fight for you."[28] Governor Mike Easley of North Carolina described Clinton as someone

---

[26] Barbara Lee Family Foundation. 2001. *Keys to the Governor's Office.* Brookline, MA: Barbara Lee Family Foundation, 28.

[27] Ibid., 29.

[28] Rick Pearson. March 2, 2008. Hillary Clinton: "A Fighter, a Doer and a Champion." *Chicago Tribune.* http://www.swamppolitics.com/news/politics/blog/2008/03/hillary clinton a fighter a do.html. Accessed February 17, 2009.

"who makes Rocky Balboa look like a pansy."[29] A union leader in Indiana even introduced her at a campaign event as a person with "testicular fortitude!"[30]

Depictions of Clinton's strength were not always positive or beneficial, however, as criticisms of her toughness fused with sexist attacks. In an egregious example of misogyny, Tucker Carlson, MSNBC's senior campaign correspondent, exhibited mock castration fears, proclaiming on more than one occasion, "When she [Hillary Clinton] comes on television, I involuntarily cross my legs."[31] Accompanying such commentary were visual portrayals of Hillary Clinton as an emasculator, such as editorial cartoons of Clinton with a whip and sales of "Hillary nutcrackers" (where the nut was cracked between her thighs.) She was repeatedly characterized as a bitch. Anti–Hillary bumper stickers proclaimed, "Stop the bitch" and "Life's a bitch so don't vote for one." In a well-publicized incident, John McCain was asked at a campaign event, "How do we beat the bitch?" His response, "That's an excellent question," received far less publicity.[32] The characterization of Clinton as a bitch occurred so often that it prompted a comedic counterattack in the form of a *Saturday Night Live* skit in which Tina Fey famously proclaimed that "bitches get stuff done" and "bitch is the new black."[33]

While the public clearly came to perceive Clinton as strong, many voters did not see her as particularly likable. Clinton's campaign, caught in a common trap for women trying to balance toughness and niceness, may ultimately have placed too much emphasis on toughness without showing enough of her humanity and humor. Clinton appears to have won over some New Hampshire voters when she teared up on the eve of that state's primary. Behind in the polls, she went on to win the primary the next day, perhaps an indication that people longed to see more of her human side. However, Clinton's boost did not last long, as some political

---

[29] Governor Mike Easley of North Carolina Endorses Hillary. http://www.youtube.com/watch?v=zbqFEaP4Vow. Accessed November 1, 2008.

[30] Fernando Suarez. April 30, 2008. From the Road: Union Boss Says Clinton Has "Testicular Fortitude." CBS News. http://www.cbsnews.com/blogs/2008/04/30/politics/fromtheroad/entry4059528.shtml. Accessed March 18, 2013.

[31] Media Matters for America. July 18, 2007. Tucker Carlson on Clinton: "[W]hen She Comes on Television, I Involuntarily Cross My Legs." http://mediamatters.org/items/200707180009. Accessed March 18, 2013.

[32] Media Matters for America. November 18, 2007. AP Reported McCain "Didn't Embrace the [Bitch] Epithet" Not That He Called the Question "Excellent." http://mediamatters.org/items/200711180001?f=h latest. Accessed March 18, 2013.

[33] Salon.com. February 25, 2008. Tina Fey: Bitch Is the New Black. http://www.salon.com/mwt/broadsheet/2008/02/25/fey/. Accessed March 18, 2013.

pundits and reporters suggested that her tears were not authentic but rather a political ploy, as though Clinton were a veteran stage actress who could turn tears off and on at will. The media's frequent interpretation of many of Clinton's moves as "calculated" reinforced perceptions that Hillary Clinton was neither genuine nor likable.

While Hillary Clinton had great difficulty walking the difficult line between toughness and niceness, Sarah Palin, in her brief two months in the 2008 campaign, seemed to fare better. In her speech before the Republican National Convention, Palin referred to herself as "just your average hockey mom" and then went on to ask, "You know, they say the difference between a hockey mom and a pit bull? Lipstick."[34] With this one metaphor Palin was able to define herself, with humor, in a way that perfectly balanced masculine and feminine; she was tough as a pit bull, but she tempered her toughness with lipstick.

Palin's convention speech helped convey her toughness in other ways. Palin presented herself as a reformer who, as governor, had "stood up to the special interests, and the lobbyists, and the Big Oil companies, and the good-old boys." She also claimed that she had taken a tough posture on a federal government earmark viewed by most as an unnecessary expenditure; as she explained, "I told the Congress, 'Thanks, but no thanks,' on that Bridge to Nowhere."[35]

Moreover, as her supporters and detractors alike frequently noted, Palin was not only a hunter but also the only candidate in the 2008 race who could field dress a moose. Even the mockery of Palin portrayed a tough but feminine woman. A widely circulated, Photoshopped picture on the Internet showed Palin's head on the shapely body of a woman clad in a bikini with a U.S. flag motif and holding a rifle with her finger on the trigger. Thus, although Clinton and Palin were both successful in conveying toughness, Palin may have been more successful in combining niceness with toughness.

Bachmann seemed to try to strike a similar stereotypical balance in 2012, emphasizing that she wanted to run as feminine while still taking hard stances on issues. She touted her toughness most clearly at the end of her campaign, in an ad airing before the Iowa caucuses, when she

---

[34] Palin's Speech at the Republican National Convention. September 3, 2008. Election 2008. *New York Times*. http://elections.nytimes.com/2008/president/conventions/videos/transcripts/20080903_PALIN_SPEECH.html. Accessed March 18, 2013.
[35] Ibid.

described herself as "America's Iron Lady."[36] She contrasted that image with cues for niceness – a feminine appearance and a constant reminder that she was a mother of five and foster mother of twenty-three children. Despite these attempts, Bachmann was less successful than Palin at combining niceness and toughness in a way that benefits female candidates and instead continued to struggle to be taken seriously as a viable presidential candidate throughout the 2012 Republican primary season.

COMMANDER IN CHIEF

Related to concerns that women may be inexperienced and weak, a third stereotype plaguing female candidates is that women are less prepared than men for the role of commander in chief and less able than men to handle the military, national security, and foreign affairs. Voters worry that women lack experience and expertise in these areas and that they will be too "soft" in dealing with U.S. enemies. For example, Geraldine Ferraro, when she was the Democratic nominee for vice president in 1984, was asked on *Meet the Press* if she would be able, if necessary, to push the button to launch nuclear weapons. No man seeking the presidency or vice presidency had ever been asked a similar question on national television.

Clinton took strong steps to counter this stereotype even before announcing her candidacy for president. From her extensive international travels while first lady to her service on the Senate Armed Services Committee, Clinton worked to gain the knowledge and experience she would need to be commander in chief. When she decided to run for president, she lined up a long list of military brass who supported her; more than thirty former admirals and generals endorsed her candidacy. As a candidate, Clinton was very careful never to show any sign of weakness on military and foreign policy issues, going so far as to say, in a very controversial statement, that if Iran attacked Israel, "we would be able to totally obliterate them."[37]

[36] Lynn Sweet. January 2, 2012. Michele Bachmann Casts Herself as "Iron Lady." *Chicago Sun-Times*. http://blogs.suntimes.com/sweet/2012/01/michele_bachmann_casts_herself.html. Accessed January 6, 2013.

[37] David Morgan. April 22, 2008. Clinton Says U.S. Could "Totally Obliterate" Iran. http://www.reuters.com/article/topNews/idUSN2224332720080422. Accessed March 18, 2013.

As a U.S. senator, Hillary Clinton voted to authorize the war in Iraq, and as a candidate, she repeatedly refused to renounce this vote, despite strong criticism by activists on the Left and by her primary opponents. The media tended to interpret her refusal as either a character flaw or a strategic mistake. But this refusal is perhaps more accurately interpreted as a response to a strong and persistent gender stereotype. Clinton and her campaign knew that, as a woman, she needed to counter the stereotype that women are soft on defense and military issues and curb the accusations of flip-flopping, weakness, and indecisiveness on defense that would inevitably follow a renunciation of her vote. She chose instead to project strength and consistency on issues of military involvement and foreign affairs, even at the cost of some votes among Democrats.

While Hillary Clinton worked hard and took serious steps to overcome the stereotype that women are weak on defense and foreign affairs, Sarah Palin was thrust onto the national stage with little knowledge or preparation in these areas. Foreign policy and military expertise do not always matter greatly for a vice presidential candidate, but the precarious state of the world in 2008, as well as John McCain's advanced age and history of melanoma, ensured that the Republican vice presidential candidate's credentials in these areas would be closely scrutinized. Governors seldom deal with international issues, and Palin's experience with the military was limited to overseeing the Alaskan National Guard and being a "military mom" whose son was sent to Iraq shortly after her nomination. Unlike Hillary Clinton, who had traveled extensively outside the United States, Palin had not obtained a passport until 2006, and other than visiting Canada, she traveled outside the United States only once, visiting National Guard troops from her state who were serving in Iraq, Kuwait, and Germany.

Moreover, in her very first major media interview as a vice presidential candidate, with Charlie Gibson of ABC News, she said of Russia, "They're our next door neighbors and you can actually see Russia from land here in Alaska, from an island in Alaska."[38] Palin's critics and detractors construed and ridiculed this as a statement of her foreign policy experience, and in her *Saturday Night Live* comedic portrayal of Palin, Tina Fey proclaimed, "And I can see Russia from my house."[39] In an astounding

---

[38] Rachel Sklar. September 29, 2008. Huffington Post. The *New Yorker* Can See Russia from Sarah Palin's House. http://www.huffingtonpost.com/2008/09/29/the-emnew-yorkerem-can-se_n_130354.html. Accessed March 18, 2013.

[39] Ibid.

example of art imitating life, made more credible by the stereotype that women are not prepared to deal with defense and foreign policy, many Americans came to believe that it was actually Palin, not Fey, who had uttered the words about seeing Alaska from her house. Because Palin had little experience to counter the stereotype that women are not prepared to be commander in chief and deal with international relations, she was particularly vulnerable to the negative gender stereotype and came to be seen as much less prepared than many men, including George W. Bush and Bill Clinton, who had assumed national executive offices with very little military or foreign policy experience.

Beyond questions of women's preparedness to make difficult foreign policy decisions, stereotypes characterizing women as less emotionally stable have fueled doubts about their ability to serve as the nation's commander in chief. In 1972, Dr. Edgar F. Berman, a member of the Democratic Party's Committee on National Priorities, argued that women's "raging hormonal imbalance" made them unfit to hold top executive positions.[40] In 2012, Michele Bachmann was repeatedly caricatured as "crazy" or unpredictable, most clearly in a *Newsweek* cover that portrayed her, wide-eyed, above the caption "The Queen of Rage." In a June 2011 profile in *Rolling Stone*, Matt Taibbi called Bachmann "completely batshit crazy ... grandiose crazy ... crazy in the sense that she's living completely inside her own mind."[41] These characterizations of Bachmann are not solely gender based, as her extreme ideological and religious beliefs played an important role. However, gendered tropes of craziness are more easily accepted for women and, in 2012, may have been more easily applied to Bachmann than to her ideologically and religiously similar competitors like Rick Santorum and Rick Perry.

Bachmann, given little credit for her experience on the House Intelligence Committee, faced another uniquely gendered critique of her preparedness to be commander in chief: the attention given to her history of migraines as a potential impediment to her ability to serve.[42] This attention was reminiscent of past claims – as recent as the 2008

[40] Patsy Mink, Veteran Hawaii Congresswoman, Dies at 74. September 30, 2002. *New York Times*. http://www.nytimes.com/2002/09/30/us/patsy-mink-veteran-hawaii-congresswoman-dies-at-74.html. Accessed March 18, 2013.

[41] Matt Taibbi. June 22, 2011. Michele Bachmann's Holy War. *Rolling Stone*. http://www.rollingstone.com/politics/news/michele-bachmanns-holy-war-20110622. Accessed January 6, 2013.

[42] Kasie Hunt and Molly Ball. July 20, 2011. Michele Bachmann Faces More Migraine Questions. *Politico*. http://www.politico.com/news/stories/0711/59433.html. Accessed January 6, 2013.

campaign – that women's menstrual cycles rendered them too volatile to be entrusted with the "red button" that could launch nuclear weapons. Such stereotypical characterizations of women as unprepared, overemotional, or unstable have long stood in sharp contrast to the demands for a strong and steady commander in chief.

CHILDREN AND SPOUSES

Private lives pose particular challenges for women candidates. Every woman who runs for office must decide how she will present her children and spouse – or the fact that she has none – to the public. Maternal roles are especially tricky for female candidates. Although voters value the communalism and compassion that they consider attached to women's familial roles, they often worry that women may neglect their maternal responsibilities in seeking office, especially if they have young children. Male candidates are rarely asked the kinds of questions that female candidates face about their parental roles. Instead, the public and the media assume the candidates' wives are taking care of day-to-day family responsibilities. But because voters still see men as playing the dominant role in family decision making while women focus on caregiving, a spouse's finances and other affairs are subject to greater scrutiny when a woman runs. The public and the media also are often concerned about how a husband will respond to seeing his wife in the political limelight.

Because the Clinton's only daughter, Chelsea, was an adult by the time Hillary Clinton decided to seek the presidency, Clinton did not have to deal with voter concerns that she might somehow be neglecting her family responsibilities in running. Nevertheless, she still had to figure out whether to highlight or downplay her maternalism. In a December 2006 memo, Mark Penn, Clinton's chief campaign strategist, wrote that voters "do not want someone who would be the first mama" because such a person would be viewed as too "soft." He added, however, that voters are "open to the first father being a woman," suggesting that Clinton should embrace this paternalistic role by displaying toughness and experience.[43] Perhaps as a result of this advice, Clinton rarely mentioned her maternal role in discussing her policy goals and qualifications for office. It was not until her concession speech, after Penn's "first father" strategy failed to secure Clinton the nomination, that she talked about the implications of

---

[43] Penn's "Launch Strategy" Ideas. December 21, 2006. *The Atlantic*. http://www.theatlantic .com/politics/archive/2008/11/penns-launch-strategy-ideas-december-21-2006/37953/. Accessed March 18, 2013.

motherhood for her candidacy. She noted, "I ran as a mother who worries about my daughter's future and a mother who wants to lead all children to brighter tomorrows."[44]

Clinton's campaign did not completely neglect the potential benefits of touting her maternal and familial roles. Seeking to reconcile the image of a tough, experienced candidate with more traditional gender stereotypes, the campaign deployed Dorothy Rodham, Clinton's mother, and Chelsea Clinton, her daughter, to campaign across the country, introducing voters to Clinton's "softer" side and reminding voters that Clinton was both an extraordinary candidate and a devoted mother and daughter.

While Hillary Clinton seldom emphasized her identity as a mother in campaign images or media coverage, Sarah Palin took to the national scene with her motherhood in tow. She confronted voters' concerns over whether a woman candidate could simultaneously be an adequate mother head-on by presenting herself as a mother-candidate. Introducing her five children to America on the day she was announced as the vice presidential candidate and labeling herself a "hockey mom" in her first national speech at the Republican National Convention, Palin attempted to turn what could have been a liability into an asset. Portraying herself as a mom would connect her to average Americans, create a sense of camaraderie with working mothers, and reassure supporters on the Right who might otherwise have been put off by an ambitious woman pursuing a high-powered career. While her children – from baby Trig to seven-year-old Piper to teenager Willow – were often with her on the trail, when they were absent Palin highlighted her maternal inclinations by mentioning the faith that she had in John McCain to command her young soldier son Track in war. She also spoke frequently about her concern for families with special-needs children, discussing her decision to carry Trig to term despite his Down syndrome diagnosis and emphasizing how her personal experience would influence the McCain-Palin policy agenda.

Nevertheless, Palin was not completely successful in turning her motherhood into an asset. Many women feared that Palin's "super-woman" or "supermom" image would create unrealistic expectations for women candidates (and women in general) who came after her. And the question of whether she could be a good mother while seeking high-level political office never really disappeared.

---

[44] Washingtonpost.com. Transcript: Hillary Rodham Clinton Suspends Her Presidential Campaign. http://www.washingtonpost.com/wp-dyn/content/article/2008/06/07/AR2008060701029.html. Accessed March 18, 2013.

As was the case for the women who preceded her in American politics, Palin's parental role was evaluated much more thoroughly than that
of her male counterparts. Although John Edwards's young children were
on the campaign trail for months during the primaries without much
public concern or scrutiny, commentators and citizens alike began asking how Palin's children were being schooled and whether Trig should
be in front of stage lights or even out in public past a certain time of
night. The concern over whether Palin was somehow a bad mother who
was putting her personal ambition ahead of her children's welfare was
amplified when the public learned that Palin's teen daughter, Bristol, was
pregnant. Female commentators were particularly critical. For example,
Campbell Brown of CNN questioned a McCain-Palin campaign adviser
about Palin's maternal responsibility, rhetorically asking, "Do you risk
putting [Bristol] through an incredibly difficult process by accepting this
job if you're her mother?"[45] The *Washington Post*'s Sally Quinn made similar claims about Palin's flawed priorities and returned to the larger question of whether Palin could or should attempt to be both candidate and
mother simultaneously. In a piece that assumes women's primordial role
as caregiver, Quinn proclaimed, "Her first priority has to be her children.
When the phone rings at three in the morning and one of her children is
really sick, what choice will she make?"[46]

While Michele Bachmann frequently emphasized her maternal role
in 2012, her children were less prominent on the campaign trail than
were Palin's children in 2008. However, Bachmann drew greater attention to her role as parent than did her male competitors, some of whom
had much younger children. Instead of asking whether Bachmann could
balance the roles of mother and president, journalists asked more questions about whether she could legitimately claim to have raised, or
even housed, twenty-three foster children. In June 2011, a *New York
Times* investigation of Bachmann's foster parenting history was unable
to find documentation that could confirm how many children she fos-
tered and for how long, only fueling skepticism of her stated motherhood
credentials.[47] While no one questioned that Bachmann had raised her

[45] CNN. September 5, 2008. Brown: Tucker Bounds Interview Becomes Lightning Rod.
     http://www.cnn.com/2008/POLITICS/09/05/brown.bounds/. Accessed March 18, 2013.
[46] Sally Quinn. August 29, 2008. Palin's Pregnancy Problem. *Washington Post*. http://
     newsweek.washingtonpost.com/onfaith/panelists/sally_quinn/2008/08/sarah_polin.
     html. Accessed August 28, 2013.
[47] Sheryl Gay Stolberg. June 22, 2011. Roots of Bachmann's Ambition Began at Home.
     New York Times. http://www.nytimes.com/2011/06/22/us/politics/22bachmann.html?
     pagewanted=all&_r=0. Accessed March 15, 2013.

five biological children, media and skeptics seemed to imply that Bachmann was not *as much of a mother* as she claimed to be.

Children are not the only private-life issue with which candidates must deal; spouses pose a challenge as well. In 2008, both Hillary Clinton and Sarah Palin sought to portray their independence from their husbands, challenging stereotypical expectations that female spouses cannot or should not act alone. Clinton struggled to separate her professional credentials from her marriage to a former governor and U.S. president, while reports circulated about Todd Palin's behind-the-scenes control during his wife's tenure as Governor of Alaska. In 2012, Michele Bachmann's marriage was also placed under greater scrutiny than those of her opponents. Citing her previous comments, reporter Byron York asked Bachmann in an August 2011 debate whether, if she were elected, she would be submissive to her husband. York's question evoked the most traditional gender roles, but roles that Bachmann herself claimed as essential to a Christian marriage. Bachmann responded affirmatively, but defined submission as a form of respect instead of ceding power to her husband.[48] Regardless of her response, no male candidate was asked about the gender role dynamics in his marriage, because the underlying assumption remains that power resides in the male partners. Moreover, male candidates are more easily assumed to act independently of their spouses, and that independence is an essential expectation for executive officeholders.

SEXUALITY

Beyond familial roles, female candidates are subjected to more blatant evaluations of femininity and sexuality based largely on their appearances. Voters want women candidates who are tough but feminine and attractive, but not too attractive. Women who are too unattractive or too unfeminine are often branded disparagingly as lesbians. Women who are too attractive can be perceived as bimbos and sex objects and find that they have a hard time being taken seriously. For years, scholars and media critics have noted the greater attention paid to female candidates' clothing, hair, age, and looks, arguing that such attention detracts from women's personas as substantive candidates for office. The same questions and criticisms emerged in the 2008 and 2012 elections, as comments

---

[48] Leslie Bennetts. August 12, 2011. Michele Bachmann Deflects "Submissive" Question at GOP Debate. *The Daily Beast.* http://www.thedailybeast.com/articles/2011/08/12/michele-bachmann-deflects-submissive-question-at-gop-debate.html. Accessed January 6, 2013.

on Hillary Clinton's pantsuits, Sarah Palin's beauty, and Michele Bachmann's sex appeal were all too common. While the attire and attractiveness of these women received far more attention than did the physical
presentation of most of their male competitors, they represent quite different examples of sexual imagery, commentary, and reaction.

Hillary Clinton has never been associated with traditional norms of
femininity. As first lady, her appearance was criticized, her sexuality
questioned, and her character profiled as masculine, tough, and bitchy.
Clinton has largely been viewed as almost asexual. Her pantsuits, the fodder for many jokes, are more symbolic of a woman who has worked to
blend the masculine and feminine, to emphasize her competence over
her appearance.

The androgyny of Clinton's self-presentation and reactions to it have
provided grist for hostile commentators who have questioned whether
Clinton was really a woman. Conservative shock jock Rush Limbaugh
has called her the only man he knows in the Democratic Party and, with
others, has perpetuated speculation that she might be a lesbian. The claim
that Clinton lacked feminine sexuality was even used in the late 1990s to
explain (and sometimes justify) her husband's infidelity. While references
to Hillary Clinton's masculine or androgynous self-presentation may have
made her seem less likable or sympathetic, her disassociation from the
traditional feminine image has afforded her a greater claim to toughness
and competence, traits vital to a campaign for commander in chief.

Whereas Hillary Clinton's public image has been largely devoid of
feminine sexuality, vice presidential candidate Sarah Palin's public image
was hypersexualized from the moment she took to the national scene in
August 2008. From her nickname "Caribou Barbie" to media emphasis
on her days as a beauty pageant contestant, Palin's image as candidate
was uncomfortably paired with her sex appeal. Much of the commentary
surrounding Palin's appearance can be described within the frame of a
Madonna-whore dichotomy. While she was often portrayed as the beau-
tiful, pure, and down-to-earth mother-politician, Palin was also viewed
as less innocent at times, strategically employing her sex appeal for political benefit. In a *Salon* article, Tom Perrotta explored these two sides
of Palin, describing her as the "sexy puritan" who symbolizes a new
Christian Right archetype of the political woman:

> Sexy Puritans engage in the culture war on two levels – not simply by
> advocating conservative positions on hot-button social issues but by
> embodying nonthreatening mainstream standards of female beauty

and behavior at the same time. The net result is a paradox, a bit of cognitive dissonance very useful to the cultural right: You get a little thrill along with your traditional values, a wink along with the wagging finger.[49]

The GOP itself emphasized Palin's attractiveness at the 2008 Republican National Convention. Selling buttons with Palin's image and the words "Hottest Governor from the Coldest State," the Republican Party linked Palin's political appeal to her physical appearance. The Republican National Committee immediately assigned a stylist to Palin and purchased thousands of dollars worth of wardrobe, hair, and makeup assistance to propagate the image that Palin had garnered in Alaska as one of America's "hottest governors."

The attention paid to Palin's image – from her hairdo to her rimless glasses – often masked both Palin's political achievements and questions about her competence for national executive office, at least early on. Media pundits, particularly men, were taken by Palin's attractiveness. Rush Limbaugh labeled Palin a "babe," Fred Barnes of the *Weekly Standard* noted she was "exceptionally pretty," Jay Nordlinger of the *National Review* described Palin as "a former beauty-pageant contestant, and a real honey, too," and Bill Kristol called her "my heartthrob."[50] The most blatant sexualization came when Donny Deutsch admitted, "I want her to lay in bed next to me," during a CNBC segment on the candidate.[51] In Palin's case, sexuality proved to be a blessing in garnering candidate attention and even favorability but a curse in that such attention and favorability were rooted in image over substance and sexuality over politics.

Though to a lesser extent than Clinton or Palin, Michele Bachmann was sexualized in similar ways in the 2012 election. In fact, pundit Bill Maher told *CNN* host Piers Morgan in July 2011 that Bachmann and Palin would "split the MILF vote" in the Republican primary.[52] In the same

[49] Tom Perrotta. September 26, 2008. How Sarah Palin Embodies the Christian Right Archetype of the Sexy Puritan. Slate. http://www.slate.com/id/ 2200814/. Accessed March 18, 2013.

[50] Amanda Fortini. November 24, 2008. The "Bitch" and the "Ditz." *New York Magazine.* http://nymag.com/news/politics/nationalinterest/52184. Accessed February 17, 2009.

[51] Rebecca Traister. September 11, 2008. Zombie Feminists of the RNC. Salon.com. http://www.salon.com/mwt/feature/2008/09/11/zombie_feminism/. Accessed March 18, 2013.

[52] Huffington Post. July 12, 2011. Bill Maher Talks Palin vs. Bachmann on Piers Morgan. http://www.huffingtonpost.com/2011/07/12/bill-maher-talks-palin-vs-bachmann_n_896204.html. Accessed January 6, 2013.

month, a guest on Maher's television show evoked a more graphic image of Bachmann. Comedian Marc Maron commented, "I hope [Marcus Bachmann] f— her angrily because, because that's how I would."[53] The backlash against these comments remained limited, demonstrating a willingness to laugh off sexist remarks instead of challenging the ease with which they are made.

CONCLUSION

Gender stereotypes present female candidates for the top executive offices in the United States with several obstacles and challenges that their male counterparts do not confront. Men who seek the presidency or vice presidency do not have to continually prove themselves qualified for office, capable of making difficult decisions and tough enough to handle the world's crises. Unlike women, men rarely face questions about their parental responsibilities interfering with their professional lives. Men are rarely burdened by questions of spousal influence and are not usually characterized by journalists or pundits on the basis of appearances or perceptions of sexuality.

While fundamentally different in ideology and persona, Hillary Clinton and Sarah Palin faced similar gender-based challenges in the 2008 election, although popular criticisms and their campaigns' reactions differed. Hillary Clinton focused her campaign on strength and experience, avoiding the stereotypic hurdles faced by women who came before her. While successful in demonstrating the qualifications and toughness necessary for executive office, Clinton's masculine emphasis failed to take advantage of the positive traits of change, warmth, compassion, and communalism often attributed to female candidates. Sarah Palin, in contrast, took full advantage of her feminine identity, becoming the mother-candidate who could appeal to new swaths of conservative voters. Although the McCain-Palin campaign attempted to balance Palin's "soft" image with a no-nonsense frontierswoman persona, it was Palin's lack of national political exposure and international experience that proved to be her Achilles' heel. Finally, the popular obsession with both women's sexuality provided unwanted attention for women asking to be taken seriously as presidential or vice presidential contenders.

---

[53] Steven Loeb. July 16, 2011. Bill Maher and his Panel Get Raunchy While Talking about the Bachmanns. *Business Insider*. http://www.businessinsider.com/maher-gay-bachmann-video-2011-7. Accessed January 6, 2013.

Three years later, Michele Bachmann – similarly distinctive in ideology and persona – confronted gender-based challenges in seeking the Republican presidential nomination. Unlike Clinton or Palin, however, Bachmann did little to directly confront negative gender stereotypes or take advantage of potentially positive ones.

Gender-based struggles are not new to female candidates, nor will they disappear for women running in the near future. However, these challenges are uniquely amplified in candidacies for the nation's highest executive offices – the presidency and the vice presidency. After 2008, many asked if Clinton and Palin's candidacies altered perceptions and expectations of gender and the presidency, easing the path – as Clinton claimed – for the next women to run. The dearth of women candidates – presidential or vice presidential – in 2012 makes it difficult to measure the impact of Clinton's and Palin's history-making candidacies. However, that near absence of women may itself demonstrate that women's candidacies are not yet normalized. Moreover, evidence from Michele Bachmann's campaign shows that the gender stereotypes faced in 2008 persisted in the 2012 contest.

What do these conclusions mean for the 2016 presidential contest? In 2016, both parties will likely have robust primary competition, and women's names are already being floated among the serious contenders. Despite her insistence that she has not made a decision to run in 2016, a July 2013 poll showed Hillary Clinton topping the list of Democratic candidate hopefuls, with 63 percent of Democrats and Democratic-leaning independents saying they would be likely to support Clinton if she runs for the Democratic nomination.[54] Asked about a 2016 bid in March 2012, Sarah Palin remarked that "anything is possible."[55] Whether or not these or other women put their names forward in 2016, both 2008 and 2012 demonstrated that while the gendered landscape may be shifting, sexism and gender stereotypes will likely continue to influence the presidential candidacies of the women who run.

[54] Marist Poll. July 24, 2013. A Look at the 2016 Presidential Contest. http://maristpoll.marist.edu/724-a-look-at-the-2016-presidential-contest/. Accessed September 2, 2013.
[55] CNN. March 6, 2012. Palin: Not ruling out run in 2016. http://cnnpressroom.blogs.cnn.com/2012/03/06/sarah-palin-to-cnn-as-i-say-anything-is-possible-and-i-dont-close-any-doors-that-perhaps-would-be-open-out-there-so-no-i-wouldnt-close-that-door-and-my-plan-is-to-be-at-that-convention/. Accessed March 18, 2013.

3 Voter Participation and Turnout

The Political Generational Divide among Women Voters

You've come a long way, baby. A century ago, your mothers, grand-mothers and great-grandmothers...and most of their sisters across the land of the free and the home of the brave were still eight years from the right to vote [1920]. *This year, the presidential [election] not only involves you, ladies, it's all about you. Both parties will spend millions courting you because whoever wins your favor likely wins...the election.*

Bob Lewis, Associated Press June 24, 2012[1]

As the 2012 general election gets under way, analysts have posited that *young, secular women are likely to be the most coveted swing group.* The degree to which the Obama campaign can win them over may well be the single most pivotal factor in the campaign.... [A]s Romney seeks to make inroads, he may need to find a new way of reaching women voters.

Molly Ball, *The Atlantic* April 2012[2]

Women make up majorities of the U.S. voting-age population, registered voters, and actual voters. These facts explain why both major political parties – Democratic and Republican – and women's advocacy groups from across the ideological spectrum worked hard to mobilize women voters in 2012.

Throughout the rough-and-tumble election year, both parties targeted the women's vote through extensive registration drives, national

---

[1] Bob Lewis. June 24, 2012. In Swing State, Women Become Both Parties' Focus. *Associated Press.*
[2] Molly Ball. April 2012. This Election Will Be All About Women. *The Atlantic.*

This work could not have been completed without the invaluable assistance of Ashleigh E. Powers and David J. Bonanza.

party conventions, presidential debates, TV and online video ads, and appearances by the candidates' wives and other strong female surrogates. Microtargeting of different slices of the female electorate was highly refined, based on massive databases and in-depth analyses of which media were most effective in reaching different age groups. The ability to "cut" and post an ad online within hours of a major event, highlighting a candidate's successful appearance or, conversely, an opponent's blatant misstep,[3] kept the campaign highly fluid – but almost always focused on women's issues.

Democrats did a better job than Republicans of getting out the women's vote, with their focus on mobilizing younger women and women of color – just as they had done in 2008. Mobilization efforts aimed at late deciders (typically young and female voters) made the difference in several key swing states in which the race had been virtually tied throughout most of the campaign, giving President Obama a second term.

This chapter examines demographic shifts within the female electorate, gives a short history of how women won the right to vote, describes mobilization efforts aimed at women voters at every stage of the campaign, and concludes with a brief summary of how and why young voters, particularly women of color, played such a major role in 2012. As the chapter shows, the get-out-the-vote game has become much more sophisticated over the years, and the women's vote is increasingly splitting along generational lines. The premium that both parties now place on winning women's votes is nothing short of amazing considering that women were denied the right to vote under the original U.S. Constitution.

THE GENDER GAP IN 2012: WIDER THAN IN 2008, BUT COMPLICATED

Exit polls showed that 55 percent of women voted for President Barack Obama, while only 45 percent voted for Governor Mitt Romney. Men preferred Romney by a margin of 52 to 45 percent. In total, the gender gap, defined by the Center for American Women and Politics as the

---

[3] Reid Wilson. November 1, 2012. U.S. Presidential Election 2012: Targeted Online Video Ads Redefine Tactics. *The Guardian*. http://www.guardian.co.uk/media-network/media-network-blog/2012/nov/01/us-presidential-election-2012-barack-obama-mitt-romney.

difference in the proportions of women and men who voted for the winning candidate, was 10 percentage points – a wider margin than the 7-point gender gap in the 2008 election.[4]

One postelection analysis proclaimed: "Of all the big winners on Election Day, one of the biggest may have been a concept: the gender gap in American politics."[5] However, the same analysis pointed out that the gender gap is complicated: "It can grow or shrink depending on a host of factors: race, age, marital status, even geography."[6]

A *USA Today* summary of exit polls contrasting characteristics of Obama and Romney supporters found that age, race/ethnicity, marital status, and religious differences, along with gender, most sharply divided the electorate in 2012:

> **Obama Supporters, 2012**: more than nine of ten African Americans and nearly seven in ten Hispanics; solid majority of women and two thirds of unmarried women; about six in ten of voters younger than thirty; more than 90 percent of Democrats and nearly 90 percent of liberals; and more than six in ten of those who never attend religious services.

> **Romney Supporters, 2012**: six of ten whites; nearly six of ten seniors; a solid majority of men and of married women, and nearly two thirds of white men; more than 90 percent of Republicans and of conservatives; and a majority of high-income voters, evangelical Christians, and those who attend religious services every week or more often.[7]

The presidential preferences of voters by age clearly showed a generational divide. Young voters (18- to 29-year-olds) preferred Obama to Romney by 23 points (60 percent to 37 percent).[8] They also tended to be more liberal on social issues. (See Figure 3.1.)

[4] CN Politics. December 10, 2012. President: Full Results, Exit Polls. http://www.cnn.com/election/2012/results/race/president.

[5] Dante Chinni. November 9, 2012. Women Are Not a Unified Voting Bloc. *The Atlantic*. http://www.theatlantic.com/sexes/archive/2012/11/women-are-not-a-unified-voting-bloc/265007/.

[6] Ibid.

[7] Susan Page. November 7, 2012. Analysis: A Nation Moving Further Apart. *USA Today*. http://www.usatoday.com/story/news/politics/2012/11/07/analysis-nation-moves-further-apart/1688031/.

[8] CNN Politics. December 10, 2012. President: Full Results, Exit Polls. http://www.cnn.com/election/2012/results/race/president.

Figure 3.1: Young voters in 2012 were more liberal on key social and fiscal issues.

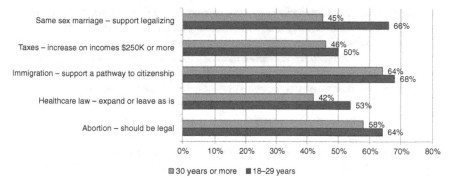

■ 30 years or more   ■ 18–29 years

Source: Analysis of the National Election Day Exit Poll data (2012), collected by Edison Research, by the Center for Information and Research on Civic Learning and Engagement (CIRCLE) Staff, "Young Voters in the 2012 Presidential Election," November 13, 2012. http://www.civicyouth.org/wp-content/uploads/2012/11/CIRCLE_2012Election_ExitPoll_OverviewFactSheet.pdf.

Among young voters, who were more ethnically diverse than older voters (Figure 3.2), those from minority populations were more likely to favor Obama over Romney.

If one looks at *women voters themselves,* the margin of preference for Obama actually narrowed. In 2008, Obama received 13 percentage points more of the female vote than his opponent, Sen. John McCain, compared to 11 points more than Romney in 2012. Romney made inroads into the white female vote, particularly that of older, married, and more religious women, but he also narrowly won the young white female vote. (See Figure 3.3.)

Figure 3.2: Young voters in 2012 were more ethnically diverse.

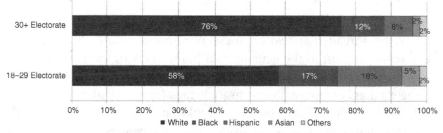

■ White ■ Black ■ Hispanic ■ Asian ▢ Others

Source: Analysis of the National Election Day Exit Poll data (2012), collected by Edison Research, by CIRCLE Staff, "Diverse Electorate: A Deeper Look into the Millennial Vote," November 14, 2012; http://www.minnpost.com/sites/default/files/attachments/CIRCLE_2012Election_GenderRace_ForWeb1.pdf.

Figure 3.3: Women of color showed the strongest support for Obama among young women voters.

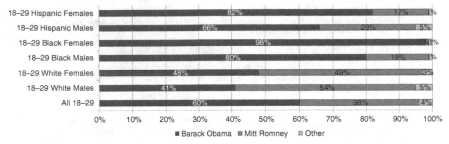

Source: Analysis of the National Election Day Exit Poll data (2012), collected by Edison Research, by CIRCLE Staff, "Diverse Electorate: A Deeper Look into the Millennial Vote," November 14, 2012; http://www.minnpost.com/sites/default/files/attachments/CIRCLE_2012Election_GenderRace_ForWeb1.pdf.

While Democrats accused Republicans of waging a "War *on* Women" in 2012, the competition for women's votes by both Obama and Romney was intense, prompting some to characterize 2012 more as the "War *for* Women." Capturing women's votes has become more challenging as the nation's demographic mix has changed.

THE CHANGING FEMALE ELECTORATE

Prior to the election, there was widespread agreement that women would be *the* key demographic group that would decide the outcome. But *which* women? Rural, suburban, or urban? Young, middle aged, or seniors? White women or women of color? College-educated or non–college educated? Married or unmarried? Religious or secular? The answer, of course, often differed across and within the fifty states.

The Age Divide
Age is the thread that tied all these personal attributes together and heightened interest in the generational political divide evident through-out the 2012 campaign. Various polls and census analyses established that younger voters are more diverse in their racial/ethnic makeup and more likely to be single, college educated, secular, and residents of metropoli-tan areas than older voters. Politically, younger women (18 to 29 years of age) from the Millennial Generation are more liberal and more heavily Democratic than their male counterparts. (See Figures 3.4 and 3.5.)

Figure 3.4: Across race and ethnicity categories, women are more liberal than men are in the Millennial Generation.

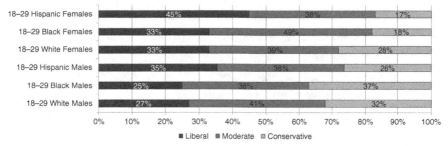

Source: Analysis of the National Election Day Exit Poll data (2012), collected by Edison Research, by CIRCLE Staff, "Diverse Electorate: A Deeper Look into the Millennial Vote," November 14, 2012; http://www.minnpost.com/sites/default/files/attachments/CIRCLE_2012Election_GenderRace_ForWeb1.pdf.

Younger women, especially 18- to 24-year-olds, are also more liberal and more Democratic than older female voters – a higher proportion of whom are white, married, more conservative, religious, and more likely to lean Republican. Consequently, the two major political parties targeted women somewhat differently.[9] The messages and messengers used to connect with younger and older women diverged considerably, primarily because of the close connection of age, political party, and candidate preference.[10]

Focusing on Young, Single Women

With women increasingly outnumbering men on college campuses and with marriage rates dropping, the emphasis on young, single female

---

[9] Obama heavily targeted younger, single women and women with postgraduate degrees. Romney focused on married women. See Karlyn Bowman and Jennifer Marsico. October 4, 2012. The Past, Present, and Future of the Women's Vote. *The American.* http://www.american.com/archive/2012/october/the-past-present-and-future-of-the-womens-vote. Both campaigns targeted suburban women, often the swing vote in presidential contests. Obama focused on contraception, abortion, and the health care law. Romney focused on the President's failure to bring back jobs. Laura Meckler and Daniel Lippman. August 8, 2012. Campaigns Put Focus on Suburban Women. *Wall Street Journal.* http://professional.wsj.com/article/SB10000872396390443517104577571300017481434.html?mg=reno64-wsj.

[10] CIRCLE. November 13, 2012. More Analysis of Young Voters on Issues, House Candidate Support, Differences from Older Voters. www.civicyouth.org/more-analysis-of-young-voters-on-issues-; CIRCLE. November 13, 2012. Young Voters in the 2012 Presidential Election. http://www.civicyouth.org/wp-content/uploads/2012/11/CIRCLE_2012Election_ExitPoll_OverviewFactSheet.pdf.

Figure 3.5: Women are more Democratic than men are in the Millennial Generation.

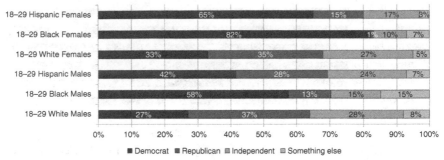

Source: Analysis of the National Election Day Exit Poll data (2012), collected by Edison Research, by CIRCLE Staff, "Diverse Electorate: A Deeper Look into the Millennial Vote," November 14, 2012; http://www.minnpost.com/sites/default/files/attachments/CIRCLE_2012Election_GenderRace_ForWeb1.pdf.

voters was stepped up – especially by Democrats.[11] The single women's vote made up nearly one-fourth (23 percent) of all voters in 2012.[12] The GOP tended to focus more on Boomer, senior, and suburban women – a larger portion of that party's traditional base and typically higher-turnout voters. The difference in outreach simply reflected the deepening *intergenerational partisan divide* evident in most polls.

While Democrats focused their mobilization efforts more heavily on younger women, *both* parties saw the importance of this diverse and growing demographic. One activist listener to a National Public Radio (NPR) program on "Wooing Women Voters" cautioned the audience three months ahead of the election against describing women as a homogeneous voting bloc and portraying all women as equally "in play" in the 2012 election.[13] The most important bloc to watch, the NPR listener correctly predicted, was "single women – more specifically, single, female, partisan Democrats – a critical voting bloc for President Obama ... [T]his is his base, and this is the basis for Sandra Fluke, the Life of Julia, and

[11] Morgan Allison. April 28, 2012. Why the Young Women's Vote Will Matter in 2012. *The Mirror.* www.erskinemirror.com/why-the-young-women-s-vote-will-matter-in-2012.

[12] Nancy Benac and Connie Cass. November 15, 2012. Face of US Changing; Elections to Look Different. *Associated Press.* http://bigstory.ap.org/article/face-us-changing-elections-look-different.

[13] Sabrina L. Schaeffer. September 24, 2012. The So-called "Women's Vote" Is Beside the Point. *The Hill's Pundits Blog.* http://thehill.com/blogs/pundits-blog/presidential-campaign/251263-the-so-called-womens-vote-is-beside-the-point.

the 'war on women' rhetoric."[14] (Sandra Fluke gained notoriety when Republicans on a House committee considering inclusion of contraception in insurance plans refused to let her testify. "The Life of Julia" on barackobama.com contrasted different effects of Obama's and Romney's policies on a fictional woman.)

The NPR listener and other Republicans well understood that to win, Romney would have to win a larger share of the women's vote in 2012 than McCain had in 2008. While they believed the poor economy would draw more women voters of all ages to Romney, they also worried that social issues like same-sex marriage and reproductive rights could effectively energize younger female voters who, for much of the campaign, were less enthusiastic about voting than in 2008, although still more interested than their male counterparts.

The 2012 election will undoubtedly go down in the history books as the "demographics is destiny" election.[15] It was the presidential election whose outcome highlighted the country's changing demographics, particularly its racial/ethnic diversity. Nowhere was that more apparent than among the Millennial Generation – the age group that gave the largest margin of victory to Obama. And it was Latina, Asian, and African-American young women who gave the biggest boost to the president. The importance of the women's vote was evident every step of the way – a world apart from the days when American women were left out of the process altogether.

A BRIEF HISTORY OF WOMEN'S SUFFRAGE

The struggle for women's voting rights began at the nation's birth. (See Text Box 3.1.) In 1776, women like Abigail Adams urged the men writing the Declaration of Independence to include women. "Remember the Ladies," wrote Adams to her husband, John, a delegate to the Continental Congress. "If particular care and attention is not paid to the ladies, we are determined to foment a rebellion, and will not hold ourselves bound by any laws in which we have no voice or representation." Was she ever right!

---

[14] Ibid.

[15] Dr. Diana E. Sheets. December 21, 2012. Obama's 2012 Victory: The Demographic Becomes the Narrative. *Huffington Post* http://www.huffingtonpost.com/dr-diana-e-sheets/obamas-2012-victory-the-demographic-becomes-the-narrative_b_2341438.html?utm_hp_ref=elections-2012.

TEXT BOX 3.1: The history of the women's vote

Today, every U.S. citizen who is 18 years of age by Election Day and a resident of the local precinct for at least thirty days is eligible to cast a ballot. However, women, African Americans, Native Americans, and members of certain religious groups were not allowed to vote during the colonial period and the early years of the country's history. In 1787, the U.S. Constitution granted each state government the power to determine who could vote. Individual states wrote their own suffrage laws. Early voting qualifications required that an eligible voter be a white man, 21 years of age, Protestant, and a landowner. Many citizens who recognized the importance of the right to vote led the suffrage movement.

ONE HUNDRED YEARS TOWARD THE WOMEN'S VOTE

Compiled by E. Susan Barber

1776

Abigail Adams writes to her husband, John, at the Continental Congress in Philadelphia, asking that he and the other men – who are at work on the Declaration of Independence – "Remember the Ladies." The Declaration's wording specifies that "all men are created equal."

1848

The first women's rights convention in the United States is held in Seneca Falls, New York. Many participants sign the Declaration of Sentiments and Resolutions, which outlines the main issues and goals for the emerging women's movement. Thereafter, women's rights meetings are held on a regular basis.

1861–1865

The American Civil War disrupts suffrage activity as women, North and South, divert their energies to "war work." The war, however, serves as a training ground as women gain important organizational and occupational skills they will later use in postwar organizational activity.

1866

Elizabeth Cady Stanton and Susan B. Anthony form the American Equal Rights Association, an organization for white and black women and men dedicated to the goal of universal suffrage.

1868

The Fourteenth Amendment is ratified. It extends to all citizens the protections of the Constitution against unjust state laws. This Amendment is the first to define citizens and voters as "male."

1870
The Fifteenth Amendment enfranchises black men.

1870–1875
Several women – including Virginia Louisa Minor, Victoria Woodhull, and Myra Bradwell – attempt to use the Fourteenth Amendment in the courts to secure the vote (Minor and Woodhull) and right to practice law (Bradwell). They all are unsuccessful.

1872
Susan B. Anthony is arrested and brought to trial in Rochester, New York, for attempting to vote for Ulysses S. Grant in the presidential election. At the same time, Sojourner Truth appears at a polling booth in Grand Rapids, Michigan, demanding a ballot; she is turned away.

1874
The Woman's Christian Temperance Union (WCTU) is founded by Annie Wittenmyer. With Frances Willard at its head (1876), the WCTU becomes an important force in the struggle for women's suffrage. Not surprisingly, one of the most vehement opponents of women's enfranchisement was the liquor lobby, which feared women might use the franchise to prohibit the sale of liquor.

1878
The Woman Suffrage Amendment is introduced in the U.S. Congress. (The wording is unchanged in 1919, when the amendment finally passes both houses.)

1890
Wyoming becomes the first women's suffrage state on its admission to the Union.

1893
Colorado becomes the first state to adopt a state amendment enfranchising women.

1896
Mary Church Terrell, Ida B. Wells-Barnett, Margaret Murray Washington, Fanny Jackson Coppin, Frances Ellen Watkins Harper, Charlotte Forten Grimké, and the former slave Harriet Tubman meet in Washington, DC, to form the National Association of Colored Women (NACW).

(continued)

TEXT BOX 3.1 (*continued*)

1903
Mary Dreier, Rheta Childe Dorr, Leonora O'Reilly, and others form the
Women's Trade Union League of New York, an organization of middle-
and working-class women dedicated to unionization for working women
and to women's suffrage. This group later becomes a nucleus of the
International Ladies' Garment Workers' Union (ILGWU).

1911
The National Association Opposed to Woman Suffrage (NAOWS) is organized. Led by Mrs. Arthur Dodge, its members include wealthy, influential women and some Catholic clergymen – including Cardinal Gibbons,
who, in 1916, sent an address to NAOWS's convention in Washington,
DC. In addition to the distillers and brewers, who work largely behind
the scenes, the "antis" also draw support from urban political machines,
Southern congressmen, and corporate capitalists – like railroad mag-
nates and meatpackers – who support the antis by contributing to their
war chests.

1912
Theodore Roosevelt's Progressive (Bull Moose/Republican) Party becomes the first national political party to adopt a women's suffrage plank.

1913
Alice Paul and Lucy Burns organize the Congressional Union, later known
as the National Woman's Party (1916). Borrowing the tactics of the radical,
militant Women's Social and Political Union (WSPU) in England, members of the Woman's Party participate in hunger strikes, picket the White
House, and engage in other forms of civil disobedience to publicize the
suffrage cause.

1914
The National Federation of Women's Clubs – which by this time includes
more than 2 million white women and women of color throughout the
United States – formally endorses the suffrage campaign.

1916
Jeannette Rankin of Montana becomes the first woman elected to represent her state in the U.S. House of Representatives.

August 26, 1920
The Nineteenth Amendment is ratified. Its victory accomplished, NAWSA
ceases to exist, but its organization becomes the nucleus of the League
of Women Voters.

Source: Adapted from *Election Focus 2004* 1, No. 8, April 14, 2004. Available at
http://usa.usembassy.de/elections04/elections04_14_043.pdf.

In the 1800s, white women began working outside the home, mostly at mills, as America changed from an agrarian to a more industrialized society. The long working hours and dangerous conditions led many women to organize. Meanwhile, stay-at-home, middle-class women began banding together for charity work, temperance, and the abolition of slavery. Black women like Sojourner Truth and Harriet Jacobs rose to oppose sexism, slavery, and the white activists who "saw themselves as the sole liberators of passive, childlike slaves."[16]

The birth of the women's suffrage movement in the United States is usually dated to July 20, 1848, at the country's first women's rights convention in Seneca Falls, New York. The three hundred attendees issued a document proclaiming that men and women were created equal and, therefore, that women should be allowed to vote.

After the Civil War, groups led by Susan B. Anthony and others organized to push for universal suffrage. They made substantial progress in 1870, when the Fifteenth Amendment extended the franchise to African-American men.

In 1890, rival suffrage groups merged to form the National American Woman Suffrage Association (NAWSA). Conservative and liberal women's groups alike – including the Woman's Christian Temperance Union, the Young Women's Christian Association, and the National Association of Colored Women – began to see that voting was the only way for women to affect public policy.

Western States Ahead of the Nation

Ultimately, it was in the Wild West that women first tasted success. Historically, most public policy innovations in America occur not at the national level but in the states. So it was with women's suffrage. In 1890, Wyoming became the first women's suffrage state on its admission to the Union. In 1893, Colorado extended the right to vote to women through an amendment to its state constitution. Neighboring western states soon jumped on the bandwagon. By 1900, women could vote in thirteen western and Midwestern states, as well as in Michigan and New York.

The Ladies Get Testy

The successes of the women's suffrage movement spurred strong opposition from anti-suffragists, many of whom were also women. Then, as

---

[16] Carol Andreas and Katherine Culkin. 2003. Women's Rights Movement: The Nineteenth Century. In *Dictionary of American History*, 3rd ed., ed. Stanley I. Kutler. New York: Charles Scribner's Sons, Vol. 8, 512.

now, different views on women's societal and political roles resulted in a traditionalist/anti-suffragist versus revisionist/suffragist schism.

Even within their own ranks, suffragists disagreed about the pace of the movement. One faction of NAWSA broke off to form another group that became the National Woman's Party in 1916. They used protests and hunger strikes to rally support for an amendment to the U.S. Constitution. (It was known as "the Anthony Amendment" in honor of Susan B. Anthony and ultimately became the Nineteenth Amendment to the U.S. Constitution in 1920.)

During World War I, women suffragists split into pro-war and anti-war blocs. (The same schism characterized women voters in 2004 over the war in Iraq.) But the leaders of suffragist groups, like Alice Paul of the National Woman's Party and Carrie Chapman Catt of the Woman's Peace Party, put aside their personal feelings about the war, fearing a backlash against women's suffrage. The tactic paid off. Their refusal to campaign against the war made it more politically palatable for President Woodrow Wilson and other politicians to support the Nineteenth Amendment.

At Last, Ratification!

On June 4, 1919, the U.S. Congress formally presented the Nineteenth Amendment to the states for ratification.[17] More than a year later, on August 18, 1920, by a single vote in its legislature, Tennessee became the thirty-sixth state to approve the amendment. The young legislator who cast the deciding vote confessed that he had been persuaded by a telegram from his mother urging him to vote for it. On August 26, 1920, the U.S. secretary of state officially proclaimed that the required thirty-six states had ratified the Nineteenth Amendment. However, it would be years before African-American women had full voting rights. Discriminatory practices such as literacy tests and poll taxes, along with threats and violence, kept many from voting until these barriers were outlawed by court rulings, voting rights acts passed by Congress, and a constitutional amendment eliminating poll taxes.

The Nineteenth Amendment as proposed and ratified read:

> The right of citizens of the United States to vote shall not be denied or abridged by the United States or by any State on account of sex.

> Congress shall have power, by appropriate legislation, to enforce the provisions of this article.

---

[17] On June 4, 1919, the U.S. Senate voted to add the Nineteenth Amendment to the U.S. Constitution by a vote of fifty-six to twenty-five. The House had passed it two weeks earlier by a vote of 304 to 89.

The suffragists finally prevailed. It had been a long haul – 144 years after the Declaration of Independence was signed in 1776 and 72 years after women had issued their first formal demand for the right to vote at Seneca Falls. In its editorial on Sunday, August 29, 1920, the *New York Times* applauded those who had worked for this right: "Women in fighting for the vote have shown a passion of earnestness, a persistence, and above all a command of both tactics and strategy, which have amazed our master politicians." But the editorial went on to warn against presuming that women would all vote alike: "It is doubtless true that women will divide much as men have done among several parties. There will be no solid 'woman vote.'"

Women Voters Are NOT Politically Monolithic

Women's voting patterns over the years have borne out the prediction of the *Times*. In the election of 2004, Democrat John Kerry won 51 percent of the women's vote and Republican George W. Bush 48 percent – a difference of only 3 percentage points. In the elections of 2008 and 2012, the women's vote was somewhat more cohesive but still by no means monolithic. Obama won 56 percent of the female vote in 2008 and 55 percent in 2012.

These results lend support to political advice given to candidates and political parties nearly a decade ago by Donna Brazile, a Democratic strategist and media commentator who managed Al Gore's 2004 presidential campaign:

> To pull more women into the voting process – and to win votes – the two major parties should drop any idea of a "one size fits all" approach to women. Instead, they should target their messages to diverse groups of women.... Political campaigns will have to address single women, married women, suburban soccer moms, security moms, on-the-go female professionals, urban-base[d] voting women, Jewish women, Latinas, senior moms, want-to-be-moms and soon-to-be moms.[18]

Since then, presidential campaigns have, by necessity, varied their outreach to women, microtargeting them differently according to age, race and ethnicity, education, and – to a lesser degree – by income and employment, marital status, parental status, and/or sexual orientation. Campaigns that rely too much on one-size-fits-all tactics can result in a candidate's defeat.

---

[18] Donna Brazile. July 3, 2004. Energize the Women's Vote in 2004. *Women's eNews*. http://www.womensenews.org/article.cfm/dyn/aid/1856/context/archive.

Throughout the 2012 campaign, political parties and advocacy groups alike used a variety of voter mobilization tools. These included everything from text messages to online social networks, recorded ("robo") phone calls from candidates and celebrities, appearances by the candidates and high-profile surrogates, and personal contacts from family and friends to precisely targeted mail, radio spots, and broadcast and cable television ads. Feedback and insights from focus groups and public opinion surveys were used to craft the content, format, and placement of political ads to reach narrowly defined groups of potential female voters. Mobilization efforts focused first on registering voters, then on getting them to vote.

REGISTRATION RATES

Convincing people to register is often more difficult than getting them to vote once they have registered. In 2012, the percentage of eligible citizens registered to vote rose only slightly from 2008 (71.2 percent from 71.0 percent).[19]

Some states, like Iowa, Maine, Minnesota, Montana, Wisconsin, Wyoming, New Hampshire, and Idaho, allow citizens to register on Election Day.[20] But most states require them to register in advance, usually fifteen to thirty days before the election.[21]

Figures from the U.S. Census show that in every election cycle since 1980, a greater percentage of women than men has registered to vote. (See Figure 3.6.) Women younger than 45 have outregistered younger men since the 1970s. It is only among the oldest cohort, 75 and older, that women's registration rates still lag behind men's, although not by much.[22]

After close presidential elections in 2000 and 2004, both the Democratic and the Republican parties realized they had to spend considerably more time and money registering voters for 2008. They continued to do

---

[19] U.S. Census Bureau, *Current Population Survey*, November 2012 and earlier reports. Table A-1. http://www.census.gov/hhes/www/socdemo/voting/publications/historical/index. html.

[20] California and Connecticut will join the list in 2013. National Conference of State Legislatures. September 24, 2012. Same-Day Voter Registration. http://www.ncsl.org/ legislatures-elections/elections/same-day-registration.aspx.

[21] North Dakota has no registration requirement.

[22] U.S. Census Bureau. October 2011. Voting and Registration in the Election of November 2010 – Detailed Tables, Table 1. http://www.census.gov/hhes/www/socdemo/voting/ publications/p20/2010/tables.html.

Figure 3.6: Women have registered to vote at higher rates than men have in recent elections.

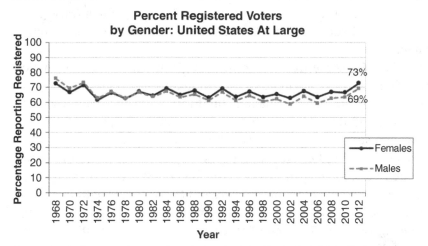

Source: U.S. Census, *Current Population Survey*, November 2012 and earlier reports.

so in Election 2012. Naturally, women were prime targets, primarily those who had never registered to vote before.

College campuses were the focus of intense registration activity in 2012 as partisan and interest groups alike became more aware of the size of the Millennial Generation and its potential political clout, as well as its diversity. The Rock the Vote organization described the Millennials: "Forty-four million strong, we are the largest generation in history and represent more than one-fifth of the electorate. We are also the most diverse generation. Sixty-one percent of Millennials identify as White, while 17 percent are Hispanic, 15 percent are Black and 4 percent are Asian."[23]

Examples of registration efforts on campuses in 2012 are abundant. But some specifically focused on registering female voters. The Feminist Majority Foundation's Campus Program supported registration drives led by students. The group encouraged and assisted with the creation of Get Out Her Vote groups on campuses by providing a tool kit and website (www.feministcampus.org/vote). Their literature used the generational divide, and specifically higher registration and turnout rates among seniors, as a rallying cry for student activism. The issue consequences of the age divide were clear: "No wonder Social Security is the

[23] Rock the Vote. Who Are Young Voters? http://www.rockthevote.com/about/about-young-voters/who-are-young-voters/.

third rail of politics while young women's issues like reproductive rights [access to abortion, birth control], peace, affirmative action, and the environment [global warming] take a back seat."[24] The gender wage gap – the pay equity issue – was another key issue in mobilizing young college women.

The AAUW (American Association of University Women) Action Fund's "It's My Vote: I Will Be Heard" campaign also focused on college campuses, with the goal of "maximiz[ing] the electoral power of women in the 2012 elections."[25] AAUW branches in nearly every state worked closely with student organizations to hold voter registration drives[26] and to convene issue and candidate forums on campuses. The group's Campus Vote Challenge helped student leaders connect with other organizations, like the League of Women Voters and NOW, that sought to educate students about voter ID laws, registration procedures, absentee voting, and polling locations. The Voter Participation Center (originally WVWV – Women's Voices. Women Vote) provided many groups with data encouraging registration drives aimed at young unmarried women and women of color[27] – groups more likely to lean Democratic.

College Republicans, more than any conservative women's advocacy groups,[28] led the charge to register young female conservatives on many campuses. Most recognized, they had a tougher job (at least on the more urban campuses) to register Republican-leaning college students but believed that once registered, they were more likely to turn out. One MTV blogger put it this way: "Conventional political wisdom has it that Democrats are great at registering new voters and Republicans are just as good at getting their already-registered base to come out and vote."[29]

---

[24] Feminist Majority Foundation, Choices Campus Leadership Program. Get Out Her Vote 2012. http://feministcampus.org/vote/2012/gohv_2012.pdf.

[25] AAUW. Campus Connections for College and University Representatives. August 2012. http://www.aauw.org/resource/campus-connections-for-college-and-university-representatives-august-2012/.

[26] The group registered more than 12,000 new voters, held seventy-two candidate forums, and contacted nearly 9,900 women to remind them to vote on Election Day. Rebecca Rutenberg. November 7, 2012. How Women Won the 2012 General Election. *Seventeen.* http://www.seventeen.com/college/presidential-election-blog/women-in-politics.

[27] Voter Participation Center, Women's Voices. Women Vote. www.voterparticipation.org/womens-voices-women-vote. December 21, 2012.

[28] Conservative women's political groups include Smart Girl Politics Action, Concerned Women for America, Independent Women's Forum, and Voices of Conservative Women.

[29] Gil Kaufman. January 31, 2012. Florida's College Republicans Taking "Right Steps" to Woo Young Voters. http://www.mtv.com/news/articles/1678216/florida-primary-college-republicans.jhtml?xrs=share_copy.

Groups like the Nebraska Federation of College Republicans held registration drives on various campuses. Their campaign, "Our Moment, Our
Future," focused on high unemployment rates and the rapidly growing
national debt as more mobilizing than social issues because they fall disproportionately on the shoulders of young voters.[30]

In general, the Obama campaign had a better organization in place
to register voters, building on the President's successes in 2008. Then,
his tremendous money advantage allowed him to open campaign offices
in key battleground states and hire young staffers to aggressively conduct registration drives on college campuses, at concerts and movies, outside churches and bookstores, at political rallies and civic group meetings – anywhere eligible but unregistered persons were likely to be. (Voter
eligibility requirements include age – 18 years or older – U.S. citizenship, and residence at the location in which one is registering. In most
states, eligibility is not extended to convicted felons and persons declared
mentally incapacitated by the state.) Many of Obama's campaign offices
never closed after the 2008 election. Keeping these offices open "allowed
Obama's campaign to remain a neighborhood presence and develop relations in critical precincts and counties."[31] It enabled staffers ("community
embeds") to maintain close contact with people less likely to be registered – the young, minorities, and the poor.[32]

The Republicans had a more difficult time registering new voters in
2008 and again in 2012. Young unregistered voters were trending more
Democratic or preferring to register as independents. And the Romney
campaign never could catch up with the Obama's grassroots organization, with its paid staffers and offices in key locations. Consequently,
the Romney campaign had to rely more on state party organizations and
unpaid volunteers. Local Republican women's clubs (part of the umbrella
National Federation of Republican Women) at the state and local levels
played the major role in registering new GOP-leaning women voters. Less
well funded than the major Democratic-leaning women's groups, Republican women's clubs reached out to friends and neighbors with whom

[30] WOWT-TV. September 26, 2012. College Republicans Hold Voter Drives. http://www
.wowt.com/news/headlines/College-Republicans-Hold-Voter-Drives-171318071.html.
[31] Frank James. November 14, 2012. Obama's Political Moneyball Could Be the Shape
of Campaigns to Come. National Public Radio. http://www.npr.org/blogs/itsallpolitics/
2012/11/13/165061652/obamas-political-moneyball-could-be-the-shape-of-campaigns-
to-come.
[32] Cameron Joseph and Niall Stanage. September 25, 2012. Obama Campaign Holds Ground-
Game Advantage as Early Voting Begins. *The Hill.* http://thehill.com/homenews/
campaign/251405-obama-holds-ground-game-edge-as-early-voting-begins-.

they regularly came in contact outside the world of politics. Specifically, they focused on married women with young children, fellow female churchgoers and social conservatives in suburban and rural areas, working women, and female small-business owners concerned about growing tax burdens.

Registration efforts aimed at women voters were not limited to college campuses. Citizens' mailboxes (postal and Internet) were flooded with voter registration forms, along with the telephone numbers and mail and e-mail addresses of election officials. Parties and advocacy group representatives went door to door offering to help people register or leaving forms for them to complete. Naturally, the registration outreach efforts were targeted at high-growth areas and places with heavier concentrations of unregistered people. Public service announcements reminding voters of how and when to register ran on just about every cable and broadcast television and radio station. These PSAs were tailored to fit the demographics of each station's viewers or listeners.

In 2012, Democrats and Republicans alike heavily targeted Spanish-language television and radio stations, reflecting Latinos' status as the fastest-growing minority group in the United States. In a number of key battleground states, such as Florida, Nevada, and New Mexico, Hispanics already outnumbered African Americans and were perceived as vital swing voters. Democrats were more successful at registering Hispanic females than Republicans. It paid off, as Latinas ended up supporting Obama more heavily than their Latino counterparts (76 percent versus 65 percent, respectively, according to the national exit poll). The turnout rate of Latinas was also higher than for Latinos, as it has been for other recent presidential elections.

TURNOUT RATES

Turnout rate is measured in two ways: (1) the percentage of the eligible voting-age population (18 and older) that voted, or (2) the percentage of registered voters that voted. The U.S. Census conducts a postelection telephone survey to determine what percentage of the 18-and-older population voted (self-reported). While official, the Census Bureau's survey inflates turnout rates, primarily because more people say they voted than actually did. State election officials generally measure turnout rates using actual voters as a percentage of registered voters. Unfortunately, not all states report turnout rates among registered voters by gender.

In spite of a closely contested election and an estimated $6 billion spent in the campaigns, turnout among eligible voters dropped in 2012. According to the U.S. Census Bureau, turnout in 2012 (61.8 percent) fell from 63.6 percent in 2008. Another study of turnout by American University's Center for the Study of the American Electorate[33] put the 2012 voter turnout rate slightly lower at 57.5 percent of all eligible voters, compared to 62.3 percent who voted in 2008, 60.4 percent who cast ballots in 2004, and 54.2 percent in 2000.

Reasons for Lower Turnout in 2012
The director of the Center for the Study of the American Electorate offered a number of reasons for the plunge in turnout nationally in 2012:

> Large drops... came in Eastern Seaboard states still reeling from the devastation from Superstorm Sandy, which wiped out power for millions and disrupted usual voting routines... In other areas not affected by the storm, a host of factors could have contributed to waning voter enthusiasm... The 2012 race was one of the nastiest in recent memory, leaving many voters feeling turned off. With Democrats weary from a difficult four years and Republicans splintered by a divisive primary, neither party was particularly enthused about their own candidate. Stricter voting restrictions adopted by many states may also have kept some voters away from the polls.[34]

Turnout Rates Slightly Higher in Competitive Swing States
Turnout among eligible voters was higher in the competitive battleground states than in other states. (See Figure 3.7.) One reason may be that the Electoral College system puts pressure on candidates to concentrate on swing states, leaving voters in nonbattleground states to view their

---

[33] Turnout data from the U.S. Census Bureau are from U.S. Census Bureau, *Current Population Survey*, November 2012 and earlier reports. Table A-1. http://www.census.gov/hhes/www/socdemo/voting/publications/historical/index.html. Turnout data from the American University study are from Curtis Gans. November 8, 2012. 2012 Election Turnout Dips Below 2008 and 2004 Levels; Number of Eligible Voters Increases by Eight Million; Five Million Fewer Votes Cast. Bipartisan Policy Center and the Center for the Study of the American Electorate. http://bipartisanpolicy.org/sites/default/files/2012%20Voter%20Turnout%20Full%20Report.pdf.

[34] Leslie Dyste summarizing comments by Curtis Gans, Center Director, in Leslie Dyste. November 7, 2012. Minnesota Has Highest Voter Turnout in Country. KSTP-TV. http://kstp.mn/64kd5.

Figure 3.7: Turnout rates are higher in swing states.

Year	Swing States	Non-Swing States	Difference (in percentage points)
2012	64.2%	56.8%	7.4
2008	66.1%	60.9%	5.2
2004	63.6%	59.2%	4.4
2000	55.1%	53.9%	1.2
1996	51.5%	51.4%	0.1
1992	57.5%	58.2%	-0.7

Note: The 10 swing states used in this analysis are Colorado, Florida, Iowa, North Carolina, New Hampshire, Nevada, Ohio, Pennsylvania, Virginia, and Wisconsin.
Source: Analysis by the Center for the Study of the American Electorate, "2012 Election Turnout Dips Below 2008 and 2004 Levels: Number of Eligible Voters Increases by Eight Million, Five Million Fewer Votes Cast," November 8, 2012; http://bipartisan policy.org/sites/default/files/2012%20Voter%20Turnout%20Full%20Report.pdf.

votes as making no difference. Turnout rates among women voters also tended to be higher in the more competitive states, no doubt driven up by intense get-out-the-vote (GOTV) efforts by both parties at virtually every stage of the campaign microtargeting various slices of the female electorate.

Women Catch Up With – and Pass – Men
For years after the passage of the Nineteenth Amendment, the participation rates of men were greater than those of women in presidential elections, even though there were more women than men of voting age. This was true whether male–female comparisons were made using the sheer number of men and women voting or the relative percentage of each gender who voted (the turnout rate). By number, women surpassed men voting in presidential elections in 1964. But by percentage, women continued to vote at a lower rate until 1980, when their percentage slightly exceeded that of men. With each successive election, women have outvoted men at increasing rates.

Early on, the civil and women's rights movements of the 1960s and 1970s played a large role in improving the turnout rate among women. More recently, GOTV efforts by women's groups and political parties have targeted females who make up a majority of the voting-age population and have a higher turnout rate than men. (See Figure 3.8.) Today women outpace men in voter turnout rate in all but the very oldest age group. In 2012, the turnout rate for young women ages 18 to 29 was

Figure 3.8: Women have voted at higher rates than men have in recent elections.

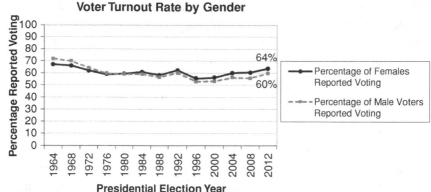

Note: The turnout rate for each gender is the percentage of the eligible population that voted.

Source: U.S. Census, Current Population Survey, November 2012 and earlier reports.

48.6 percent compared to 41.5 percent for their young male counter-parts – a 7.1 percent gender gap.[35]

In 2012, the Women for Obama part of the campaign had vote directors in ten battleground states. The operation used phone banks, house parties, and Women Vote 2012 Summits featuring discussion of the issues of paycheck fairness, health care (including birth control), abortion rights, and education[36] to get out the women's vote in these key swing states. Similarly, the Romney campaign's Women for Mitt operation hosted roundtables, forums, and town hall meetings and conducted extensive phone-banking. It, too, was led by women vote directors in key battleground states. Both campaigns also relied on women-to-women networking.[37]

[35] CIRCLE. May 10, 2013. The Youth Vote in 2012. http://www.civicyouth.org/only-12-3-million-young-people-18-29-voted-for-president-obama-in-%E2%80%9812-down-from-14-8-million-in-%E2%80%9808/.

[36] David Jackson. June 27, 2012. Obama '12 Targets Women Where They Live. *USA Today.* http://usatoday30.usatoday.com/NEWS/usaedition/2012-06-27-Women-summits_ST_U.htm.

[37] Lynn Sweet. October 13, 2012. Election Could Come Down to What Women Want. *Chicago Sun-Times.* http://www.suntimes.com/news/sweet/15721901-452/election-could-come-down-to-what-women-want.html.

Early "Convenience" Voting

Educating women about early and absentee voting was a major component of GOTV efforts in many states. Since 2000, a number of states have adopted or expanded laws making it easier to vote by mail (absentee voting) or in person at designated voting sites. Both forms of pre–Election Day balloting are jointly referred to as early voting.

Early voting is a growing trend throughout the United States. It is popular with voters and appears to have a negligible impact on actual voter turnout. It is, simply, "convenience" voting that more Americans are choosing. One postelection survey of voters found that 37 percent had voted early (19 percent in person, 17 percent by mail) in 2012, up from 34 percent in 2008.[38] Only eight percent of voters, both for Romney and Obama, were late deciders, making up their minds within a week of Election Day.

WINNING WOMEN VOTERS: FROM PRIMARY TO ELECTION DAY

Efforts to sway and mobilize women voters began in earnest during the primary season and continued right up to Election Day. Throughout the campaign, timing proved to be a critical and sometimes unpredictable factor.

The GOP Primary: Romney Chose to Be More Conservative

As the incumbent in the 2012 election, President Obama faced no serious challengers for his party's nomination – the reverse of 2008 when he and Hillary Clinton battled it out for the Democratic nomination right up to the convention. In 2012, it was the Republicans with the highly competitive primary season, and the primary calendar was not particularly kind to the eventual nominee. To win the nomination against a field of more conservative, social-issue-focused Republican contenders like Rick Santorum and Newt Gingrich in small, more rural states like Iowa, New Hampshire, and South Carolina, Romney chose to take stances on reproductive rights that clashed with his previous actions as governor of Massachusetts on a variety of women's health issues.

---

[38] The percentages voting in person and by mail do not add to 37 percent because of rounding. The Pew Research Center for the People & the Press. November 15, 2012. Low Marks for the 2012 Election. Washington, DC: Pew Research Center http://www.people-press. org/2012/11/15/section-3-the-voting-process-and-the-accuracy-of-the-vote/.

It was during the GOP primaries when the former governor, eager to court social conservatives (including many pro-life women), "said he supported a 'personhood' amendment that would confer full legal rights on a fertilized egg and potentially criminalize some forms of contraception, and that if elected president he would 'get rid of' Planned Parenthood."[39] While effective in mobilizing conservative pro-life women, statements of this type worked equally well in mobilizing more liberal pro-choice women – a slightly larger force in some key swing states in the general election. Romney ended up losing the swing states of Ohio, Florida, Virginia, Colorado, Nevada, and others.

The National Party Conventions: Focus on Women
Republicans held their party convention in Tampa, Florida, in late August (27–30). Democrats followed a week later (September 4–6) in Charlotte, North Carolina. Both states had gone for Obama in 2008, although narrowly. Neither convention site would deliver its state to the host party. But at each party's convention, strong, aggressive appeals to women voters across the United States were made by an impressive array of female speakers via prime-time broadcast TV networks, cable TV news programs, and online videos, including YouTube.

Predictably, the issue focus of each convention differed. The Democratic convention "devoted a huge chunk of its messaging to social issues," while Republicans homed in on the economic failures of the Obama administration.[40] The Republicans also worked hard to repair the damage that had been done to the party the weekend before the convention began by Missouri GOP Senate candidate Todd Akin. Asked in an interview whether abortion is justified in a pregnancy resulting from rape, he replied: "[I]t's really rare. If it's a legitimate rape, the female body has ways to try to shut the whole thing down."[41] U.S. Sen. Olympia Snowe, a well-respected and influential Republican from Maine, laid out the challenge for Romney: "[He] must work to overcome what others in our party

---

[39] Eleanor Clift. November 8, 2012. Republicans Learn the Cost of Alienating Women Voters. *The Daily Beast.* http://www.thedailybeast.com/articles/2012/11/08/republicans-learn-the-cost-of-alienating-women-voters.html.

[40] Mytheos Holt. September 7, 2012. Convention Role Reversal: Did Romney Put Obama on Defense? *The Blaze.* www.theblaze.com/stories/convention-role-reversal-did-romney-put-obama-on-defense/.

[41] Lori Moore. August 20, 2012. Rep. Todd Akin: The Statement and the Reaction. *New York Times.* http://www.nytimes.com/2012/08/21/us/politics/rep-todd-akin-legitimate-rape-statement-and-reaction.html?_r=0.

TABLE 3.1: Women accounted for one-third of the speakers at 2012 national party conventions

Convention	Day 1	Day 2	Day 3	Total	%
Republican					
Male Speakers	22	11	11	44	66.7
Female Speakers	14	4	4	22	33.3
Total	36	15	15	66	100.0
Democratic					
Male Speakers	25	35	24	84	63.6
Female Speakers	18	17	13	48	36.4
Total	43	52	37	132	100%

Source: List of Speakers was provided by CNN; http://www.cnn.com/interactive/2012/08/politics/rnc.schedule/index.html;   http://www.cnn.com/interactive/2012/09/politics/dnc.schedule/index.html.

have done to undermine our standing with women, and he must restore the image of who we are as Republicans."[42] Predictably, the Democrats highlighted the damaging statement at every turn during and after their convention, along with other insensitive comments made by Republican men later in the campaign.[43]

The proportion of women speakers at each convention differed little: 33 percent at the GOP convention and 36 percent at the Democratic convention. (See Table 3.1.) Female speakers at both conventions were racially and ethnically diverse. But there were sharp contrasts otherwise. Republicans allotted more time to their speakers, meaning they had far fewer speakers than the Democrats. A large proportion of Republican speakers were women elected officials from key states. In contrast, the Democrats featured a noticeably larger number of new faces, often young path breakers, telling personal stories of how they had been helped by policies promoted during Obama's first term or hindered by Republican proposals (Sandra Fluke). Debbie Wasserman Schultz, Democratic National Committee chair and a congresswoman from Florida, and

[42] Olympia J. Snowe. August, 24, 2012. Sen. Olympia Snowe on How the GOP Can Mend Its Image Among Women. *Washington Post.* http://articles.washingtonpost.com/2012-08-24/opinions/35492298_1_romney-ryan-mitt-romney-gop-platform.

[43] Indiana Republican Richard Mourdock, a U.S. Senate candidate, remarked that when a woman becomes pregnant as a consequence of being raped, "that's something God intended."

Kamala Harris, California's state attorney general, appeared before the delegates twice.

Each approach was effective. Republican women were energized by stronger, diverse officeholders, like Governors Nikki Haley (S.C.) and Susana Martinez (N.M.), who created a different image of Republican women politicos than Sarah Palin. Democratic women were elated to see the emphasis on mobilizing younger women. (At that time, polls were showing less enthusiasm for voting among younger voters than in 2008.)

The candidates' wives, Ann Romney and Michelle Obama, were both given prime-time speaking slots the first nights of their party's conventions. They each received standing ovations from the delegates and drew sizable television audiences. According to Nielsen, on the first night of the Democratic National Convention, 26.2 million people tuned in; night one of the Republican National Convention drew 22.3 million viewers.[44] Both wives made strong appeals to women by elaborating on their marriages, their children, and their spouses' caring and compassion – themes they would repeat when they hit the campaign trail as popular surrogates.[45] Their husbands, too, frequently returned to the love-of-family theme in speeches, debates, and media appearances right up to Election Day.

Ann Romney described her marriage in this way: "I read somewhere that Mitt and I have a 'storybook marriage.' Well, in the storybooks I read, there were never long, long, rainy winter afternoons in a house with five boys screaming at once. And those storybooks never seemed to have chapters called MS or breast cancer (alluding to herself). A storybook marriage? No, not at all. What Mitt Romney and I have is a real marriage."[46]

The First Lady spoke of her apprehensions when her husband first thought about running for office: "I loved the life we had built for our girls and I deeply loved the man I had built that life with, and I didn't want

[44] Jilian Fama. September 7, 2012. The Fight for the Spotlight in 2012 National Conventions. *ABC News.* http://abcn.ws/15eRwsG.

[45] Colleen McCain Nelson. July 20, 2012. Political Perspectives: Michelle Obama, Ann Romney Hit the Trail. *Wall Street Journal.* http://blogs.wsj.com/washwire/2012/07/20/political-perspectives-michelle-obama-ann-romney-hit-the-trail/.

[46] Caitlin Dickson and Kevin Fallon. November 7, 2012. The Most Popular DNC, RNC Speeches Ranked Using Twitter Data. *The Daily Beast.* http://www.thedailybeast.com/galleries/2012/09/07/most-tweeted-convention-speakers-obama-romney-clinton-and-more-photos.html#fdc40fe9-2935-4cb1-8dc1-2e82cbc148ba.

that to change if he became President. Well, today, after so many struggles and triumphs and moments that have tested my husband in ways I could never have imagined, I have seen firsthand that being President doesn't change who you are. No, it reveals who you are.... [L]et me tell you today, I love my husband even more than I did four years ago, even more than I did 23 years ago, when we first met."[47]

The Democrats got the much-desired convention bounce, while Republicans did not. The reasons, Republicans said, included their storm-shortened convention, cutbacks in prime-time media coverage, and overly negative media coverage because of the extensive visuals of security barricades, along with the short time between conventions. Democrats countered that their prime-time speakers, most notably former president Bill Clinton, were bigger draws than those who appeared at the Republican convention and that the camera shots panning over the Democratic delegates revealed a much more diverse America than similar shots of GOP convention delegates. The latter, in combination with the increases in the minority (especially Hispanic and Asian) and youth shares of the electorate, will undoubtedly prompt Republicans to find a way to recruit and select a more diverse-looking array of Republican convention delegates in 2016.[48]

The Presidential/Vice Presidential Debates

The nonpartisan Commission on Presidential Debates (CPD) sponsored and produced the national debates – three presidential and one vice presidential. On July 25, 2012, the CPD announced the dates, locations, topics, rules, and formats of the debates to be held in the fall; the debate moderators were selected in August. The CPD, under considerable pressure, selected two female moderators: CNN's Candy Crowley moderated the second presidential debate (a town hall format) and ABC's Martha Raddatz moderated the vice presidential debate. Conservative groups complained that all the moderators, including the two women, were from liberal news outlets.

The high-stakes nature of the debates virtually guaranteed that from the outset, viewers would look for partisan and ideological bias in each

---

[47] Ibid.
[48] Susan A. MacManus. 2013. From 2012 to 2016: Concluding Thoughts on the Permanent Campaign. In Larry Sabato, ed., *Barack Obama and the New America*. Lanham, MD: Rowman & Littlefield, 195–226.

moderator's questions and refereeing of candidate responses, as well as in the media's postdebate coverage. No moderator escaped criticism; predictably, critiques (and defenses) fell more often along party rather than gender lines.

Interest in the debates ran high. The first presidential debate (domestic policy) drew 67.2 million viewers, the second (town hall) 65.6 million, and the third (foreign policy) 59.2 million.[49] The vice presidential debate drew 51.4 million – down considerably from the Joe Biden–Sarah Palin debate in 2008, the most watched of all debates in 2008 with 69.9 million viewers.

Romney's surprisingly strong performance in the first debate stunned even the most seasoned political observers and changed the momentum of the race almost overnight. The gender gap closed somewhat and polls in the swing states narrowed. According to veteran Democratic pollster Celinda Lake, "Women went into the debate actively disliking Romney, and they came out thinking he might understand their lives and might be able to get something done for them."[50] Up to that point, many women had highly negative impressions of Romney based on negative ads run against him by the Obama campaign. But during the debate, Romney "appeared nothing like the candidate that was essentially a caricature in the advertising by the Obama campaign."[51] Although Obama rebounded in the second and third debates, nearly every postelection analysis identified the first debate as a "momentum changer" that kept the contest close right up until Election Day.

Not surprisingly, it was during the second debate that the two candidates clashed most over women's issues, with each touting his stronger level of support among women voters in reaction to questions posed by the female town hall participants. Romney's reference to receiving "binders full of women" as governor of Massachusetts when he requested more female applicants for jobs in his administration became prime fodder for Obama attack ads against him. The day after the debate, Obama, campaigning in Iowa, said: "I've got to tell you, we don't have to collect a bunch of binders to find qualified, talented, driven *young women*,

---

[49] In fairness, the third debate was pitted against two major sporting events (Monday Night Football on ESPN and Major League Baseball playoffs on FOX).

[50] Susan Page. October 15, 2012. Swing States Poll: Women Push Romney into Lead. *USA Today*. www.usatoday.com/story/news/politics/2012/10/15/swing-states-poll-women-voters-romney-obama/1634791/.

[51] Neil Newhouse, a Republican pollster, quoted in Ibid.

ready to learn and teach in these fields [science and technology] right now. And when *young women* graduate, they should get equal pay for equal work"[52] (author's emphasis). The binder comment, along with the president's stances on contraception, unequal pay, and Planned Parenthood funding,[53] helped Obama regain his footing with some women voters who were sorely disappointed with his performance in the first debate.

Romney, in turn, pivoted back to his argument that women were more concerned about the failing economy: "This is a presidency that has not helped America's women, and as I go across the country and ask women, 'What can I do to help?' what they speak about day in and day out is, 'Help me find a good job, or a good job for my spouse.' That's what the women of America are concerned about. And the answers are coming from us and not from Barack Obama."[54]

The Romney campaign knew from the outset that winning a majority of the women's vote would be a challenge. In fact, Romney spent a lot of time trying to cast an image of himself as more woman sensitive than the picture the Obama campaign had painted of him. Even in the third debate, focused on foreign policy, "many political observers read Mr. Romney's noninterventionist foreign policy stance – a shift from more-bellicose Republican primary rhetoric – as an effort to reassure women voters."[55]

Campaigns Place More Ads on TV and in Swing States
Postelection surveys by the Pew Research Center found that the debates had a bigger impact on voter choice than ads but that commercials moved voter opinions as well, especially in swing states that saw more of them. The candidates and their campaign strategists created effective television, online (Facebook, YouTube), direct mail, and radio ads. Very little advertising was done in newspapers and magazines.

---

[52] Rosalind S. Helderman and Nia-Malika Henderson. October 17, 2012. Women's Issues Help Shape Presidential Debate. *Washington Post.* http://articles.washingtonpost.com/2012-10-17/politics/35501441_1_romney-campaign-female-voters-presidential-debate.

[53] Laura Meckler and Carol E. Lee. October 18, 2012. Candidates Zero in on Women Voters. *Wall Street Journal.* http://professional.wsj.com/article/SB10000872396390444592704578062963511441022.html?mg=reno64-wsj.

[54] Helderman and Henderson, Women's Issues Help Shape...

[55] Peter Hruby. November 6, 2012. The Race Was on for Independent Women Voters. *Washington Times.* http://www.washingtontimes.com/news/2012/nov/6/the-race-was-on-for-independent-women-voters/print/#ixzz2Fkx99ISr.

With television the most common source of campaign news, it was not surprising that the candidates spent more money and placed more political ads on local broadcast and national cable television. (Many of these ads were also placed online.) It was estimated that more than 1 million ads were aired in the presidential general election by the two candidates, their party committees, and support interest groups. This was a 39 percent increase over 2008 and a 41 percent increase over 2004.[56] However, they were more concentrated in the key swing states than was the case in 2008.

The Obama campaign out-advertised the Romney campaign by a 2.6-to-1 margin. Their strategy was to advertise more heavily in the early part of the campaign (summer), while Romney aired more ads in the latter half of the campaign. Many analysts believe the earlier negative branding ("carpet-bombing") of Romney by Obama was effective and might have cost Romney the election.[57] Romney was somewhat disadvantaged by federal campaign finance rules stating that a candidate must be officially nominated by the party before receiving federal funds for the general election phase of a campaign. Thus, the late-summer convention deprived Romney of resources to counter the massive number of attack ads the Obama campaign launched against him before the GOP convention.

Targeting Media Ads to Women Voters. Television and radio ads are especially powerful in reaching young and new voters, the majority of whom are female. Both the Obama and Romney campaigns selected the stations whose viewers or listeners the candidates most wanted to reach and the times those viewers would most likely tune in. In each ad, the words and images focused sharply on a desired group of viewers – often women voters – whose faces appeared in the ads.

Direct mail can also aim specific campaign messages to specific audiences. Traditional postal-delivered mail reaches far narrower audiences (by ZIP code, for example) and can be sent to only registered voters eligible to vote in a particular electoral contest – a more efficient

---

[56] Pew Research Center. October 25, 2012. Internet Gains Most as Campaign News Source But Cable TV Still Leads. http://www.journalism.org/commentary_backgrounder/social_media_doubles_remains_limited.

[57] Thomas M. DeFrank. November 7, 2012. Obama Campaign Attack Ads Appeared Effective in Defeating Mitt Romney. *New York Post.* http://www.nydailynews.com/news/election-2012/obama-campaign-attack-ads-appeared-effective-article-1.1198517.

approach than broadcasting to larger audiences made up of a siz-able number of unregistered voters. Campaign managers subdivide or cross-reference registered voter lists according to personal characteristics such as gender or race or membership in religious or environmental groups and mail pieces to only those names. The same microtargeting approach can be used to send online ads, videos, and e-mails. Often, the ad theme is the same, regardless of how it is transmitted to potential voters.

Overall, analysts agree that the 2012 election was characterized by the most precise demographic targeting in American campaign history. Ads were specially crafted to appeal to different groups of women on the basis of their age, race or ethnicity, marital and parental status, employment and income, ideology, and religion, among others. Reflective of the dom-inant issue of the campaign, the economy, both campaigns created ads featuring women worried about a job, equal pay for equal work, rising gas prices, the prospects for Social Security and Medicare, college educa-tion and health care for their children, and/or reproductive rights. (See Photo 3.1 and Photo 3.2.)

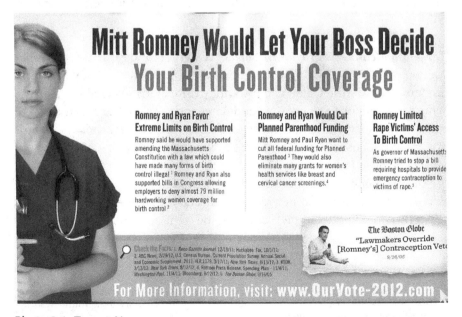

Photo 3.1: Target: Young women
Sponsor: Organizing for America Florida, a project of the Florida Democratic Party

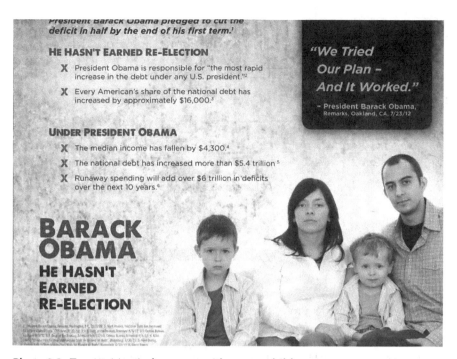

Photo 3.2: Target: Married women with young children
Sponsor: Republican Party of Florida; for Romney/Ryan

The goal of any ad is to capture attention by enabling the recipient to immediately see something of herself and her sentiments. That means compelling pictures and a simple, straightforward message. Ads that look more like human-interest informational pieces are often more effective than "political" ads because politics is a lower priority with many voters than are children, work, health, and other aspects of their lives. Repetition is critical, whether for mail, ads aired on television and radio, or those appearing online.

What About Those Negative Ads? From the voter's perspective, there was considerably more mudslinging (negative ads) in 2012 than in 2008. Analyses of the actual content of the ads confirmed a record number of negative ads run by both presidential candidates. (See Figure 3.9.)

Many believe that negative ads are particularly alienating to younger and women voters. If so, then why did both candidates run so many negative ads against each other on women's issues (Obama against Romney on subjects like abortion, contraception, pay equity; Romney

Figure 3.9: Television ads were more negative in 2012 than in previous elections.

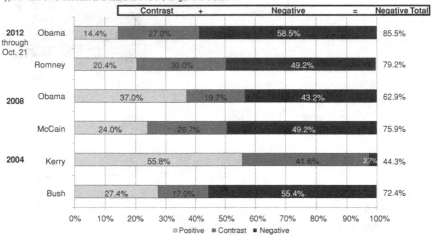

Type of ads on broadcast and cable television, for general elections.

Source: Wesleyan Media Project analysis of Kantar Media/CMAG presidential ad airings (2012); Wisconsin Advertising Project (2004 and 2008), "2012 Shatters 2004 and 2008 Records for Total Ads Aired," October 24, 2012; http://mediaproject .wesleyan.edu/2012/10/24/2012-shatters-2004-and-2008-records-for-total-ads-aired.

against Obama on the plummeting job market and unemployment)? The answer may lie in new research from Montreal's Centre for Studies on Human Stress suggesting that women remember negative ads more than men *if* women are emotionally engaged in the subject and inclined to vote. Thus, if a woman deeply cares about an issue, she might be more effectively swayed to vote against a candidate painted as opposing her view on the issue. "If you don't care about the election, it probably won't touch you," one of the researchers said. "But if it's a matter you care about and the ad is negative, it could have an impact."[58]

The bottom line is that the record number of negative ads aimed at women voters simply reflected the character of the entire presidential election: "[I]t was primarily a contest for the female portion of the electorate, with Mr. Obama's campaign attempting to exploit and expand a potentially decisive Democrat-Republican gender gap – the same gap Mitt Romney's campaign sought to minimize and narrow."[59]

[58] Jason Koebler. October 12, 2012. Do Negative Ads Work Better on Women? *US News & World Report.* http://www.usnews.com/news/articles/2012/10/12/do-negative-ads-work-better-on-women_print.html.
[59] Peter Hruby. The Race Was on ...

TABLE 3.2: Late deciders broke for President Obama in 2012

When did you finally decide for whom to vote in the presidential election?	Total	Obama	Romney
Just today	3%	51%	44%
In the last few days	6%	50%	45%
In October	11%	49%	48%
In September	9%	45%	53%
Before that	69%	53%	46%
Sample: 5,439 respondents			

Note: Late deciders are typically disproportionately young and women voters.
Source: 2012 Edison Research National Exit Poll.

According to journalist Susan Page, "as a group, women tend to start paying attention to election contests later and remain more open to persuasion by the candidates and their ads."[60] While this was true in 2012, the oversaturation of TV ads in key swing states limited their effectiveness in mobilizing late deciders. These ads – running virtually nonstop and aired back to back – seemed to cancel each other out and confuse less-informed voters. So, too, did the various fact-checking exercises of journalists and advocacy groups. This left visits by the candidates and their influential surrogates, as well as personal contacts by respected family members, friends, and neighbors (the ground game), to get these less-than-enthusiastic voters to the polls.

Mobilizing the Late Deciders

In a close contest, victory goes to the team that ends the game with the better performance. In presidential politics, the victor is the candidate who can mobilize more late deciders, or low-propensity voters. As shown in Table 3.2, the Obama campaign bested Romney's in winning over late deciders, who were disproportionately Democratic-leaning young women voters, especially minorities.

Appearances by the Candidates and Their Surrogates. One way of measuring how important a state is to a candidate is the number of visits or

---

[60] Susan Page. October 15, 2012. Swing States Poll: Women Push Romney into Lead. *USA Today.* www.usatoday.com/story/news/politics/2012/10/15/swing-states-poll-women-voters-romney-obama/1634791/.

Figure 3.10: The Obama campaign made fewer swing state visits than the Romney campaign did.

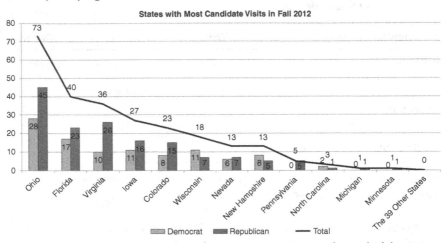

Note: This chart shows the number of campaign events since the end of the Democratic National Convention.

Source: "Presidential Tracker," The Center for Voting and Democracy, November 16, 2012. http://www.fairvote.org/presidential-tracker#.ULNroYbe-Sp.

campaign stops the candidate makes there.[61] The states that receive the most attention are often the battleground states, although some visits are made to one-party states to raise money (California and New York for Democrats and Texas for Republicans.)

The Obama-Biden team targeted its visits more strategically and ended up with fewer total visits to fewer swing states. (See Figure 3.10.) There were two major reasons for the visit differential. First, Romney had a much tougher road to the White House than Obama and needed to carry almost all the swing states to win – a daunting task. Second, the Obama campaign used a voter database far superior to Romney's that generated much more accurate polls (internal) and turnout projections. This enabled the campaign to more precisely pinpoint locations at which strategic last-minute visits by Obama, Bill Clinton, and Michelle Obama could turn out traditionally late-deciding young, minority, and women voters (college campuses, urban core areas with large concentrations of minorities, union-dominated Midwestern states).

---

[61] Andrea Levien, November 14, 2012. Tracking Presidential Campaign Field Operations. Fairvote.org. http://www.fairvote.org/tracking-presidential-campaign-field-operations.

On the day before the election, Obama had 181 surrogates on the trail, including many elected officials and stars from the Hollywood and music worlds like Bruce Springsteen, Rashida Jones, Ashley Judd, Jon Bon Jovi, Morgan Freeman, and Eva Longoria, to name but a few.[62] (Noticeably missing was Oprah Winfrey, who had been a major figure in the 2008 campaign.) Obama also turned to Sandra Fluke, still fresh from her starring role at the Democratic National Convention, to reach out to women voters in Colorado and Nevada.[63]

Romney had 100 surrogates campaigning for him in swing states during the final four days. The most prominent were political figures rather than entertainers: Secretary of State Condoleezza Rice, Louisiana Gov. Bobby Jindal, former New York City Mayor Rudy Giuliani, Sen. Marco Rubio (FL), Sen. John McCain (AZ), Sen. Rob Portman (OH), Sen. John Thune (SD), Sen. Lindsey Graham (SC), and Sen. Kelly Ayotte (NH). He also heavily relied on his five adult sons to represent him throughout the campaign. Son Craig, fluent in Spanish, addressed the Republican convention in Spanish and recorded numerous Spanish-language radio ads for his father.[64] Some analysts criticized the Romney campaign for failing to give more prominent surrogate roles to the women governors who had won impressive victories in 2010 and spoken at the Republican National Convention but were seldom seen on the campaign trail thereafter.

Personal Contacts at the Grassroots Level. Visits by the candidates and their surrogates, while helpful, were not as crucial as the last-ditch personal-contact efforts by grassroots-level staffers and volunteers. The Obama campaign relied more on in-person contacts with young "low propensity" voters who needed "extra nudges and last-minute reminders"[65] to get them to vote, while the Romney campaign relied on

[62] For a detailed list of Obama's surrogates from the entertainment industry as well as from the political world, see Dominic Patten. November 5, 2012. Hollywood for Obama & Romney: Star Surrogates Out on Final Campaign Day. *Deadline Hollywood*. http://www .deadline.com/2012/11/hollywood-for-obama-romney-star-surrogates-out-on-final-campaign-day/.

[63] Julie Pace. October 23, 2012. The Big Story: Campaign Surrogates Shore up Support in Final Days. *Associated Press*.

[64] Ibid. Romney did have some entertainer surrogates, but far fewer and less visible than those tapped by the President.

[65] Travis Pillow. November 11, 2012. Obama's Florida Election Edge. *Tallahassee Democrat* http://www.tallahassee.com/article/20121111/POLITICSPOLICY/311110026/Obama-s-Florida-election-edge.

less effective phone calls. The Obama campaign reveled in pointing out the difference:

> [On Election Day], our volunteers are not driving to some large office miles from their homes and handed a phone and a call sheet. Instead, Canvass Captains, Phone Bank Captains and scores of local volunteers will be knocking on the doors of the very voters they registered, have been talking to for months and know personally. And they will be directing them to polling locations in their communities – the schools their kids go to, the places of worship they attend each week and community centers they know well.[66]

Even if the Republicans' database had been operating up to speed (which it was not), it is not clear whether it would have been as effective as the Democrats' database in convincing the late deciders or unenthusiastic voters to go to the polls. They were more Obama's natural base than Romney's. But the relative superiority of the Obama campaign's database (nicknamed Narwhal) left some Republicans calling for their own party to spend less on TV ads and invest equally or more on "micro-targeted voter mobilization campaigns and support organizations that execute those campaigns."[67]

The irony was that in the most highly technological campaign ever run in the United States, personal contacts at the grassroots level in key battleground states made the difference in who won the presidency. Perhaps the best account of the successful mobilization efforts of the Obama campaign in 2012 is one by Associated Press reporter Julie Pace:

> In the end, President Barack Obama won re-election exactly the way his campaign had predicted: running up big margins with women and minorities, mobilizing a sophisticated registration and get-out-the-vote operation, and focusing narrowly on the battleground states that would determine the election.[68]

[66] Sam Stein. November 3, 2012. Obama Campaign: We've Contacted One Out of Every 2.5 People in the Country. *Huffington Post*. http://www.huffingtonpost.com/2012/11/03/obama-voter-contact_n_2069289.html.

[67] Brian J. Wise. November 11, 2012. Republicans Lost the Ground Game. *Washington Times*. http://www.washingtontimes.com/news/2012/nov/11/republicans-lost-the-ground-game/.

[68] Julie Pace. November 8, 2012. Obama 2012: President Wins the Way His Campaign Predicted. *Huffington Post*. http://www.huffingtonpost.com/2012/11/08/obama-2012-campaign_n_2092452.html.

One example of the impact of intense mobilization efforts occurred in Florida, where the presidential race was virtually tied for months. (Obama ultimately won by only 0.88 percent.) Exit polls showed that women made up 55 percent of all Florida voters, up from 52 percent in 2008. Prior to Election Day, Florida was home to four GOP primary televised debates, one nationally televised presidential debate (the last), and forty visits from presidential/vice presidential candidates. More money was spent on TV ads in Florida's ten media markets than in any other state. A large share of these ads featured women. A similar pattern characterized GOTV efforts in other key swing states.

The Obama campaign's ultimate success in battleground states was largely based on mobilization efforts aimed at younger women, especially minority and single women. The campaign fully recognized that there is, indeed, a generational divide among women voters, with the younger, more liberal women tending to vote Democratic and the older, more conservative and less racially/ethnically diverse women leaning more Republican.

A FINAL WORD

Women were not included in the "We the people" opening of the U.S. Constitution when it was originally written. But after a seventy-two-year struggle (longer for black women), women won the right to vote with the Nineteenth Amendment in 1920. By 1964, more women than men were voting, and by 1980, the percentage of women voting was greater than the percentage of men voting. The larger number and higher turnout of women voters account for their growing clout. One must not make the mistake, however, of assuming that women form a unified voting bloc.

In the election of 2012, it was clear from the outset that women voters would be the deciding factor in the outcome. Consequently, candidates, political parties, and women's advocacy groups all worked to get more women registered and to the polls, using virtually every advertising and mobilization tool available in this high-tech era. Democrats proved particularly adept at targeting different slices of the female electorate, including the late deciders who are typically young, single women. In spite of a drop in the turnout rate overall, the female share of the electorate actually increased in some of the key swing states.

What became obvious from the exit polls was a deepening generational divide, particularly between the two largest generations – the younger Millennials and the older Baby Boomers – best distinguished by their racial/ethnic and lifestyle diversity. This divide is now being described as "the new normal" in presidential politics.[69]

But perhaps the most lasting impacts of the 2012 election were realizations that, first, fielding an all-white-male ticket is no longer pragmatic, and, second, given the current partisan generational divide, choosing a woman candidate who has broad appeal to *all* women voters is probably not possible.

---

[69] Stacy Teicher Khadaroo. November 7, 2012. Youth Vote Decides Presidential Election – Again. Is This the New Normal? *Christian Science Monitor*. http://www.csmonitor.com/ USA/Elections/President/2012/1107/Youth-vote-decides-presidential-election-again.-Is-this-the-new-normal.

4 Voting Choices

How and Why the Gender Gap Matters

Women voters have received special attention from the presidential candidates in recent elections primarily because of differences between women and men in their political preferences, a phenomenon commonly referred to as the gender gap. Statistically, a gender gap can be defined as the difference in the proportion of women and the proportion of men who support a particular politician, party, or policy position. In the 2012 election, Barack Obama received 55 percent of women's votes compared with 45 percent of men's, resulting in a gender gap of 10 percentage points.

A gender gap in voting has been evident in every general election for president since 1980. In each of the last nine presidential elections, a greater proportion of women than men has voted for the Democratic candidate. For example, in 2008, when Barack Obama was first elected, 56 percent of women, compared with only 49 percent of men, cast their votes for him, resulting in a gender gap of 7 percentage points – somewhat smaller than the gap in 2012.[1]

Prior to the 1980 election, it was widely believed that women and men took similar positions on most issues, had similar political preferences, and voted in much the same ways. In other words, the assumption before 1980 was that gender did not matter much in voting. Today, the assumption is exactly the opposite – that gender does matter for politics. Women and men, in the aggregate, have different positions on many issues and tend to vary in their party identification and support for political candidates. The gender gap is now viewed as an enduring part of

---

[1] Center for American Women and Politics. 2009. The Gender Gap. http://www.cawp .rutgers.edu/fast_facts/voters/documents/GGPresVote.pdf. Accessed March 15, 2013.

the political landscape, and candidates, parties, and politicians must pay specific attention to women voters if they want to win elections.

This chapter begins with an overview of the role that women voters and the gender gap played in the 2012 presidential elections. It then traces the origins of and explores possible explanations for the gender gap. It also examines the strategies candidates have employed in attempting to appeal to women voters. The gender gap has led to increased political influence for women, although that influence has been somewhat tempered by the fact that candidates have often used symbolic appeals rather than strictly issue-based appeals to respond to the growing influence of women voters.

WOMEN VOTERS AND THE 2012 PRESIDENTIAL ELECTION

Women voters received more attention in 2012 than in any previous election. Women occupied center stage throughout much of the primary and general election campaigns.

Of course, women voters received considerable attention in the 2008 election, largely because of Hillary Clinton. Although Clinton ultimately lost her bid for the Democratic Party's nomination for president to Barack Obama, she nevertheless attracted strong support from female voters throughout her many months of campaigning. Once Clinton was out of the race, Democrat Barack Obama and Republican John McCain competed to win the support of the women who had backed her. Obama did so largely by emphasizing his economic initiatives to help working women and support for equal pay. However, he also talked about how women in his family had played critical roles in his personal development, and he had Hillary Clinton and other well-known women campaign on his behalf in an effort to shore up support among women voters. McCain also attempted to appeal to women voters by emphasizing his support for small businesses, many of which are owned by women, and by using women surrogates – perhaps most prominently Carly Fiorina, the former chief executive officer of Hewlett-Packard – to campaign on his behalf. However, McCain's most significant attempt to attract women voters, especially disaffected Hillary Clinton supporters, was his selection of Sarah Palin as his vice presidential nominee. Although the choice of Palin did provide the McCain campaign with a burst of energy and a short-term surge in the polls, in the end issues and policy positions mattered more to women voters than did the gender of the vice presidential candidate. As the economy eroded over the course of the fall, so too did women's support for McCain's candidacy, and on Election Day a majority of women voters opted for Barack Obama and a new direction for the country.

The dynamics around gender and women voters in the 2012 presidential contest were very different. Incumbent President Barack Obama was, of course, unopposed in his party's primary. The lone female contender in the field of candidates in the Republican primary, Michele Bachman, who withdrew after an early defeat in the Iowa caucuses, never attracted the kind of support from women voters that Hillary Clinton received in 2008. Nevertheless, attention to women voters in the 2012 race began very early in the primary season when the Democrats and the Obama campaign began to weave together a series of extreme statements and missteps by Republicans into a narrative about a Republican "war on women."

The idea of a Republican war on women first began to gain traction in the presidential race in early 2012 with Senator Rick Santorum's rise in popularity among the Republican contenders. Increased media attention to Santorum brought his somewhat extreme views on social policy to the forefront. Santorum asserted that the states have the right to ban contraception[2] and that contraception is "not okay" because it is "a license to do things in the sexual realm that is counter to how things are supposed to be."[3] He also expressed his disapproval of women in combat roles, abortion even in the case of rape, and "radical feminism's misogynistic crusade to make working outside the home the only marker of social value and self-respect" as expressed in a book he had authored.[4]

When the Obama administration mandated that employers must include contraception in their health care coverage, Republicans in Congress introduced controversial legislation, known as the Blunt Amendment, which would have allowed employers to deny women contraceptive health coverage on the basis of moral or religious objections. This amendment failed in a very close U.S. Senate vote on March 1, 2012,

---

[2] Jake Tapper. Santorum Explains '06 Loss, Still Supports State Right to Outlaw Contraception. *ABC News*. http://abcnews.go.com/blogs/politics/2012/01/santorum-explains-06-loss-still-supports-state-right-to-outlaw-contraception/. Accessed March 15, 2013.

[3] Michael Scherer. Santorum Wants to Fight the "Dangers of Contraception." *Time*. http://swampland.time.com/2012/02/14/rick-santorum-wants-to-fight-the-dangers-of-contraception/. Accessed March 15, 2013.

[4] Santorum's Quotes on the Role of Women. *Washington Post*, http://www.washingtonpost.com/politics/santorums-quotes-on-the-role-of-women/2012/02/10/gIQABbMu4Q_story.html. Accessed March 15, 2013.

with all Republican senators except for Olympia Snowe of Maine voting in favor of the amendment.[5] The attempt to pass the Blunt amendment provided ammunition for those who wished to portray the Republican party as anti-woman. However, about the same time, talk-show host Rush Limbaugh set off an even greater firestorm of adverse publicity for Republicans when he called Sandra Fluke, a law student who testified at a congressional hearing on contraception coverage, a "slut" and a "prostitute."

A few months later, just when things seemed to calm down for the Republicans, GOP Congressman Todd Akin, who was mounting a seemingly successful challenge to Democratic Senator Claire McCaskill in Missouri, again created a public controversy that raised questions about the extreme views of some Republicans regarding women's reproductive rights. In an August television interview Akin explained, "If it's a legitimate rape, the female body has ways to try to shut the whole thing down."[6] Although many mainstream Republicans expressed disagreement with his comments and tried to get him to step down as a Senate candidate, Akin refused to exit the race and ultimately went down to a resounding defeat. In a similar episode only two weeks before the general election, another Republican U.S. Senate candidate, Richard Mourdock of Indiana, claimed, "even when life begins in that horrible situation of rape, that is something that God intended to happen."[7] These incidents, like the flap over insurance coverage for contraception, added fuel to the Democrats' narrative that the Republican Party had moved far to the right and was hopelessly out of touch with contemporary women.

Governor Mitt Romney, first as a Republican primary candidate and then as the party's nominee, was asked repeatedly about his views regarding each of these incidents, and his campaign never seemed to find an effective way to deal with them. When asked in a January 2012 Republican presidential debate if he agreed with Santorum's view that the states have the right to ban contraception, Romney danced around the question, telling moderator George Stephanopoulos that it was "kind of a

[5] Robert Pear. Senate Rejects Step Targeting Coverage of Contraception. *New York Times.* http://www.nytimes.com/2012/03/02/us/politics/senate-kills-gop-bill-opposing-contraception-policy.html?pagewanted=all&_r=0. Accessed March 15, 2013.

[6] John Eligon and Michael Schwirtz. Senate Candidate Provokes Ire with "Legitimate Rape" Comment. *New York Times.* http://www.nytimes.com/2012/08/20/us/politics/todd-akin-provokes-ire-with-legitimate-rape-comment.html. Accessed March 15, 2013.

[7] Gregory J. Krieg. Murdock Rape Comment Puts GOP on Defense. *ABC News,* http://abcnews.go.com/Politics/OTUS/richard-mourdock-rape-comment-puts-romney-defense/story?id=17552263. Accessed March 15, 2013.

silly thing" to ask him.[8] Romney first said he was not in favor of the Blunt amendment but soon reversed his position and said he was for it. Perhaps not wanting to alienate the right wing of his party during primary season, Romney refused to denounce Rush Limbaugh for his comments about Sandra Fluke, saying only, "it's not the language I would have used."[9] Although Romney did criticize Akin's comments regarding "legitimate" rape, it was soon revealed that the doctor whose views Akin relied on in making his remarks had endorsed and campaigned for Romney in 2008.[10] And Romney had actually made a televised campaign ad endorsing Richard Mourdock, which the media played over and over again in the aftermath of Mourdock's statement about rape. All of these incidents adversely influenced the Romney campaign, at best merely pulling him off message from the campaign's focus on economic issues and at worst tainting him as the leader of a party that did not understand women.

The Obama campaign took advantage of Republican missteps and the fact that Obama's views on key women's issues were more popular with female voters than were Romney's. Although Romney had taken varying positions on the abortion issue over the course of his political career, he campaigned in 2012 as strongly pro-life. He pledged to eliminate federal funding for Planned Parenthood, asserting to a reporter in March 2012, "Planned Parenthood, we're going to get rid of that."[11] However, polls showed a majority of Americans were opposed to ending funding for family planning clinics, [12] and Obama took advantage by expressing his support for the besieged organization, mentioning Planned Parenthood five times in the second debate alone. Obama stressed his support for equal pay and the fact that the Lilly Ledbetter Fair Pay Act of 2009 was the first bill he signed into law after he was elected in 2008. Romney's position on the Ledbetter Act was less straightforward. When

---

[8] Felicia Sonmez. 2012 ABC/Yahoo!/WMUR New Hampshire GOP primary debate (Transcript). *Washington Post.* http://www.washingtonpost.com/blogs/post-politics/post/2012-abcyahoowmur-new-hampshire-gop-primary-debate-transcript/2012/01/07/gIQAk2AAiP_blog.html. Accessed March 15, 2013.

[9] Emily Friedman. Romney on Rush: Not the Language I Would Have Used. *ABC News,* http://abcnews.go.com/blogs/politics/2012/03/romney-on-rush-not-the-language-i-would-have-used/. Accessed March15, 2013.

[10] Tomer Ovadia. Akin Source Was Romney Surrogate. *Politico.* http://www.politico.com/news/stories/0812/79986.html. Accessed March 15, 2013.

[11] Jake Tapper. Democrats Seize on Romney Pledge to "Get Rid of" Planned Parenthood. *ABC News.* http://abcnews.go.com/blogs/politics/2012/03/dems-hit-romney-on-planned-parenthood-funding/. Accessed March 15, 2013.

[12] Ibid.

asked by a reporter if Governor Romney supported the bill, a Romney campaign spokesman replied, "We'll get back to you on that." The campaign never got back to the reporter. Romney did not directly answer a question posed to him by Diane Sawyer of ABC News about whether he, if president, would have signed the Ledbetter Act, saying instead that he had "no intention of changing that law."[13] When asked in the second debate to explain what he would do to rectify the situation that women make less than men in the workplace, Romney chose not to address the issue of pay equity. Instead, he talked about how many women he had appointed to positions in his administration as governor of Massachusetts, explaining that women's groups had brought him "binders full of women" to consider.

Romney's strategy for appealing to women voters seemed to rest largely on a general economic appeal – that his policies would help grow the economy, thereby helping women. For example, during the second debate, Romney cited statistics showing that women had lost jobs during the Obama administration and that the numbers of women living in poverty had increased. He argued:

> We're going to have to have employers in the new economy, in the economy I'm going to bring to play, that are going to be so anxious to get good workers they're going to be anxious to hire women.... What we can do to help young women and women of all ages is to have a strong economy...[14]

The state of the economy was also a major concern for the Obama campaign. However, Obama frequently turned Romney's economic argument on its head, suggesting that focusing on women's economic security and helping women get ahead was good for American families and the economy more generally – that is, helping women would strengthen the economy. For example, in the second debate Obama argued:

> ...women are increasingly the breadwinners in the family. This [pay equity] is not just a women's issue, this is a family issue, this is a middle-class issue, and that's why we've got to fight for it.... And one

[13] *Tampa Bay Times* PolitiFact.com, Obama: Mitt Romney refused to say whether he supports Lilly Ledbetter Act. October 25, 2012. http://www.politifact.com/truth-o-meter/ statements/2012/oct/16/barack-obama/obama-mitt-romney-refused-say-whether-he-supports-/. Accessed March 15, 2013.

[14] *ABC News*, October 17, 2012. Second Presidential Debate Full Transcript. http:// abcnews.go.com/Politics/OTUS/2012-presidential-debate-full-transcript-oct-16/story? id=17493848&page=5. Accessed March 15, 2013.

of the things that makes us grow as an economy is when everybody participates and women are getting the same fair deal as men are.[15]

Also, in contrast to the Romney campaign, Obama talked frequently about women's issues, especially women's reproductive health care and pay equity, in an attempt to appeal to women voters, sometimes linking these issues to the health of the economy. Again in the second debate, Obama explained:

> In my health care bill, I said insurance companies need to provide contraceptive coverage to everybody who is insured. Because this is not just a – a health issue, it's an economic issue for women. . . . Romney says that we should eliminate funding for Planned Parenthood, there are millions of women all across the country, who rely on Planned Parenthood for, not just contraceptive care, they rely on it for mammograms, for cervical cancer screenings. That's a pocketbook issue for women and families all across the country. And it makes a difference in terms of how well and effectively women are able to work . . . These are not just women's issues. These are family issues. These are economic issues.[16]

Thus, while Romney appealed to women voters mostly by arguing that he would take steps to improve the overall economy, Obama employed what might be considered an "economy plus" strategy to win support from women. He, too, appealed to women voters in terms of general economic policy, but he also hit hard on issues of women's health and pay equity where he knew he had an advantage, sometimes highlighting the economic implications of these issues as well. In the end, more women seem to have opted for Obama's "economy plus" appeal, reelecting him with a majority of their votes and the second-largest gender gap (10 percentage points) ever recorded in a presidential election. Only Bill Clinton in his 1996 reelection bid had a larger gender gap (11 percentage points).

THE ORIGINS OF THE GENDER GAP

In Chapter 3 of this volume, Susan A. MacManus describes the suffrage movement that led to the addition of the Nineteenth Amendment to the Constitution in 1920, granting women the right to vote. Over the course of the several decades that it took to win the right to vote, suffragists used a variety of arguments to win support from different segments of

[15] Ibid.
[16] Ibid.

the all-male electorate and political structure. Some approaches stressed fundamental similarities between women and men and demanded the vote for women as a matter of simple justice. Suffragists observed that women were human beings just as men were, and therefore women, like men, were created equal and had an inalienable right to political equality and thus the vote.

However, suffragists also used arguments that focused on how women were different from men and would use their votes to help make the world a better place. Suffragists claimed that women's experiences, especially their experiences as mothers and caregivers, gave them special values and perspectives that would be readily apparent in their voting decisions. They argued that women would use their votes to stop wars, promote peace, clean up government, ban the sale of liquor, and bring justice to a corrupt world.

The use of such arguments led some people to eagerly anticipate and others to greatly fear the consequences of women's enfranchisement. Many observers at the time expected women to go to the polls in large numbers and thought that their distinctive impact on politics would be immediately apparent. However, the right to vote, in and of itself, proved insufficient to bring about a distinctive women's vote. Rather, a women's vote would emerge only decades later after other changes in society and women's perceptions of themselves took place. In the elections immediately following women's enfranchisement in 1920, women voted in much lower numbers than men, and there were few signs that women were voting much differently than men or using their votes to express a distinctive perspective.

As the decades passed after 1920, it seemed that the women's vote, feared by some and longed for by others, would never materialize. However, by the early 1980s, a sufficient number of women finally achieved the social and psychological independence necessary to bring about a divergence in the voting patterns of women and men. In the decades since 1980, the women's vote promised by the suffragists has finally arrived, although with underlying issues and dynamics somewhat different from those anticipated during the suffrage era.

In the decades between 1920 and 1980, the vast majority of women, particularly white women,[17] remained economically dependent on men,

[17] This account applies largely to white women who constituted a large majority of women in the United States throughout these decades. The situation for African-American women and other women of color was somewhat different. African-American women

not necessarily by choice but because society offered them few options. As a result, women's political interests were intertwined with, even inseparable from, the political interests of men, and for the most part, women did not make political decisions that differed from those made by men. However, since the 1960s and 1970s, women's dependence on men has begun to unravel, and as this unraveling has taken place, women have started making political choices that are more independent of men's wishes and interests.

At least three critical developments over the past several decades have contributed to the increased independence of women from men and have made possible the emergence of a distinctive women's vote. The first is the fact that, for a variety of reasons, including higher divorce rates and longer life spans, more women are living apart from men, often heading households on their own. The second development is that more women have achieved professional and managerial positions that, even when they live with men, provide them with sufficient incomes to support themselves and allow them a substantial degree of financial independence from men. The third critical development is the contemporary women's movement, which began with the founding of the National Organization for Women (NOW) in 1966 and the development of women's liberation groups around the country in 1967 and 1968. Although even today a majority of women in American society do not call themselves feminists, the women's movement has changed the way most women in the United States see themselves and their life options. Most women now recognize that they have concerns and interests that are not always identical to those of the men in their lives, and they are aware that these concerns can be relevant to their political choices.

Brief glimpses of gender differences in voting had been apparent from time to time before 1980. For example, women were slightly more likely than men to vote for Dwight Eisenhower, the victorious Republican candidate, in the 1952 and 1956 elections. However, these pre–1980 gender differences in voting were not persistent, nor were they accompanied by consistent gender differences in evaluations of presidential performance, party identification, or voting for offices other than president. A textbook on public opinion commonly used in political science courses, published

---

were less likely than white women to be economically dependent on men because they more often worked outside the home (although usually in low-paying jobs). However, the political interests of African-American women and men still were generally intertwined because society offered limited options for African Americans of either gender.

just before the 1980 election, reflected the conventional thinking about gender differences at that time. This 324-page textbook devoted only a half page to women and gender, concluding, "Differences in the political attitudes of men and women are so slight that they deserve only brief mention....In political attitudes and voting, people are seldom different because of their sex."[18]

Even though women had achieved a substantial degree of independence from men and their attitudes about themselves were changing throughout the 1970s, it was not until 1980 that a political candidate came along who could crystallize political differences between women and men into a gender gap. Governor Ronald Reagan, the Republican who was elected president in 1980 and reelected in 1984, proved to be the catalyst for the gender gap. In contrast to the 1976 presidential campaign, in which most positions taken by the Republican and Democratic candidates were not starkly different, the 1980 presidential campaign presented voters with clear alternatives. Reagan offered policy proposals that contrasted sharply with the policies of then-incumbent President Jimmy Carter. Reagan promised to cut back on the size of the federal government, greatly reduce government spending, increase the strength of the U.S. military, and get tough with the Soviet Union. When offered such clear-cut alternatives, women and men expressed different preferences. Although Reagan defeated Carter in 1980 and was elected president, he received notably less support from women than from men. Exit polls conducted by the major television networks on Election Day showed that women were between 6 and 9 percentage points less likely than men to vote for Reagan. For example, an exit poll conducted jointly by CBS and the *New York Times* showed that only 46 percent of women, compared to 54 percent of men, voted for Reagan, resulting in a gender gap of 8 percentage points. Clearly, women were less attracted to the candidacy and policies of Reagan than men were. (Alternatively, looking at the gender gap from the flip side, the polls showed that the policies and candidacy of Reagan resonated more with men than with women.)

Many commentators in the early 1980s thought that this gender gap in presidential voting might be short lived and would disappear in subsequent presidential elections, much like earlier glimpses of gender differences (e.g., those in the presidential elections of the 1950s), but this time the gender gap was here to stay. As Table 4.1 shows, in every presidential

[18] Robert S. Erikson, Norman R. Luttbeg, and Kent L. Tedin. 1980. *American Public Opinion: Its Origins, Content, and Impact*, 2nd ed. New York: John Wiley & Sons, 186.

TABLE 4.1: A gender gap in voting has been evident in every presidential election since 1980

Election year	Winning presidential candidate	Women voting for winner (%)	Men voting for winner (%)	Gender gap (in percentage points)
2012	Barack Obama (D)	55	45	10
2008	Barack Obama (D)	56	49	7
2004	George W. Bush (R)	48	55	7
2000	George W. Bush (R)	43	53	10
1996	Bill Clinton (D)	54	43	11
1992	Bill Clinton (D)	45	41	4
1988	George H. W. Bush (R)	50	57	7
1984	Ronald Reagan (R)	56	62	6
1980	Ronald Reagan (R)	46	54	8

Source: Data are from exit polls conducted by CBS/*New York Times*, 1980, 1984, 1988; Voter News Service, 1992, 1996, 2000; Edison Media Research and Mitofsky International, 2004, 2008; Edison Research 2012.

election since 1980, differences have been apparent in the proportions of women and men who voted for the winning candidate, ranging from a low of 4 percentage points in 1992 to a high of 11 percentage points in 1996. In each of these elections, women have been more likely than men to support the Democratic candidate for president.

If the suffragists who had worked so hard to achieve voting rights for women were able to return today to see the results of their efforts, they would surely say, "I told you so." It may have taken sixty years to arrive, but the women's vote that the suffragists anticipated is now clearly evident and has been influencing the dynamics of presidential elections for more than three decades.

THE BREADTH AND PERSISTENCE OF THE GENDER GAP

The gender gap has become an enduring feature of American politics, evident across a wide variety of political attitudes, preferences, and behaviors. Since 1980, the gender gap has been apparent not only in voting in presidential elections but also in voting at other levels of office, in party identification, and in the performance ratings of various presidents. The exit polls conducted on each Election Day have asked voters not only about their selections in the presidential contest but also about their choices in U.S. House, U.S. Senate, and gubernatorial elections. In every election since 1982, women have been more likely than men to vote for Democrats in races for the U.S. House of Representatives. For example, according to the 2012 exit poll conducted by Edison Research, a majority (55 percent) of women but only a minority (45 percent) of men voted for the Democratic candidate for Congress in their district, resulting in a gender gap of 10 percentage points.[19]

Gender gaps also have been evident in a majority of races for U.S. Senate and gubernatorial seats in recent elections. Thirty-three of the 100 seats in the U.S. Senate were up for election in 2012, and eleven of the fifty states elected governors. Women and men had significantly different candidate preferences in most of these races. In twenty-two of the twenty-three U.S. Senate races in which exit polls were conducted by Edison Research, gender gaps ranging from 4 to 19 percentage points were evident. In all seven of the gubernatorial races in which exit polls were conducted, there were gender gaps of 3 to 11 percentage points. The largest gender gap in a race for governor was in New Hampshire, where the sole female 2012 gubernatorial candidate, Democrat Maggie Hassan, defeated Republican Ovide Lamontagne. Women were 11 percentage points more likely than men to vote for Hassan, while men favored Hassan over her opponent by only 1 point. In each of the U.S. Senate and gubernatorial elections in which a notable gender gap was present, women were more likely than men to vote for the Democratic candidate.[20]

Not only are women more likely than men to vote for Democratic candidates, but also they are more likely than men to identify with the Democratic Party. When asked whether they think of themselves as Democrats, Republicans, or independents, more women than men call themselves Democrats. For example, the Pew Research Center for the People and the Press reported in August 2012 that among registered voters, 40 percent of women, compared with 29 percent of men, identified with or leaned toward the Democratic Party, a gender gap of 11 percentage points. Moreover, men did not have a strong preference for one party over the other. They split about evenly, with 29 percent of men identifying as Democrats and 29 percent as Republicans. However, women showed a clear preference for the Democratic Party over the Republican Party, with

---

[19] CNNPolitics.com. Election Center 2008. Exit Polls. http://www.cnn.com/ELECTION/ 2008/results/polls/#USP00p1. Accessed March 1, 2009.
[20] Ibid.

40 percent of women identifying as Democrats and only 27 percent as Republicans.[21]

Some observers have argued that the gender gap is the result of changes in men's, not women's, political behavior, and the data on party identification offer strong evidence in support of this point of view. In the 1970s, both women and men were more likely to identify as Democrats than Republicans, and no significant gender gap in party identification was apparent. However, that pattern changed beginning in the early 1980s, following the election of Ronald Reagan. Men shifted in the direction of the Republican Party, becoming more likely to identify as Republicans and less likely to identify as Democrats than they had been in the 1970s. In contrast, women's party identification remained more stable, showing less dramatic changes since the 1970s. Women were more likely to identify as Democrats than as Republicans in the 1970s, and they remained more likely to be Democrats in 2012.

Although the gender gap in party identification apparent today seems largely the result of changes among men, this does not mean that the gap is the result of men's behavior alone; the behavior of women also has been critical. Prior to 1980, when shifts occurred in the political environment, women and men generally responded similarly. But with the increasing independence of women from men, the politics of the 1980s produced a different result. When men chose to shift their party identification, women chose not to follow them.

Just as a gender gap has been evident in party identification, a gender gap has also been apparent in evaluations of the performance of presidents who have served since 1980. On surveys conducted throughout the year, the Gallup Poll asks whether people approve or disapprove of the way the incumbent is handling his job as president. Some presidents have had higher approval ratings than others, and the ratings for each president have varied across his tenure in office. For example, although George W. Bush ended his time in office as one of the most unpopular presidents in recent history, his approval ratings soared in the months following September 11, 2001, when the World Trade Center was attacked and the American people rallied behind their leader. Even though Bush's approval ratings varied greatly during his eight years in office, women and men differed in their evaluations of his performance across most of

---

[21] Pew Research Center for the People and the Press. August 23, 2012. A Closer Look at the Parties in 2012. http://www.people-press.org/2012/08/23/a-closer-look-at-the-parties-in-2012/. Accessed March 15, 2013.

his tenure. For example, a Gallup Poll conducted November 11-14, 2007, when Bush's popularity was low, found that 29 percent of women, compared with 35 percent of men, approved of the way Bush was handling his job as president (a 6-percentage-point gender gap).[22]

A similar gender gap has been apparent in Barack Obama's approval ratings. Shortly after his first inauguration in January 2009, when support for Obama was very high, Gallup found that 71 percent of women, compared with 64 percent of men, approved of Obama's performance as president (a 7-percentage-point gender gap).[23] Throughout Obama's first term, women were consistently more likely than men to give Obama favorable job performance ratings.[24] Similarly, in the week following his second inauguration in January 2013, Gallup found that 57 percent of women, compared with 47 percent of men, approved of Obama's performance (a 10-percentage-point gender gap).[25]

Gender gaps have been apparent in the performance ratings of all other recent presidents as well. Women have been more critical than men of Republican presidents and more approving than men of the lone Democrat other than Obama who has served as president since 1980. Thus, women were less likely than men to approve of the way Republicans Ronald Reagan and George H. W. Bush handled their jobs as president but more likely than men to evaluate favorably Democrat Bill Clinton's performance.

THE GENDER GAP AND WOMEN CANDIDATES

As other chapters in this volume document, the number of women running for public office has increased over the past several decades. Every election year, women are among the candidates who run for the U.S. House, U.S. Senate, and governor. What happens to the gender gap in the general election when one (or both) of the candidates for one of these offices is a woman?

[22] Gallup. November 20, 2007. Congress' Approval Rating at 20%; Bush's Approval at 32%. http://www.gallup.com/poll/102829/Congress-Approval-Rating-20-Bushs-Approval-32.aspx#2. Accessed February 28, 2008.
[23] Gallup. January 6, 2009. Obama's Initial Approval Ratings in Historical Context. http://www.gallup.com/poll/113968/Obama-Initial-Approval-Ratings-Historical-Context.aspx. Accessed February 28, 2008.
[24] Gallup. May 9, 2012. Gender Gap in Obama Approval Constant Since Term Began. http://www.gallup.com/poll/154562/gender-gap-obama-approval-constant-term-began.aspx. Accessed March 15, 2013.
[25] Gallup. January 21-17, 2013. Presidential Job Approval Center. http://www.gallup.com/poll/124922/Presidential-Approval-Center.aspx. Accessed March 15, 2013.

Unfortunately, there is no straightforward, easy answer to this question. It depends on whether the woman candidate is a Democrat or a Republican, and if she is a Republican, how moderate or conservative she is. The answer may also depend on the state or district in which she runs and the larger context of the election.

Years ago, voter prejudice may have been a major problem for the few women who were brave enough to seek public office. However, bias against women candidates has declined significantly. Since 1937, pollsters have asked voters whether they would be willing to vote for a "qualified" woman for president. In 1937, only about one-third of voters said that they would vote for a woman. In contrast, by the beginning of the twenty-first century, about nine of every ten Americans reported that they would vote for a woman for the nation's highest office (although there is some evidence that this high level of support dipped for a while in the aftermath of the attack on the World Trade Center in 2001).[26] Thus, voter prejudice against women candidates, even for the most powerful office in the United States, has declined considerably, although it has not disappeared completely.

But if there are still some voters predisposed to vote against women, there are also voters predisposed to cast affirmative votes for women candidates. Moreover, research has shown that women are more likely than men to be predisposed to support women candidates.[27] This predisposition on the part of some voters to vote for or against a woman candidate, all other things being equal, becomes an additional factor that can alter the size of the gender gap when women run for office.

In general, women candidates who are Democrats tend to have gender gaps (with women voters more likely than men to vote for them) that are similar in size to or sometimes larger than those for male Democratic candidates. In contrast, women candidates who are Republicans tend to have gender gaps (with women voters more likely than men to vote against them) that are similar in size to or sometimes smaller than those for male Republican candidates. An analysis of U.S. House races in three elections in the early 1990s found that the gender gap was, on average, greater in races in which the Democratic candidate was a woman candidate than in races in which a Democratic man ran against a Republican

---

[26] Jennifer L. Lawless. 2004. Women, War, and Winning Elections: Gender Stereotyping in the Post–September 11th Era. *Political Research Quarterly* 53(3): 479–90.

[27] Kira Sanbonmatsu. 2002. Gender Stereotypes and Vote Choice. *American Journal of Political Science* 46: 20–34.

TABLE 4.2: A gender gap in voting was evident in the races of all women who won election to the U.S. Senate in 2012 in states where exit polls were conducted

	Women voting for winner (%)	Men voting for winner (%)	Gender gap (in percentage points)
U.S. Senate Winners			
Dianne Feinstein (D-CA)	64	57	7
Elizabeth Warren (D-MA)	59	47	12
Debbie Stabenow (D-MI)	62	55	7
Amy Klobuchar (D-MN)	72	59	13
Claire McCaskill (D-MO)	58	51	7
Kirsten Gillibrand (D-NY)	77	65	12
Maria Cantwell (D-WA)	62	57	5
Tammy Baldwin (D-WI)	56	46	10

Source: Edison Research National Exit Poll, 2012.

man. Similarly, on average, the gender gap was smaller in races in which the Republican candidate was a woman than in races in which a Republican man ran against a Democratic man.[28]

Table 4.2 shows the gender gap in races won by the eight women elected to the U.S. Senate in the 2012 elections in races in which exit polls were conducted, and the generalizations presented here hold up fairly well for these victorious candidates. All the women in Table 4.2 are Democrats; only one Republican woman, Deb Fischer of Nebraska, was elected to the U.S. Senate in 2012, and unfortunately no exit poll was conducted in her race.

The average gender gap in the ten U.S. Senate races with exit polls in 2012 in which the major candidates were a Democratic man and a Republican man was just more than 7 percentage points, with female voters more likely than male voters to vote for the Democratic candidate. No man-versus-man race had a gender gap larger than 10 points.

As Table 4.2 shows, four of the Democratic women senators (Elizabeth Warren, Amy Klobuchar, Kirsten Gillibrand, and Tammy Baldwin) not only had gender gaps greater than the average for races involving two male candidates but also had gender gaps as large as or larger than the

[28] Elizabeth Adell Cook. 1998. Voter Reaction to Women Candidates. In *Women and Elective Office: Past, Present, and Future,* ed. Sue Thomas and Clyde Wilcox. New York: Oxford University Press, 56–72.

biggest difference evident in a man-versus-man race. Three Democratic women senators had gender gaps that were about average, and only one had a gender gap notably smaller than the average for races involving two men.

No Republican women were elected in 2012 in statewide races in which exit polls were conducted, but the previous elections of Olympia Snowe of Maine, a Republican Senator who chose not to seek reelection in 2012, demonstrate that it is possible – although unusual – for a Republican woman candidate to position herself on issues in such a way that she reduces the size of or even eliminates the gender gap. Snowe served in the U.S. House from 1979 until she was elected to the U.S. Senate in 1994. She was reelected to the Senate in both 2000 and 2006. In 2000, no gender gap was apparent in Snowe's race; she was reelected with 69 percent of the votes of women and 69 percent of the votes of men in her state. In 2006, Maine's senior Republican senator actually attracted slightly more votes from women than from men; 75 percent of women and 73 percent of men cast their ballots for her.[29]

Snowe was a champion for women and had a moderate, pro-choice voting record during the years she served in both the Senate and the U.S. House. For example, in the U.S. House of Representatives, she co-chaired the Congressional Caucus for Women's Issues. Moreover, during her thirty-three years in the U.S. House and Senate, Snowe voted with the American Conservative Union (ACU) less than 50 percent of the time; no other Republican serving in the U.S. Senate in 2012 more often voted in opposition to the positions favored by the ACU during his or her tenure in office.[30] It is largely because of her moderate, pro-choice voting record and her advocacy on behalf of women that Snowe was able to effectively neutralize the gender gap, eliminating the deficit that Republican candidates, female as well as male, usually experience with women voters.

EXPLANATIONS FOR THE GENDER GAP

One observation about the gender gap can be made with a high degree of certainty: the gender gap is not limited to one or even a few demographic subgroups. In an attempt to undermine women's voting power, political

[29] CNN.com. 2006. AmericaVotes2006 Exit Polls. http://www.cnn.com/ELECTION/2006/pages/results/states/ME/S/01/epolls.0.html. Accessed March 1, 2009.
[30] American Conservative Union. Ratings of Congress, 2011. http://conservative.org/ratingsarchive/uscongress/2011/. Accessed March 15, 2013.

TABLE 4.3: A gender gap in voting was evident across a range of demographic groups in the 2012 presidential election

Demographic group	Women voting for Obama (%)	Men voting for Obama (%)	Gender gap (in percentage points)
Race or ethnicity			
White	42	35	7
African American	96	87	9
Latino	76	65	11
Marital status			
Married	46	38	8
Unmarried	67	56	11
Parental status			
Children under 18 in household	56	45	11
No children under 18 in household	54	47	7

Source: Edison Research National Exit Poll, 2012.

commentators have sometimes claimed that the gender gap is not a broad-based phenomenon but rather one that can be fully explained by the voting behavior of some particular subgroup of women in the electorate – for example, women of color or unmarried voters. Table 4.3 reveals the obvious problem with such claims. When compared with men who shared their demographic characteristics, women of different races and ethnicities, marital statuses, and parental statuses more often voted for Barack Obama in 2012 than men did (and less often voted for Mitt Romney). In fact, voting differences between women and men are found in most subgroups of the electorate. Consequently, no single demographic category of voters can be designated as responsible for the gender gap. Rather, the gender gap is clearly a phenomenon evident across most of the various subgroups that comprise the American electorate.

Beyond the fact that the gender gap is not limited to one particular subgroup but rather widespread across the electorate, definitive statements about the gender gap are difficult to make. Indeed, the gender gap appears to be a rather complex phenomenon. Nevertheless, a number of different explanations have been put forward to account for the gender gap in voting. None of these explanations seems sufficient by itself. Moreover, the explanations are not mutually exclusive; in fact, they are somewhat overlapping. However, several of the explanations offered by

academic and political analysts do seem to have some validity and are useful in helping account for the fact that women and men make somewhat
different voting choices. Four of the most common explanations – compassion, feminism, economics, and the role of government – are reviewed
briefly here.

The compassion explanation focuses on women's roles as mothers and
caregivers. Despite recent changes in gender roles, women still bear disproportionate responsibility for the care of children and the elderly in
their families and in the greater society. Mothers are still called more often
than fathers when children become ill at school, and women are still a
large majority of health care workers, teachers, child care providers, and
social workers. Women's roles as caregivers may lead them to be more
sympathetic toward those in need and more concerned with the safety
and security of others. Women's caregiving responsibilities may also lead
them to put greater emphasis than men on issues such as education and
health care.

Consistent with this compassion explanation, education and health
care were two of the top issues in the 2000 presidential election, which
focused largely on domestic politics rather than foreign affairs. Polls
showed that these issues were of greater concern to women voters in the
election than they were to men, and both presidential candidates spent
a great deal of time talking about these issues. In an obvious attempt to
appeal to women voters, the Bush campaign suggested that George W.
Bush was not an old-style conservative but rather a "compassionate conservative" who genuinely cared about the well-being of Americans.

While concerns over the economy trumped all other issue concerns
for both women and men in 2012, women voters in 2012, as in 2000,
continued to express more concern over health care and education than
did men. For example, a poll conducted in September 2012 by the Pew
Research Center for People and the Press found that women were 10
percentage points more likely than men to say that the issue of education
would be very important to their vote; women were also 14 percentage
points more likely to say that health care would be very important in
determining their choice for president.[31]

Also consistent with the compassion explanation is the greater reluc-
tance of women than men to use military force to resolve foreign

[31] Pew Research Center for People and the Press. September 24, 2012. For Voters
It's Still the Economy. http://www.people-press.org/2012/09/24/for-voters-its-still-the-
economy/. Accessed March 15, 2013.

conflicts. In 1980, when the gender gap first became apparent, Americans were being held hostage in Iran, tensions were running high with the Soviet Union, and foreign policy had become a central issue in the presidential campaign. Women reacted more negatively than men to Ronald Reagan's tough posture in dealing with other nations, and women feared more than men that Ronald Reagan might involve the country in a war. These gender differences were important in explaining why Reagan received stronger support from men than from women.[32] Similarly, in both 2008 and 2004, which was the first presidential election since 1980 in which foreign policy was central, gender differences were evident in women's and men's attitudes toward the war in Iraq. For example, a Rasmussen Reports survey released in June 2008 found that just 26 percent of women, compared with 45 percent of men, believed that troops should stay in Iraq until the mission is finished. Similarly, 67 percent of women but only 50 percent of men wanted to see the troops come home within a year.[33] Heading into the 2012 election, a similar pattern was evident in support for the war in Afghanistan. A CNN/ORC Poll conducted in October 2011 found that 71 percent of women, compared with 55 percent of men, opposed the war in Afghanistan, and 49 percent of women, compared with 32 percent of men, believed that the United States had made a mistake in sending military forces to Afghanistan.[34]

Polls have consistently shown gender gaps on questions such as these, with women having more reservations than men about U.S. involvement in Iraq, Afghanistan, and other international conflicts. In fact, one of the most persistent and long-standing political differences between women and men is in their attitudes toward the use of military force. For as far back as we have public-opinion polling data, women have been significantly more likely than men to oppose the use of force to resolve international conflicts.

As a second explanation for the gender gap, some observers have suggested the influence of the feminist movement. The discovery of the contemporary gender gap in voting in the aftermath of the 1980 presidential

---

[32] Kathleen A. Frankovic. 1982. Sex and Politics: New Alignments, Old Issues. *PS* 15(Summer): 439–448.

[33] Rasmussen Reports. June 3, 2008. 59% of Adults Want Troops Home from Iraq within the Year. http://www.rasmussenreports.com/public_content/ politics/current_events/the_war_in_iraq/59_of_adults_want_troops_home_from_iraq_within_the_year. Accessed March 1, 2009.

[34] CNN/ORC Poll. October 14-16, 2011. http://i2.cdn.turner.com/cnn/2011/images/10/28/rel17h.pdf. Accessed March 15, 2013.

election coincided with intensive efforts by women's organizations, especially NOW, to have the Equal Rights Amendment (ERA) ratified in the necessary thirty-eight states before the June 30, 1982, deadline. In addition, NOW undertook an intensive effort to publicize the gender gap and women's lesser support for Ronald Reagan relative to men's. As a result, the ERA and the gender gap became associated in many people's minds, and there was speculation that women were less supportive than men of Ronald Reagan because he opposed the ERA. However, scholarly analyses of voting and public opinion data have consistently shown that so-called women's issues – those issues most closely associated with the organized women's movement, such as the ERA and abortion – do not appear to be central to the gender gap. In part, this may be because women and men in the general electorate have very similar attitudes on these issues, and in part, this may be because candidates for president and other offices usually do not choose to campaign on these issues. Interestingly, the 2012 presidential election may be an exception in that women's reproductive health issues such as insurance coverage for contraception, and to a lesser extent, pay equity, were discussed frequently in the campaign. These issues may well have influenced the votes of some women and helped produce a larger gender gap than in most previous elections.

However, even if women's issues such as the ERA or abortion are not central to the gender gap, feminism may still play a role. As explained earlier in this chapter, the contemporary women's movement has altered the way most women in the United States see themselves and their life options. The movement has provided women with more awareness about their political interests and greater self-confidence about expressing their differences from men. Compelling empirical evidence suggests that women who identify with feminism are more distinctive from men in their political values than are other women, and that for women, a feminist identity may, in fact, foster the expression of the compassion differences described previously. Women influenced by feminism appear more likely than either men or other women to express attitudes sympathetic to those who are disadvantaged and in need and consequently more predisposed to support the Democratic Party.[35]

Other explanations for the gender gap have focused on economic factors. More women than men live below the poverty line, and women earn only seventy-seven cents for every dollar men earn. Because women

---

[35] Pamela Johnston Conover. 1988. Feminists and the Gender Gap. *Journal of Politics* 50(November): 985–1010.

on average are poorer than men, they are more dependent on government social services and more vulnerable to cuts in these services. Similarly, women are disproportionately employed in jobs that involve the delivery of human services (health, education, and welfare). Although most women in human services jobs are not directly employed by the government, their employers often receive substantial government funding, and thus their jobs are, to varying degrees, dependent on the continuation of government subsidies. As the principal providers of social welfare services, women are more likely than men to suffer loss of employment when these programs are cut.

Beginning with Ronald Reagan and continuing through the 1990s with the Republican Congress's Contract with America, Republicans at the national level argued that government (with the exception of defense) had grown too large and that cutbacks in domestic spending were necessary. When candidates and politicians propose to cut back on big government or the welfare state, the cuts they propose fall heavily on women who are disproportionately both the providers and the recipients of government-funded services. Consequently, economic self-interest could lead women to favor the Democrats more than the Republicans.

However, women's economic concerns do not appear to be merely self-interested. Evidence shows that women are less likely than men to vote on the basis of economic considerations, but when they do, they are less likely than men to vote on the basis of their own self-interest and more likely to vote on the basis of how well off they perceive the country to be financially.[36] Thus, women are more likely than men to think not just of their own financial situation but also of the economic situation that others are facing.

The final explanation for the gender gap, focusing on the role of government, is clearly related to the economic explanation but extends beyond economic considerations. In recent years, some of the most consistent and important gender differences in public opinion have shown up on questions about the role that government should play in Americans' lives. Both women and men agree that government, especially the federal government, does not work as effectively as they would like. Beyond that, however, their attitudes are quite different. Men are more likely than women to see government as the problem rather than the solution, and

---

[36] Susan J. Welch and John Hibbing. 1992. Financial Conditions, Gender, and Voting in American National Elections. *Journal of Politics* 54(February): 197– 213.

they are considerably more likely than women to favor serious cutbacks in federal government programs and federal spending on non–defense-related projects. Men more than women prefer private-sector solutions to societal problems. In contrast, women are more likely to want to fix government rather than abandon it. Women are more worried than men that government cutbacks may go too far; they are more concerned than men about preserving the social safety net for the people who are most in need in the United States. As an example of this gender difference in perspective, Pew Research Center for the People and the Press found in an October 2011 poll that 45 percent of women but only 36 percent of men favored a bigger government providing more services; similarly, women were notably more likely than men to believe that the government does not do enough for older people, children, and the poor.[37] The Republican Party, which receives greater support from men, is commonly perceived as the party that wants to scale back the size of government, whereas the Democratic Party, which has more women among its supporters, is more commonly perceived as the party that defends government programs and works to preserve the social safety net.

POLITICAL STRATEGIES FOR DEALING WITH THE GENDER GAP AND APPEALING TO WOMEN VOTERS

Given the foregoing explanations for the gender gap, it would appear that the best way for candidates and parties to appeal to women voters is by talking very specifically, concretely, and frequently about issues, whether they be compassion issues (e.g., health care and education), economic concerns, or foreign policy. However, presidential candidates and campaigns often use symbolic appeals in addition to and sometimes in lieu of issue-based appeals to win support from women voters.

One of the ways candidates and campaigns have attempted to appeal to women voters symbolically is by showcasing prominent women. In the 2012 election, both Obama and Romney attempted to appeal to women voters by having widely admired and accomplished women campaign for them. For example, New Hampshire Senator Kelly Ayotte, Washington Congresswoman Cathy McMorris Rodgers, South Carolina Governor Nikki Haley, and the candidate's wife, Ann Romney, all served as

---

[37] Pew Research Center for the People and the Press. March 29, 2012. The Gender Gap: Three Decades Old, as Wide as Ever. http://www.people-press.org/2012/03/29/the-gender-gap-three-decades-old-as-wide-as-ever/. Accessed March 15, 2013.

important surrogates for Romney. Women who campaigned for Obama included actresses Eva Longoria and Rashida Jones, singer Katy Perry, Caroline Kennedy, Sandra Fluke, Democratic National Committee chair and Florida Congresswoman Debbie Wasserman Schultz, and Michelle Obama. As Barbara Burrell notes in Chapter 8 of this volume, both political parties also featured prominent women at their 2012 presidential nominating conventions.

Beyond the use of well-known women, recent presidential campaigns have used symbolic strategies to appeal to women voters. The presidential campaign of George W. Bush, in particular, was very clever in its use of symbolic appeals to woo women voters. In the 2004 campaign and especially the 2000 campaign, the Bush campaign employed a new term, describing their candidate as a compassionate conservative. Bush himself suggested, "I am a compassionate conservative, because I know my philosophy is full of hope for every American."[38] Although ambiguous as to what concrete policy proposals might flow from this philosophy, the use of the term *compassionate conservative* clearly invoked the image of a candidate who cared about people, and the term undoubtedly was coined, entirely or in part, as a strategy to appeal to women voters. However, the cleverest symbolic strategy of all may have been the name that the Bush campaign chose for its organized effort to win women voters. At Bush campaign events across the country, signs appeared with the slogan "W Stands for Women," a double entendre suggesting that Bush's middle initial and nickname, "W," indicated his supportive posture toward women.

Another use of symbolic appeals in campaigns has focused on the targeting of specific groups of women (and occasionally groups of men, such as NASCAR dads) to the exclusion of large numbers of other women voters. Two examples are the targeting of so-called soccer moms in the 1996 and, to a lesser extent, the 2000 elections, and so-called security moms in the 2004 elections. Both soccer moms and security moms were social constructions – a combination of demographic characteristics, assigned a catchy name by political consultants, with no connection to any existing self-identified group or organizational base. When consultants and the media first started referring to soccer moms in 1996, women did not identify themselves as such, but the term has subsequently entered into popular usage and some women now refer to themselves this way.

---

[38] Joe Conason. September 15, 2003. Where's the Compassion? *The Nation.* http://www .thenation.com/doc/20030915/conason. Accessed July 26, 2009.

Similarly, women did not self-identify as security moms before the term was introduced in the context of the 2004 elections.

Although the definition of a soccer mom varied somewhat, she was generally considered a white, married woman with children (presumably of soccer-playing age), living in the suburbs. She also was often described in media coverage as stressed out and driving a minivan. The soccer mom was considered important politically because she was viewed as a swing voter – a voter whose demographics had traditionally led her to vote Republican but who could be persuaded to vote Democratic. One of the most important characteristics of the soccer mom was that she was not primarily concerned about her own self-interest but about her family and, most important, her children. As Kellyanne Fitzpatrick, a Republican pollster, noted, "If you are a soccer mom, the world according to you is seen through the needs of your children."[39]

The security mom, who became a focus of attention during the last several weeks of the 2004 presidential campaign, shared many of the demographic characteristics of the soccer mom. Like the soccer mom, she was considered white and married, with young children. Also like the soccer mom, the security mom did not put her own needs first but rather those of her family and children. She was repeatedly described as preoccupied with keeping her family safe from terrorism. The Republican presidential campaign, in particular, openly campaigned for the votes of these women in 2004. For example, on October 10, 2004, on CNN's *Late Edition with Wolf Blitzer*, Vice President Dick Cheney's daughter, Liz, urged women to vote for the Republican ticket, explaining, "You know, I'm a security mom. I've got four little kids. And what I care about in this election cycle is electing a guy who is going to be a commander-in-chief, who will do whatever it takes to keep those kids safe."[40]

The intensive campaign and media attention devoted to soccer moms in 1996 and 2000 and to security moms in 2004 deflected attention from the concerns of many other subgroups of women, including feminists, college-age women, older women, women on welfare, women of color, and professional women. Ironically, it even deflected attention from the concerns of white, middle-class women themselves except in their role as moms. Both the campaigns and the media were able to appear to be

[39] Neil MacFarquhar. October 20, 1996. Don't Forget Soccer Dads; What's a Soccer Mom Anyway? *New York Times*.

[40] CNN. October 10, 2004. Late Edition with Wolf Blitzer. http://cnnstudent-news.cnn.com/TRANSCRIPTS/0410/10/le.01.html. Accessed March 21, 2005.

responsive to the concerns of women voters by talking about soccer moms and security moms while actually ignoring the vast majority of women. As a result, Clinton was reelected in 1996 and Bush was twice elected to the presidency in 2000 and 2004 without campaigning aggressively on (or, in some cases, even seriously addressing) many of the issues of greatest importance to the majority of women in this country who are not white, middle-class mothers of young children.

CONCLUSION: WHY THE GENDER GAP MATTERS AND A LOOK TOWARD 2016

The gender gap has increased the political influence wielded by women voters. Candidates now must pay attention to women voters to win elections. As Susan A. MacManus observes in Chapter 3 of this volume, in recent elections, women have voted at slightly higher rates than men. Women also are a greater proportion of the population. These two facts combined mean that there have been many more female than male voters in recent elections. In the 2012 election, for example, about 9.8 million more women than men voted.[41] The fact that there are so many more female voters than male voters adds power to the so-called women's vote, and clearly the more women who turn out to vote, the more clout women are likely to have.

Women voters received more attention in 2012 than in any previous presidential election, and the presidential campaigns used not only symbolic appeals but also substantive policy-based appeals in an attempt to win over women voters. While Romney tried to appeal to women voters largely on the basis of economic issues, Obama emphasized economic issues plus his support for women's reproductive health policies and pay equity. Obama's "economy plus" strategy seems to have paid off, because he won a clear majority of women's votes and was the beneficiary of one of the largest gender gaps ever in presidential voting.

In the first few months following the 2012 elections, Hillary Clinton emerged in polls as the frontrunner for the Democratic presidential nomination in 2016. Obviously, much can change in the many months before the 2016 election. Clinton may ultimately choose not to run for president in 2016, and other candidates will certainly enter the race for the

---

[41] United States Census Bureau. Voting and Registration in the Election of 2012 – Detailed Tables. Table 1. http://www.census.gov/hhes/www/socdemo/voting/publications/p20/2012/tables.html. Accessed May 9, 2013.

Democratic nomination. But if Clinton runs, attention will almost assuredly be paid to how women voters respond to her candidacy. Will the votes of women propel her to victory in the Democratic primary? If she becomes her party's nominee, will she be able to attract general election votes not only from Democratic women but from large numbers of Independent women and some Republican women as well? Will the Republicans nominate a candidate who can appeal to women voters? Will they devise an effective strategy to reduce the size of the gender gap? Much can change before 2016, but early signs suggest that women voters will play an interesting and important role in the next presidential contest, just as they did in 2012.

5 Latinas and Electoral Politics

Expanding Participation and Power in State and National Elections

INTRODUCTION

Latina and Latino[1] political participation in the 2012 election reached new heights, proving to be a significant factor in the electoral outcomes of several battleground states and ultimately the reelection of President Obama. Both Latinas and Latinos played pivotal roles in the 2012 election, increasing their share of the national electorate and their support for President Obama over 2008 election levels. In the end, President Obama received 71 percent of the Latina/o vote (compared with 27 percent for Mitt Romney), surpassing all previous presidential candidates with the exception of Bill Clinton, who garnered 72 percent of the Latina/o vote

---

[1] The terms *Latino* and *Hispanic* are used interchangeably by the federal government. Within the U.S. Census, the population is defined to include any person of "Mexican, Puerto Rican, Cuban, South or Central American or other Spanish culture or origin, regardless of race" and reflect "self-identification by individuals according to the group or groups with which they most closely identify" (American Community Survey 2006, American Community Survey Reports 2007).

However, the inability of these designations to properly account for the complexity of persons whose ancestry stems from Latin America but are living in the United States has generated considerable debate and dissension. Central to this discourse is whether the population constitutes its own separate racial group, a coherent ethnic group, or something else. Moreover, longstanding concern about the imprecision of pan-ethnic labels has led many to gravitate to specific national origin references (i.e., Mexican American, Cuban American).

For the purposes of this chapter, I use the term *Latina/o* to mean persons with ancestral, genealogical, or cultural origins in Latin American currently residing primarily in the United States. Moreover, in describing the population at large, I use the "a/o" ending to signify the mutual presence of men and women, as opposed to the default masculine "o." On occasions when the data are reported using the label *Hispanic* or specific national origin identifiers, I duplicate the same terms here for consistency.

TABLE 5.1: Contrary to the patterns for other groups, a larger proportion of Latinas/os voted for Obama in 2012 than did in 2008

% of vote			2012		2008	
	2012	2008	Obama (%)	Romney (%)	Obama (%)	McCain (%)
Latinas/os	10	9	71	27	67	31
Whites	72	74	39	59	43	55
Blacks	13	13	93	6	95	4
Women	53	53	55	44	56	43
18–29 year olds	19	18	60	27	66	32
Independents	29	29	45	50	52	44
Total			50	48	53	46

Sources: Pew Hispanic Research Center, "Latino Voters in the 2012 Election," and the National Election Exit Poll conducted by Edison Research.

in 1996.[2] In fact, among key demographic groups comprising the "new electorate" – African Americans, Latinas/os, women, younger voters, and independents – Latinas/os were the only group whose level of turnout and support for Obama substantially surpassed those of the 2008 presidential election.[3] Table 5.1 compares voting in 2008 and 2012 across several demographic groups and demonstrates the growth of Latina/o support for Obama. Ultimately, while President Obama's favorability ratings were affected by a bruising first term, resulting in decreased support among key constituents and whites generally, Latina/o turnout and support for Obama, particularly in Florida, Colorado, New Mexico, and

[2] Data on rates of Latina/o political participation in the 2012 election draw primarily from the National Election Exit Poll conducted by Edison Research, with additional information from the Pew Hispanic Research Center and the ImpreMedia/Latino Decisions 2012 Latino Election Eve Poll. (See specifically Mark Hugo Lopez and Paul Taylor. Latino Voters in the 2012 Election. Pew Hispanic Research Center. November 7, 2012. http://www.pewhispanic.org/2012/11/07/latino-voters-in-the-2012-election/; Matt Barreto and Gary Segura. 2012. ImpreMedia/Latino Decisions 2012 Latino Election Eve Poll. ImpreMedia/Latino Decisions. November 7, 2012. http://www.latinodecisions.com/files/3513/5232/9137/LEE_PRESENTATION_2012.pdf. While the National Election Exit Poll continues to be the standard-bearer for news agencies like CNN and for research centers like Pew, the accuracy of their results regarding Latinos has been called into question for more than a decade. These findings are used with a degree of caution and, where possible, balanced against other data including exit polling from Impremedia/Latino Decisions and Gallup.
[3] Mark Hugo Lopez and Paul Taylor. 2012. Latino Voters in the 2012 Election. Pew Hispanic Research Center. November 7, 2012. http://www.pewhispanic.org/2012/11/07/latino-voters-in-the-2012-election/.

Nevada, were vitally important in overcoming setbacks elsewhere. As one political scientist and pollster put it, "for the first time in U.S. history, [the] Latino vote can plausibly claim to be nationally decisive."[4]

Latinas proved to be a key factor driving President Obama's increased support among Latinas/os. In the years leading up to the election, Latinas outpaced Latinos in rates of naturalization, and in both 2008 and 2012, larger proportions of Latinas voted in the election and supported Obama. While Obama's favorability ratings among both Latinas and Latinos were consistently strong throughout the 2012 election season, in the end Latina support outpaced that of men, with 76 percent of Latinas voting for Obama compared with 65 percent of Latino men. Tracking polls conducted in the months leading up to the election suggested other important differences between Latinas and Latinos on women's policy issues and perceptions of Republicans in Congress. These differences fueled new discussions of a "Latina/o gender gap" which, unlike previous gaps among Latinas/os, turned out to be statistically significant in states such as Colorado. In addition, the gendered nature of heated immigration policy debates and reaction to a late intervention by President Obama in the form of the Deferred Action for Childhood Arrivals further strengthened Latina support for Obama's immigration policies.

Latinas also played a significant role in the Obama administration leading up to the election and were featured in the national election strategy teams and the party conventions. Moreover, Latinas achieved important electoral success as candidates in several national and state races, joining with their male counterparts to become the largest contingent of Latina/o members in the U.S. Congress and producing the first Latina governor. Ultimately, this suggests that while gender was significant to the campaign and women voters were an important part of the election outcomes, particular attention must be paid to how the intersection of gender and race in the lives of Latinas played a part in the 2012 election season.

In the following chapter, I examine the state of Latinas within contemporary electoral politics, paying particular attention to their role in the 2012 presidential election. Focusing on their expanded electoral strength and specific participation as voters, the emergence of a significant Latina/o gender gap, and their role as advisors and surrogates in the

[4] Matt Barreto and Gary Segura. 2012. ImpreMedia/Latino Decisions 2012 Latino Election Eve Poll. ImpreMedia/Latino Decisions. November 7, 2012. www.latinodecisions.com/files/3513/5232/9137/LEE_PRESENTATION_2012.pdf.

election, I argue that 2012 was a pivotal year for Latinas/os generally and Latinas in particular. Throughout the essay, I examine how Latinas' role in the 2012 election season compared and contrasted with their participation in 2008 and how this affected their overall electoral strength.

INCREASE OF LATINA/O VOTERS: THE STATE OF THE LATINA/O ELECTORATE IN 2012

By 2010, Latinas/os comprised more than 16 percent of the total U.S. population, or approximately 50.5 million persons.[5] This figure represents a 43 percent increase over 2000 data and a growth of more than five million persons since 2008.[6] In addition, this rapid growth reflects the status of Latinas/os as the largest and fastest-growing racial/ethnic minority population in the country.[7] While this growth was apparent across almost every individual national origin group, the Mexican population increased by 54 percent, accounting for approximately three fourths of the total increase, followed by Puerto Ricans, who grew from 3.4 million to 4.6 million, and Cubans, who grew from 1.2 million persons in 2000 to 1.8 million by 2010.[8]

Latinas make up just less than half of the total Latino community, or approximately 49.3 percent of the population. More importantly, Latinas are central to the growth of the population, both as new immigrants and as mothers. That is, two factors in particular explain much of the growth of Latinas/os in the United States: a steady flow of immigrants from Latin America and a strong fertility rate among Latinas/os already in the United States. Among legal adult migrants from Latin America, women have outnumbered men since 2004, leading to the "feminization of immigration."[9] In addition, Latinas possess a higher fertility rate than non–Hispanic whites, with Guatemalan women and Mexican women

---

[5] Sharon R. Ennis, Merarys Rios-Vargas, and Nora G. Albert. 2011. The Hispanic Population: 2010. 2010 Census Briefs. U.S. Department of Commerce: United States Census Bureau. May 2011.

[6] Pew Hispanic Center. 2012. *Statistical Portrait of Hispanics in the United States, 2010: Table *: Race and Ethnicity, by Sex and Age: 2010.*

[7] Elizabeth M. Grieco and Rachel C. Cassidy. 2001. Overview of Race and Hispanic Origin: Census 2000 Brief. U.S. Department of Commerce, Economics and Statistics Administration. March 2001. http://www.census.gov/prod/2001pubs/c2kbr01-1.pdf.

[8] Sharon R. Ennis, Merarys Rios-Vargas, and Nora G. Albert. 2011. The Hispanic Population.

[9] Richard Fry. 2006. *Gender and Migration*. Washington, DC: Pew Hispanic Center. pewhispanic.org/files/reports/64.pdf.

TABLE 5.2: Larger proportions of Latinas than Latinos voted for Obama in both 2012 and 2008

% of voters		2012		2008	
2012	2008	Obama (%)	Romney (%)	Obama (%)	McCain (%)
Latinas	6	5	76	23	68	30
Latinos	5	4	65	33	64	33

Sources: 2012 National Election Exit Poll conducted by Edison Research and 2008 National Election Exit Poll conducted by Edison Media Research and Mitofsky International.

reporting some of the highest levels of fertility in the country.[10] In short, Latinas lie at the heart of these expanding demographics but are often overlooked.

Another way of examining the growth of Latinas generally is in relationship to all women in the United States. Since 2000, Latinas have been the fastest-growing female population in the country. The National Association of Latino Elected and Appointed Officials (NALEO) reported that "between 2000 and 2010, the nation's female population grew from 143.4 million to 157.0 million, an increase of 9.5 percent. During the same period, the Latina population grew from 17.1 million to 24.9 million, an increase of 45.0 percent."[11]

The share of Latinas and Latinos participating in the national electorate also grew in the past decade, from approximately 8 percent in 2004 to more than 10 percent in 2012.[12] Latinas in particular continued to comprise a larger percentage of the electorate than Latino men, as they have in every presidential election since 1996; however, the number of Latino male voters grew at a faster pace than the number of Latina voters. Approximately 6.4 million Latinas voted in the 2012 election, constituting more than one in twelve of all female voters. As Table 5.2 demonstrates, this increase of voters, coupled with targeted outreach directed

[10] American Community Survey Reports. 2007. *The American Community-Hispanics: 2004.* U.S. Census Bureau. U.S. Department of Commerce. www.census.gov/prod/2007pubs/acs-03.pdf.

[11] Rosalind Gold. 2012. Election Profile: Latina Voters. National Association of Latino Elected and Appointed Officials. http://www.naleo.org/2011_downloads/Latina_NALEO_Profile_2012.pdf.

[12] Lopez and Taylor. 2012. Latino Voters in the 2012 Election. See also Mark Hugo Lopez. 2008. The Hispanic Vote in the 2008 Election. Pew Hispanic Center. November 5, 2008. www.pewhispanic.org/files/reports/98.pdf.

specifically at Latinas, resulted in a greater share of Latinas than Latinos voting for Obama in both 2008 and 2012.

The growing political capacity of Latinas and Latinos, while tied to resources and mobilization strategies, was also linked directly to increased rates of naturalization among the ten largest Hispanic-origin groups and the declining foreign-born population.[13] Specifically, between 2000 and 2010, the percentage of foreign-born persons within the Latina/o population fell from 40 percent in 2000 to 37 percent in 2010. Similarly, the percentage of foreign-born persons declined among each of the top ten Hispanic-origin groups in the same period, with the largest decline occurring among Salvadorans (from 76 percent to 62 percent).[14]

At the same time, the share of Hispanics with U.S. citizenship increased from 71 percent in 2000 to 74 percent in 2010, with notable spikes in the rates of naturalization in 2000, 2006, and in the months leading up to the historic 2008 election. As the Pew Hispanic Research Center notes, "Among all foreign-born Hispanics, the share holding U.S. citizenship increased from 28 percent in 2000 to 29 percent in 2010."[15] In this same period, Latina immigrants outpaced their male counterparts in rates of naturalization, thus overcoming a key obstacle to participation and political incorporation at a faster pace than Latinos.[16] In short, in 2010, a greater share of the Latina/o population in the United States held

---

[13] The ten largest Hispanic origin groups are Mexicans (who make up 65 percent of all Hispanics in the United States), Puerto Ricans (9.2 percent), Cubans (3.7 percent), Salvadorans (3.6 percent), Dominicans (3.0 percent), Guatemalans (2.2 percent), Colombians (1.9 percent), Hondurans (1.4 percent), Ecuadorians (1.3 percent), and Peruvians (1.2 percent). Collectively, these ten groups comprise 92 percent of the total U.S. Hispanic population. Seth Motel and Eileen Patten. 2012. The 10 Largest Hispanic Origin Groups: Characteristics, Rankings, Top Counties. Pew Research Hispanic Center, June 27, 2012. http://www.pewhispanic.org/files/. Seth Motel and Eileen Patten. 2012. The 10 Largest Hispanic Origin Groups: Characteristics, Rankings, Top Counties. Pew Research Hispanic Center, June 27, 2012. http://www.pewhispanic.org/2012/06/27/the-10-largest-hispanic-origin-groups-characteristics-rankings-top-counties/.

[14] Seth Motel and Eileen Patten. 2012. The 10 Largest Hispanic Origin Groups: Characteristics, Rankings, Top Counties. Pew Research Hispanic Center, June 27, 2012. http://www.pewhispanic.org/files/2012/06/The-10-Largest-Hispanic-Origin-Groups.pdf. See also Statistical Abstract of the U.S. 2012. Table 47. Petitions for Naturalization Filed, Persons Naturalized, and Petitions Denied: 1990–2010. http://www.census.gov/compendia/statab/2012/tables/12s0047.pdf.

[15] Seth Motel and Eileen Patten. 2012. The 10 Largest Hispanic Origin Groups: Characteristics, Rankings, Top Counties. Pew Research Hispanic Center, p. 5. http://www.pewhispanic.org/files/2012/06/The-10-Largest-Hispanic-Origin-Groups.pdf.

[16] Felicia Gonzales. 2008. Hispanic Women in the United States, 2007. Pew Hispanic Center. pewhispanic.org/files/factsheets/42/pdf; Immigration Policy Center. 2010. Immigrant Women in the United States. Washington, DC. www.immigrationpolicy.org/just-facts/immigration-women-united-states-portrait-demographic-diversity.

citizenship as compared with 2000, with the largest change taking place among Dominicans. Thus, while nationally the Democratic Party and the Obama campaign did a better job of targeted outreach and mobilization among Latina/o voters than the Republican Party and the Romney campaign did, their strategies were aided by growth of the pool of eligible voters – an increase driven by Latinas.

THE SIGNIFICANCE OF SELECT STATES TO LATINA/O ELECTORAL POWER IN 2012

The outcome of the national election and the surge of Latina/o electoral power in 2012 rested disproportionately with the outreach, mobilization, and investment of both campaigns in select states. Of particular significance to Latinas/os was the focus on Colorado, New Mexico, Nevada, and Florida. While Latinas/os reside disproportionately in large states such as California, Illinois, New Jersey, New York, and Texas, none of these states was competitive in 2012, resulting in less attention and outreach to Latinas/os in those locations. In contrast, the competitive presidential race as well as key House and Senate contests in Colorado, New Mexico, Nevada, and Florida meant that every vote counted and both campaigns expanded outreach to Latinas/os. In this context, Latinas/os emerged as important targets because they represented a critical mass of voters, because there was a high percentage of eligible non-voters among the population, and because despite their tendencies to support Democrats, as voters they remained fluid.

Latinas, particularly newly naturalized voters, those registered to vote who did not do so in the previous general election, and low-propensity voters eligible to vote but marginalized from the electoral process, became key targets of various campaigns looking to expand their mobilization strategies in these battleground states. For example, civic engagement campaigns such as Voto Latino (spearheaded by actress Rosario Dawson) worked in partnership with labor unions and local nonprofits in Colorado, Florida, and Nevada to mobilize young voters and Latinas through a combination of registration, fundraising, and get-out-the-vote (GOTV) efforts, coupled with expanded use of social networking and community relationships. Similarly, Mi Familia Vota – a civic engagement effort led by the Service Employees International Union (SEIU) – partnered with local nonprofits in several battleground states to mobilize Latino families, hoping to increase Latina participation specifically through its efforts.[17] All of these advocacy organizations were active in the 2008 presidential campaign, building capacity and mobilizing Latinas to participate as both voters and candidates in battleground states. Mirroring the 2008 election, the organizations worked collaboratively with state and local campaigns (both partisan and nonpartisan) and even with the national party coordinating committees to drive turnout in 2012. Thus, in many ways the increase of Latina and Latino voters, along with the gains made by Latinas elected to state and national office, reflects the culmination of a much longer process of outreach stretching back to at least 2008 and, in many cases, to even earlier organizational mobilization.[18]

In Colorado, mobilization campaigns aimed at Latina and Latino voters resulted in their increased electoral presence as well as increased support for President Obama. In particular, Latina/o vote share increased from 13 percent in 2008 to 14 percent in 2012, and Latina/o support for Obama swelled from 61 percent in 2008 to 75 percent.[19] While Latina/o voting capacity increased in response to targeted mobilization efforts, the Latina/o proportion of the vote also grew because the Obama campaign lost support among whites (50 percent in 2008 to 44 percent in 2012) and independents (54 percent in 2008 to 45 percent in 2012) – key segments of his 2008 winning coalition.[20] In the end, Obama carried Colorado 51.2 percent to 46.5 percent over Mitt Romney but won by a much smaller margin than his 54 percent to 45 percent victory over John McCain in 2008.[21] The increased mobilization of Latina and Latino voters in Colorado also translated to a surge of Latina/o candidates elected in various

---

[17] In addition to an increased focus on Latinas, several of these campaigns increased outreach to low-propensity voters (including those nonregistered or who were eligible to vote but never voted), populations in small or rural counties, and individuals who were newly naturalized.

[18] For a thorough examination of contemporary Latina electoral success, particularly elections to local and state offices, see Christina Bejarano. 2013. *The Latina Advantage: Gender, Race, and Political Success*. Austin: University of Texas Press.

[19] Lopez and Taylor. 2012. Latino Voters in the 2012 Election.

[20] Estimates drawn from exit polls. CNN: Election Center. 2008. Exit Polls: Florida. http://www.cnn.com/ELECTION/2008/results/individual/#FLP00; CNN: Election Center. 2012. Florida Exit Polls 2012. http://www.cnn.com/ELECTION/2012/.

[21] Obama's 2008 victory represented an important shift, as Colorado had consistently supported Republican candidates in eight of nine previous presidential elections. However, it is important to note that Obama's 2008 victory built on the strength of an emerging Latina/o electorate (marked in 2006 by the election of Latino Representative John Salazar in the conservative 3rd Congressional district and the election of Ken Salazar to the U.S. Senate) and a bolstered Democratic party that took over both the lower house of the state legislature and the governor's office by 2008.

state races, subsequently giving Democrats control over both houses of the legislature and signaling a rise of a Latina/o political elite with agenda-setting power in the state.

Latina/o mobilization efforts in Florida paralleled campaigns in Colorado with similar effect. That is, Latina/o vote share in Florida increased from 14 percent in 2008 to 17 percent in 2012, and overall Latina/o support for Obama grew from 57 percent in 2008 to 60 percent in 2012.[22] Latina voters also increased their capacity (from 8 percent of the electorate in 2008 to 9 percent by 2012) and support for Obama (from 55 percent to 61 percent in 2012).[23] In fact, exit polls suggest that the increased support among Latinas/os in the state came disproportionately from Latina voters, as Obama lost some ground among Latino male voters (60 percent in 2008 to 58 percent in 2012). Obama also lost support among white voters in the state (42 percent in 2008 to 37 percent in 2012), while support among the state's African Americans remained consistent.[24] As a result, Obama's margin of victory was reduced to less than 1 percent in 2012 (50 percent to 49.1 percent) compared with the 3-point advantage he held in 2008 over John McCain (51 percent to 48 percent).[25]

The stories of Latina and Latino mobilization and voting in Nevada and New Mexico are a bit more complex. Latinas'/os' electoral presence in Nevada grew by 3 percent in 2012, comprising 18 percent of the state's electorate in 2012 compared to 15 percent in 2008; however, in contrast to the situations in Colorado and Florida, exit polls indicate that Obama lost support among Latinas/os in Nevada (76 percent in 2008 to 70 percent in 2012).[26] As in other battleground states, Latina voters increased their share of the state's electorate from 9 percent in 2008 to 10 percent in 2012, but reports from the National Election Survey indicate that fewer Latinas voted for Obama in Nevada in 2012 than in 2008 (from 76 percent to 72 percent). While fewer Latinas supported the Democratic presidential candidate in 2012, support for Republicans remained the same (21 percent), suggesting that while Latinas may have felt less enthusiasm or approval of President Obama, they were not more inclined to support

[22] Matt Barreto and Gary Segura. 2012. ImpreMedia/Latino Decisions 2012 Latino Election Eve Poll. ImpreMedia/Latino Decisions. November 7, 2012. www.latinodecisions.com/files/3513/5232/9137/LEE_PRESENTATION_2012.pdf.

[23] CNN: Election Center. 2008, 2012.

[24] Lopez and Taylor. 2012. Latino Voters in the 2012 Election.

[25] Lopez and Taylor. 2012. Latino Voters in the 2012 Election.

[26] Lopez and Taylor. 2012. Latino Voters in the 2012 Election.

Mitt Romney or the Republican party as an alternative.[27] In the end, President Obama's margin of victory shrank by half as he won the state with a 6-point lead over Romney, compared with his 12-point victory over McCain in 2008.

New Mexico has always been an important site of Latina and Latino political power, generating a consistently large electorate, electing the first Latina governor in 2010 (Republican Susana Martinez), and producing the first competitive Latino presidential candidate in 2008 (former Democratic Governor Bill Richardson). By 2012, New Mexico, like Colorado and Nevada, was a competitive battleground for Democrats and Republicans, but Democrats were steadily gaining an advantage. The election of Michelle Lujan Grisham from New Mexico's 1st Congressional District in 2012 is symbolic of the rise of Latina/o electoral strength in the state and the concomitant increase in Democratic Party power. Originally created in 1969, the 1st CD was dominated by Republicans until the first successful election of a Democrat in the district in 2008. While Lujan Grisham ran in that election, she was easily defeated in the primary by Martin Heinrich, a well-funded party insider who went on to win election to the U.S. Senate in 2012. By 2012, the district that encompasses Albuquerque and most of its suburbs leaned strongly Democratic, and Latinas/os represented 48 percent of the electorate. Reflecting the growth of Latina/o power as both voters and candidates in the district, Lujan Grisham faced off in the primary against two other Latinos – state legislators Marty Chavez and Eric Griego. After winning the primary, she went on to defeat Republican Janice Arnold-Jones, a former member of the New Mexico House of Representatives, in the November general election 59 percent to 41 percent.

The share of Latina/o voters in New Mexico's 2012 presidential election decreased (from 41 percent of the electorate in 2008 to 37 percent in 2012), and their support for Obama tapered off from 69 percent in 2008 to 64 percent in 2012. Early exit polls suggest that the loss of support occurred more prominently among Latinas, as fewer voted in 2012 (down from 25 percent in 2008 to 21 percent in 2012) and fewer supported President Obama (from 72 percent in 2008 to 67 percent in 2012). Latino male turnout and support for Obama remained virtually the same in this period.

Notably, while Latina support for President Obama decreased in New Mexico in 2012, this did not translate into greater support for Republican candidate Mitt Romney. Despite Republican Party outreach efforts in

[27] CNN: Election Center. 2008, 2012.

the state, only 27 percent of Latina voters supported Romney – the same percentage that voted for McCain in 2008. The relatively low unemployment rate in New Mexico and failure of Republicans to support meaningful immigration reform undoubtedly helped distance Latina voters from the party.

However, the trend toward Democratic dominance in the state was interrupted briefly by Republican gains made in the 2010 midterm election. In that year, Republican Susana Martinez was elected governor, the first female governor of New Mexico and the first Latina governor in the United States. In only the third woman-versus-woman gubernatorial race in U.S. history, Martinez defeated former Lieutenant Governor Democrat Diane Denish. Martinez, a former district attorney in the state, won the Republican nomination in a crowded five-way contest that included business and political elites – among them Pete Domenici, Jr., son of long-term New Mexico Senator Pete Domenici. She handily won the nomination, garnering 51 percent of the vote, along with the endorsement of former Alaska Governor Sarah Palin. Moreover, despite early tracking polls indicating a lead for Denish, Martinez quickly emerged in the general election as the leader, highlighting economic reform and emphasizing Denish's connections to long-time governor and political elite Bill Richardson. By late September of 2010, Martinez out-fundraised and outspent Denish, and a concentrated mobilization and advertising campaign resulted in a swell of voter support that carried through to Election Day.

Despite supporting the Republican Party's restrictive positions on various immigration measures, Martinez was able to connect with and mobilize Latina/o supporters, who proved significant to her victory. Garnering 38 percent of the Latina/o vote in the state, Martinez earned more Latina/o support than Nevada gubernatorial candidate Brian Sandoval and nearly all other Republican gubernatorial candidates that year (with the exception of Rick Scott in Florida.) Moreover, data collected among Latina/o voters in the state indicate that Martinez's win wasn't simply a referendum on Richardson or a pattern of Democratic party discontent in a midterm election, because a sizable percentage (67 percent) of those polled said their vote was motivated by a desire to support the Republican candidate.[28]

Since her victory in 2010, Governor Martinez has continued to oppose various features of immigration reform, including driver's licenses for undocumented immigrants. She signed an executive order in her first

[28] Latino Decisions Election Eve Poll – State by State Results, November 02, 2010.

month in office rescinding "sanctuary" status for "illegal immigrants who commit crimes in New Mexico" and spoke out in support of Arizona's restrictive measures to crack down on undocumented immigrants. However, Martinez also deviated from her Republican counterparts, openly criticizing Republican proposals to deport Mexican immigrants, including Mitt Romney's suggestion during the 2012 campaign that the 11 to 12 million undocumented immigrants in the United States should "self-deport." In an interview with *Newsweek*, Martinez replied to Romney's suggestion by saying: "'Self-deport'? What the heck does that mean? I have no doubt Hispanics have been alienated during this campaign, but now there's an opportunity for Governor Romney to have a sincere conversation about what we can do and why."[29] Governor Martinez's comments echoed similar sentiments captured in Impremedia/Latino Decisions tracking polls, reflecting the inability of the GOP to connect with Latina/o voters in New Mexico and other battleground states. Her comments were particularly surprising given her own immigration battles in the state and rumors she was being considered as a vice presidential running mate at the time of the interview.

However, her ascension to statewide office, her ability to mobilize strong support from Latina/o voters at a time of Democrat party dominance, and her willingness to critique the more restrictive positions within the GOP on deportation of Latin American immigrants also add up to an important lesson for the future of the national Republican Party. As the party leadership regroups in the wake of resounding losses in the 2012 election cycle, one area in which there is clearly room for growth is in Latina/o outreach. The election of Susana Martinez provides evidence that it is possible to expand the base of Latina/o Republicans, both as candidates for office and as voters.

Ultimately, the net contribution of Latinas/os to President Obama's reelection campaign was enough to overcome deficits elsewhere and secure New Mexico's five electoral votes for Obama.[30] Moreover, like Latinas/os in Colorado, Florida, and Nevada, Latina voters were a crucial component of the winning coalitions in these battleground states that resulted in President Obama's reelection. However, their presence in the 2012 elections went beyond this important contribution; Latinas also helped shape strategic decisions in both parties, a status reflected both

[29] Andrew Romano. 2012. Susana Martinez: What New Mexico's Governor Can Teach the GOP. *Newsweek Magazine*.

[30] Lopez and Taylor. 2012. Latino Voters in the 2012 Election.

in their expanded role in the Obama administration and their leadership
roles in both parties' campaign structures.

PRESENCE WITHIN LEADERSHIP OF THE OBAMA ADMINISTRATION
AND 2012 PRESIDENTIAL CAMPAIGNS

Latinas/os were important fixtures in the 2008 presidential campaigns of
both Barack Obama and Hillary Clinton, serving as surrogates, advisors,
and managers and providing critical endorsements, particularly during
the primary races. In 2008, Latinas and Latinos were notably present
as official surrogates (including labor leaders Maria Elena Durazo and
Linda Chavez-Thompson; U.S. Representatives Xavier Becerra, Loretta
Sanchez, and Linda Sanchez; and actresses America Ferrera and Eva Longoria for Obama; and Maria Echeveste, Supervisor Gloria Molina, activist
Dolores Huerta, and Congresswoman Hilda Solis for Hillary Clinton),
and as statewide leaders and key advisors. Both campaigns also benefitted from Latina/o Advisory Councils that included several high-profile
Latinas such as Congresswomen Linda Sanchez, Hilda Solis, and Nydia
Velasquez and labor leader Geocanda Arguell-Kline. Two of the more
notable placements within the 2008 campaigns included former Transportation and Energy Secretary Federico Pena, who served as both an
advisor and co-chair of Obama's transition committee after the election,
and Patti Solis Doyle, who briefly served as Hillary Clinton's campaign
manager, the first Latina to hold that title in a presidential campaign.[31]

After the election, Latinas and Latinos figured prominently among
President Obama's appointments during his first term in office and within
the subsequent 2012 reelection campaign. The Obama administration
nominated more Latinas/os to senior government positions than any previous White House. The most significant high-ranking Latina appointments included California Congresswoman Hilda Solis as Secretary of
Labor, former National Council of La Raza president Cecilia Munoz as
director of the White House Domestic Policy Council, and Justice Sonia
Sotomayor as the first Latina to serve on the Supreme Court.[32]

Attention to the increasing strength of Latina/o voters, especially within select battleground states, also prompted more Latina/o

---

[31] Christine Marie Sierra. 2010. Latinas and Electoral Politics: Movin' on Up. In *Gender and
Elections: Shaping the Future of American Politics*, Second Edition, ed. Susan J. Carroll and
Richard L. Fox. New York: Cambridge University Press.

[32] Former Colorado Senator Ken Salazar was also appointed to the Obama cabinet as
Secretary of the Interior.

appointments within the 2012 Obama reelection campaign. Specifically, Katherine Archuleta, chief of staff to Secretary of Labor Hilda Solis, was appointed as the national political director of Obama for America 2012 – the first Latina to hold that position on a major presidential campaign. Other Latina leaders included Angela Barranco, who served as the national western regional director of Obama for America, and Alida Garcia, who was national Latino vote deputy director for the campaign (second to Adrian Saenz, who was director of the national Latino vote of OFA.) Additionally, in 2012, seven of the thirty-five co-chairs of Obama's reelection campaign were Latina/o, including San Antonio Mayor Julian Castro; prominent labor leader Maria Elena Durazo; former chair of the Congressional Hispanic Caucus Congressman Charles A. Gonzalez; former Energy and Transportation Secretary Federico Pena; Los Angeles Mayor Antonio Villaraigosa; Florida activist Lynette Acosta; and actress Eva Longoria. Villaraigosa also served as chair of the 2012 Democratic National Convention Committee.

In addition to serving as a co-chair, Longoria reprised her 2008 role as an outspoken surrogate for Obama and expanded her political capacity by co-founding a new fund-raising venture aimed at Latina and Latino political elites, the Futuro Fund. The fund aimed to raise $6 million for Obama's reelection but ultimately brought in more than $30 million. More important, the fund signaled a new level of political impact by creating a Latina/o fund-raising network that used its clout to push the administration for commitments on immigration reform. Through her work with the fund, Longoria established herself as one of the campaign's top "bundlers" and as a Latina with national political influence. In turn, Obama named Longoria as co-chairwoman of his inaugural committee.[33]

Latinas were also present within the Republican presidential campaign, although their involvement on the GOP side paled in comparison to their engagement with the Democrats. Bettina Inclan was appointed as director of Hispanic outreach for the Republican National Committee, and political consultant Anna Navarro reprised her role as campaign advisor on Hispanic affairs for Romney. In addition, the Romney campaign launched a national women's coalition titled Women for Mitt, led by his wife and represented through an advisory board including Latina reality television personality Rachel Campos-Duffy (who is also the wife of

---

[33] Matea Gold. 2013, January 21. With Obama fundraising, Latinos demonstrate growing clout. *Los Angeles Times*. http://articles.latimes.com/2013/jan/21/nation/la-na-inaug-latino-20130121.

Wisconsin Republican congressman Sean Duffy) and Jovita Carranza, former vice president of air operations for UPS.

Latinas/os also made their mark during both the Democratic and Republican national conventions. Of particular importance was Julian Castro, mayor of San Antonio, Texas, who was the first Latino to give a keynote speech at the DNC (introduced by his twin brother, Representative Joaquin Castro) and a promising candidate for future leadership within the party. Other prominent Latinas/os who delivered remarks included Representatives Charles Gonzalez and Nydia Velasquez, who spoke to the convention on behalf of the Congressional Hispanic Caucus (of which Gonzalez is the chair), Secretary of the Interior Ken Salazar, Representative Xavier Becerra, who delivered remarks as the vice chair of the Democratic caucus, and California Assembly Speaker John A. Perez. While Latino men captured many coveted speaking slots during the convention, both actress Eva Longoria and Representative Nydia Velasquez addressed the convention during prime time. (Cuban American journalist and talk show host Cristina Saralegui addressed the convention outside the featured period.) Arguably one of the most enduring, if brief, speeches of the convention came from Benita Veliz, an undocumented student from St. Mary's University and leader within the movement supporting passage of the DREAM Act:

> My name is Benita Veliz, and I'm from San Antonio, Texas. Like so many Americans of all races and backgrounds, I was brought here as a child. I've been here ever since. I graduated as valedictorian of my class at the age of 16 and earned a double major at the age of 20. I know I have something to contribute to my economy and my country. I feel just as American as any of my friends and neighbors. But, I've had to live almost my entire life knowing I could be deported just because of the way I came here.[34]

Benita Veliz's speech marked the first time an undocumented person had addressed a national convention and the highest-profile appearance representing the student movement. Moreover, her story of success, struggle, and the pressing need for immigration reform signaled the degree to which Latina/o policy concerns were influencing the Democratic Party's positions.

---

[34] Transcript of Benita Veliz remarks as prepared for delivery, Democratic National Convention. 2012. Daily Kos. http://www.dailykos.com/story/2012/09/05/1128253/ -Transcript-of-Benita-Veliz-remarks-as-prepared-for-delivery-Democratic-National- Convention.

The Republican National Committee selected Tampa, Florida, as its convention site, a location that drew greater attention to the established and complex Latina/o community of the state, and the program featured several prominent Latina/o speakers.[35] Among the most notable was Florida's Senator and rumored vice presidential candidate Marco Rubio, who introduced presidential nominee Mitt Romney. By August, Rubio had emerged as the GOP's leading voice on immigration reform and a strong contender for the 2016 election. Puerto Rico Governor Luis Fortuno, Texas Senate Republican candidate Ted Cruz, and Nevada Governor Brian Sandoval all scored prime-time speaking roles. Much like the Democratic National Convention, Latinas featured less prominently in the convention, with the exception of New Mexico Governor Susana Martinez. While Governor Martinez's role in the convention was overshadowed by tensions over the party's position on immigration reform, including her criticisms of Mitt Romney and the party's failure to mount a successful Latina/o outreach campaign, she nonetheless gave an impassioned speech that wove together elements of race and gender with a partisan critique aimed at President Obama:

> Growing up I never imagined a little girl from a border town could one day become a governor. But this is America *y en America, todo es posible!* My parents taught me to never give up and to always believe that my future could be whatever I dreamt it to be ... As the first Hispanic female governor in history, little girls they often come up to me in the grocery store or in the mall. They look and they point, and when they get the courage to come up, they ask, "Are you Susana?" and they run up and they give me a hug. And I wonder, how do you know who I am? But they do. And these are little girls. It's in moments like these when I'm reminded that we each pave a path. And for me it's about paving a path for those little girls to follow. No more barriers.[36]

Finally, Latinas/os were successful as candidates for national office, expanding their presence in both the U.S. House of Representatives and the U.S. Senate. Owing to their electoral successes, the 113th Congress "features the largest class of Latinas/os in the U.S. House of

[35] Unfortunately for the RNC, the first day of the convention was postponed in the wake of Tropical Storm Isaac, resulting in several speakers being displaced or rescheduled during less prominent speaking times.

[36] Susana Martinez RNC speech. 2012. Politico. http://www.politico.com/news/stories/0812/80421.html.

TABLE 5.3: Latinas from four states serve in the 113th Congress

California	Grace Flores Napolitano	Democrat, District 32
	Gloria Negrete McLeod	Democrat, District 35
	Linda Sanchez	Democrat, District 38
	Lucille Roybal-Allard	Democrat, District 40
	Loretta Sanchez	Democrat, District 46
Florida	Ileana Ros-Lehtinen	Republican, District 27
New Mexico	Michelle Lujan Grisham	Democrat, District 1
New York	Nydia Velazquez	Democrat, District 7

Sources: National Association of Latino Elected and Appointed Officials (NALEO), http://www.naleo.org/downloads/US_Congress_Table_2012.pdf.

Representatives."[37] This combination of reelected Latina/o representatives coupled with newly elected members means that Latinas and Latinos will exert greater influence on the national agenda during an important moment for immigration reform. The 113th Congress features twenty-eight Latinas/os with nine new members, two of whom are Latinas: former California State Senator Gloria Negrete McLeod (D), who won in the 35th congressional district, and former New Mexico County Commissioner Michelle Lujan Grisham (D), who was elected in the first congressional district, becoming the first Latina to represent the state in the U.S. House.[38] These women join California Representatives Grace Flores Napolitano (D), Linda Sanchez (D), Loretta Sanchez (D), and Lucille Roybal-Allard (D), Florida Representative Ileana Ros-Lehtinen (R), and New York Representative Nydia Velasquez (D). (See Table 5.3.)

THE LATINA GENDER GAP

While Latinas took their political participation to new heights with their leadership in the national presidential contest, it was a widening gender gap between Latinas and Latinos that bolstered Democratic mobilizing efforts in the last few months of the campaign. Tracking data from Impremedia/Latino Decisions polls showed that while both Latinas and Latinos

[37] National Association of Latino Elected and Appointed Officials (NALEO). 2012. Latino Candidates Make History on Election Night. November 7, 2012. http://us1.campaign-archive1.com/?u=c1a51befb8159efb3bbd1f2620f9e1&id=995bc2c942&e=bt7gXpS6oS.
[38] Ibid.

strongly favored Obama throughout the campaign, by mid September 2012, Obama held a 53-point lead over Romney among Latinas, compared to a 29-point lead with Hispanic men. The gender gap between Latinas and Latinos who favored Obama was 13 points, as compared to a 9-point gender gap among all voters.

This gap extended beyond Obama and Romney's favorability to the entire Republican Party, as only 20 percent of Latinas held a favorable view of the party, compared with 29 percent of Latino men. In addition, 68 percent of Latinas said they would vote Democratic in the upcoming House elections, while 59 percent of Latino men said they would vote for a Democratic candidate in these races.

Even more significant was the broad advantage that Latinas conferred on Democrats with regard to "women's issues," what political scientist Sylvia Manzano described as "the largest gap on any policy issue our polling data has ever revealed".[39] Specifically, when asked "who do you trust to make the right decisions and address issues of concern to women?" 78 percent of Latinas favored Democrats, while only 13 percent of Latinas favored Republicans. Similarly, 68 percent of Latino men said Democrats could better handle women's issues, while only 19 percent said they thought Republicans were better suited. In short, Latinas gave Democrats a 65-point advantage over Republicans on issues of specific concern to them.

Finally, in addition to a substantial gender gap for Obama and the Democrats, Latina responses indicated more enthusiasm for turning out; 59 percent reported being very enthusiastic about voting in the upcoming election (as compared with 51 percent of Latino men). This enthusiasm gap was a significant bolster for many Democrats, as earlier tracking and field reports suggested a lackluster response to the Obama campaign in 2012 as compared with 2008. Advisors and pundits worried openly that the lack of enthusiasm among Latinas/os could result in a poor turnout in competitive states, swinging the popular vote to Romney and the Republicans. However, Obama's action in June creating a bold new option for undocumented minors breathed new life into Latina/o support while simultaneously undermining Republican gestures toward Latinas/os

---

[39] Sylvia Manzano. 2012. The Latino gender gap: Latino voters prefer Obama by 53 point margin. Latino Decisions. September 17, 2012. http://www.latinodecisions.com/blog/2012/09/17/latina-voters-prefer-obama-by-53-point-margin/. See also Summer Ballantine. 2012. The New Gender Gap: Polls show Obama with 52 point lead among Latinas, 29 among Hispanic men. *The Houston Chronicle*.

voters through a modified DREAM act proposal floated by Florida Senator Marco Rubio.[40]

A significant Latino/a gender gap was also reported in the key battleground state of Colorado. A June tracking poll found a gender gap in Latina and Latino evaluations of both President Obama's job approval and support for his reelection. With respect to job approval, 76 percent of Latina voters in Colorado approved of President' Obama's performance, compared with 69 percent of Latino men. This 7-point gender gap paralleled national scores on Obama's job performance but was not statistically significant. However, when asked about their presidential candidate preference, 80 percent of Colorado Latinas indicated support for Obama over Romney, compared with 65 percent of Colorado Latino men. This 15-point gender gap was much wider than the national average, which hovered at approximately 8 percent at the time, and proved to be statistically significant.[41] In the end, Latina/o support for Obama in Colorado increased by more than 10 points over his margin in 2008, with 75 percent of Latinas and Latinos in the state voting for President Obama and only 23 percent supporting Mitt Romney.[42]

---

[40] In June 2012, President Obama used executive authority to create Deferred Action for Childhood Arrivals – a policy cousin to the DREAM Act, an effort to provide paths to legalization for undocumented children in the United States. The new policy permits undocumented immigrants 30 or younger who have clean criminal records, have lived in the United States for at least five years, are in school (or are high school graduates or military veterans in good standing), and who came to the United States before age sixteen to remain in the United States without fear of deportation. For immigrants who come forward and qualify, DHS will grant deferred action – preventing their deportation through a two-year reprieve. Moreover, the policy clears the way for these young immigrants to work legally, specifically permitting them to apply for work permits and possibly to obtain other significant documents such as driver's licenses. The Pew Hispanic Center estimates that as many as 1.4 million immigrants might benefit from the new policy. The program was seen by many as a strategic move intended to undermine Republican advances toward Latina/o voters with plans for immigration reform while simultaneously mollifying critics of the Obama administration's aggressive criminal alien apprehension program that had resulted in record numbers of immigrant deportations. See Julia Preston and John H. Cushman. 2012, June 15. Obama to Permit Young Migrants to Remain in the U.S. *The New York Times.*

[41] Rob Preuhs. 2012. Colorado Latina/Latino Gender Gap. Latino Decisions. September 13, 2012. http://www.latinodecisions.com/blog/2012/09/13/colorados-latinalatino-gender-gap/.

[42] Lopez and Taylor. 2012. Latino Voters in the 2012 Election. As with the data on national Latina/o turnout and vote choice, there is considerable debate about the actual growth of the Latina/o vote in Colorado in 2012. Specifically in 2008, the National Election Poll reported that Obama secured 61 percent of the Latina/o vote in the state, while more comprehensive exit polls in the state reported that 67 percent of Colorado Latinas/os voted for Obama. Similarly, in 2012, NEP data indicate that 75 percent of Colorado Latinas/os supported Obama (and 23 percent Romney) as compared with 87 percent

Ultimately, examining the Latina gender gap reveals some important differences between Latina and white female voters. In particular, Susan J. Carroll in Chapter 4 of this volume traces the appearance of a national gender gap since 1980, noting that the gap typically hovers between 7 and 8 points. More importantly, the gap typically translates into a greater likelihood that female voters would support a Democratic candidate for office while male voters would more likely favor a Republican candidate. However, the gender gap among Latinas and Latinos is a far more recent phenomenon (owing in part to the more recent availability of data), but even more significantly it reflects a difference between Latinas and Latinos on the *depth* of their support for Democratic candidates and issues and not on a partisan divide, as exists among white voters. In other words, both Latinas and Latinos overwhelmingly support Democratic candidates and issues, and the tracking data compiled over the 2012 elections suggest that more than 50 percent of both Latinas and Latinos consistently preferred Obama to Romney. Despite differences in their levels of support within the party, both Latinas and Latinos also indicated a strong likelihood of voting and consistently evaluated the outreach efforts of Democrats as superior to Republicans.[43]

Thus, the Latino/a gender gap that appeared in the 2012 election revealed important variations in Latino/a political participation (particularly for the Democratic Party) and demonstrated the significance of simultaneous attention to both race and gender. Recent research by Latina political scientists and women of color on the Latina/o gender gap extends our understanding of this important political phenomenon, examining variations by age, generational cohort, race, national origin, and immigration status.[44] Utilizing an intersectional analysis, this research raises new questions about the causes and directions of the gap while heightening the profile of Latinas as political agents and advancing research on Latina political participation.

---

support indicated in the Impremedia/Latino Decisions exit data. In the end, the point is most significant to academics and campaign strategists, because in both studies Latinas/os overwhelmingly favored President Obama over the Republican challenger.

[43] Sylvia Manzano. 2012. The Latino gender gap.

[44] Christina Bejarano, Sylvia Manzano, and Celeste Montoya. 2011. Tracking the Latino Gender Gap: Gender Attitudes across Sex, Borders, and Generations. *Politics and Gender* (7), 521–549; Lisa Garcia Bedolla, Jessica Lavariega Monforti, and Adrian D. Pantoja. 2006. A Second Look: Is There a Latino/a Gender Gap? *Journal of Women, Politics, and Policy,* 28 (January); 147–171; Pei-te Lien. 1998. Does the Gender Gap in Political Attitudes and Behavior Vary Across Racial Groups? *Political Research Quarterly* 51 (December): 869–894.

CONCLUSION

Latinas and Latinos played a substantial role in the 2012 national election, securing reelection for President Obama and demonstrating their power in key battleground states. Owing in large part to the showing of electoral strength, Latina/o policy preferences – especially on immigration – took center stage on the national agenda by January 2013.[45] Moreover, in states such as Colorado and Florida, the surge of Latina and Latino voters also gave new strength to an elected base of Latina/o elites within the state and placed Latina/o political interests on the legislative agenda.

However, the story of Latina/o electoral success is not uniform; that is, Latina/o voting power rested significantly on the mobilization and distinct voting preferences of Latinas, as demonstrated in the emerging gender gap in the elections. That is, Latina voters were disproportionately driving the increased turnout of Latina/o voters as well as the increased support for President Obama. Preferences among Latinas for humane, comprehensive immigration reform and their negative evaluation of Republicans on this issue helped explain the increased support for the President.

Finally, the story of Latina/o electoral success is also a story about targeted outreach and mobilization in the specific states of Colorado, Florida, New Mexico, and Nevada. While efforts aimed at expanding Latina/o electoral presence in those states existed long before 2012 and were strongly present in 2008, they bore new fruit in 2012, making the Latina/o vote nationally decisive for the first time in U.S. history.

---

[45] Comprehensive immigration reform became a recurring feature in the Election Night speech of President Obama, in his inauguration speech in January, and in the first State of the Union address to Congress that same month. The president also convened multiple working groups on various aspects of immigration reform in the months after the election and delivered a rousing speech outlining his plan for immigration reform in late January. Moreover, by early February 2013, both the president and a bipartisan group of senators had outlined plans for comprehensive immigration reform legislation they planned to introduce in that session of Congress. Finally, immigration reform gained so much momentum that it even featured prominently in the Republican rebuttal to the State of the Union address delivered by Senator Marco Rubio of Florida.

6 African-American Women and Electoral Politics

Translating Voting Power into Officeholding

Evidence of dynamic shifts in the American electorate evolved as the biggest story of the 2012 presidential election. The electoral power of women, African Americans, Latinos, and Asian Americans showed the political parties that these groups are considerable forces in American politics today and are likely to shape the future of elections. According to the U.S. Census, minority groups and women of color in particular generated record highs in voter turnout in 2012. African Americans increased their voter turnout rates more than any other group among the electorate, surpassing white voters for the first time. African-American women's high vote share largely accounted for voter turnout among African Americans. Latinos and Asian Americans also increased their voter turnout rates, while whites were the only group to experience a decrease in voter turnout.[1] The historic turnout rates prompted many to scramble for explanations to account for these changes in the electorate.

Explanations surfaced to help account for these historic dynamics among each group. Some point to the growing size of the voting-age population among minority groups and particularly among Latinos. Others explain the high voter turnout among African Americans as a response to mobilizations against voter suppression tactics in urban areas reminiscent of historic attacks on the black vote. Women's strong voter turnout coupled with women's strong support for the Democratic candidate is explained in part by the volatile, ill-conceived comments from conservative politicians hostile toward women's issues overall and reproductive rights in particular. Regardless of whether these explanations fully account for these shifts, it is without question that this presidential

---

[1] U.S. Census. 2013. The Diversifying Electorate-Voting Rates by Race and Hispanic Origin in 2012 (and Other Recent Elections.).

election, even more than the historic election of 2008, produced the most diverse electorate in the nation's history. The 2012 election also signaled the long-term electoral power of voters beyond traditional white men voters, who have long determined the outcomes of presidential elections.

President Obama benefitted from the makeup of this electorate, over-whelmingly receiving the support of minorities and women, and this elec-toral coalition is indeed credited with his reelection. Minority voters sup-ported Obama with 80 percent of their votes.[2] The power of minority voters in this election cycle forecasts the changes in the American eli-gible voting population, which by 2050 will represent a majority of the nation's population and the majority of voters in the nation's elections.[3] In 2012, every minority group expanded its electoral power by increas-ing its turnout by as much as a 4.9 percent between 2004 and 2012. In addition to minority groups, women are very much a key component of the coalition that pushed the President to victory. At the nexus of those described as minorities and women are women of color, who were par-ticularly strong in their support of the president and proved exceedingly important as the threads weaving together the tapestry of the new Amer-ican electorate.

African-American women first showed their political heft as voters in 2008 when they made history in that election cycle with the highest voter turnout rate among all groups of eligible voters.[4] The excitement surrounding the campaign of the nation's first black presidential nomi-nee on a major ticket is credited with galvanizing black women's mobi-lization. Although their voter turnout was expected to be significantly lower in 2012, African-American women actually maintained their level of mobilization in the 2012 election with high voter turnout rates. They also led all other groups in their support of President Obama just as they did in 2008.

While African-American women played a pivotal role in President Obama's victories in both 2008 and 2012, the questions now turn to the extent to which they are able to translate their support for win-ning candidates into policy positions that improve the lives of women and girls of color. It is also an open question whether African-American

[2] Pew Research Center. 2012. *Changing Face of America Helps Assure Obama Victory.* Washing-ton, DC: Pew Research Center.

[3] Paul Taylor and D'Vera Cohn. 2012. *A Milestone En Route to a Majority Minority Nation.* Pew Research Center.

[4] Mark Hugo Lopez and Paul Taylor. 2009. *Dissecting the 2008 Electorate: Most Diverse in U.S. History.* Washington, DC: Pew Research Center.

women can translate their political power as voters into political strength as candidates for elected office at all levels of government. In this chapter, I explore African-American women's political participation in electoral politics as candidates and their potential to move through the political pipeline to higher offices. As black women increase their power as voters, are they also increasing their numbers as elected representatives?

   Although African-American women are politically active as voters, there is still a gap between their political participation as voters and their participation as candidates. We still have far to go to achieve racial and gender parity in American politics. In this chapter, I focus on African-American women in politics, noting that both structural barriers and Americans' race and gender preferences still affect the success of women of color in securing political office. I chart how African-American women are faring in electoral politics at the national, state, and local levels, illustrating the considerable challenges they continue to face. Traditional measures and indicators of political participation suggest that African-American women would be among the least likely to participate in politics, yet they are heavily engaged in a range of political activities. After identifying what I term the *paradox of participation*, I trace African-American women's participation in formal electoral politics from Shirley Chisholm's 1972 presidential campaign to the present day. African-American women are still experiencing a number of firsts in electoral politics, which signifies that their journey from the shadows to the spotlight in American politics is not yet complete. In response to the many barriers they encounter, African-American women are organizing and exploring new strategies to ensure their future leadership in American politics. By focusing on their experiences, we can examine the extent of America's progress toward political inclusiveness along both race and gender lines and toward a society in which race and gender are less significant as determinants of electoral success.

AFRICAN-AMERICAN WOMEN AND THE PARADOX OF PARTICIPATION

African-American women have consistently participated in American politics despite formidable barriers to their participation in formal electoral roles as voters and candidates. At its inception in 1787, the U.S. Constitution limited the citizenship rights of African Americans, both women and men, regarding each one as only three-fifths of a person. Later, as Mamie Locke argues, African-American women would move

from three-fifths of a person under the Constitution to total exclusion
from constitutional protections with the passage of the Fifteenth Amendment in 1870, which extended the right to vote to African-American men
only.[5] When women earned the right to vote in 1920 with the passage of
the Nineteenth Amendment, large numbers of African-American women
remained restricted from the franchise through the cultural norms of
the Jim Crow South. African Americans were disenfranchised through
literacy tests, poll taxes, grandfather clauses, and all-white primaries. It
was not until the passage of the Voting Rights Act of 1965 that African-
American women secured the right to freely practice the franchise.

The impact of the Voting Rights Act was keenly apparent in the states
of the Deep South. African-American voter registration in Mississippi, for
example, increased from 6.7 percent in 1964 to 64 percent in 1980.[6]
The Voting Rights Act of 1965 was arguably the single most important
piece of legislation in securing the franchise for African-American voters and realizing political empowerment. The rapid growth in the numbers of African-American elected officials is further evidence of the Act's
impact. At the time the Voting Rights Act passed, fewer than 500 African-
American elected officials held office nationwide. Today, the number of
African-American elected officials has grown to more than 9,000.[7]

Studies of American politics have defined political participation narrowly in terms of electoral participation. As Cathy Cohen argues, such a
limited definition of political participation has hindered the development
of research on African-American women's political activism because their
political participation tends to extend beyond electoral politics to community organizing and civic engagement.[8] Because African-American
women were excluded from participation in formal politics until the passage of the Voting Rights Act of 1965, first by the condition of their
enslavement and then by equally oppressive systems of exclusion, their

[5] Mamie Locke. 1997. From Three Fifths to Zero. In *Women Transforming Politics*, ed. Cathy
Cohen, Kathleen B. Jones, and Joan Tronto. New York: New York University Press, 377–
386.

[6] Frank R. Parker. 1990. *Black Votes: Count Political Empowerment in Mississippi after 1965*.
Chapel Hill: University of North Carolina Press.

[7] Linda F. Williams. 2001. The Civil Rights-Black Power Legacy: Black Women Elected
Officials at the Local, State, and National Levels. In *Sisters in the Struggle: African Ameri-
can Women in the Civil Rights-Black Power Movement*, ed. Bettye Collier-Thomas and V. P.
Franklin. New York: New York University Press, 306–332.

[8] Cathy J. Cohen. 2003. A Portrait of Continuing Marginality: The Study of Women of
Color in American Politics. In *Women and American Politics: New Questions, New Directions*,
ed. Susan J. Carroll. New York: Oxford University Press, 190–213.

nontraditional political activism developed outside the electoral system and was informed by their political, economic, and social conditions.[9]

Defining political participation beyond the narrow framework of voting and holding elected office allows us to see the consistent levels of African-American women's political participation across history. By asking new questions and examining the nontraditional spaces of women's activism, such as churches, private women's clubs, and volunteer organizations, feminist historians have uncovered countless activities of women of color involved in social movements. African-American women have been central to every effort toward greater political empowerment for both African Americans and women. As the historian Paula Giddings attests, African-American women were the linchpin in struggles against racism and sexism. They understood that the fates of women's rights and black rights were inextricably linked and that one would be meaningless without the other.[10]

In spite of this rich legacy of activism, African-American women's political participation represents a puzzle of sorts. African-American women appear to be overrepresented in elective office while simultaneously holding the characteristics that would make them least likely to be politically engaged. African-American women account for a greater proportion of black elected officials than white women do of white elected officials.[11] In the 113th Congress (2013–2014), 30 percent of African Americans in the House are women, compared with only 18 percent of all members of the House who were women. Further, as Figure 6.1 illustrates, since the early 1990s, there has been a steady increase in the number of African-American women elected officials. The steady increase in African-American women reverses the trends of the 1970s immediately following the passage of the Voting Rights Act, when 82 percent of the growth in black elected officials was attributed to African-American men.[12]

Scholars who study the intersection of race and gender argue that African-American women suffer from a "double disadvantage" in

---

[9] See Paula Giddings. 1984. When and Where I Enter: The Impact of Black Women on Race and Sex in America. New York: Bantam Books; Darlene Clark Hine and Kathleen Thompson. 1998. A Shining Thread of Hope: The History of Black Women in America. New York: Broadway Books; Dorothy Sterling. 1997. We Are Your Sisters: Black Women in the Nineteenth Century. New York: W. W. Norton.

[10] Giddings, 1984.

[11] Williams, 2001.

[12] David A. Bositis. 2001. *Black Elected Officials: A Statistical Summary 2001*. Washington, DC: Joint Center for Political and Economic Studies.

Figure 6.1: The number of African-American women elected officials has increased in recent elections while the number of African-American men elected to office has leveled off.

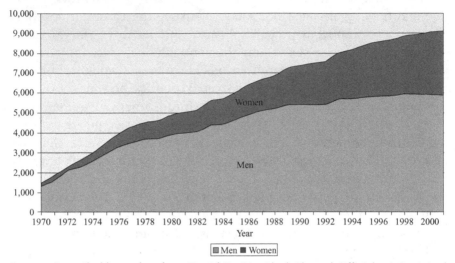

Source: Compiled by author from David Bositis, *Black Elected Officials: A Statistical Summary*, Washington, D.C.: Joint Center for Political and Economic Studies, 2001.

politics, in that they are forced to overcome the ills of both sexism and racism.[13] Darcy and Hadley, however, conclude that African-American women defied expectations, proving more politically ambitious than their white counterparts and enjoying greater success in election to mayoral, state legislative, and congressional office in comparison with white women throughout the 1970s and 1980s. These authors link the puzzle of African-American women's achievement to their activism in the civil rights movement and the skills developed during the movement, which African-American women quickly translated into formal politics once passage of the Voting Rights Act opened opportunities.[14]

Studies of political participation have consistently concluded that the affluent and the educated are more likely to participate in politics at higher rates.[15] However, for African-American women, the usual

[13] See Robert Darcy and Charles Hadley. 1988. Black Women in Politics: The Puzzle of Success. *Social Science Quarterly* 77: 888–898; Gary Moncrief, Joel Thompson, and Robert Schuhmann. 1991. Gender, Race and the Double Disadvantage Hypothesis. *Social Science Journal* 28: 481–487.

[14] Darcy and Hadley, 1988.

[15] See Andrea Y. Simpson. 1999. *Taking Over or Taking a Back Seat? Political Activism of African American Women.* Paper delivered at the annual meeting of the American Political Science

determinants of political participation – education and income – are not strong predictors of their participation.[16] African-American women's high level of officeholding contrasts with their material conditions, which suggest that they would be far less politically active. As of the 2000 U.S. Census, 43 percent of black families were headed by a single mother, and the poverty rate among African-American women was more than twice that of non–Hispanic white women.[17] Regardless of their socioeconomic status, African-American women are far more likely than African-American men to engage in both traditional forms of political participation (including voting and holding office) and nontraditional forms of participation (such as belonging to organizations and clubs, attending church, and talking to people about politics). For example, the proportion of voters who were African American increased from 11 percent in 2004 to 13 percent in 2008 and 2012. In 2012, African-American women were 61.5 percent of the black vote.[18] Social scientists do not fully understand these inconsistencies in African-American women's political participation.[19] The 2012 elections present an opportunity to better understand their political participation by focusing on their experiences as candidates for elected office.

AFRICAN-AMERICAN WOMEN AND THE PRESIDENCY

African-American women have a long-established history of seeking political inclusion via the highest office in the land, the presidency. Across history, at least six African-American women have had their names on the general election ballot for the presidency, including Cynthia McKinney, who ran in 2008 representing the Green Party (see Table 6.1).[20] As was the case with McKinney in 2008, most of these candidates represented fringe or third parties. Two African-American women have run

---

Association, Atlanta, GA, September 1–5. For an extensive discussion of political participation, see Sidney Verba, Kay Lehman Scholzman, and Henry E. Brady. 1995. *Voice and Equality: Civic Volunteerism in American Politics*. Cambridge, MA: Harvard University Press.

[16] Sandra Baxter and Marjorie Lansing. 1980. *Women and Politics: The Invisible Majority*. Ann Arbor: University of Michigan Press.

[17] U.S. Bureau of the Census. 2003. U.S. Census. *The Black Population in the United States*. http://www.census.gov/prod/2003pubs/p20-541.pdf. Accessed September 13, 2013.

[18] David A. Bositis. 2012. *Blacks and the 2012 Elections: A Preliminary Analysis*. Washington, DC: Joint Center for Political and Economic Studies.

[19] Simpson, 1999.

[20] Jo Freeman. *The Women Who Ran for President*. http://jofreeman.com. Accessed January 15, 2009.

TABLE 6.1: Six African-American women have appeared on general election ballots for president

Candidate	Political Party	Year
Charlene Mitchell	Communist Party	1968
Lenora Fulani	New Alliance Party	1988 and 1992
Margaret Wright	People's Party	1976
Isabel Masters	Looking Back Party	1992 and 1996
Monica Morehead	Workers World Party	1996 and 2000
Cynthia McKinney	Green Party	2008

Source: Compiled by author using data from http://www.jofreeman.com.

for the presidency seeking to represent the Democratic Party. Shirley Chisholm ran in 1972, and more than thirty years later, Carol Moseley Braun ran in 2004. Both Chisholm and Braun's candidacies were declared nonviable from the onset, but in both of these cases, these women offered serious challenges to the status quo that suggests that presidential politics is not the domain of women of color. In this section, I highlight the candidacies of Chisholm, Braun, and McKinney, showing the differences among their campaigns and the challenges that mark women of color's ascension to the highest political office.

In 1972, Congresswoman Shirley Chisholm broke barriers as the first African-American woman to make a serious bid for the presidency.[21] Chisholm was well positioned to run for president, with political experience at the community, state, and national levels. She served in the New York General Assembly before becoming the first African-American woman elected to Congress. As the lone African-American woman in Congress, she joined her twelve African-American male colleagues in founding the Congressional Black Caucus (CBC).[22]

After two terms in the House of Representatives, Chisholm decided to run for president. Her run came at a point when the civil rights leadership was calling for greater political engagement and the women's movement

[21] Although Shirley Chisholm's 1972 run for the White House is most often cited, there is a long legacy of African Americans running for the presidency, largely as third-party candidates. For a full discussion, see Hanes Walton Jr. 1994. Black Female Presidential Candidates: Bass, Mitchell, Chisholm, Wright, Reid, Davis, and Fulani. In *Black Politics and Black Political Behavior: A Linkage Analysis,* ed. Hanes Walton Jr. Westport, CT: Praeger, 251–276.

[22] Katherine Tate. 2003. Black Faces in the Mirror: African Americans and Their Representatives in the U.S. Congress. Princeton, NJ: Princeton University Press.

was at its height. In running for president, Chisholm hoped to bring the concerns of these communities to the forefront of national politics. She spoke out for the rights of African Americans, women, and gays. She was quickly dismissed, perceived as not a serious candidate.

Chisholm faced a 1970s America that was just becoming accustomed to women in the workforce and in politics. She challenged notions of women's proper place. On the campaign trail, she routinely encountered hecklers who were happy to tell her the proper place for a woman. She told the story of a man at a campaign stop who questioned whether she had "cleaned her house" and "cared for her husband" before coming there.[23] Chisholm often faced such blatant sexism and, in other encounters, racism in her campaign, but she continued to press toward the Democratic National Convention.

Although Chisholm fashioned herself as both the "black candidate" and the "woman candidate," she found herself shunned by black leaders in both Congress and the feminist community. Far from supporting her, members of the CBC, an organization she had helped found, charged that her run was detrimental to the black community, dividing it along gender lines at a time when the black community could not afford such divisive politics. Chisholm, a founder of the National Organization for Women (NOW), was dealt an equally devastating blow when prominent feminists such as the cofounder of NOW, Gloria Steinem, and fellow U.S. Congresswoman Bella Abzug decided not to endorse her candidacy publicly. Instead, they opted to protect their political leverage by supporting Senator George McGovern, who was considered at that time the more viable candidate of the Democratic contenders and the candidate most capable of defeating then-President Nixon.[24]

Deserted by both the leaders of the CBC and the feminist community, Chisholm survived the primaries and remained a candidate at the outset of the Democratic National Convention. She received 151 delegate votes on the first ballot, far short of the roughly 2,000 needed to secure the nomination. In the end, Chisholm acknowledged that her bid for the White House was less about winning and more about demanding full inclusion for African Americans and women. By waging a national presidential campaign, her candidacy had shown the world what was possible

---

[23] Shirley Chisholm. 1973. *The Good Fight*. New York: Harper & Row.
[24] For a more elaborate discussion of Chisholm's supporters and detractors during the 1972 presidential campaign, view *Chisholm '72 Unbought and Unbossed*, a documentary by the filmmaker Shola Lynch.

for women and men of color with increased access to political empowerment in a more democratized America. Indeed, Chisholm blazed the trail
that would eventually lead to the election of Barack Obama.

More than three decades later, there was no doubt that Carol Moseley
Braun benefited from Chisholm's pioneering candidacy. The differences
between the two experiences signify some progress for African-American
women as high-profile candidates, even as they bring to light enduring problems African-American women face in achieving greater political
empowerment.

Carol Moseley Braun's treatment in the 2004 election cycle symbolizes some progress from the blatant, overt sexism and racism that Shirley
Chisholm encountered in 1972. Moseley Braun experienced more sub-
versive, structurally embedded sexism and racism, which are more difficult to recognize. Her experiences reflect the extent to which the office of
the president is consistently associated with white men, a pattern Georgia Duerst-Lahti documents in Chapter 1 of this volume. There is an
understanding that the president of the United States will be a man and
white, and this sentiment has dominated thinking about the presidency.[25]
Because Moseley Braun was neither a man nor white, she struggled con-
stantly to convince the public that her candidacy was, in fact, viable. The
doubts surrounding the feasibility of her candidacy affected all aspects of
her campaign, but they were most devastating to her fund-raising efforts.
The negligible and trivializing media coverage she received reinforced
doubts and further stymied her campaign. Such struggles are reflective
of the remaining institutional racism and sexism that continue to impede
qualified candidates who differ from societal expectations about who
should serve as president. Moseley Braun campaigned promising to "take
the 'men only' sign off the White House door," but this seemed to be a
challenge America was not ready to accept.

By objective measures, Moseley Braun was well positioned to run for
the presidency. Once questioned as to why she was running, Moseley
Braun quickly responded, "Why not?" adding, "If I were not a woman – if
I were a guy – with my credentials and my experience and what I bring to
the table, there would be no reason why I wouldn't think about running
for president."[26] In the field of Democratic contenders, Moseley Braun's

[25] Georgia Duerst-Lahti and Rita Mae Kelly, eds. 1995. *Gender Power, Leadership, and Gover-
nance.* Ann Arbor: University of Michigan Press.
[26] Monica Davey. December 18, 2003. In Seeking Presidency, Braun Could Win Back
Reputation. *New York Times.*

political record was among the most stellar. She was the only candidate to have experience at the local, state, national, and international levels of government.

Despite the energetic responses Moseley Braun drew from crowds at campaign stops, political pundits remained dismissive of her campaign. According to her, this was nothing new, "Nobody ever expected me to get elected to anything. For one thing, I'm black, I'm a woman and I'm out of the working class. So the notion that someone from my background would have anything to say about the leadership of this country is challenging to some."[27] Like Shirley Chisholm, she also faced charges of running a purely symbolic campaign to establish that women are capable of running for the country's top executive office.

Fund-raising plagued Moseley Braun's campaign from the onset, and her fund-raising efforts continuously lagged behind those of most other candidates, even after she gained impressive endorsements from the National Women's Political Caucus (NWPC) and NOW, two of the leading feminist organizations. Notable white feminists, including the legendary Gloria Steinem and Marie Wilson, director of the White House Project, a nonprofit organization dedicated to getting a woman into the White House, publicly supported the campaign. Black women's organizations, including the National Political Congress of Black Women, invested in Moseley Braun's campaign, and she enjoyed public endorsements from notable legendary African-American women from the late Coretta Scott King to the late Dr. Dorothy Height, president emerita of the National Council of Negro Women. Receiving such ardent support from the women's community and black women's organizations, Braun's candidacy represented progress over the struggles faced by Shirley Chisholm's campaign.

Garnering media attention proved to be an equally challenging problem for Moseley Braun's campaign, creating a circular effect; without media visibility, her ability to raise funds was limited, and with minimal funding, her campaign drew less media attention. She had extreme difficulty getting her message to the voters. When she received any coverage at all, it most often referred to her as "improbable," "nonviable," a "long-shot" candidate, or at worst an "also-ran."

Whatever its challenges, Moseley Braun's campaign was certainly not confronted with the overt sexism and racism that Chisholm had

[27] Nedra Pickler. May 2, 2003. Washington Today: Braun Appears with the Presidential Candidates, but Isn't Running Like One. Associated Press State and Local Wire.

experienced. Instead, a much more subtle, indirect brand of racism and sexism plagued her campaign, characterized by the outright dismissal of her candidacy as a serious bid for the White House. Consistent slights affected all facets of her campaign. The failure to garner media attention, along with fund-raising challenges, forced Carol Moseley Braun to formally pull out of the race in January 2004, even before the first primary.

David Bositis of the Joint Center for Political and Economic Studies may have best captured her predicament when he argued, "Part of Carol Moseley Braun's problem is that she is a black woman." Bositis observed that Democratic voters were looking for a candidate who could beat George H. W. Bush, and unfortunately, she was not perceived as a candidate who could do that.[28] Further, the political scientist Paula McClain argues that Moseley Braun was disadvantaged from the onset in crafting a name for herself in this campaign, given the Democratic Party leadership's preference that candidates forgo more leftist politics. As she argues, Moseley Braun's identity as an African-American woman positioned her clearly as a "left-of-center candidate" and subsequently constrained her ability to establish an alternative identity as a candidate in the minds of voters.[29]

The 2008 presidential election was considered by all accounts one of the most memorable presidential contests in modern history. That election is certainly remembered for electing the first African-American man, Senator Barack Obama, to the presidency. It will also be historicized for Senator Hillary Clinton's remarkable run, during which she won more than 18 million votes. Moreover, that presidential election cycle is noted for giving rise to the vice presidential candidacy of Alaska Governor Sarah Palin, only the second woman to be named to a major party's presidential ticket. Buried among all the historic firsts of this election cycle, few noted that the 2008 presidential election cycle also marked the first time two women of color – an African American and a Latina – ran on a political party's ticket as the presidential and vice presidential candidates.

Former Congresswoman Cynthia McKinney, an African American, was tapped as the Green Party's presidential candidate. McKinney

[28] Adam Reilly. December 12–18, 2003. Hitting with Her Best Shot. *Portland Phoenix.* http://www.portlandphoenix.com/features/other_stories/multi1/documents/03404038. asp. Accessed September 13, 2005.

[29] Paula McClain. 2004. *Gender and Black Presidential Politics: From Chisholm to Moseley Braun Revisited.* Comments made at Roundtable on Black and Presidential Politics, American Political Science Association meeting, September 1–5, Chicago.

selected Rosa Clemente, a Latina, New York–based hip-hop community activist, as her vice presidential running mate. McKinney and Clemente appeared on the ballot in thirty-one states and the District of Columbia, ultimately receiving 157,759 votes to finish sixth among all tickets. During their campaign, they raised a range of social justice–based issues, including an end to racial disparities in health, housing, education, and incarceration. They supported a right-of-return policy for New Orleans residents displaced by Hurricane Katrina; greater access to reproductive choice, including the right to bear children for poor women and women of color; and an end to Social Security policies that disproportionately harm women. Their platform pushed beyond the Green Party's more familiar stances on the environment to include a broad, progressive social justice–based platform.

Like most third-party candidates, McKinney and Clemente struggled to gain attention from media outlets and raise critical campaign dollars to execute a robust campaign. With so much attention focused on the major-party candidates, the 2008 election cycle was especially hard for third-party candidates. As a progressive, McKinney was particularly pressed to articulate a rationale for posing even the potential of a threat to Obama's campaign success. McKinney and her supporters were challenged to make an argument for supporting their ticket in the face of Obama's historic run. The Green Party advocated a strategy of supporting Obama in critical states, even campaigning on his behalf, but in Democratic Party strongholds or states in which polls showed Obama well ahead of McCain (such as California, Illinois, and New Jersey), Green Party activists urged voters to open the dialogue to the Green Party by supporting their candidates. With a dismal showing in the polls, the Green Party failed to obtain the 5 percent of the national vote that would make it eligible to obtain federal matching funds for the 2012 election.

Although McKinney is a former member of the Democratic Party and a six-term congresswoman (serving from 1993 to 2003 and again from 2005 to 2007), by most all accounts, McKinney's run for the presidency was a long shot. Not only her third-party candidate status but also her own reputation in politics placed her outside the mainstream. McKinney has long articulated a politics to the left of most members of the Democratic Party. She garnered national attention for her outspoken support of Palestine and for one of her final acts as a member of Congress – the filing of impeachment charges against President Bush on the grounds that he misled the American people in going to war in Iraq. Many argue that her extreme leftist politics and brazen approach accounted for the loss of her congressional seat in 2003.[30] After an altercation with a congressional security guard who failed to recognize her as a member of Congress and attempted to detain her, McKinney's reputation was further tarnished.

McKinney's fate was sealed in many ways by running as a third-party candidate in a two-party electoral system. Yet even in coverage of those who "also ran" during the 2008 presidential race, McKinney hardly garnered a mention from most press outlets, particularly in comparison to Ralph Nader, who ran as an independent, or even the former congressman Bob Barr, who ran on the Libertarian Party ticket during the 2008 election. Green Party activists launched a strong critique of mainstream and even progressive media outlets for their refusal to recognize the historic nature of the McKinney-Clemente ticket, even in the midst of an election cycle marked by a continuous nod to history.

McKinney's experiences in 2008 were somewhat reminiscent of those of Chisholm and Braun, who were treated as nonviable candidates, thus diminishing their chances of reaching the American people. Although the 2008 presidential election is heralded for all the ways it disrupted the status quo in politics, on some level, that election cycle continued the legacies of past elections by reaffirming the belief that African-American women are not appropriate, viable contenders for the presidency.

AFRICAN-AMERICAN WOMEN AND ELECTED OFFICE: ON THE PATH TO HIGHER OFFICE?

The presidential candidacies of Chisholm, Moseley Braun, McKinney, and the other African-American women who have sought the presidency across history compel us to ask whether there are African-American women poised to run for the presidency in future elections. Women and politics scholars and activists discuss increasing the numbers of women elected to public office at lower levels as the first step toward moving women into higher offices.[31] Feeding the political pipeline has become a critical strategy in preparing women to successfully seek the highest offices, including the presidency. Are African-American women moving through that pipeline? Are they securing offices at the local, state, and national levels in preparation for the highest political offices? Are they

---

[30] See Wendy Smooth. 2005. African American Women in Electoral Politics: Journeying from the Shadows to the Spotlight. In *Gender and Elections*, ed. Susan J. Carroll and Richard L. Fox. New York: Cambridge University Press, 117–142.

[31] For a full discussion on getting women into the political pipeline, see Jennifer Lawless and Richard L. Fox. 2005. *It Takes a Candidate*. New York: Cambridge University Press.

poised to run for the presidency in future elections? In light of the contributions of African-American women in 2012 to making up the new American electorate, are they also contributing to diversifying elected offices from national to local levels? Are they seeking political office in step with their participation as voters?

To date, African-American women's engagement in electoral politics as a means of securing greater political empowerment and placing their concerns on the political agenda has produced mixed results. On the one hand, they are gaining increased access to political offices, often outpacing African-American men in winning elections. On the other hand, they continue to face considerable obstacles to securing high-profile offices at both the state and the national levels.

AFRICAN-AMERICAN WOMEN IN STATE AND LOCAL POLITICS

Of the more than 3,000 African-American women elected officials, most are elected to sub–state-level offices, such as regional offices, county boards, city councils, judicial offices, and local school boards. African-American women have gained increasing access to leadership positions at the local level. In 2008, forty-eight African-American mayors led cities with populations of 50,000 or more, and twelve of those were women. At that time, three African-American women – Shelia Dixon (Baltimore), Shirley Franklin (Atlanta), and Yvonne Johnson (Greensboro, North Carolina) led large cities with populations of more than 200,000. As of 2013, Stephanie Rawlings-Blake of Baltimore is the only African-American woman leading a city of more than 100,000. As of 2010, only six African-American women were mayors cities with a population of more than 50,000 (see Table 6.2). Although African-American women have held these significant leadership posts, few scholars have devoted attention to women of color in sub–state-level offices, largely because variations among localities make comparisons difficult.

As African-American women move beyond the local level, they face greater challenges in winning office. In many ways, statewide offices are more difficult for African-American candidates to secure, especially for African-American women. No state has ever elected an African-American woman as governor, and only four African-American women currently hold statewide offices. Democrat Denise Nappier of Connecticut made history in 1998 as the first African-American woman elected as state treasurer, and in 2013, she continues to serve in that capacity. Sandra Kennedy was elected in 2008 to serve as corporation commissioner in

TABLE 6.2: Six African-American women were mayors of cities with populations of more than 50,000 in 2012

Mayor	City	Population
Stephanie Rawlings-Blake	Baltimore, Maryland	651,154
Shirley Gibson	Miami Gardens, Florida	105,414
Dana Redd	Camden, New Jersey	79,904
Brenda L. Lawrence	Southfield, Michigan	78,296
Patricia A. Vance	Evanston Township, Illinois	74,239
Terry Bellamy	Ashville, North Carolina	68,889

Source: Data provided by David Bositis of the Joint Center for Political and Economic Studies (http://www.jointcenter.org).

Arizona and continues to hold that post. In 2011, Jennifer Carroll, Lieutenant Governor of Florida, became the first woman elected to that office and the first African-American elected to a statewide office in the state. She continues to serve in that position. Elected in 2012, Kamala Harris, who was elected Attorney General, became the first African-American woman to serve in statewide office in California.[32]

In running for statewide offices, African-American candidates do not have the benefit of African-American majority electorates, as they often do when they run in smaller districts. As a result, they must depend on the support of white majorities for election. Because African Americans are generally significantly more supportive of African-American candidates than whites are, attracting white voters is a significant challenge. African-American candidates, who must depend on racially tolerant whites to win,[33] face the dual challenge of offering strong crossover appeal for white voters while maintaining a connection to communities of color to ensure their high voter turnout.

In state legislatures, African-American women are steadily increasing their numbers, yet their gains still appear minuscule, especially relative to the number of available legislative seats. As of 2013, there were 7,382 state legislators, of whom only 365 were women of color. African-American women led women of color in holding state legislative seats

[32] Center for American Women and Politics. 2013. *Fact Sheet. Women of Color in Elective Office 2013.* http://www.cawp.rutgers.edu/fast_facts/levels_of_office/documents/color.pdf. Accessed January 2013.
[33] See Lee Sigelman and Susan Welch. 1984. Race, Gender, and Opinion toward Black and Female Candidates. *Public Opinion Quarterly* 48: 467–75; Ruth Ann Strickland and Marcia Lynn Whicker. 1992. Comparing the Wilder and Gantt Campaigns: A Model of Black Candidate Success in Statewide Elections. *PS: Political Science and Politics* 25: 204–212.

with 241 (236 D; 4 R; 1 NP), followed by 79 (70 D; 9 R) Latinas, 32
(26 D; 6 R)Asian American–Pacific Islander women, and 13 (11 D; 2 R)
Native American women.[34] Although the numbers of women of color
in state legislatures remain small, they have increased steadily, while
the overall numbers of women in state legislatures, as reported in Kira
Sanbonmatsu's Chapter 10 in this volume, seems to have reached a
plateau. In 1998, for example, only 168 African-American women served
as state legislators, and today their numbers have increased by seventy-
three.[35] Similar trends hold for Asian American–Pacific Islander, Latina,
and Native American women.

African-American women's influence in state legislatures is concentrated in a limited number of states (see Table 6.3). Forty-four state legislatures have African-American women currently serving. Georgia leads
the states, with twenty-six African-American women serving in its legislature, followed by Maryland (twenty), Illinois (fourteen), and Mississippi
(thirteen).[36] Overall, women have traditionally fared poorly in Southern and border-state legislatures, yet the trend is different for African-
American women, who have experienced some of their greatest successes
in these states. This is largely a result of the significant concentrations of
African-American voters in these states.

AFRICAN-AMERICAN WOMEN IN CONGRESSIONAL POLITICS

When Congress convened its 113th session in January of 2013, it was
the most diverse congress in the history of the body in terms of gender, ethnicity, race, religion, and sexual orientation. This diversity is especially evident within the Democratic Party Caucus, which is likely to spur
more robust debate on the issues before the body. House Representative
Donna Edwards of Maryland contends that the diversity of the Democratic Caucus is more representative of the American electorate. According to Edwards:

> Come January, women and minorities for the first time in U.S. history
> will hold a majority of the party's House seats, while Republicans will

[34] Center for American Women and Politics. 2013. Fact Sheet. Women of Color in Elective
Office 2013.
[35] See Center for American Women and Politics. Women of Color in Elected Office
Fact Sheets for 1998 and 2013. http://www.cawp.rutgers.edu/fast_facts/levels_of_office/
documents/color.pdf. Accessed July 31, 2013.
[36] See Center for American Women and Politics. African American Women in Electoral
Politics. http://www.cawp.rutgers.edu/fast_facts/levels_of_office/documents/color.pdf.

TABLE 6.3: The proportion of African-American women among state legislators varies across the states

	No African-American Women in State Legislature	0.1–4% African-American Women in State Legislature	4% African-American Women in State Legislature
States with African American population of less than 5%	Washington Alaska Hawaii South Dakota Main North Dakota Utah Vermont Montana	Minnesota Nebraska Arizona Colorado West Virginia Iowa New Mexico Oregon New Hampshire Wyoming Idaho	
States with African American population of 5–15%	Kentucky	Arkansas Michigan Pennsylvania Connecticut Indiana Nevada Oklahoma Massachusetts Rhode Island California Kansas	New Jersey Ohio Texas Missouri
States with African American population of 15.1–20%		Wisconsin	Tennessee Mississippi Louisiana Georgia
States with African American population greater than 20%		South Carolina Delaware	Maryland Alabama North Carolina Virginia New York Florida Illinois

Note: In each cell, states are listed in descending order by African-American population. Georgia has the highest proportion of African-American women in its state legislature (11.4 percent), followed by Maryland (10.1 percent), Mississippi (8.1 percent), and New Jersey (7.5 percent).

Source: Center for American Women and Politics, 2013 Fact Sheets. State percentage of African-American population is drawn from 2010 U.S. Census data.

TABLE 6.4: Fourteen African-American women were serving in the U.S. House of Representatives in 2013

Congresswoman	Party	District	Major City in the District	Year First Elected to Congress
Rep. Karen Bass	D	33rd/37th	Los Angeles, CA	2011
Rep. Joyce Beatty	D	3rd	Columbus, OH	2012
Rep. Corrine Brown	D	3rd	Jacksonville, FL	1992
Rep. Yvette Clark	D	11th	New York, NY	2006
Rep. Donna Edwards	D	4th	Ft. Washington, MD	2008
Rep. Marcia Fudge	D	11th	Cleveland, OH	2008
Rep. Eddie Bernice Johnson	D	30th	Dallas, TX	1992
Rep. Barbara Lee	D	9th	Oakland, CA	1997
Rep. Sheila Jackson Lee	D	18th	Houston, TX	1994
Rep. Gwen Moore	D	4th	Milwaukee, WI	2004
Del. Eleanor Holmes Norton[a]	D	–	Washington, D.C.	1991
Rep. Terri Sewell	D	7th	Birmingham, AL	2010
Rep. Maxine Waters	D	35th	Los Angeles, CA	1990
Rep. Frederica Wilson	D	17th/24th	Miami, FL	2010

[a] Eleanor Holmes Norton is a nonvoting delegate representing the District of Columbia.
Source: Compiled by author from Center for American Women and Politics, 2013 Fact Sheets.

continue to be overwhelmingly white and male. The chamber, already politically polarized, more than ever is going to be demographically polarized, too. One thing that's always been very startling to me is to see that on the floor of the House of Representatives when you look over on one side where the Democrats caucus and you look to the other side and it looks like two different visions of America.[37]

For the 113th Congress, fourteen African-American women members are serving the same as the 112th Congress (see Table 6.4). Although the number of African-American women in Congress goes unchanged, the state of Ohio sent a new African-American woman to congress, Representative Joyce Beatty. For the first time in history, Ohio will be

[37] Timothy Homan. Nov. 8, 2012. White Guys Running the U.S. House Face Diverse Democrats. *Bloomberg Business Week.*

represented by two African Americans, both women, as Beatty joins Representative Marcia Fudge of the Ohio 10th congressional district.

Beatty's campaign was nothing less than strategic taking advantage of a significant change in the political opportunity structure in Ohio following the 2010 redistricting process, which created new congressional districts. Her electoral success was due in part to running for an open seat in which she did not challenge a seated incumbent, a typical path for emergent candidates.

She would not have been able to take full advantage of the changes in the political opportunity structure had she not been a seriously prepared candidate. The level of her preparedness is also typical of many women who enter Congress. Beatty served in the Ohio state legislature for five terms representing the same constituents who elected her to Congress. As an Ohio legislator, she made history as the first woman to serve as the Democratic House leader. Going into the 2012 election, Beatty benefited from far-reaching name recognition in the district. She had a well-established record on the civil rights and equality issues that matter significantly to her constituents.

Running for an open seat and running as an experienced legislator are typical for all women elected to Congress. Beatty's path is also the prototypical route for African-American women elected to Congress. The district in which she ran, the Ohio's 3rd congressional district, is a majority-minority district, newly created following the 2010 redistricting process. Majority-minority districts remain the primary means of electing African Americans to Congress.

Most African-American candidates are still elected from districts in which African Americans make up the majority of eligible voters. Majority-minority districts resulted from provisions in the Voting Rights Act of 1965 and its subsequent extensions, which allowed for the formation of new districts in which African Americans consisted of a plurality or majority of the electorate. In these new districts, African Americans could run for open seats, which not only alleviated the incumbency advantage but also freed them from dependence on white voters. Many scholars concede that historically, it has been nearly impossible for African-American candidates to win in districts without black majorities, as some whites continue to resist voting for African-American candidates.[38]

---

[38] Bernard Grofman and Chandler Davidson, eds. 1992. *Controversies in Minority Voting: The Voting Rights Act*. New York: Cambridge University Press.

The number of African-American women serving in Congress today is largely a result of creating majority-minority districts. Although 1992 was widely proclaimed the "Year of the Woman" in politics, reflecting the phenomenal success of women candidates for Congress, for African-American women, 1992 was also the "Year of Redistricting." A number of open seats were created nationally as a result of redistricting following the 1990 Census, and most were majority-minority districts. African-American women (including Cynthia McKinney) claimed five additional seats in the U.S. House of Representatives in 1992, more than doubling their numbers.[39] Four of the five African-American women won in newly created majority-minority districts. The fifth African-American woman elected in 1992, Eva Clayton of North Carolina, won a special election for a seat that was vacant because of the death of the incumbent, also in a majority-minority district.

While majority-minority districts have helped secure African-American women's place in Congress, these districts have been challenged in the courts as a means of increasing black representation. As a result of a string of cases in the 1990s from Georgia, Louisiana, North Carolina, and Texas, the future of majority-minority districts is now in question. Many scholars insist that African Americans' continued success in winning elective office, particularly congressional seats, is dependent on the preservation of majority-minority districts. Because of the precarious future of such districts, the number of African-American women elected to Congress is likely to grow at a considerably slower pace than it did in the 1990s. To the extent that the number of African-American women does grow in future years, the increase in their numbers will likely come largely at the expense of African-American men who must compete with them for the limited number of seats available in majority-minority districts.[40]

THE FUTURE OF AFRICAN-AMERICAN WOMEN IN POLITICS

African-American female elected officials are enduring symbols of the long fight for political inclusion in U.S. electoral politics. Although legal barriers preventing their participation in politics have been removed,

---

[39] Tate, 2003.

[40] Irwin N. Gertzog. 2002. Women's Changing Pathways to the U.S. House of Representatives: Widows, Elites, and Strategic Politicians. In *Women Transforming Congress*, ed. Cindy Simon Rosenthal. Norman: Oklahoma University Press, 95–118.

African-American women continue to confront considerable barriers when seeking political office. The higher profile the office, the more formidable barriers they face to being considered viable candidates.

In light of the formidable challenges as they seek higher-profile offices, African-American women are not leaving their political futures to chance. They are forming political action committees to address serious barriers to fund-raising. One group, Women Building for the Future (Future PAC), formed in 2002 to capitalize on the growing voting power of African-American women. Future PAC's major objective is to increase the numbers of African-American women elected at every level of government by supporting candidates financially and identifying women to run for office. In describing the purpose of the group, Donna Brazile, a strategist for the Democratic Party, argues that African-American women face three major hurdles in seeking office: achieving name recognition, overcoming the tendency of the "old-boy network" to endorse other men, and garnering financial support. Brazile adds, "Our objective is to try to help women overcome one of the major barriers – financial – which will hopefully break down the other two."[41] Future PAC endorses African-American women who have proven records in their communities and who share the group's views on a range of issues from education to health care.[42]

This type of organizing is essential if African-American women are to continue increasing their representation. Such organizing efforts hold the promise of translating African-American women's high voting rates into increased officeholding. Other national groups, such as the Black Women's Roundtable, established by the National Coalition on Black Civic Participation, are also working to increase political participation by mobilizing African-American organizations, including Greek-letter fraternities and sororities, around voter education and civic empowerment.[43] During the 2012 campaign when efforts to suppress voter participation surfaced in minority communities across the country and particularly in the battleground states Florida, Ohio, Michigan, and Virginia, African-American women organized to protect voter rights and to educate African-American women about their rights as voters. These groups are invested in the important work of empowering citizens, mobilizing voters, and identifying likely candidates. These mobilization efforts

[41] Joyce Jones. January 2004. The Future PAC. *Black Enterprise*.
[42] Robin M. Bennefield. July/August 2004. Women Join Forces to Support Black Female Politicians. *Crisis* (The New) 111: 12.
[43] See the Black Women's Roundtable (BWR), a part of the National Coalition on Black Civic Participation, at http://ncbcp.org/programs/bwr/. Accessed September 10, 2013.

have focused on maintaining and fully realizing the potential of African-American women as voters. The challenge remains to translate African-American women's power as voters into increasing their numbers from the local to the national levels.

The most difficult work for these groups remains transforming American society to fully embrace African-American women as political leaders. This issue must be addressed both inside the African-American community and in the greater American society. The public's willingness to regard these well-prepared women as viable, appropriate political leaders is essential. The political parties, in particular the Democratic Party, which is the party affiliation of most African-American women, must end their practice of assuming that African-American women are left of center by virtue of their intersecting identities as both African Americans and women. Many African-American women elected officials prioritize both women's issues and minority issues and build on their ties to multiple communities. In this way, their intersectional identities represent a strength that results in greater representation across underrepresented groups. Not until such core cultural issues are addressed will we see women of color fully excel in politics with well-qualified women of color successfully moving through the political pipeline to hold elected offices at the local, state, and federal levels.

7 Congressional Elections

Women's Candidacies and the Road to Gender Parity

Recent congressional elections have been turbulent for women candidates. Many analysts viewed the 2012 election as a major achievement for women's progress in politics, as the campaign ended with a record twenty women serving in the U.S. Senate. Headlines such as this one in the *Christian Science Monitor* were common: "Election 2012 results: Women to reach landmark – 20 percent of senators." The new crop of women senators was headlined by Democrat Elizabeth Warren in Massachusetts, who had become a national figure speaking out on the excessive influence of big banks. Warren defeated incumbent Republican Scott Brown, who had defeated another woman, Massachusetts Attorney General Martha Coakley, to win his seat in a 2010 special election. Even Democrat Heidi Heitkamp in North Dakota surprised the political establishment by winning her open-seat contest against Republican Scott Berg. Women's success in running for the U.S. Senate came during an election in which women voters and women's issues were at the heart of the discourse in the presidential race. Ironically, women's greatest gains in the Senate came in an electoral environment in which Democrats were accusing Republicans of engaging in a "war on women" by repeatedly advocating what the Democrats considered to be draconian policies on reproductive rights.

But the historic gains in the Senate in 2012 came on the heels of the 2010 midterm elections in which women candidates for Congress did not fare very well. The 2010 election was the first in two decades in which the number of women in Congress actually decreased. The two elections illustrate quite clearly how the success of women running for Congress is

I would like to thank Hallie Spoor for assistance in data collection

TABLE 7.1: Over time, more Democratic women than Republican women have emerged as House candidates and winners

	1970	1980	1990	1992	2000	2004	2006	2008	2010	2012
General election candidates										
Democratic women	15	27	39	70	80	88	95	95	91	118
Republican women	10	25	30	36	42	53	42	38	47	48
Total women	25	52	69	106	122	141	137	133	138	166
General election winners										
Democratic women	10	11	19	35	41	43	50	58	56	58
Percentage of all Democratic winners	3.9	4.5	7.1	13.6	19.4	21.4	21.5	22.6	29	28.9
Republican women	3	10	9	12	18	23	21	17	17	19
Percentage of all Republican winners	1.7	5.2	5.4	6.8	8.1	9.9	10.4	9.6	7	8.1

Note: Except where noted, entries represent the raw number of women candidates and winners for each year.
Source: Center for American Women and Politics, 2012 Fact Sheets, http://www.cawp .rutgers.edu/fast_facts/index.php.

increasingly tied to the successes of the political parties. More specifically, women do well when the Democrats have a good year, and women fare less well when Republicans make gains. In 2010, the Republicans had a triumphant election, gaining sixty-three seats in the House and six in the U.S. Senate. But the proportion of Republican women candidates remains very low (see Table 7.1). The Republican majority that emerged from the 2010 congressional election also ended the historic Democratic speakership of Nancy Pelosi, the first woman to head one of the major parties in the 220-year history of the Congress.

As these recent elections suggest, women are having some successes in electoral politics, but they continue to face many of the same challenges that have plagued women's candidacies throughout modern U.S. electoral history. This chapter examines the evolution of women's candidacies for Congress and the role gender continues to play in congressional elections. Ultimately, I focus on one fundamental question: Why are there still so few women serving in the House and Senate? In exploring the persistence of gender as a factor in congressional elections, I divide the chapter into three sections. In the first section, I offer a brief historical overview of the role of gender in congressional elections. The second section compares male and female candidates' electoral performance and success in House and Senate races through the 2012 elections. The results of this analysis confirm that, when considered in the aggregate, the electoral playing field has become largely level for women and men. But if that is the case, why are there still so few women in Congress? In the final section of the chapter, I provide some answers, examining the subtler ways that gender continues to affect congressional elections. The combination of gendered geographic trends, women's presence in different types of congressional races, the scarcity of women running as Republicans, and the gender gap in political ambition suggests that gender is playing an important role in congressional elections.

THE HISTORICAL EVOLUTION OF WOMEN'S CANDIDACIES FOR CONGRESS

Throughout the 1990s, women made significant strides competing for and winning seats in the U.S. Congress. The 1992 elections, often referred to as the Year of the Woman, resulted not only in a historic increase in the numbers of women in both the House and the Senate but also in the promise of movement toward some semblance of gender parity in our political institutions (see Table 7.1). After all, in the history of the U.S. Congress, there have been more than 11,700 men but only 297 women. Only forty-four women have ever served in the U.S. Senate, nineteen of whom either were appointed or won special elections.

However, the gains of 1992 were not repeated at a steady pace. Currently, 80 percent of the members of the U.S. Senate and 82 percent of the members of the U.S. House are male. This places the United States roughly ninetieth worldwide in terms of the proportion of women serving in the national legislature, a ranking far behind that of many other democratic governments.[1] Further, the overwhelming majority of women elected to Congress have been white. Of the 78 (out of 435) women elected to the U.S. House in the 2012 election, there are 14 African Americans, 9 Latinas, and 7 Asian Pacific–Pacific Islander Americans. There is one women of color among the twenty women currently serving in the U.S. Senate, Mazie Hirono, a Hawaii Democrat.

The continued dearth of women in Congress suggests that a masculine ethos, ever present across the history of Congress, still permeates the congressional electoral environment. A host of interrelated factors – money, familiarity with power brokers, political experience, and support

[1] Inter-Parliamentary Union. 2013. Women in National Parliaments. http://www.ipu.org/wmn-e/classif.htm. Accessed May 1, 2013.

from the political parties – contribute to a winning campaign. Traditional candidates are members of the political or economic elite. Most emerge from lower-level elected offices or work in their communities, typically in law or business. They tend to receive encouragement to run for office from influential members of the community, party officials, or outgoing incumbents. And these same elites who encourage candidacies also contribute money to campaigns and hold fund-raisers. These norms have been in place for most of the recent history of congressional candidacies and, for obvious reasons, have served men well and women very poorly.

Because they have been excluded from their communities' economic and political elites throughout much of the twentieth century, women often take different paths to Congress. Widows of congressmen who died in office dominated the first wave of successful female candidates. Between 1916 and 1964, twenty-eight of the thirty-two widows nominated to fill their husbands' seats won their elections, for a victory rate of 88 percent. Across the same time period, only 32 of the 199 nonwidows who garnered their parties' nominations were elected (a 14 percent victory rate).[2] Overall, roughly half the women who served in the House during this period were widows. Congressional widows were the one type of woman candidate that was readily acceptable to party leaders at this time.

The 1960s and 1970s marked the emergence of a second type of woman candidate – one who turned her attention from civic volunteerism to politics. A few women involved in grassroots community politics rode their activism to Washington. Notable figures (all Democrats) who pursued this path include Patsy Mink in Hawaii, elected in 1964; Shirley Chisholm in New York, elected in 1968; Bella Abzug in New York, elected in 1970; and Pat Schroeder in Colorado and Barbara Jordan in Texas, both elected in 1972.

We are currently in the third and possibly final stage of the evolution of women's candidacies. The prevailing model of running for Congress is far less rigid. The combination of decreased political party power and growing media influence facilitates the emergence of a more diverse array of candidates competing successfully for their parties' nominations. Converging with this less rigid path is an increase in the number of women who now fit the profile of a "traditional" candidate. Women's presence in fields such as business and law, from which candidates have often emerged, has increased dramatically. Further, the number of women

[2] Irwin Gertzog. 1984. *Congressional Women*. New York: Praeger, 18.

serving in state legislatures, often a springboard to Congress, has roughly tripled since 1975 (although it is important to note that women's presence in the state governments has stalled in recent elections; for more on this, see Kira Sanbonmatsu's Chapter 10 in this volume.) Together, these developments help explain why the eligibility pool of prospective women candidates grew substantially throughout the 1990s.

Despite the growth in the number of eligible women who could run for Congress, the most recent congressional election cycles indicate that women's progress has continued only in fits and starts. The 2010 elections marked the second time since 1990 that women did not increase their presence in the House. In 2012, there were modest gains for women, with net increases of five new House members. In the Senate, the rate of increase had been just as slow until 2012 saw a jump from seventeen to twenty Senators. Perhaps more important, though, 2010 and 2012 saw record numbers of women win major party nominations for the U.S. House of Representatives. Similar patterns exist for U.S. Senate races. A record eighteen women won their parties' U.S. Senate nominations in 2012, surpassing the 2010 record of fifteen candidates. This was after a mere seven women won major party Senate nominations in 2008.

Table 7.1 presents the numbers of women candidates that won their party nominations and ran in House general elections from 1970 through 2012. As mentioned above, the 2012 election did set a record, with 166 women candidates winning their party nominations for House seats. But to put this number into perspective, it is helpful to recognize that roughly 650 male candidates garnered their parties' nominations. It is also important to recognize that the 2012 record was the result of a more than 20 percent increase in the number of Democratic women running for office. Table 7.1 illustrates the divergent paths of the Democratic and Republican parties. The Democrats have been on a slow and steady path, continually increasing the number of women candidates and winners. The Republicans, in contrast, have put forward significantly fewer women over the past two decades, and the percentage of women among House Republicans has not grown since 2000.

Overall, the historical evolution of women's candidacies demonstrates that we are in a period of increasing opportunities for women candidates, yet progress is slow. From this point, we turn our attention to examining the potential challenges facing women candidates, focusing on the question of why there continue to be so few women elected to the U.S. Congress.

MEN AND WOMEN RUNNING FOR CONGRESS: THE GENERAL INDICATORS

In assessing why so few women serve in Congress, most researchers have turned to key election statistics and compared female and male congressional candidates. Looking first at overt voter bias against women candidates, the research is mixed. In a series of experimental studies in which participants are presented with a hypothetical matchup between men and women candidates, researchers have identified bias against women.[3] But studies that focus on actual vote totals fail to uncover evidence of bias.[4] Barbara Burrell, a contributor to this volume, concluded in an earlier study that candidates' sex accounts for less than 1 percent of the variation in the vote for House candidates from 1968 to 1992. Kathy Dolan, who carried out a comprehensive 2004 study of patterns in gender and voting, concluded that candidates' sex is a relevant factor only in rare electoral circumstances.[5] Jennifer Lawless and Kathryn Pearson, in an analysis of congressional primary elections between 1958 and 2004, found that women candidates are more likely to face more crowded and competitive primaries, although they did not find evidence of voter bias.[6] The previous edition of this book, focusing on the 2006 and 2008 elections, also found no systematic evidence of voter bias.

If we look at the performance of men and women in House elections in 2010 and 2012, we arrive at a similar conclusion. The data presented in Table 7.2 confirm that there is no widespread voter bias against women candidates. In the most recent House races, women and men fared similarly in terms of raw vote totals. In fact, Democratic women running as incumbents, challengers, and in open seats in 2010 and 2012 performed as well as or better than their Democratic male counterparts. Conversely,

---

[3] For examples of experimental designs that identify voter bias, see Leonie Huddy and Nadya Terkildsen. 1993. Gender Stereotypes and the Perception of Male and Female Candidates. *American Journal of Political Science* 37: 119–47; Leonie Huddy and Nadya Terkildsen. 1993. The Consequences of Gender Stereotypes for Women Candidates at Different Levels and Types of Office. *Political Research Quarterly* 46: 503–25; and Richard L. Fox and Eric R. A. N. Smith. 1998. The Role of Candidate Sex in Voter Decision-Making. *Political Psychology* 19: 405–419.

[4] For a comprehensive examination of vote totals through the mid-1990s, see Richard A. Seltzer, Jody Newman, and M. Voorhees Leighton. 1997. *Sex as a Political Variable*. Boulder, CO: Lynne Reinner.

[5] Kathleen A. Dolan. 2004. *Voting for Women*. Boulder, CO: Westview.

[6] Jennifer Lawless and Kathryn Pearson. 2008. The Primary Reason for Women's Under-Representation: Re-evaluating the Conventional Wisdom. *Journal of Politics* 70(1): 67–82.

TABLE 7.2: Women and men House candidates have similar vote shares for 2010 and 2012

	2010		2012	
	Women (%)	Men (%)	Women (%)	Men (%)
Democrats				
Incumbents	64*	59	70	66
	(53)	(182)	(50)	(143)
Challengers	36	32	38	37
	(29)	(105)	(50)	(138)
Open seats	52	40	53	53
	(9)	(32)	(11)	(14)
Republicans				
Incumbents	65	68	62	65
	(19)	(137)	(17)	(197)
Challengers	37	39	36	35
	(31)	(201)	(27)	(151)
Open seats	60	55	52	43
	(2)	(39)	(4)	(23)

Notes: Candidates running unopposed are omitted from these results. Entries indicate mean vote share won. Parentheses indicate the total number of candidates for each category. Significance levels: *$p < .05$; difference of means test.
Source: Compiled from *New York Times* listing of election results.

on the Republican side, incumbent Republican women fared a little worse in 2010 and 2012 than did male incumbents. But Republican women performed better than their male counterparts in open-seat races and about the same in the challenger category. None of the comparisons for Republicans was statistically significant. In the Senate, the record-setting fifteen women major party general election candidates in 2010 was surpassed in 2012 with eighteen candidates. Ultimately, this is too few candidates for a meaningful statistical analysis, but general trends reveal no general bias for or against women Senate candidates in 2010 or 2012.

Turning to the second most important indicator of electoral success – fund-raising – we see similar results. In the 1970s and 1980s, because so few women ran for office, many scholars assumed that women in electoral politics simply could not raise the amount of money necessary to mount competitive campaigns. Indeed, older research that focused mostly on anecdotal evidence concluded that women ran campaigns with lower levels of funding than did men. More systematic examinations of campaign receipts, however, have uncovered few sex differences in fund-raising for similarly situated candidates. An early study of congressional candidates from 1972 to 1982 found only a "very weak" relationship between gender and the ability to raise campaign funds.[7] More recent research indicates that, by the 1988 House elections, the disparity between men and women in campaign fund-raising had completely disappeared.[8] In cases in which women raised less money than men, the differences were accounted for by incumbency status: male incumbents generally held positions of greater political power and thus attracted larger contributions.[9] Since 1992, political action committees such as EMILY's List have worked to make certain that viable women candidates suffer no disadvantage in fund-raising. (See Chapter 8, by Barbara Burrell, in this volume for a discussion of EMILY's List.)

If we examine fund-raising totals of male and female general election House candidates in 2010 and 2012, we see few gender differences (see Table 7.3). In fact, the discrepancies that do exist reveal an advantage for women candidates in several instances. Women Democratic challengers, for instance, substantially outraised their male counterparts in 2010 and 2012. The number of women Senate candidates is too small for meaningful statistical comparisons with men. If we look at the three most competitive Senate races in 2012 in which women ran against men, the results do not suggest any clear gender patterns in fund-raising. In the 2012 Massachusetts race, Democratic challenger Elizabeth Warren raised $42,505,349, compared to $28,159,602 for Republican incumbent Scott Brown. In the hotly contested race for Missouri's U.S. Senate seat, Republican challenger Todd Akin was outspent by Democratic incumbent Claire McCaskill $21,131,801 to $5,676,248. Akin had been cut off from party funds after he made much-publicized comments about abortion and what he referred to as "legitimate rape" (see the Introduction for a fuller description of Akin's remarks). Akin's comments allowed an initially vulnerable woman incumbent to win in an electoral romp, with

---

[7] Barbara Burrell. 1985. Women and Men's Campaigns for the U.S. House of Representatives, 1972–1982: A Finance Gap? *American Political Quarterly* 13: 251–272.

[8] Barbara Burrell. 1994. *A Woman's Place Is in the House*. Ann Arbor: University of Michigan Press, 105.

[9] Carole Jean Uhlaner and Kay Lehman Schlozman. 1986. Candidate Gender and Congressional Campaign Receipts. *Journal of Politics* 52: 391–409.

TABLE 7.3: Women and men House candidates have similar fund-raising patterns for 2010 and 2012

	2010		2012	
	Women	Men	Women	Men
Democrats				
Incumbents	$1,404,476	$1,627,261	$1,295,467	$1,536,735
	(53)	(182)	(50)	(143)
Challengers	656,854*	249,547	645,145*	428,686
	(29)	(105)	(50)	(137)
Open seats	792,159	859,424	1,565,040	909,684
	(9)	(32)	(11)	(14)
Republicans				
Incumbents	1,971,510	1,332,131	2,844,476	1,754,366
	(19)	(137)	(17)	(197)
Challengers	523,175	660,823	646,462	782,524
	(31)	(201)	(27)	(150)
Open seats	1,262,130	1,146,655	1,262,130	909,684
	(2)	(39)	(2)	(14)

Notes: Candidates running unopposed are omitted from these results. Entries indicate total money raised. Parentheses indicate the total number of candidates in each category. Significance levels: * $p < .05$ in difference of means test.
Source: Compiled from 2012 Federal Election Commission (FEC) reports.

McCaskill notching a 16-point victory. Finally, in North Dakota's open-seat race, Democratic candidate Heidi Heitkamp raised $5,638,438 but was outraised by Rick Berg, who took in $6,502,926. In a year of many Democratic success stories, Heitkamp eked out a narrow victory. Overall, though, no clear gender differences emerged in House or Senate competition for funds. As Barbara Burrell suggests in her chapter on party organizations and interest groups, women and men may turn to different fund-raising sources, but the net results appear to be similar levels of financial success.

On the basis of general indicators, we see what appears to be a largely gender-neutral electoral environment. Women are slowly increasing their numbers in Congress, and men and women perform similarly in terms of vote totals and fund-raising. The data certainly suggest that men have lost their stranglehold over the congressional election process and that women can now find excellent political opportunities. But these broad statistical comparisons tell only part of the story.

ARE WOMEN MAKING GAINS EVERYWHERE? STATE AND REGIONAL VARIATION

Women have not been equally successful running for elective office in all parts of the United States. Some regions and states appear to be far more amenable to the election of women than others. But across the 2010 and 2012 congressional elections, women made significant break-throughs, with none more dramatic than in New Hampshire.

Heading into the 2012 election, New Hampshire had already elected two women to the U.S. Senate: Democrat Jeanne Shaheen in 2008 and Republican Kelly Ayotte in 2010. But when female Democratic challengers Carol Shea-Porter and Ann McLane Kuster defeated Republican incumbent U.S. House members Frank Guinta and Charlie Bass, New Hampshire became the first state in U.S. history to have an all-woman congressional delegation.

While New Hampshire was making history, other states maintained their poor records of failing to elect women. Delaware, Iowa, Mississippi, and Vermont remain the only four states that have never sent women to Congress. As the results of recent elections in places like Iowa and Mississippi suggest, women may face disadvantages when running for office in some parts of the United States. If we examine the prevalence of male and female House candidates by region and state, we see that the broader inclusion of women in high-level politics has not extended to all regions of the country equally. Table 7.4 tracks women's electoral success in House races since 1970 but breaks the data down by four geographic regions. Before 1990, the Northeast saw two and three times as many women candidates as any other region in the country. The situation changed dramatically with the Year of the Woman elections in 1992.

The number of women winning election to Congress from western states more than doubled; and in the South, the number more than tripled. Gains were much more modest in the Midwest and the Northeast. Since the late 1990s, only the West continues to show clear gains for women. A lot of the gains in the West can be attributed to the high number of women from California holding House seats, but women also have strong records of success in other western states such as Wyoming, Nevada, and Washington. The geographic breakdown in Table 7.4 puts the 1992 elections, as well as the modest increases in women's numbers in Congress since that time, into perspective. The 1992 Year of the Woman gains were largely in the West and the South.

TABLE 7.4: The proportion of U.S. Representatives who are women varies sharply by region

	West (%)	South (%)	Midwest (%)	Northeast (%)
1970	3.9	0.0	2.5	4.9
1980	2.6	1.6	3.3	8.1
1990	8.2	2.3	6.2	9.6
1992	17.2	7.9	6.7	12.4
2000	25.8	9.2	10.9	11.3
2002	25.5	8.7	11.5	9.8
2004	26.5	11.0	14.0	10.9
2006	28.6	9.9	18.0	11.6
2008	28.6	9.2	18.0	14.7
2010	27.4	13.8	12.7	14.9
2012	29.4	10.5	18.1	14.9
Net percentage change (1970 to 2012)	+25.5	+10.5	+15.6	+10.0

Notes: Percentages reflect the proportion of House members who are women.
Source: Compiled by author from Center for American Women and Politics, 2012 Fact Sheets.

Looking more closely, there are also several striking differences among individual states. Consider, for example, that after the 2012 elections, twenty states had no women representatives in the U.S. House and fifteen states had no women representatives in either the House or Senate. Further, twenty-two states had never been represented by a woman in the U.S. Senate. Table 7.5 identifies the states with the best and worst records in sending women to serve in the House of Representatives following the 2012 elections. Through the 2010 and 2012 elections, women continue to have trouble getting elected in a number of larger states. Georgia with fourteen House seats, New Jersey with twelve House seats, and Virginia with eleven have no women representatives. Also, among some of the largest states, women are still scarce – only one of Pennsylvania's eighteen House members is a woman, as are just three of the thirty-six House members from Texas.

Table 7.5 also demonstrates that women congressional candidates have succeeded in a number of high-population states, like California and New York. Why have women done well in these states and not others? California and New York are among the states with the biggest

TABLE 7.5: Forty percent of the states had no women serving in the U.S. House of Representatives in 2012

States with no women in the House of Representatives	States with high percentages of women representatives (20% or higher)
Georgia (14)	New Hampshire (2) – 100%
New Jersey (12)	South Dakota (1) – 100%
Virginia (11)	Wyoming (1) – 100 %
South Carolina (7)	Maine (2) – 50%
Kentucky (6)	Connecticut (5) – 40%
Louisiana (6)	Missouri (8) – 38%
Oklahoma (5)	California (53) – 34%
Arkansas (4)	New Mexico (3) – 33%
Iowa (4)[a]	Washington (10) – 30%
Mississippi (4)[a]	West Virginia (3) – 33%
Utah (4)	Alabama (7) – 29%
Nebraska (3)	New York (27) – 26%
Idaho (2)	Kansas (4) – 25%
Rhode Island (2)	Minnesota (8) – 25%
New Hampshire (2)	Nevada (4) – 25%
Alaska (1)	Arizona (9) – 22%
Delaware (1)[a]	Florida (27) – 22%
Montana (1)	Indiana (9) – 22%
North Dakota (1)	Tennessee (9) – 22%
Vermont (1)[a]	Oregon (5) – 20%

Notes: Number in parentheses is the number of House seats in the state as of 2012. [a] Indicates states that have never sent a woman to either the House or Senate.
Source: Compiled by author from Center for American Women and Politics, 2012 Fact Sheets.

delegations, so perhaps we can assume that more political opportunities for women drive the candidacies. But this would not explain women's lack of success in large states like Texas and Pennsylvania. Moreover, what explains women's success in states like Missouri, where, for much of the 1990s and again in 2012, three of the state's House members were women? Missouri borders Iowa, which has never elected a woman House candidate. By the same token, why has Connecticut historically elected so many more women than neighboring Massachusetts?

Some political scientists argue that state political culture serves as an important determinant of women's ability to win elective office. The researchers Barbara Norrander and Clyde Wilcox have found considerable disparities in the progress of women's election to state legislatures across various states and regions. They explain the disparities by pointing to differences in state ideology and state culture.[10] States with conservative ideologies and "traditionalist or moralist" cultures are less likely to elect women.[11] A strong correlation between the percentage of women in the state legislature and the number of women in Congress, however, does not always exist. Massachusetts and New Jersey, for example, are better than average in terms of the number of women serving in the state legislature, yet each has a very poor record of electing women to the House of Representatives.

Barbara Palmer and Dennis Simon, in their book, *Breaking the Political Glass Ceiling: Women and Congressional Elections*, propose specific causes of regional and state differences in electing women U.S. House members. Examining all congressional elections between 1972 and 2006, Palmer and Simon introduce the idea of women-friendly districts. They find that several district characteristics are important predictors of the emergence and success of women candidates. For example, U.S. House districts that are not heavily conservative, are urban, are not in the South, have higher levels of racial minorities, and have higher levels of education are much more likely to have a record of electing women candidates. Palmer and Simon's findings suggest that the manner in which gender manifests itself in the political systems and environments of individual states is an important part of the explanation for the paucity of women in Congress.[12]

ARE WOMEN RUNNING FOR BOTH PARTIES AND UNDER THE BEST CIRCUMSTANCES?

Most congressional elections feature hopeless challengers running against safely entrenched incumbents. Reporters for *Congressional Quarterly* completed an analysis of all 435 U.S. House races in June 2004, five months before the 2004 elections, and concluded that only 21 (out of 404) races

---

[10] Barbara Norrander and Clyde Wilcox. 1998. The Geography of Gender Power: Women in State Legislatures. In *Women and Elective Office*, ed. Sue Thomas and Clyde Wilcox. New York: Oxford University Press.

[11] Kira Sanbonmatsu. 2002. Political Parties and the Recruitment of Women to State Legislatures. *Journal of Politics* 64(3): 791–809.

[12] Barbara Palmer and Dennis Simon. 2008. *The Political Glass Ceiling: Women and Congressional Elections*, 2nd ed. New York: Routledge.

with incumbents running were competitive.[13] Even in the more tumultuous elections of 2010 and 2012, only roughly 20 percent of House races were rated as competitive by the parties and experts. More specifically, in the 2010 elections in which Republicans retook the house, the Cook Political Report identified eighty-seven competitive House seats, the highest number in over a decade.[14] In 2012, a *New York Times* analysis found that only twenty-five, less than six percent of all House races, could be rated as tossups.[15]

Predictably, political scientists often identify the incumbency advantage as one of the leading explanations for women's slow entry into electoral politics. Low turnover, a direct result of incumbency, provides few opportunities for women to increase their numbers in male-dominated lxegislative bodies. Between 1946 and 2002, only 8 percent of all challengers defeated incumbent members of the U.S. House of Representatives.[16] In most races, the incumbent cruised to reelection with well over 60 percent of the vote. Accordingly, as congressional elections scholars Ronald Keith Gaddie and Charles Bullock state, "Open seats, not the defeat of incumbents, are the portal through which most legislators enter Congress."[17]

To begin to assess whether women are as likely as men to take advantage of the dynamics associated with an open-seat race, we can examine the presence and performance of women in open-seat House contests. Table 7.6 compares women's presence in House elections by time period, party affiliation, and type of seat. In this analysis, I divide the data into two earlier time periods and then show the four most recent elections to more clearly examine the evolution of women's candidacies. As expected, women were significantly more likely to run for office in the later eras, although the increase in women candidates is not constant across parties. In the 1980s, the parties were very similar in terms of the types of races in which women ran. Between the first and second time period,

---

[13] Republicans Maintain a Clear Edge in House Contests. June 4, 2004. *CQ Weekly*.

[14] Nate Silver. October 10, 2010. Number of Competitive House Races Doubles from Recent Years. http://fivethirtyeight.blogs.nytimes.com/2010/10/10/number-of-competitive-house-races-doubles-from-recent-years/. Accessed March 30, 2013.

[15] House Race Ratings. *New York Times*. http://elections.nytimes.com/2012/ratings/house. Accessed March 30, 2013.

[16] Gary C. Jacobsen. 2004. *The Politics of Congressional Elections*, 6th ed. New York: Longman, 23.

[17] Ronald Keith Gaddie and Charles S. Bullock. 2000. *Elections to Open Seats in the U.S. House*. Lanham, MD: Rowman and Littlefield, 1.

TABLE 7.6: Types of seats contested by women candidates in the U.S. House vary by years and party

Type of seat	1980–1990		1992–2004		2006		2008		2010		2012	
	Democrat (%)	Republican (%)	Democrat (%)	Republican (%)	Democrat (%)	Republican (%)	Democrat (%)	Republican (%)	Democrat (%)	Republican (%)	Democrat (%)	Republican (%)
Open seat	11 (24)	8 (16)	25 (88)	15 (49)	32 (12)	19 (7)	28 (10)	6 (2)	19 (9)	5 (2)	32 (11)	15 (4)
Challengers	10 (80)	9 (98)	21 (230)	12 (153)	21 (41)	8 (12)	22 (35)	10 (19)	28 (29)	13 (31)	27 (50)	15 (273)
Incumbents	4 (59)	5 (52)	14 (224)	8 (101)	22 (42)	11 (23)	22 (50)	10 (17)	23 (53)	12 (19)	26 (50)	8 (17)

Note: Entries indicate the percentage of all candidates for that electoral category who were women. The number of candidates for each category is in parentheses.

Source: Compiled by author from Center for American Women and Politics, 2012 *Fact Sheets* and *New York Times* listing of election results.

however, the number of women Democrats running in all types of races more than doubled, whereas the increases among the Republicans were quite small. The disparities between the parties became even starker in recent open-seat elections. In 2010, Democrats nominated almost four times as many open-seat candidates as Republicans, and in 2012, there were more than twice as many Democratic women running for open seats as Republican women. The Republicans had their highest share of women open-seat candidates in 2006, at almost 20 percent, but in 2008 and again in 2010, the Republicans nominated only two women for open-seat races. With open-seat races usually providing the best opportunities for electoral pickups, Democrats are nominating women to run for these seats, but Republicans are not.

Aside from open-seat races in recent election cycles, the Democrats have been much more likely than the Republicans to nominate women to run for all seats (see also Table 7.1). This carries serious long-term implications for the number of women serving in Congress. For women to achieve full parity in U.S. political institutions, women must be represented fully in both parties.

ARE MEN AND WOMEN EQUALLY AMBITIOUS TO RUN FOR CONGRESS?

The decision to run for office and ultimately seek a seat in Congress is a critical area of inquiry for those interested in the role of gender in electoral politics. Examples abound of political women who report that they had some difficulty taking the plunge. Wisconsin Congresswoman Gwen Moore never thought of herself as someone who would run for office until she was coaxed to run for a state legislative seat in the 1990s.[18] Even House Democratic Leader Nancy Pelosi claims that she had never thought of running for office until she was encouraged to do so in 1987.[19]

Until recently, very little empirical research had explored the initial decision to run for office. But if the general election playing field is largely level, then gender differences in political ambition likely provide a crucial explanation for women's underrepresentation in Congress. In 2001 and 2011, Jennifer Lawless and I conducted separate waves of the Citizen Political Ambition Study. This series of surveys asks women and

[18] Reluctant to Take the Plunge. May 29, 2008. *USA Today*, 10A.
[19] Dana Wilkey. November 13, 2002. From Political Roots to Political Leader, Pelosi Is the Real Thing. Copley News Service.

TABLE 7.7: Among potential candidates, women are less interested than men in seeking elective office

	2001		2011	
	Women (%)	Men (%)	Women (%)	Men (%)
Has thought about running for office	43	59	46	62
Discussed running with party leaders	4	8	25	32
Discussed running with friends and family	17	29	27	38
Investigated how to place your name on the ballot	4	10	13	21
Sample size	1,796	1,969	1,796	1,969

Notes: Sample is composed of lawyers, business leaders and executives, and educators. Entries indicate percentage responding "yes." All differences between women and men are significant at $p < .05$.

Sources: Adapted from the Citizen Political Ambition Study. For 2001, see Richard L. Fox and Jennifer L. Lawless, "Entering the Arena: Gender and the Decision to Run for Office," *American Journal of Political Science*, 2004, 48(2): 264–280. For 2011, see Jennifer L. Lawless and Richard L. Fox, "Men Rule: The Continued Under- Representation of Women in U.S. Politics," *School of Public Affairs, American University*, Washington, DC: 2011.

men working in the four professions most likely to precede a career in Congress (law, business, politics, and education) about their ambition to someday run for elective office. Table 7.7 shows some of the results of the survey, focusing on whether women and men have ever thought about running for office and whether they have ever taken any of the steps that usually precede a candidacy, such as speaking with party officials and community leaders. On the critical question of interest in running for office, the results of the study highlighted a substantial gender gap in political ambition. The results of the most recent survey in 2011 reveal that there has been almost no change in the gap across the past decade. In 2001, there was a 16 percent gap, with men more likely than women to have thought about running for office. In 2011, the gap again stood at 16 percent, virtually unchanged. The gender gaps on concrete steps that a potential candidate might take before running for office were roughly unchanged across the time period. Even though all of the empirical evidence shows that women who run for office are just as likely as men to be victorious, a much smaller number of women than men are likely

TABLE 7.8: Among potential candidates, women are less interested than men in running for the U.S. House or Senate

	2001		2011	
	Women (%)	Men (%)	Women (%)	Men (%)
Interested in someday running for...				
U.S. House of Representatives	15	27	9	19
U.S. Senate	13	20	6	11
Sample Size	816	1,022	1,766	1,848

Notes: Sample is composed of lawyers, business leaders and executives, and educators who expressed some interest in running for office. Entries indicate percentage responding "yes." All differences between women and men are significant at $p < .05$.

Sources: Adapted from the Citizen Political Ambition Study. For 2001, see Richard L. Fox and Jennifer L. Lawless, "Entering the Arena: Gender and the Decision to Run for Office," *American Journal of Political Science,* 2004, 48(2): 264–280. For 2011, see Jennifer L. Lawless and Richard L. Fox, "Men Rule: The Continued Under-Representation of Women in U.S. Politics," *School of Public Affairs, American University,* Washington, DC: 2011.

to emerge as candidates because women are far less likely than men to consider running for office.

Further, when we consider male and female potential candidates' interest in running for Congress, the gender gap in political ambition is amplified. Table 7.8 shows the interest of potential candidates in running for the U.S. House and Senate in both waves of the survey. Potential candidates were asked to identify which offices they might ever be interested in seeking. For both questions, men were significantly more likely than women to demonstrate an interest in running for Congress. Again, the gender gap in interest in congressional office persisted across both time periods. The one change between 2001 and 2011 was that both women and men expressed less interest in running for Congress overall, likely a result of the increasingly negative and partisan view of politics in Washington.

Ultimately, three critical factors uncovered in the Citizen Political Ambition Study explain the gender gap in ambition. First, women are significantly less likely than men to receive encouragement to run for office. This difference is very important, because potential candidates are twice as likely to think about running for office when a party leader, elected official, or political activist attempts to recruit them as candidates. Second, women are significantly less likely than men to view themselves as

qualified to run for office. In other words, even women in the top tier
of professional accomplishment tend not to consider themselves qualified to run for political office, even when they have the same objective credentials and experiences as men. Third, even among this group
of professionals, women were much more likely to state that they were
responsible for the majority of child care and household duties. Although
many of the women in the study had blazed trails in the formerly male
professions of law and business, they were still serving as the primary
caretakers in their households. Although family roles and responsibilities were not significant predictors of political ambition, interviews with
potential women candidates suggested that traditional family roles are
still an impediment.[20]

CONCLUSION AND DISCUSSION

When researchers and political scientists in the late 1970s and early
1980s began to study the role of gender in electoral politics, concerns
about basic fairness and political representation motivated their inves-
tigations. For many, the notion of governing bodies overwhelmingly
dominated by men offends a sense of simple justice. In this vein, some
researchers argue that the reality of a male-dominated government suggests to women citizens that the political system is not fully open to them.
These concerns are as pertinent today as they were in the past. As Susan
J. Carroll and I noted in the introduction to this volume, a growing body
of empirical research finds that a political system that does not allow
for women's full inclusion in positions of political power increases the
possibility that gender-salient issues will be overlooked. Ample research
has shown that women are more likely than men to promote legislation
geared toward ameliorating women's economic and social status, especially concerning issues of health care, poverty, education, and gender
equity.[21] Despite the substantive and symbolic importance of women's
full inclusion in the electoral arena, the number of women serving in
elected bodies remains low. This chapter's overview of women's performance in congressional elections makes it clear that we need to adopt a

---

[20] Jennifer L. Lawless and Richard L. Fox. 2010. *It Still Takes a Candidate: Why Women Don't Run for Office.* New York: Cambridge University Press.
[21] For one of the most recent analyses of how women in Congress address different policy issues from those that men address, see Michele L. Swers. 2002. *The Difference Women Make.* Chicago: University of Chicago Press.

more nuanced approach if we are to understand gender's evolving role in the electoral arena.

As to answering this chapter's central question – why there are still so few women in Congress – two broad findings emerge from the analysis.

First, on a more optimistic note, women now compete in U.S. House and Senate races more successfully than at any previous time in history. The last two election cycles saw record numbers of women candidates seeking and winning major party nominations. The key to increasing women's representation is to get more women to run for office. For as this study found, there are almost no gender differences in terms of the major indicators of electoral success – vote totals and fund-raising. The evidence presented in this chapter continues to show that women and men perform similarly as general election candidates. On the basis of recent congressional election results, the findings presented in this chapter confirm, as a number of other studies have found, that there is no evidence of widespread gender bias among voters and financial contributors.

The second broad finding to emerge from this chapter, however, is that gender continues to play an important role in the electoral arena and, in some cases, works to keep the number of women running for Congress low. Notably, there are sharp state and regional differences in electing men and women to Congress. Women cannot emerge in greater numbers until the candidacies of women are embraced throughout the entire United States and by both parties.

Additionally, women's full inclusion will not be possible if the overwhelming majority of women candidates continue to identify with the Democratic Party. Recent declines and stagnation in the number of women running as Republicans bode very poorly for the future, at least in the short term. Republicans have made very little progress in recent decades in promoting and facilitating the election of women candidates. As long as the fortunes of women candidates are tied so heavily to one political party, women's movement toward parity in officeholding will prove illusory.

Finally, gender differences in political ambition – particularly in the ambition to run for the U.S. Congress – suggest that gender is exerting its strongest impact at the earliest stages of the electoral process. Many women who would make ideal candidates never actually consider running for office. The notion of entering politics still appears not to be a socialized norm for women. A recent study of full time college students ages 18 to 25 reveals that women continue to show far less interest in ever running for office than their male counterparts. Table 7.9 shows

TABLE 7.9: A large gender gap in future interest in running for office among college students

2012	Women (%)	Men (%)
Have you ever thought that, when you're older, you might want to run for political office?		
Thought about it many times	10	20
Has crossed my mind	27	37
Never thought about it	63	43
Sample Size	1,097	1,020

Source: Adapted from Jennifer L. Lawless and Richard L. Fox, "Girls Just Wanna Not Run," *School of Public Affairs, American University,* Washington, DC: 2012.

that young men are twice as likely as young women to say they might someday like to run for elective office. These results highlight some of the long-term challenges in creating an environment in which women and men are equally likely to be interested in pursuing a seat in the U.S. Congress.

As these findings suggest, gender permeates the electoral environment in subtle and nuanced ways. Broad empirical analyses often tend to overlook these dynamics, yet the reality is that these dynamics help explain why so few women occupy positions on Capitol Hill.

BARBARA BURRELL

8 Political Parties and Women's Organizations

Bringing Women into the Electoral Arena

The dominance of party organizations in campaigns declined in the 1960s and 1970s. Candidate-centered campaigns became the principal approaches for those seeking elective office, especially national positions. In recent decades, national party organizations have been reinvigorated, emerging once again as major players.[1] They have been joined by other political organizations, including women's groups that recruit and train candidates and provide financial and logistical support to their campaigns. Contemporary electoral campaigns take place within a vibrant and complex organizational world, one that shapes women's quests for political leadership, whether in public office or within party organizations.

This chapter chronicles the historical development of women's involvement in the major political party organizations, considers their emergence as leaders within those organizations, and provides an overview of trends in party efforts to elect women to national office. It also offers a parallel narrative of the emergence and growth of women's organizations whose goal has been to recruit and support women candidates. Such organizational efforts have sometimes operated in tandem with party organizations but also often as independent and even challenging forces to the parties. An assessment of the current state of women's quests for political leadership from these organizational perspectives is woven into this narrative, with organizational activity in the 2012 election highlighted.

---

[1] Gary Jacobson. 2009. *The Politics of Congressional Elections*, seventh edition. New York: Pearson Longman; Paul Herrnson. 2008. *Congressional Elections*, fifth edition. Washington, DC: CQ Press.

WOMEN WITHIN THE PARTIES: HISTORICAL BACKGROUND

Beginning with the suffragists, women have a long and complex history of working within party organizations to become voters, attain political influence, and help other women win electoral office. Table 8.1 presents a chronology of important dates in the history of parties, women's organizations, and women's candidacies for public office from suffrage to the contemporary period.

Suffragists lobbied party organizations to include planks supporting the women's vote in their platforms. By their account, they undertook 277 such campaigns in the seventy-two-year effort to secure the right to vote.[2]

In the years immediately preceding the passage of the Nineteenth Amendment, party leaders feared the entrance of women onto the voter rolls. The major political parties worried that women, armed with the vote, might form their own parties and act independently in the political process, undermining the capacity of major parties to control elections and the spoils of victory. William Chafe notes that parties were concerned about the creation of a "petticoat hierarchy which may at will upset all orderly slates and commit undreamed of executions at the polls" and viewed the formation of the nonpartisan League of Women Voters as threatening to their hegemony in the electoral process.[3]

For these reasons, as Kristi Andersen notes:

> The national party organizations, sensitive to the demands and the potential influence of a new element in the electorate, responded to the imminent granting of suffrage with organizational changes designed to give women nominally equal roles in the party hierarchy and to allow for the efficient mobilization of women voters by women leaders.[4]

Fearing the independence of women voters, the parties undertook a dual effort, establishing distinct organizations led by women to work with women voters and making efforts to integrate women into their leadership committees through expansion of those organizations.

---

[2] Aileen Kraditor. 1965. *Ideas of the Woman Suffrage Movement, 1890–1920.* New York: Columbia University Press.

[3] William Chafe. 1972. The American Woman: Her Changing Social, Economic, and Political Roles, 1920–1970. New York: Oxford University Press, 25.

[4] Kristi Andersen. 1996. After Suffrage: Women in Partisan and Electoral Politics before the New Deal. Chicago: University of Chicago Press, 80–81.

TABLE 8.1: Important dates in the history of parties, women's organizations, and women's candidacies for public office

1918   Republican Women's National Executive Committee established.

1919   Democratic National Committee passes a resolution recommending that the Democratic State Committees "take such practical action as will provide the women of their respective states with representation, both as officers and as members thereof;" also passes a resolution calling for equal representation of the sexes on the Executive Committee of the Democratic National Committee.

Republican National Committee urges state and county committees to select "one man and one woman member" as "the principle of representation."

1920   Delegates to the Democratic National Convention vote to double the size of their national committee and "one man and one woman hereafter should be selected from each state."

1924   Republican National Committee votes for one male and one female representative from each state.

1940   The Republican Party endorses an Equal Rights Amendment to the Constitution in its party platform for the first time.

1944   The Democratic Party includes a plank endorsing the Equal Rights Amendment in its platform for the first time.

1966   The National Organization for Women (NOW) is founded.

1971   The National Women's Political Caucus (NWPC) is founded with the major aim of increasing the number of women in public office.

1972   U.S. Representative Shirley Chisholm seeks the Democratic nomination for president.

Frances "Sissy" Farenthold's name is placed in nomination for vice president at the Democratic National Convention. She receives 420 votes.

Jean Westwood is appointed chair of the Democratic National Committee.

1974   The Women's Campaign Fund is founded, the first women's PAC. Mary Louise Smith is appointed chair of the Republican National Committee.

1975   NOW forms a PAC to fund feminist candidates.

1976   Democrats mandate equal division between men and women in their national convention delegations, effective in 1980.

1977   The NWPC forms a PAC, the Campaign Support Committee.

1979   The NWPC forms a second PAC, the Victory Fund.

1980   The Republican Party removes support for the Equal Rights Amendment from its platform.

1984   Democrats nominate U.S. Representative Geraldine Ferraro for vice president.

The National Political Congress of Black Women is founded.

(continued)

TABLE 8.1 *(continued)*

1985   EMILY's List is founded on the principle that "Early Money Is Like
        Yeast – it makes the dough rise."

1991   Clarence Thomas, a nominee for associate justice of the U.S. Supreme
        Court, is accused of sexual harassment by former staffer Anita Hill.
        Many women are disturbed by the absence of women senators and the
        dismissive attitude toward Hill during Thomas's confirmation hearings,
        and one result is a record number of women seeking office.

1992   Media dub 1992 the "Year of the Woman" in American politics as the
        number of female U.S. senators grows from two to six and the number
        of female U.S. representatives climbs from twenty-eight to forty-seven.

        The WISH List is founded.

        The NWPC sponsors the Showcase of Pro-Choice Republican Women
        Candidates at the Republican convention, with thirteen GOP
        candidates.

        NOW adopts the Elect Women for a Change campaign and raises
        about $500,000 for women candidates.

        NOW also initiates the formation of a national third party, the 21st
        Century Party.

1999   Elizabeth Dole enters the Republican race for president but drops out
        before the first caucuses and primaries.

2003   Former U.S. Senator Carol Moseley Braun enters the Democratic race
        for president but drops out before the first caucuses and primaries.

2006   U.S. Representative Nancy Pelosi is chosen by her Democratic
        colleagues to be Speaker of the House, putting her second in line for
        the presidency and making her the highest female constitutional officer
        ever in the United States.

2007   U.S. Senator Hillary Clinton enters the Democratic primary for
        president of the United States.

2008   In June at the end of the primary season, Hillary Clinton drops out,
        conceding the race to Barack Obama after putting "18 million cracks
        into the political glass ceiling."

        U.S. Senator John McCain, Republican nominee for president, chooses
        Alaska Governor Sarah Palin as his vice presidential running mate,
        making her the first Republican female nominee for that position.

2011   U.S. Representative Debbie Wasserman Schultz becomes chair of the
        Democratic National Committee.

2012   U.S. Representative Michelle Bachman enters the Republican race for
        president but drops out after several debates and primaries.

Source: Compiled by author.

The Democratic Party acted first, creating in 1916 a Women's Bureau to mobilize women voters in the western states in which they had already gained the right to vote. In 1917, the Democratic National Committee (DNC), the main governing body of the party, created a women's version of itself, staffed by appointed female members from the states that had already granted women full suffrage.[5] In 1919, they adopted a plan for an Associate National Committee of Women. The DNC also agreed that year to appoint a woman associate member from each state based on the nomination of the state committeeman. In addition, the DNC recommended that Democratic state committees provide women with similar representation at the state and local levels and equal representation of men and women on the executive committee. At their 1920 national convention, delegates voted to double the size of their national committee and stipulated that "one man and one woman hereafter should be selected from each state."[6]

In 1918, the Republicans created the Republican Women's National Executive Committee. The next year, they adopted a plan calling for state chairmen to appoint "a State Executive Committee of women numbering from five to fifteen members to act with the State Central Committee" and established a women's division.[7] But in 1920, they rejected equal representation for women on the Republican National Committee (RNC), although eight women were appointed to its twenty-one-member Executive Committee. In 1924, Republican leaders agreed to enlarge the RNC and elect male and female members from each state.

Women came to represent about 10 to 15 percent of the delegates to the parties' national conventions in the years after they won the vote. Although they gained some measure of formal equality in the party organizations in those days, women activists struggled for many years to gain respect and influence within the parties, in part because women did not vote sufficiently differently from men or in large enough numbers to cause the party organizations to worry about their influence.

By the latter part of the 1960s, women were still only marginally represented within party leadership ranks. Party organizations had not made any particular effort to promote women as candidates for public office,

[5] Anna Harvey. 1998. Votes without Leverage: Women in American Electoral Politics, 1920–1970. New York: Cambridge University Press.
[6] Ibid., 85.
[7] Ibid., 113.

and women were encouraged to run primarily in situations in which the party had little chance of winning.

As the second women's rights movement took off, however, activists adopted the strategy of engaging in partisan politics. The National Women's Political Caucus (NWPC), established in 1971 to "help elect women and also men who declare themselves ready to fight for the needs and rights of women and all underrepresented groups," pressured both parties to increase their representation of women as national convention delegates in 1972. NWPC created Democratic and Republican party task forces and challenged both parties to help women achieve positions of public leadership.

The Democratic Party undertook a reform effort in the wake of the debacle of its 1968 national convention and its subsequent loss in the presidential election, establishing the McGovern-Fraser Commission to spearhead changes. In its 1971 report, the commission included a recommendation that racial minorities, youths, and women be represented in state delegations "in reasonable relationship to their presence in the population of the state." The NWPC pushed the Democratic Party to interpret "reasonable representation" as meaning matching a group's proportion in a state's population. As a result, they succeeded in substantially increasing the percentage of female convention delegates. Prior to the reform effort, at the 1968 Democratic National Convention, only 13 percent of the delegates had been women; in 1972, women constituted 40 percent of the delegates. The push for greater representation of women among delegates continued throughout the 1970s, and since 1980, Democratic Party rules have mandated gender equity within all state delegations to its national conventions.

The Republicans have not followed the Democrats in mandating equal numbers of men and women in convention delegations. But in the 1970s, under pressure from the delegates, the GOP adopted affirmative steps to encourage state parties to elect more women as convention delegates. The percentage of female Republican delegates increased from 17 percent in 1968 to 30 percent in 1972.

Jo Freeman, one of the founders of the women's liberation movement in the United States and an astute observer of U.S. political parties, describes the parties as having become completely polarized around feminism and their reaction to it. In her view, "On feminist issues and concerns the parties are not following the traditional pattern of presenting different versions of the same thing, or following each other's lead into new territory. They are presenting two different and conflicting visions of how Americans should engage in everyday life."[8] The Republican Party has become more hospitable to antifeminism, while the Democratic Party is perceived as the more pro-feminist party.[9] The "war on women" rhetoric that structured much of the debates between the parties in the 2012 election highlights the current polarity between the parties on women's issues.

But both parties want to appear to promote women in political leadership positions. Thus, in an example Freeman cites, the 1992 national conventions emphasized showcasing women candidates and raising money to elect more women far more than discussing polarizing issues. National party conventions, once venues for political power struggles and ideological battles with uncertain outcomes fought before the public on television, have become staged media events to spotlight candidates and promote a favorable impression of the party among the general public. Party platforms and party nominees are decided before the convention convenes, requiring only formal ratification. In this new style of convention, highlighting of party support for women in political leadership positions has become a staple, presumably in an effort to attract the support of women voters. In the next section, I describe the efforts of the two parties in this regard at their 2012 conventions.

WOMEN IN THE SPOTLIGHT AT THE 2012 NATIONAL PARTY CONVENTIONS

Winning women's votes was a major and much publicized goal of the 2012 election. A major theme of the Democratic Party on the campaign trail and within Congress was that the Republicans were engaged in a "war on women." The Republicans insisted in return that it was really the Democrats who were "anti-women." The essence of this debate involved federal funding of reproductive health services and the effect of national government spending on women's economic status. The symbolism of showcasing female leaders during prime time at their conventions became highly significant for both parties. Media headlines in 2012 spotlighted the two parties' attempts to win over women

---

[8] Jo Freeman. 1993. Feminism vs. Family Values: Women at the 1992 Democratic and Republican Conventions. *PS: Political Science and Politics* 26 (March): 21–27.
[9] Jo Freeman. 2008. *We Will Be Heard*. Lanham, MD: Rowman & Littlefield, 121–132.

voters through high profiling at the convention. Examples of headlines included

- "News Analysis: GOP convention underscores efforts to tap Hispanics, blacks and women"[10]
- "Republicans are parading their party's women, taking full advantage of these women's power with delegates and voters"[11]
- "Democrats Seek to Fire Up Female Voters: At the Democratic National Convention in Charlotte, every night is ladies' night"[12]

The parties' main convention strategy to appeal to women in the electorate was a prime-time lineup heavily featuring female speakers. The contemporary practice of presidential wives giving opening-night speeches continued with great fanfare. Both Ann Romney's and Michelle Obama's addresses were considered successes, receiving much positive media coverage. Beyond those events, a count of the sex breakdown of prime-time presentations between 7 and 11 p.m. Eastern Time shows that women made up a nearly equal proportion of the two parties' speakers. Women were sixteen of the fifty-one prime-time individuals making remarks at the Republican National Convention (31 percent) and thirty-one of the eighty-eight prime-time Democratic National Convention speakers (35 percent).

In addition to individual appearances, U.S. Senator Barbara Mikulski, the longest-serving female senator ever, led eleven of the twelve Democratic women senators in a group presentation on Wednesday night at the convention. Senator Mikulski spoke for the group, highlighting the Obama administration's record on women's issues. When her speech ended, the women joined hands above their heads to the tune of Katy Perry's "Firework." Marquee senatorial candidate Elizabeth Warren (running against Massachusetts Republican Senator Scott Brown) received major billing, appearing before former President Bill Clinton on Wednesday night.

Female governors were the most prominent women in the Republican Party in 2012, especially the two women of color – Governor Nikki Haley of South Carolina and Governor Susana Martinez of New Mexico. Along with Governor Mary Fallin of Oklahoma, they were given prime-time

---

[10] Matthew Rusling. 2012. News Analysis: GOP convention underscores efforts to tap Hispanics, blacks and women. Xinhua General News Service, August 25.
[11] Barbara Lee. 2012. Democratic National Convention: Where Are the Women? *Huntington Post,* August 16.
[12] Nancy Cook. 2012. *National Journal,* September 4.

speaking roles at their party's convention. Former Secretary of State Condoleezza Rice also received a prominent slot. Mia Love, the African-American, Mormon mayor of Saratoga Springs, Utah, who was mounting a very competitive challenge to Democratic U.S. Representative Jim Matheson in Utah's 4th Congressional District, also gave a prime-time address.

The Democrats, in addition to featuring their female officeholders and campaign stars such as Warren and Rep. Tammy Baldwin (running for the U.S. Senate in Wisconsin), strategically showcased prominent members of the reproductive rights movement: Nancy Keenan, president of the National Abortion Rights Action League-Pro-Choice America; Cecile Richards, president of Planned Parenthood Federation of America; and Sandra Fluke, a Georgetown University law student and birth control advocate. Fluke had made national headlines when conservative radio host Rush Limbaugh called her a "slut;" she had come to his attention when Republican members of the House Oversight Committee refused to allow her to speak at a hearing considering an Obama administration mandate related to insurance coverage of contraception. Only five men, all opposed to the mandate, were allowed to address the committee, leading Democratic Rep. Carolyn Maloney to ask, "Where are the women?" She and two of her colleagues walked out of the hearing, which attracted considerable media coverage and commentary.

Women also served as convention officials. Congresswoman Cathy McMorris Rodgers was the Republicans' official convention host, introducing each night's theme. The role was created to enhance her status and visibility within the party.[13] On the Democratic side, Congresswoman Debbie Wasserman Schultz, chair of the Democratic National Committee, played a prime leadership role in organizing, opening, and managing the convention.

PARTY EFFORTS TO ELECT MORE WOMEN

The Democratic Party's distinct culture made it the site of early efforts to recruit and promote women.[14] Feminists, as an accepted organized group within the party, had the attention of leadership and gained a sympathetic

[13] Spin Control. 2012. McMorris Rodgers Convention Host. August 27.

[14] Jo Freeman. 1987. Whom You Know Versus Whom You Represent: Feminist Influence in the Democratic and Republican Parties. In *The Women's Movements of the United States and Western Europe: Consciousness, Political Opportunity, and Public Policy*, ed. Mary Fainsod Katzenstein and Carol McClurg Mueller. Philadelphia: Temple University Press, 215–244.

ear within the party's liberal wing. As early as 1974, the Democratic Party sponsored the Campaign Conference for Democratic Women, aimed at electing more women to political office.[15] The 1,200 women who attended the workshop passed resolutions urging their party to do more for potential female candidates. Most of the female members of the U.S. House of Representatives in the 1970s were Democrats, including a number who won their seats by challenging and defeating the local party organizations.

The Republican Party did not initiate similar women's conferences until nearly a decade later. However, this later start does not mean that the GOP has been less receptive to female candidacies. Indeed, at one time, feminist leaders Eleanor Smeal, former chair of the National Organization for Women (NOW), and former Congresswoman Bella Abzug argued just the opposite.[16] Republican women in the 1980s tended to credit men for bringing them into the organization.[17]

Wanting to appear supportive of women in the face of an emerging gender gap in the 1980s, the parties saw it as expedient to champion women candidates. Republican leaders, in particular, publicly acknowledged this fact. The Republican Senatorial Campaign Committee (RSCC) chair Senator Richard Lugar issued a press statement in 1982 declaring:

> A concerted drive by the Republican Party to stamp itself as the party of the woman elected official would serve our nation as well as it serves our own political interests. The full political participation of women is a moral imperative for our society and intelligent political goal for the Republican Party.

He pledged to

> commit the RSCC to the maximum legal funding and support for any Republican woman who is nominated next year, regardless of how Democratic the state or apparently formidable the Democratic candidate. I am prepared to consider direct assistance to women candidates even prior to their nomination, a sharp departure from our usual policy.[18]

[15] Austin Scott. 1974. Democratic Women See Gains in 1974. *Washington Post,* March 31.

[16] Jo Freeman. 1989. Feminist Activities at the Republican Convention. *PS: Political Science and Politics* 22 (March): 39–47; Bella Abzug. 1984. *The Gender Gap: Bella Abzug's Guide to Political Power for American Women.* Boston: Houghton Mifflin.

[17] Ronna Romney and Beppie Harrison. 1988. *Momentum: Women in America Politics Now.* New York: Crown Publishers.

[18] Richard Lugar. August 21, 1983. A Plan to Elect More GOP Women. *Washington Post.*

The Democrats in 1984 included a section in their party platform on political empowerment for minorities and women. It stated:

> We will recruit women and minorities to run for governorships and all state and local offices. The Democratic Party (through its campaign committees) will commit to spending maximum resources to elect women and minority candidates and offer these candidates in-kind services, including political organizing and strategic advice. And the bulk of all voter registration funds will be spent on targeted efforts to register minorities and women.

In 1988, both national party platforms included statements recommending support for women's candidacies. The Democrats endorsed "full and equal access of women and minorities to elective office and party endorsement," while the Republicans called for "strong support for the efforts of women in seeking an equal role in government and [commitment] to the vigorous recruitment, training and campaign support for women candidates at all levels." However, these pledges did not include any action plans for implementation. Prior to 1990, the calls for increasing the number of women candidates were only rhetoric, as there were few substantive actions to ensure that women were nominated in favorable electoral circumstances.

Then, for a variety of reasons, 1992 emerged as the Year of the Woman in American politics. With the end of the Cold War, attention was increasingly turning away from foreign policy and defense and toward domestic issues on which women were perceived to have more expertise. The confirmation hearings for Clarence Thomas's nomination to the U.S. Supreme Court shone a spotlight on the absence of women in the Senate and upset women who thought that Anita Hill's charges of sexual harassment against Thomas were trivialized. The reapportionment and redistricting process of that election resulted in more open seats than usual, creating new electoral opportunities. These forces stimulated the parties to direct a greater share of their recruitment activity than in previous years toward women. The leadership of both parties' congressional campaign committees made special efforts to seek out qualified female House candidates. The Democratic Senatorial Campaign Committee (DSCC) formed a women's council that raised approximately $1.5 million for Democratic women running for the Senate. These affirmative steps did not, however, spur the parties to clear the field of primary competition for women or discourage anyone, male or female, from running against women.[19]

Republican women have initiated specific efforts in their party to recruit and train women as political and public leaders. These include the work of the National Federation of Republican Women (NFRW) and the Republican National Committee's Excellence in Public Service Series.

The NFRW provides training for potential Republican women candidates. As early as 1976, it published the booklet *Consider Yourself for Public Office: Guidelines for Women Candidates*. It now offers Campaign Management Schools that local groups can bring to their areas.

The Excellence in Public Service series is a political leadership development program offered to Republican women in a number of states. Most of the programs are named for prominent Republicans. The initial program was the Lugar Series started in 1989 in Indiana, named for Senator Richard Lugar, who encouraged his party to promote women's candidacies. Now, nineteen additional states have such programs, although not all are offered every year. Typically, a yearlong series of programs, with eight monthly sessions and a three-day leadership seminar in Washington, DC, is offered to selected women willing to make a commitment to play active roles in the political arena. Classes are designed to encourage, prepare, and inspire women leaders to seek new levels of involvement in government and politics. The extra edge these programs afford is very much needed, because research has shown that the biggest hurdle for Republican women has been winning their party's primaries.

Training sessions for potential female candidates have become a central and multifaceted aspect of contemporary women's rights activism. A description of various such programs is included later in this chapter.

CONGRESSIONAL CAMPAIGN COMMITTEES, WOMEN'S LEADERSHIP, AND WOMEN'S CANDIDACIES

The parties' four congressional campaign committees – the Democratic Congressional Campaign Committee (DCCC), the National Republican Congressional Committee (NRCC), the Democratic Senatorial Campaign Committee (DSCC), and the National Republican Senatorial Committee (NRSC) – have achieved significant roles in the contemporary campaign

---

[19] Robert Biersack and Paul S. Herrnson. 1994. Political Parties and the Year of the Woman. In *The Year of the Woman: Myths and Realities*, ed. Elizabeth Adell Cook, Sue Thomas, and Clyde Wilcox. Boulder, CO: Westview Press.

era. They participate in recruiting candidates in opportune races, whether by taking on vulnerable incumbents of the opposite party or by contesting open seats. They are also major sources of campaign money, services, and advice for congressional candidates.[20] In recent election cycles, both parties have promoted women into leadership positions within their campaign committees and have established subgroups to promote the candidacies of women. The trend has also been to include female contenders in their more general candidate support programs.

Female lawmakers headed both of the Democratic campaign committees in the 107th Congress at the beginning of the new millennium (2001–2002). Rep. Nita Lowey of New York chaired the Democratic Congressional Campaign Committee and Senator Patty Murray of Washington State chaired the Democratic Senatorial Campaign Committee. Senator Murray returned as chair of the DSCC in the 112th Congress.

In 1999, Rep. Lowey had founded Women Lead, a fund-raising subsidiary of the DCCC targeting women donors and contributors to women candidates. When Lowey became chair of the DCCC, she appointed Rep. Jan Schakowsky of Illinois to head Women Lead. In the 2001 to 2002 election cycle, that committee raised approximately $25 million for women candidates. Lowey had admired Schakowsky's fund-raising prowess in her initial run for an open House seat in 1997. Schakowsky had approached all the female law partners in the greater Chicago area, asking for donations in what she called "an untapped constituency" of women contributors. "The strategy paid off. . . . Schakowsky raised 57 percent of her campaign funds from women donors that year – a higher percentage than any other congressional candidate in the 1998 election cycle."[21] In office, Rep. Schakowsky hosts an annual Ultimate Women's Power Lunch at a downtown Chicago hotel (featuring a keynote speaker from the entertainment world or the political world) that has raised hundreds of thousands of dollars for female candidates. The DCCC's Women Lead program continues with Reps. Jackie Speier and Karen Bass as co-chairs during the 2012 election cycle.[22] Rep. Allyson Schwartz was responsible for the Committee's overall recruitment program in that election cycle.

[20] Paul Herrnson. 1995. Congressional Elections: Campaigning at Home and in Washington. Washington, DC: CQ Press.

[21] Allison Stevens. January 14, 2002. Both Parties Say Women's Wallets Ripe for Tapping. http://www.now.org/eNews/jan2002/011402donors.html. Accessed September 10, 2013.

[22] A clip promoting their program can be found at http://www.dccc.org/pages/women_lead.

Prior to being appointed to chair the DSCC, Sen. Murray had launched a program in 1999 called Women on the Road to the Senate, which helped elect four women senators in 2000. In 2002, the program, renamed the Women's Senate Network and headed by Michigan Senator Debbie Stabenow, raised $1.3 million on top of some $2 million collected through separate events earlier in that election cycle. Fund-raising activities included $1,000-per-person issue conferences that showcased Senators Hillary Clinton, Dianne Feinstein, and other "prominent senators who happen to be women" in a series of discussions on topics such as terrorism, national security, and the economy. Senator Stabenow commented that it irked her that her female colleagues are so rarely interviewed on such topics.[23] The Women's Senate Network continues as a DSCC program, headed by Senator Kay Hagan in the 2012 election cycle. Its current activities are monthly policy luncheons held in Washington, DC, as fund-raising events.

Through the 108th Congress (2003–2004), no woman had chaired a corresponding Republican campaign committee, although Representative Anne Northup of Kentucky headed recruitment for the National Republican Congressional Committee. However, for the 109th Congress (2005–2006), Republicans elected Senator Elizabeth Dole of North Carolina to head the National Republican Senatorial Committee (NRSC). She won the position by defeating Minnesota Senator Norman Coleman by one vote in the Senate Republican caucus. Dole had campaigned for the presidency in the early stages of the 2000 election before winning her Senate seat in 2002. She had also served in two cabinet positions in earlier Republican presidential administrations. Described as "about as close to a rock star as the Republican Senate has," she was considered a celebrity within the party.[24] She had helped raise more than $16 million for the NRSC in the 2004 election cycle.[25] In addition, "Dole's supporters argued that she would help Republicans win over female and minority voters by putting a 'different face on the party.'"[26]

---

[23] Sheryl Gay Stolberg. April 28, 2004. Partisan Loyalties and the Senate Women's Caucus. *New York Times*.

[24] Jamie Dettmer. November 12, 2004. Senator Dole Is Eyeing Leadership of Key Senate Committee, GOP Post. *New York Sun*.

[25] David Dolan. November 18, 2004. Dole to Lead GOP Senate Efforts; N.C. Senator Will Raise Money for 2006 Campaigns, Recruit Candidates. *Herald-Sun, Durham*, North Carolina.

[26] Frederic J. Frommer. November 17, 2004. Republicans Choose Elizabeth Dole to Head 2006 Senate Campaigns. http://usatoday30.usatoday.com/news/washington/2004-11-17-dole-senate_x.htm. Accessed December 3, 2004.

Dole's leadership of the NRSC proved otherwise. The committee fell $30 million behind the DSCC. Some of the losing Republican Senate candidates blamed Dole and her committee for a lack of support and for making bad decisions regarding advertising in support of their campaigns and against their opponents. The Associated Press reported:

> President Bush's low approval ratings, the unpopular war on Iraq, voter concern about corruption and Democratic fundraising all figured in the GOP loss of Senate control in last month's elections. But among Republicans, long-hidden tensions are spilling into view, with numerous critics venting their anger at the GOP Senate campaign committee headed by North Carolina Sen. Elizabeth Dole.[27]

Other than Senator Dole's campaign to chair the NRSC, no female members appear to have sought these party leadership positions, but they have been tapped by leadership to head up informal efforts to get more Republican women to run. In 2007, the NRCC chair Rep. Tom Cole appointed Rep. Candice Miller of Michigan to lead an effort to recruit women as candidates for the House.[28] Little appeared in the media after this announcement about any follow-up recruitment activities, and the miniscule number of Republican women who mounted candidacies for House seats in the 2008 election, especially in the twenty-six House districts vacated by Republican incumbents, suggests that this effort was anemic at best. Republicans have continued with informal efforts to recruit and support female candidates. In recent elections, Rep. Cathy McMorris Rodgers has been appointed to spearhead such efforts. In a *National Journal* interview in 2010, she offered the following advice to her party: "If we want women to run for office, it's important that we're doing the outreach, that we're talking with women and just encouraging them to run for office. There's a recognition ... that we want to encourage a broader face for our party."[29]

The party campaign committees comprise staffs of "many highly skilled political professionals" run by executive directors in addition to the elected legislative chair. A recent account of their organizational structure reported that the two Senate committees each had more than 50 staff,

---

[27] David Espo. December 23, 2006. In Wake of Senate Loss, Republicans Turn Anger on Campaign Committee Led by Elizabeth Dole. Associated Press.

[28] Aaron Blake. January 22, 2007. House Republicans Aim for More Recruitment of Women in 2008. *The Hill*.

[29] Erin McPike. May 28, 2010. Women's Prospects Still Lackluster. http://www.highbeam.com/doc/1G1-227666647.html. Accessed May 30, 2013.

while the DCCC had more than 100 employees and NRCC had approximately 75. The staffs are responsible for administration, fund-raising, research, communications, and campaign activities.[30] Women's visibility as organizational leaders within these party committees has grown in recent election cycles. In 2012, the NRCC appointed Joanna Burgos to head its independent expenditures division. Burgos was the first woman and the first Hispanic to achieve such an appointment. She had moved up through the party organization. The first woman to head the DSCC independent expenditure unit, Martha McKenna, was also appointed in 2012, and Anna Cu was hired as the DSCC's policy director. As will be shown later in this chapter, decisions regarding independent expenditures are among the most significant acts of the party organizations in their support role for candidates' campaigns in contemporary elections.

For the 2014 elections, women will be directing both parties' House campaign committees. Liesl Hickey has been appointed executive director of the NRCC. She served as the head of the NRCC's incumbent-retention Patriot Program during the 2012 cycle and had previously served as chief of staff for U.S. Rep. Mark Kirk from 2003 to 2007. Kelly Ward will serve as DCCC executive director. She had served as political director of the DCCC in the 2012 electoral cycle. A significant feature of women's increasing influence in the political world has been their movement into professional political organizational positions as well as elective office posts. *Campaigns and Elections* magazine reports that female managers ran more than half of the thirteen most competitive Senate campaigns on the Democratic side in 2012. Only one female manager worked on the top thirteen most competitive races on the Republican side.[31] These advances into organizational leadership are important for individual careers, and women campaign professionals serve as role models for young women thinking about political careers other than running for public office.

PARTY CAMPAIGN COMMITTEE SUPPORT FOR WOMEN CANDIDATES

In 2012, the DSCC created a series of joint fund-raising committees titled Women On the Road to the Senate: 12 and Counting. Each committee was designated to a particular city such as Washington, DC, New York,

---

[30] Paul Herrnson. 2008. *Congressional Elections: Campaigning at Home and in Washington*, fifth edition. Washington, DC: CQ Press.

[31] Shira Toeplitz. 2012. Women in the War Room. *Campaign and Elections Magazine*. July 23.

and Boston and included a subset of the twelve candidates. As part of this fund-raising effort, for example, in early March four western regional fund-raisers were organized under the Women on the Road banner.

In addition, as part of this campaign, the DSCC produced a video asserting that "it is time to end the culture wars and get to work for the middle class." Each of the twelve candidates was introduced, and the video ended with the tag line "If you don't like what the Republicans are doing, send a Democratic woman to the Senate. In fact, send them all."

U.S. Senators Barbara Boxer and Kirsten Gillibrand joined this effort with their own fund-raising projects for female candidates. Senator Boxer created Win with Women 2012 (www.winwithwomen2012.com) as part of her leadership PAC, endorsing all eleven Democratic female Senate candidates and providing each with the maximum amount allowed in direct contributions. A music video, "A Woman's Voice," promotes the program.[32] Senator Gillibrand has created an Off the Sidelines PAC and empowerment program (www.offthesidelines.org).

The Democratic female Senate contenders did very well. All of the incumbents were reelected, and four new women were elected. The media dubbed the Democratic female senate candidates stars of the 2012 election.[33]

Beyond these specific programs to fund women's campaigns in recent elections, in 2004 the DCCC created the Red to Blue Program, mounting major efforts to recruit and support strong Democratic candidates of both sexes in normally Republican districts. The program has since become an ongoing Democratic Party effort.

Twenty-seven Democratic House candidates benefited from Red to Blue in 2004, receiving an average rate of $250,000 per campaign. In 2012, Democrats had fifty-three candidates in the Red to Blue program, thirteen of whom were women.

In 2008, Republicans in the U.S. House initiated a counterorganization, the Young Guns, to recruit and support strong challengers and open-seat contenders in an attempt to win back majority control of the House. They designated eighteen candidates as Young Guns in that election, including two women. In 2012, the Republican Young Guns program had forty-two candidates, five of whom were women.

The number of candidates in each of these programs varies by election cycle, depending on opportunities available to a party in that campaign

---

[32] The video can be watched at www.winwithwomen2012.com/video.
[33] See for example, Hotline's The Meaning of Deb, May 17, 2012.

season. Candidates nominated in districts considered safe for a party are not part of these programs, because they are less in need of assistance.

Federal law restricts the amount of money the parties and other organizations, as well as individuals, can contribute directly to candidates running for federal offices, but unlimited independent expenditures are allowed on behalf of or in opposition to a candidate. The law also mandates that candidates and organizations report amounts raised and spent and the sources of those funds. The law and court decisions interpreting it have altered the financial world of congressional campaigns in the last few decades.

By federal law, these groups may contribute directly to any one candidate's campaign only $5,000 for a primary race and $5,000 for the general election. In addition, these organizations can contribute much larger amounts in coordinated expenditures (e.g., financing a public opinion poll for several candidates) and in independent expenditures (e.g., buying television ads supported by the party committee and shown "independently" of the candidates' campaigns). The independent expenditure aspect of federal campaign financing is of greatest consequence to campaigns for the U.S. House and Senate in recent elections. The Mc-Cain-Feingold Bipartisan Campaign Reform Act in 2002 required that independent expenditures be reported. Since the 2004 election, this reporting has allowed researchers to analyze independent expenditures to determine whether party leaders see women and men as equally viable candidates and assist them in winning to the same extents. For example, we can examine whether party organizations allocate their expenditures during the final weeks before an election, including advertising on behalf of candidates and against their opponents, in similar ways for women and men. My analyses of campaign contributions in recent elections show that the parties' congressional campaign committees have provided comparable direct financial support (limited by federal law) to similarly situated female and male Congressional nominees.[34] And looking at the larger base of funding, including coordinated and independent expenditures, the national party committees appear to have poured significant resources into the campaigns of female candidates in recent elections. Candidate sex has not made a difference in expenditure of independent funds once other factors have been taken into account. This support has important

---

[34] Biersack and Herrnson, 1994; Barbara Burrell. 1994. *A Woman's Place Is in the House: Campaigning for Congress in the Feminist Era.* Ann Arbor: University of Michigan Press.

implications not only for encouraging women to enter the electoral arena but also for increasing the likelihood of their success.

Reports through the end of November for the 2012 election indicate that the DCCC had spent $500,000 or more in independent expenditures on the campaigns of twenty-five of its fifty-five Red to Blue designated candidates. Eight of the thirteen female candidates in the program were the beneficiaries of such levels of expenditures. For example, nearly $3 million was spent against Cherie Bustos's opponent incumbent, Bobby Shilling, in Illinois' 17th district. She received the second-highest DCCC independent expenditure. Ann Kirkpatrick (AZ1) and Carol Shea Porter (NH1), both working to regain House seats lost in 2010, also received more than $2 million each from the DCCC, along with Krysten Sinema (AZ9) and Ann Kuster (NH2). The DSCC spent more than $5.6 million in negative advertising against former Wisconsin governor Tommy Thompson on behalf of Rep. Tammy Baldwin's campaign for the state's open Senate seat. Heidi Heitkamp also benefited from $2.8 million in DSCC expenditures against her opponent in the North Dakota Senate race. Nearly $3 million was spent against initially embattled incumbent Sen. Claire McCaskill's ultimately infamous opponent, U.S. Rep. Todd Akin, whose reference to "legitimate rape" in a television interview subjected him to widespread scorn and caused him to lose Republican support.

On the Republican side, the NRCC spent more than $1.5 million in advertising against Rep. Jim Matheson in Utah's 4th Congressional District to benefit challenger Mia Love. None of the other female Young Guns benefitted from large party independent expenditures. Most of the NRCC independent expenditures of $500,000 or more were spent on the campaigns of their incumbents. The GOP was on the defensive, while the House Democrats were able to go on offense.

None of the three Republican women seeking Senate seats in the general election were NRSC independent expenditure beneficiaries. However, Linda McMahon, the Republican candidate for an open Senate seat in Connecticut, contributed $40,000,000 to her own campaign, far outspent her opponent, Rep. Christopher Murphy, who raised $9,000,000. Although being vastly outspent, Rep. Murphy won the election.

Elizabeth Warren was the champion Senate fund-raiser on the Democratic side. She raised more than $39,000,000, 98 percent in individual contributions. She and her opponent, U.S. Senator Scott Brown (who raised $29,000,000 himself), had made an agreement that if any outside group ran ads for them or against their opponent, they would pay a fine. Neither party's campaign organization violated the pact with independent advertising.

WOMEN'S ORGANIZATIONS, WOMEN'S PACs, AND WOMEN'S CANDIDACIES

To approach numerical parity among elected officials, an underrepresented group must recruit candidates, often training them and providing them with sufficient early resources to mount viable campaigns. Women's political organizations have increasingly engaged in this process, becoming significant actors in contemporary elections. Going beyond prodding the parties to advance women's candidacies, they have taken matters into their own hands, undertaking recruitment, training, and development of resource bases for women candidates and grassroots support. The women's campaign community has grown, becoming more diverse in ideology and focus as it applies its resources to candidates for national, state, and local offices. They engage in the most sophisticated campaign techniques, using social media as well as grassroots organizing. They have formed their own political action committees (PACs) in the 2012 election.

The National Women's Political Caucus, founded in 1971, was the first organization to recruit and train female candidates and provide resources for their campaigns. In 1974 it conducted its first Win With Women campaign to recruit, train, and support feminist women candidates for local, state, and congressional office. The Women's Campaign Fund (WCF) was established that same year. It was the first group to establish a PAC specifically to provide resources for female candidates. These two groups are bipartisan, supporting both Democratic and Republican candidates who are pro-choice. The vast majority of their money has gone to Democratic candidates, who are more likely than Republicans to support reproductive rights. Indeed, at the federal level, all of the candidates the NWPC endorsed in 2012 were Democrats and all but one of the Women's Campaign Fund–supported candidates were Democrats. Rep. Judy Biggert of Illinois was the only WCF–endorsed Republican.

In 1984, EMILY's List was founded with the mission of "building a progressive America by electing pro-choice Democratic women to office." It has become *the* preeminent campaign organization dedicated to electing female candidates, legendary for the resources it has acquired to achieve its goal and affect the campaign world. Its political muscle has brought

Figure 8.1: EMILY's List contributions increased dramatically in contemporary elections.

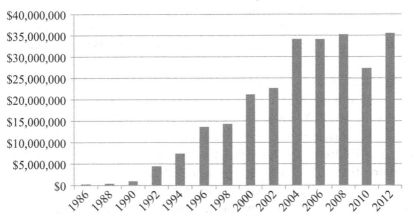

dismay and complaints from political foes[35] Figure 8.1 shows the organization's receipts in elections since 1986.

EMILY's List initiated the idea of a donor network that collects checks from individuals written directly to candidates and "bundles" them to present to endorsed candidates. Bundling has proven widely successful for EMILY's List. Members of the organization are encouraged – and in some cases asked to commit – to support endorsed candidates in this fashion. While PACs themselves are limited to a total of $10,000 in direct contributions to candidates for national office, bundling greatly expands a PAC's clout by allowing it to deliver larger sums made up of individual contributions – for example, a $20,000 package consisting of 200 $100 checks written directly to the candidate. For a number of election cycles, EMILY's List was joined by the WISH List on the Republican side. EMILY's List founder Ellen Malcolm even advised the organizers of the WISH List. The WISH List provided support to pro-choice female Republican candidates. However, the number of such candidates dwindled in recent election cycles, and the WISH List has ceased to exist as a separate organization and PAC.

EMILY's List has come to wield considerable power within Democratic circles because of its accumulated financial clout and campaign expertise. It is the "grand dame" of the PAC world, classified as a "heavy hitter"

---

[35] My parallel chapter in the second edition of Gender and Elections describes these complaints.

among PACs.[36] In recent elections, it has been among the leading PACs (not just women's PACs) in the amount of money raised. In the 2012 election cycle, it ranked sixth. Indeed, one scholar suggests that Democratic Party efforts to recruit women candidates have become virtually indistinguishable from the candidate recruitment strategies of EMILY's List.[37] In 2012 it also created a super PAC (discussed below), WOMEN VOTE!

The 2012 election was a very good campaign cycle for EMILY's List. Indeed, in promoting its endorsed candidates, EMILY's List took to calling the election W.H.Y. (Women's Historic Year) 2012. It endorsed and financially supported eleven Senate candidates, nine of whom won, and twenty-nine House candidates, nineteen of whom won. EMILY's List raised more than $1 million for both Elizabeth Warren and Tammy Baldwin in its bundling operation. In addition to direct PAC money that it contributed to campaigns, it put organizational muscle into these campaigns, delivering grassroots personnel and direct mail and phone programs aimed at informing female voters as well as Internet targeting and advertising of its endorsed candidates.

EMILY's List issued individual press releases immediately following the election congratulating each of the Senate candidates it had backed in tough competitive campaigns. Each release described the effort EMILY's List had made on behalf of that individual. For example, its press release congratulating Rep. Baldwin on her Senate victory highlighted that it had raised $1,170,312. Its super PAC, WOMEN VOTE!, ran the single largest independent effort in the history of EMILY's List, running a total of six different ads, spending more than $3 million in paid media over the course of the campaign. WOMEN VOTE! also created a Wisconsin women vote website, advertised online to swing women statewide and targeted nearly 116,000 women statewide.

Beyond EMILY's List, the NWPC, and the Women's Campaign Fund, women organizing for women have taken on a broader and increasingly significant role in political campaigns. Women's PACs that raise money primarily or exclusively for female candidates stand "at the nexus of

[36] "Heavy hitter" is a designation the Center for Responsive Politics that runs the Opensecrets.org website providing extensive data on the financing of federal election campaigns gives to the highest-funded PACs.
[37] Rosalyn Cooperman. 2001 (September). Party Organizations and the Recruitment of Women Candidates to the U.S. House since the Year of the Woman. Paper presented at the Annual Meeting of the American Political Science Association, San Francisco, CA.

TABLE 8.2: Contributions to federal candidates by PACs concerned with women's issues went predominantly to Democrats in 2012

PAC Name	Total	Democrats	Republicans
EMILY's List	$ 248,980	$ 248,980	$ 0
Value in Electing Women PAC	$ 166,241	$ 0	$ 166,241
Women's Political Committee	$ 161,000	$ 161,000	$ 0
Tri-state Maxed Out Women	$ 115,000	$ 115,000	$ 0
Women's Campaign Forum	$ 59,500	$ 58,000	$ 1,500
National Organization for Women	$ 44,381	$ 44,381	$ 0
Maggie's List	$ 39,500	$ 0	$ 39,500
WomenWinning/Minnesota Women's Campaign Fund	$ 15,000	$ 15,000	$ 0
Feminist Majority Foundation	$ 14,250	$ 14,250	$ 0
Women's Action for New Directions	$ 13,850	$ 13,850	$ 0
National Organization for Women	$ 13,301	$ 13,301	$ 0
Women under Forty PAC	$ 10,000	$ 7,500	$ 2,500
National Women's Political Caucus	$ 7,000	$ 6,500	$ 500
Women in Leadership	$ 6,200	$ 6,200	$ 0
Santa Barbara Women's PAC	$ 3,500	$ 3,500	$ 0

Note: Based on data released by the FEC on November 12, 2012.

political change and politics as usual: bringing women into positions of power by mastering the political money game."[38] They have encouraged women to run, trained them in campaign tactics and strategy, raised vital early money to start their campaigns, and provided a network of supportive organizations that can sustain a campaign during the final weeks of an election.[39] Table 8.2 describes the federal women's issue PAC world in the 2012 election as compiled by the Center for Responsive Politics. Contributions to federal candidates by PACs concerned with women's issues went predominately to Democrats in that election as in the past.

[38] Christine L. Day and Charles D. Hadley. 2005. *Women's PACs: Abortion and Elections*. Upper Saddle River, NJ: Pearson Prentice Hall.

[39] Candice J. Nelson. 1994. Women's PACs in the Year of the Woman. In *The Year of the Woman: Myths and Realities*, ed. Elizabeth Adell Cook, Sue Thomas, and Clyde Wilcox. Boulder, CO: Westview Press, 181–196. See also Mark Rozell. 2000. Helping Women Run and Win: Feminist Groups, Candidate Recruitment and Training. *Women & Politics* 21(3): 101–116.

TEXT BOX 8.1: Sarah Palin, SarahPAC, and Mama Grizzlies

The biggest challenge to liberal feminist dominance of the world of women's campaign organizations since the 2008 election has undoubtedly been former Alaska Governor and Republican vice-presidential nominee Sarah Palin's campaign for "common-sense conservative" female candidates in 2010 and 2012. Her rhetorical invocation of what she calls "mama grizzlies" in the midst of the 2010 election challenged not only the liberal feminist establishment but Republican mainstream organizations as well. In a speech at a Susan B. Anthony List fund-raiser in May of 2010, she issued a clarion call to mama grizzlies to rise up, issuing a warning that a herd of "pink elephants" was stampeding to Washington with an "e.t.a. of November 2 . . . You don't want to mess with moms who are rising up." "If you thought pit bulls were tough, you don't want to mess with mama grizzlies she intoned. Mama grizzly candidates became part of the Republican campaign landscape in that election, with Palin endorsements and characterizations of a number of the female candidates as mama grizzlies, tough conservative women. "She brought to the Republican Party what some members had once complained did not exist: a concerted effort to tap female candidates for promotion and lift them out of obscurity," Anne Kornblut noted in the *Washington Post* (2010).

Illustrative is Palin's endorsement of CeCe Heil in the 2012 election, one of eleven Republican primary contenders and the only woman competing to oppose Democratic Rep. Jim Cooper in the general election. In her endorsement, Palin described Heil (who had previously run for a seat in the House) as "another tough 'mama grizzly' with the experience, passion, and integrity to restore some common sense to Washington. As a small business owner, attorney, constitutional scholar, and proud mother of two, she will fight tirelessly to protect our freedoms and rein in the excesses of an out-of-control federal government that seems set on spending away our children's future" (CeCe Heil's campaign website).

SarahPAC, her political action committee, then produced a video highlighting the mama grizzly phenomenon to raise money for their campaigns. In addition to making direct contributions to thirteen Republican women running for House seats and five Republican female Senate candidates, Palin provided a priceless boost to the momentum of many of these 2010 candidacies with her endorsement. In her video and speeches, Palin explicitly invoked women's status as mothers as a central reason they would be good political representatives. Palin argued that voters should support her mama grizzly candidates "because moms kind of just know when there's something wrong." Moreover, she argued that the mama grizzlies represented an emerging conservative feminist ideology that would bring important and underrepresented perspectives to the policy table.

In 2012, the number of mama grizzlies to endorse was quite small. In that election, SarahPAC, reported raising nearly $5 million. It made direct contributions totaling $134,500 to seven senate candidates (six men and one woman) and seventeen House candidates (ten men and seven women). In only one case did the endorsement come with reference to being a mama grizzly. In a thirty-second ad that featured Palin praising Sarah Steelman running in the Republican primary to challenge Missouri Senator Claire McCaskill, she praised Steelman as a "conservative maverick" who would defend tax dollars "like a mama grizzly defending her cubs." Steelman lost the primary to Rep. Todd Akin.

COMPETING IN THE SUPER-PAC WORLD

Super PACs are a new type of political action committee created in 2010. In its *Citizens United v. Federal Election Commission* decision, the U.S. Supreme Court overturned sections of the 2002 McCain-Feingold Reform Act that had prohibited corporate and union political expenditures in political campaigns. The *Citizens United* ruling has made it legal for corporations and unions to spend funds from their general treasuries to finance independent expenditures related to campaigns but did not alter the prohibition on direct corporate or union contributions to federal campaigns. Organizations seeking to contribute directly to federal candidate campaigns must still rely on traditional PACs for that purpose. This ruling opened the way for outside groups to organize into what have come to be called "super" PACs, which can raise and spend unlimited amounts of money. No limits have been put on individual contributions to these PACs.

The creation of super PACs dramatically increased the role of money in the 2012 election. The "independence" of these PACs has allowed them to fill airwaves, phone lines, mailboxes, and websites with unprecedented negative advertising, their predominant mode of influencing voters. Super PACs spent more than $630 million in that election, according to Federal Election Commission reports. Conservative super PACs dominated the election. These organizations may pose challenges to women's candidacies and opportunities for women's campaign organizations in the new financial milieu.

There is not yet evidence to suggest that this flow of money has disproportionately hurt female candidates or that they are disproportionately negatively targeted. But because Democrats have fielded more female candidates and conservatives have so far dominated among super PACs, it would seem that their involvement might have had a negative impact on the election of women to federal office. The outcome of the 2012 elections, in which four new Democratic women were elected to the Senate and all of the Democratic female incumbents running for reelection emerged victorious, suggests that negative conservative super PAC advertising was effectively countered. And in fact, a couple of women's groups, She-PAC and Women Vote!, formed their own super PACs.

She-PAC was created in 2012 as both a traditional political action committee that gives directly to campaigns and a super PAC planning "to pour millions of dollars into the campaigns of conservative women running for state and federal office." According to its mission statement, it has a two-fold purpose: to make contributions directly to the campaigns of principled conservative women running for federal office and to make expenditures on behalf of principled conservative women running for federal and statewide office. "She" stands for "support," "honor," and "elect." Its aim for 2012 was to raise $25 million.[40] Condoleezza Rice served as the group's star attraction at fund-raising events. At the end of the 2012 election cycle, it reported having raised $154,860, far short of its initial goal, and spending $113,749. It reported contributing $5,000 in traditional PAC contributions to five candidates: Deb Fischer and Heather Wilson running for the U.S. Senate and three U.S. House candidates – Karen Harrington, Mia Love, and Kim Vann. As a super PAC, it must be considered a failure, because it reported only $430 in independent expenditures.

EMILY's List's super PAC, WOMEN VOTE!, was the dominant super PAC supporting women's campaigns in 2012. It reported $7.9 million in independent expenditures for that election. It entered five Senate races and nineteen House races.

"DON'T GET MAD, GET ELECTED": FOSTERING GREATER FEMALE POLITICAL LEADERSHIP

As noted earlier, women have implemented a variety of strategies to bring more women into political leadership positions with the goal of gender equity in elective office. Some groups focus on fostering leadership skills among girls and young women, while others aim to increase the candidacies of older women. Universities have established campaign training

---

[40] Chris Moody. 2012. "ShePAC": Republican women get their own super PAC. *The Ticket.* February 12. And see Naureen Khan. 2012. Can She-PAC Help Republicans Solve Their Woman Problem? *National Journal.* February 24.

academies, and local and state programs have proliferated alongside the national efforts that have been the focus of this chapter to this point.

Why is it that twenty years after the Year of the Woman in American politics, even more groups are being created across the political spectrum to recruit, train, and elect women to public office? Why are distinct efforts still needed to effect women's empowerment and political parity, especially when female candidates in contemporary elections are just as seasoned and professional campaigners as men and run sophisticated fund-raising operations?

A fascinating array of projects to find, recruit, train, and finance women as political candidates characterizes the current election terrain in the United States. Their names include such titles as Political Parity, She Should Run, Real Women Run, Smart Girl Politics, the White House Project, and Emerge America.

Consider, for example, the 2012 Project's rallying cry, "Don't Get Mad, Get Elected." The 2012 Project was a national, nonpartisan campaign of the Center for American Women and Politics (CAWP). The Project's goal was to increase the number of women in Congress and state legislatures by taking advantage of newly drawn and newly created districts resulting from redistricting and reapportionment. Its initial aim was to reach out to women in professions such as finance, science, technology, health, the environment, small business, and international affairs and encourage them to consider running for office, although as it evolved, the focus was increasingly on more general outreach to women candidates, particularly through state-based efforts. As Debbie Walsh, director of CAWP, described it using the words of one of the project's initiators, Mary Hughes, "We all stand in a circle and look at each other, and at some time we need to turn around and look outside the circle and bring in some new faces, and that is hard" (personal interview).

Other groups employed a variety of strategies. Some, such as Smart Girl Politics and Emerge America, ran webinars in which women could learn campaign skills online from home. A coalition of women's rights leaders under the banner of Political Parity launched a bipartisan campaign to double the number of women elected to the highest levels of government by 2020. The group held a press conference on January 19, 2012, to announce the initiative, chaired by Democrat activist Swanee Hunt and former Lieutenant Governor Republican Kerry Healey. Healey dubbed the campaign a "grand experiment."

Efforts to bring women into the electoral arena have expanded downward to encourage young women and girls to become political leaders. A number of universities and organizations around the country

have developed such programs. The CAWP, for instance, has offered
the NEW Leadership™ summer institute since 1991. This intensive resi-
dential program educates college women about politics and policy making and encourages them to participate in the political process. In 1999,
CAWP began partnering with colleges and universities across the country to offer state or regional versions of the program (see http://www
.cawp.rutgers.edu/education_training/NEWLeadership/index.php). And
in 2004, building on the NEW Leadership™ model, CAWP began collab-
orating with Girl Scouts of the USA on Pathways to Politics, a two-week
program for high school students from across the nation. That program
was repeated in 2006 and 2008.

Others have initiated similar efforts to educate younger women and
girls about politics. Inaugurated in 2007, Running Start hosts an annual
Women's Political Leadership Retreat at American University in Washington, DC, for high school girls from across the country, with the goal
of encouraging them to enter political office. Future Frontrunners, a segment of Lifetime Networks' nonpartisan Every Woman Counts campaign,
held a high school and college leadership contest in which contestants
submitted written or video essays answering the question, "What would
you do if you were president?" The winners attended the Democratic
and Republican National Conventions in 2008, where they participated
in leadership training workshops with women elected officials.

The Girl Scouts of the USA has also developed a Ms. President Patch
in cooperation with the White House Project. Girls participate in a variety
of projects to learn about women in leadership both within their troops
and on their own. Such activities can be undertaken locally rather than
by attending a national or regional program.

CosmoGirl, working with the White House Project, took another
approach with *What's Your Point, Honey?* a film that premiered in 2008.
The documentary, created by Amy Sewell and Susan Toffler, tells the
stories of seven young women who were leaders on college campuses
or local communities and in 2006 participated in Project 2024. The concept of the film is that by 2024 – the year when the magazine's youngest
readers will reach the age of thirty-five and be eligible to run for U.S.
president – one "CosmoGirl" from each year of the program will stand on
the presidential debate floor as a real candidate.[41]

[41] Besa Luci. June 23, 2008. Tweens and Twenties See Future Led by Women. http://www
.truth-out.org/archive/item/78803:tweens-and-twenties-see-future-led-by-women. Accessed June 28, 2008.

Organized efforts to increase the numbers of women in public office have also reached outward, encouraging women to think of themselves as potential candidates and prepare themselves to run. The CAWP lists a number of these programs and itself offers one such model, its Ready to Run™ campaign training. Held annually, Ready to Run is a bipartisan program for women who want to run for office, work on a campaign, get appointed to office, become community leaders, or learn more about the political system.[42] As it does with NEW Leadership™, CAWP trains state-based partners to present their own versions of the Ready to Run™ model.

In July 2007, the Women's Campaign Forum (WCF) launched the She Should Run campaign. The campaign is mainly an online effort to stimulate individuals to nominate women who they believe would make good candidates. WCF follows up, approaching viable nominated women and encouraging them to consider running. They also provide informational resources for prospective candidates. By September 2009, the names of more than 1,000 women had been submitted to an online database that lists women who have been identified by friends or colleagues as potential candidates who should run for office. The WCF is working to build on the research finding that women may not put themselves forward as candidates and may need encouragement to consider running.

CONCLUSION

Long gone are the days when women candidates won party nominations primarily as "sacrificial lambs" in districts in which their party had little prospect of winning. The parties have found it to their advantage to promote women candidates, and once women become nominees, they are as likely as male candidates to have access to party resources, particularly in highly competitive races in which they can often count on substantial support in the final days of the campaign. Women candidates, particularly those who are pro-choice, also have the advantage of access to women's PACs, which have become formidable players in campaigns; conservative women are also gaining increasing access to PAC money and training from their end of the spectrum. A continuing problem for women candidates, however, is reaching the point of becoming competitive. Research suggests that women are more hesitant than men to run

---

[42] See   http://www.cawp.rutgers.edu/education_training/ReadytoRun/RtoR_New_Jersey. php.

for office, and the limited opportunity structure for newcomers in the form of open seats, competitive districts, and vulnerable incumbents has offered few opportunities for women to expand their numbers as national lawmakers.

Party organizations no longer control the nomination process in most states. While they are involved in recruiting candidates, few have taken concerted steps to recruit women candidates as an overt strategy to increase women's numbers in elective office. Members of Congress and the campaign committees' staffs do appear to encourage some prospective candidates to run. As congressional scholar Paul Herrnson has observed, "Armed with favorable polling figures and the promise of party assistance in the general election they search out local talent. Promising individuals are invited to meet with the members of Congress and party leaders in Washington and to attend campaign seminars."[43] At this early stage of the campaign process, women's groups are especially valuable. They recruit and train women candidates to make them more viable candidates. They work aggressively in primary elections and provide a substantial resource base.

In the world of political campaigns, women have come a long way and are now strong and competitive players. Several factors have advanced women's prospects: the rise of PACs promoting women's candidacies for public office and funding their campaigns; the lessening of party discrimination against women candidates; and the availability of substantial support from congressional campaign committees in competitive situations. None of these positive factors, however, offsets such negatives as the paucity of women presenting themselves as candidates and the advantages afforded incumbents, most of whom are male. Thus, gender continues to matter in political campaigns; fortunately, a multitude of organized efforts are now promoting women's candidacies, and an increasing number of female professionals are joining the world of campaign organizing.

[43] Paul Herrnson. 1998. Congressional Election: Campaigning at Home and in Washington. Washington, DC: CQ Press.

9 Advertising, Websites, and Media Coverage

Gender and Communication along the Campaign Trail

Twenty years after 1992's "Year of the Woman" campaign, in which record numbers of women ran for and were elected to political office, female political candidates recorded several significant political firsts in 2012. A new record was set in the number of women running for and elected to the U.S. Congress. New Hampshire became the first state to have an all-female delegation in the U.S. Congress as well as a woman governor. And the first openly gay woman was elected to the U.S. Senate.

Still, women running for state and federal political office continue to confront age-old challenges in their media coverage and, subsequently, how they frame their communication to voters through television advertising and websites. Three U.S. Senate candidates – incumbent Claire McCaskill (Democrat-Missouri), open-seat contender Deb Fischer (Republican-Nebraska), and challenger Elizabeth Warren (Democrat-Massachusetts) – demonstrate how successful women candidates used communication strategies to win their elections in 2012.

McCaskill, who became the first woman elected to the U.S. Senate from Missouri when she narrowly defeated the male incumbent in 2006, faced a serious reelection challenge in 2012 against U.S. Representative Todd Akin of Missouri's second congressional district. The Tea Party-backed Akin led McCaskill in polls taken in March through late August, when his comment in a television interview that victims of "legitimate rape" rarely get pregnant because the female body "has ways to try to shut that whole thing down" derailed his campaign. Republicans – including presidential nominee Mitt Romney – were quick to denounce Akin for his remarks and demand that he leave the U.S. Senate race.

McCaskill quickly capitalized on the turn of events in her speeches and political ads. In one ad, her campaign used clips of statements by some of the most prominent Republicans who came out against Akin at the time: "Is Todd Akin fit to serve in the Senate? Mitt Romney doesn't think so," a voiceover says at the opening, which is followed by a clip of Romney disavowing Akin soon after his comments came to light. "What he said was indefensible, was wrong, it was offensive, and he should step out of the race," Romney says. The ad also cites remarks made by Arizona Republican Senator John McCain that Akin "would not be welcome by Republicans" in the Senate.

In addition to capitalizing on Akin's remarks to turn the race around and eventually win by a 55 percent-to-39 percent margin, McCaskill emphasized her bipartisan accomplishments in her television ads and on her website: "Earning accolades from Republicans and Democrats alike, Claire has tackled issues of accountability and transparency, earmark reform, national security and consumer protection, among many others."

Fischer, the first woman elected to the U.S. Senate from Nebraska by a 58 percent-to-42 percent margin, also highlighted her record as a "bipartisan problem solver" in her open-seat race against former Nebraska Governor and former U.S. Senator Bob Kerrey. Serving her second term in the state legislature when she defeated two better-known and better-financed male challengers in the primary, Fischer was described by lawmakers of both political parties as a tough legislator and an unwavering advocate for her district covering a vast area of north-central Nebraska. Fischer highlighted this reputation in an ad titled "New Leader" featuring Nebraska Governor Dave Heineman. While Fischer is shown in a montage of scenes talking to voters – women, men, seniors, and young professionals – in a variety of indoor and outdoor settings, Heineman says: "She's a smart, bipartisan problem solver who sticks to her principles.... America faces big challenges and Deb Fischer will work the Nebraska way to change Washington, balancing the budget, stopping higher taxes, repealing Obamacare. Deb Fischer is a strong leader Nebraska can trust."

Fischer also was portrayed as a tough political candidate by the state's largest newspaper, the *Omaha World Herald*. In an article titled "Deb Fischer's Path to Politics Fueled by Grit, Determination," Matthew Hansen described the candidate's "brief and fleeting moment of fear" when door-knocking for votes during her first campaign for a seat in the Nebraska legislature. "If there is a second true thing about Fischer, it is this: When she encounters this emotion, she puts on work boots and stomps it into dust." The article also quotes longtime friend Joyce Simmons, a national committeewoman for the Republican Party: "Deb is as tough as barbed wire. She can be warm and friendly, but at her core she's made of steel.

People used to underestimate her. They used to underestimate her toughness. They don't do that so much anymore."[1]

Warren also emphasized her toughness and strength as a Washington outsider fighting for the middle class in her campaign against incumbent Massachusetts Senator Scott Brown. For example, on her website, she noted:

> There are plenty of people in Washington looking out for the billion dollar corporations and lobbying for Wall Street. I've been an outsider, but for years, I've been fighting for middle class families, taking on big banks, putting forward new ideas, and working to turn those ideas into a reality that makes a difference for people. That's what I'll keep doing once I'm in the U.S. Senate. I'll be there fighting for small businesses and middle class families.

Trailing Brown in the early months of the race, Warren went on to win by a 53 percent-to-46 percent margin as the first woman elected to the U.S. Senate from Massachusetts.

From its very beginning, the Massachusetts Senate race attracted national attention from the media, especially after it was revealed that Warren had identified herself as a minority professor in a law faculty directory but did not have proof of the 1/32 Cherokee heritage that she claimed. Conservative bloggers and commentators were quick to make derogative comments about Warren's claims, with Russ Limbaugh calling her a "heap big squaw Indian giver," "not even an honest Injun," and the "high-cheek boned priestess" on his nationally syndicated radio talk show.[2] Opponent Brown also ran a television ad, titled "Who Knows," which included a series of news clips reporting Warren's claims of undocumented Native American heritage and argued that she lacked credibility.

Warren directly responded to allegations that she improperly identified as Native American to further her career by releasing a thirty-second-spot in which she addresses the issue head on: "Let me be clear. I never asked for, never got any benefit because of my heritage. The people who hired me have all said they didn't even know about it," she says. "Scott

---

[1] Matthew Hansen. September 30, 2012. Deb Fischer's Path to Politics Fueled by Grit, Determination. *Omaha World Herald*. http://www.omaha.com/article/20120930/NEWS/709309936.

[2] Media Matters for America. Search for articles on Russ Limbaugh's comments about Elizabeth Warren. http://mediamatters.org/search/index?qstring=Elizabeth+warren&tags=&tags=&tags=rush-limbaugh&issues=&from=MM%2FDD%2FYYYY&to=MM%2FDD%2FYYYY.

Brown can continue attacking my family, but I'm going to keep fighting for yours."

Through their televised political ads, websites, and media coverage, McCaskill, Fischer, and Warren demonstrated how a candidate's communications can create a positive, integrated message that connects with voters. From the time a candidate contemplates her candidacy to the day of the election, she will be engaged in some aspect of communication – including person-to-person, speeches, interviews with the media, debates, television ads, e-mail, and websites. Further complicating the campaign communication process is the recent rise of online media sources – such blogs, Facebook, Twitter, YouTube, and political websites – for campaign news and the concurrent decline of some traditional media sources, especially newspapers.

In this chapter, I examine the three major communication channels through which voters see candidates – media coverage, television commercials, and websites. In today's political campaign, these three media are powerful and important sources of information, not necessarily because they influence voting behavior, although there is some evidence that they do, but because they draw attention to the candidates and their campaigns. Moreover, candidates, especially for federal and statewide elected office, have found that these media provide efficient ways to reach potential voters, and thus their campaigns use all three channels to get their messages out.

By comparing how female and male political candidates navigate the campaign communication environment, we can see how both are presented to voters and speculate about how differences in media use and coverage might affect their voter support. Ultimately, examining gender differences in candidate communication reveals that both women and men are using television and online communication strategies to define their images and issues – at some times confronting and at other times capitalizing on gender stereotypes held by voters and the news media.

MEDIA COVERAGE OF WOMEN POLITICAL CANDIDATES

Women forging new political ground often struggle to receive media coverage and legitimacy in the eyes of the media and, subsequently, the public. According to some observers, journalists often hold female politicians accountable for the actions of their husbands and children, although they rarely hold male candidates to the same standards. They ask women questions they don't ask men, and they describe them in ways and with words that emphasize their traditional roles and focus on their appearance and behavior.

Twenty years ago, in 1992's Year of the Woman campaign, news stories nonetheless commented on female candidates' hairstyles, wardrobes, weight and other physical attributes, children, and the men in their lives. For example, a story in the *Washington Post* described unsuccessful U.S. Senate candidate Lynn Yeakel from Pennsylvania as a "feisty and feminine fifty-year-old with the unmistakable Dorothy Hamill wedge of gray hair . . . a congressman's daughter [with] a wardrobe befitting a first lady . . . a former full-time mother."[3]

In 1992, the *Chicago Tribune* described Carol Moseley Braun, who was elected to the U.S. Senate from Illinois, as a "den mother with a cheerleader's smile."[4] Six years later, the *Chicago Tribune* was still focusing on Moseley Braun's personality and appearance, as this story from her 1998 reelection campaign shows: "Though she boasts that her legislative record is one of the best in the Senate, it is not her votes that make many of her supporters go weak in the knees. It is her personality, featuring a signature smile that she flips on like a light switch, leaving her admirers aglow."[5]

And it does not seem to make a difference – in terms of stereotypical media coverage – if two women are running against each other rather than a male opponent, as these excerpts from stories in the *Seattle Times* covering the 1998 U.S. Senate campaigns of incumbent U.S. Senator Patty Murray and challenger U.S. Representative Linda Smith illustrate: "Murray has been airing soothing television commercials that make her look so motherly and nonthreatening, in her soft pinks and scarves, that voters might mistake her for a schoolteacher." Murray and Smith, the story further noted, are different "in style as well as politics. Even the shades of their blue power suits hinted at the gap between the women. Murray's was powder blue; Smith's royal."[6]

Beginning with the 2000 election, there appears to have been less emphasis on the physical appearance and personality of women political candidates, particularly those running for governor and U.S. Senate.

[3] Linda Witt, Karen M. Paget, and Glenna Matthews. 1995. *Running as a Woman: Gender and Power in American Politics*. New York: Free Press.

[4] Ibid.

[5] Michael Dorning. October 22, 1998. Carol Moseley Braun for Senator, Image Is Asset and Curse: Though She Stresses Her Record, the Democrat Finds Her Personality and a Series of Missteps in the Spotlight. *Chicago Tribune*.

[6] James Devitt. 1999. *Framing Gender on the Campaign Trail: Women's Executive Leadership and the Press*. Washington, DC: Women's Leadership Fund.

However, examples of such coverage can still be found. For instance, the weight, wardrobe, and hairstyles of former First Lady Hillary Clinton – who ran successfully for the U.S. Senate in New York in 2000 and 2006 and unsuccessfully for the Democratic nomination for president in 2008 before serving as U.S. Secretary of State from 2008 to 2012 – have been a constant source of media comment. In coverage of her 2000 race, an article in the *Milwaukee Journal Sentinel* declared that Clinton had "whittled her figure down to a fighting size 8" by "touching little more than a lettuce leaf during fundraisers."[7] An article in the *New York Times*, reflecting on her victory, was titled "First Lady's Race for the Ages: 62 Counties and 6 Pantsuits," and referred to retiring U.S. Senator Daniel Patrick Moynihan as walking the newly elected Senator Clinton "down the road to a gauntlet of press like a father giving away the bride."[8]

Comments by the news media on Clinton's appearance and personality continued as she campaigned for the Democratic Party nomination for president in 2008. For example, three articles in the September 30, 2007, *New York Times* commented on Clinton's laugh – calling it a "cackle," "calculating," and transitioning the candidate "from nag to wag"[9] – evoking negative stereotypes about women. On cable television news shows, Clinton was referred to as a "white bitch" on MSNBC and CNN; the "wicked witch of the west" on CNN; and a "she devil" and the castrating Lorena Bobbitt on MSNBC.[10]

The 2012 presidential campaign also produced some anecdotal evidence that Minnesota U.S. Representative Michele Bachmann was covered in stereotypical ways by the media in her bid for the Republican nomination for president. For example, an article in the *New York Daily News* titled "Palin's Hair Apparent! Bachmann Politics Aren't N.Y.C. Fave, but Locks Are" focused on Bachmann's hairstyle: "It's redder. It's fuller. It's more chic."[11] A story on The Huffington Post website titled "Michele

---

[7] Jennifer L. Pozner. March 13, 2001. Cosmetic Coverage. http://www.alternet.org./story/10592.

[8] Ibid.

[9] See Patrick Healy. September 30, 2007. The Clinton Conundrum: What's Behind the Laugh? *New York Times*. http://www.nytimes.com/2007/09/30/us/politics/30clinton.html; Frank Rich. September 30, 2007. Is Hillary Clinton the New Old Al Gore? *New York Times*. http://www.nytimes.com/2007/09/30/opinion/30rich.html?_r=0; and Maureen Dowd. September 30, 2007. The Nepotism Tango. *New York Times*. http://www.nytimes.com/2007/09/30/opinion/30dowd.html?_r=0

[10] Media Matters for America. Search for articles on Hillary Clinton. http://mediamatters.org/.

[11] Joanna Malloy, August 30, 2011. Palin's Hair Apparent! Bachmann Politics Aren't N.Y.C. Fave, But Locks Are. *New York Daily News*. http://www.nydailynews.com/news/national/palin-hair-apparent-bachmann politics-aren-n-y-fave-locks-article-1.951037.

Bachmann Wears Tons of Makeup for CNN Debate" – which was picked up by several newspapers – noted that the candidate "sported heavily made-up eyes for the debate – is that blue eye shadow? – and frosty pink lips, along with her silver necklace and diamond earrings."[12]

Such examples of the media's attention to the appearance of women political candidates are backed by more than thirty years of research by scholars from political science, journalism, and communication. Even though the media coverage of female politicians has improved over the years, they are still treated differently than male politicians by the media, suggesting that gender stereotypes continue to pose problems for women in politics.

For example, women candidates who ran for election in the 1980s and 1990s were often stereotyped by newspaper coverage that not only emphasized their feminine traits and feminine issues but also questioned their viability – that is, their ability to win the election. In an experiment in which fictitious female candidates were given the kind of media coverage usually accorded to male incumbents, respondents rated them equally likely as men to win.[13]

In the mid to late 1990s and into the twenty-first century, women political candidates began to receive more equitable media coverage, in terms of both quantity and quality, when compared with male candidates. In 1998, for example, female and male candidates for governor received about the same amount of coverage, but women received less issue-related coverage than men did.[14]

In the 2000 primary and general election races, women running for the U.S. Senate and governor received more coverage than men, and the quality of their coverage – slant of the story and discussion of their viability, appearance, and personality – was mostly equitable. Still, women candidates in 2000 were much more likely to be discussed in terms of their gender, marital status, and children, which can affect their viability in the eyes of voters.[15]

The media coverage of women political candidates running for the U.S. Senate and governor continued to improve in the 2002 and 2004

[12] Jessica Misener, November 23, 2011. Michele Bachmann Wears Tons of Makeup for CNN Debate. *The Huffington Post*. http://www.huffingtonpost.com/2011/11/23/michele-bachmann-makeup_n_1109553.html.

[13] Kim F. Kahn. 1992. Does Being Male Help? An Investigation of the Effects of Candidate Gender and Campaign Coverage on Evaluations of U.S. Senate Candidates. *Journal of Politics* 54: 497–517.

[14] Devitt, 1999.

[15] Dianne G. Bystrom, Mary C. Banwart, Lynda Lee Kaid, and Terry Robertson. 2004. *Gender and Candidate Communication: VideoStyles, WebStyles, NewsStyles*. New York: Routledge.

elections, especially in terms of the number and length of stories written about their campaigns. However, the media continued to link some issues – particularly those that resonate with voters – with male candidates more often than with female candidates. For example, in the media coverage of their race for governor in 2003, Kathleen Blanco was associated with stereotypically feminine issues and Bobby Jindal with stereotypically masculine ones, despite her expertise on the economy and his on health and education.[16]

In 2008, contradicting recent research trends, women running for governor and mayors of cities of 100,000 or more received less media coverage than their male opponents. Although they were covered similarly in terms of their image attributes, male candidates were linked more often with the masculine issues of budget and crime. And, while both female and male candidates were covered most often in the strategy (or game) frame, women candidates for governor and mayor were more likely than men to be covered in the issue frame and men were more likely than women to be covered in the candidate frame.[17]

An analysis of the newspaper coverage of twelve female-versus-male U.S. Senate races in 2012 found that these candidates received mostly similar coverage of their images and issues. Female candidates were more often portrayed as compassionate and intelligent and were more likely to discuss the middle class and birth control than were male candidates. Female candidates received more positive coverage than did male candidates, but the men received significantly more coverage.

Female candidates were more likely to be covered in the candidate frame and less likely to be covered in the issue frame than were male candidates.

Overall, although some stereotyping still exists, the playing field for female candidates is becoming more level, at least when they are running for governor and for the U.S. Senate. However, as the 2000, 2008, and 2012 campaigns show, women running for vice president or for the major political parties' nomination for president receive less equitable coverage than do their male opponents.

[16] Lesa Hatley Major and Renita Coleman. 2008. The Intersection of Race and Gender in Election Coverage: What Happens When the Candidates Don't Fit the Stereotypes? *The Howard Journal of Communication* 19: 315–333.

[17] Dianne Bystrom, Narren Brown, and Megan Fiddelke. 2012. Barriers Bent but Not Broken: Newspaper Coverage of Local and State Elections. In *Women and Executive Office: Pathways and Performance*, ed. Melody Rose, 159–179. Boulder, CO: Lynne Rienner.

For example, Elizabeth Dole received less coverage in terms of quality and especially quantity than her male opponents during her eight-month run in 1999 for the 2000 Republican nomination for president. Polls consistently showed Dole as a distant runner-up to eventual nominee George W. Bush, but her coverage lagged behind not only that of Bush but also that of Steve Forbes and John McCain, who at the time were behind her in the polls. Dole also received less issue coverage than her top male opponents. However, Dole's issue coverage was balanced between such masculine issues as taxes, foreign policy, and the economy and such feminine issues as education, drugs, and gun control. She also received more personal coverage than her male opponents, including references to her appearance and, especially, personality.[18]

In 2008, Democratic presidential candidate Clinton and Republican vice presidential candidate Sarah Palin both received negative and often stereotypical media coverage. Clinton's newspaper coverage in Iowa and New Hampshire in the months leading up to the Iowa caucus and New Hampshire primary was significantly more negative than Barack Obama's, with 22 percent of the stories focusing on Clinton coded as negative compared to just 2 percent of the stories focusing on Obama. In addition, stories focusing on Clinton were more likely to emphasize her campaign strategies and personal characteristics – or game frame – than issues in her newspaper coverage in the *Des Moines Register*, *Concord Monitor*, *New York Times*, and *USA Today*.[19]

In their 2010 book, *Hillary Clinton's Race for the White House: Gender Politics & the Media on the Campaign Trail*, Regina Lawrence and Melody Rose document findings of their content analysis of Clinton's newspaper and television coverage. Not only were negative comments more frequently directed at Clinton, the media's overwhelming game-framed coverage of

---

[18] See Sean Aday and James Devitt. 2001. Style over Substance. Newspaper Coverage of Female Candidates: Spotlight on Elizabeth Dole. Washington, DC: Women's Leadership Fund; Dianne Bystrom. 2006. Media Content and Candidate Viability: The Case of Elizabeth Dole. In *Communicating Politics: Engaging the Public in Democratic Life*, ed. Mitchell S. McKinney, Dianne G. Bystrom, Lynda Lee Kaid, and Diana B. Carlin, 123–133. New York: Peter Lang; and Caroline Heldman, Susan J. Carroll, and Stephanie Olson. 2005. "She Brought Only a Skirt": Print Media Coverage of Elizabeth Dole's Bid for the Republican Presidential Nomination. *Political Communication* 22: 315–335.

[19] See Dianne Bystrom. 2008. *Gender and U.S. Presidential Politics: Early Newspaper Coverage of Hillary Clinton's Bid for the White House*. Presentation at the annual meeting of the American Political Science Association, Boston, MA, August 29; and Daniela V. Dimitrova and Elizabeth Geske. 2009. *To Cry or Not to Cry: Media Framing of Hillary Clinton in the Wake of the New Hampshire Primary*. Presentation at the annual meeting of the International Communication Association, Chicago, IL, May 29.

the presidential primaries also highlighted her campaign as a struggling one, even when she was the decisive front-runner.[20]

A study that examined the media coverage of both Clinton and Palin through examples from print media, television, and social networking found that Clinton was attacked for her lack of femininity (e.g., overly ambitious, cold, calculating, scary, or intimidating), while Palin was portrayed as a sex object.[21] Another study that compared Palin's media coverage to that received by Democratic vice presidential candidate Joe Biden in 2008 and Democratic vice presidential candidate Geraldine Ferraro in 1984 found that Palin's media coverage, especially on television, focused more extensively on her appearance and family; was more critical on personal as well as substantive issues; and reinforced gender stereotypes by focusing on feminine traits and issues, even though she emphasized masculine issues in her speeches. Palin's coverage in 2008 mirrored the treatment of Ferraro as the first woman to run for vice president on a major party ticket.[22]

In the race for the 2012 Republican nomination for president, Bachmann appears to have received more equitable coverage than Clinton and Palin in 2008, at least in the early stages of her campaign. For example, the Pew Research Center's Project for Excellence in Journalism found that mainstream media coverage of Bachmann was more positive than negative between May 2 and October 9, 2011. She received 47 percent neutral coverage, 31 percent positive coverage, and 22 percent negative coverage compared to eventual Republican presidential nominee Romney's coverage, which was 47 percent neutral, 26 percent positive, and 27 percent negative during that time period.[23]

However, while the tone of Romney's media coverage remained consistent over those 23 weeks, the "trajectory of Bachmann's coverage was...bumpy" with "distinctly good weeks and bad weeks," according

[20] Regina G. Lawrence and Melody Rose. 2010. *Hillary Clinton's Race for the White House: Gender Politics and the Media on the Campaign Trail*. Boulder, CO: Lynne Rienner.

[21] Diana B. Carlin and Kelly L. Winfrey. 2009. Have You Come a Long Way, Baby? Hillary Clinton, Sarah Palin, and Sexism in 2008 Campaign Coverage. *Communication Studies* 60(4): 326–343.

[22] Kim Fridkin, Jill Carle, and Gina Serignese Woodall. 2012. The Vice Presidency as the New Glass Ceiling: Media Coverage of Sarah Palin. In *Women and Executive Office: Pathways and Performance*, ed. Melody Rose, 33–52. Boulder, CO: Lynne Rienner.

[23] Pew Research Center's Project for Excellence in Journalism. October 17, 2011. The Media Primary: How News Media and Blogs Have Eyed the Presidential Contenders during the First Phase of the 2012 Race. http://www.journalism.org/node/26958.

to the Pew report. Bachmann's coverage became more negative when the media began to focus on personal matters – including reports that she suffered from debilitating migraines and accusations that her husband operated a counseling practice that tried to convert homosexuals to heterosexuals through prayer.[24]

Another study comparing Bachmann's media coverage on national network and cable television stations to that of six male opponents seeking the 2012 Republican nomination for president found mostly similarities and just a few differences. For example, although mentions of such image attributes as appearance, family, and marital status were rare for all candidates, Bachmann received less coverage of these attributes as compared to her male opponents. And she received less personal criticism than former Speaker of the House of Representatives Newt Gingrich, Texas Governor Rick Perry, and Romney. Bachmann was twice as likely to be linked with masculine issues as feminine ones overall. Specifically, she was most often linked with foreign relations (28 percent of her issue coverage), taxes (20 percent), and health care (18 percent.) Bachmann did receive much less coverage than most of her male opponents; although she was mentioned in 56 percent of the 557 television news stories studied, she was was quoted in only 19 percent and was the focus of just 5 percent.[25]

Thus, as we embark on the beginning of the twenty-first century, we find mostly equitable media coverage of female and male candidates for governor and U.S. Senate in terms of quantity as well as quality (e.g., assessments of their viability, positive versus negative slant, and mentions of their appearance). However, women running for president or vice president mostly receive less equitable and often more sexist and stereotypical coverage than their male opponents.

The differences that persist in the media coverage of female and male candidates for federal and statewide executive and legislative office may mesh with gender biases in the electorate to put women candidates in untenable positions. By reinforcing some of the traditional gender stereotypes held by the public, the media affect the outcomes of elections and, thus, how the nation is governed.

---

[24] Ibid.

[25] Dianne Bystrom and Daniela V. Dimitrova. (Forthcoming). Marriage, Migraines, and Mascara: Media Coverage of Michele Bachmann in the 2012 Republican Presidential Campaign. *American Behavioral Scientist.*

TELEVISED POLITICAL ADVERTISING OF WOMEN CANDIDATES

Because women political candidates are often framed in stereotypical terms by the media, television advertising – and the control it affords candidates over campaign messages about their images and issues – may be even more important for female candidates. Over time, researchers have found both differences and similarities in the ways in which female and male candidates use this campaign communication medium.

In the 1980s, female candidates' political ads were more likely to emphasize social issues, such as education and health care, whereas men were more likely to focus on economic issues such as taxes. In highlighting their personal traits, women were more likely to emphasize compassion and men to stress their strength, although sometimes both sexes emphasized stereotypically masculine traits such as competence and leadership. Men were more likely to dress in formal attire, while women preferred "feminized" business suits and office or professional settings.[26]

From the 1990s to the present, as more women ran for political office, my colleagues and I found that female and male candidates were strikingly similar in their uses of verbal, nonverbal, and film or video production techniques, although some differences were discovered.[27] Female and male candidates were increasingly similar over time in their use of negative ads as well as in the issues discussed in their ads and, especially, in the image traits emphasized and appeal strategies used.

The similarities and differences that did emerge over the past twenty-two years are interesting from a gender perspective. For example, although female and male candidates have used attacks similarly in recent years, they differ in the purpose of the attacks and employ different strategies. Both female and male candidates now use negative ads primarily to

---

[26] See Anne Johnston and Anne Barton White. 1994. Communication Styles and Female Candidates: A Study of Political Advertisements of Men and Women Candidates for U.S. Senate. *Political Research Quarterly* 46: 481–501; Kim F. Kahn. 1993. Gender Differences in Campaign Messages: The Political Advertisements of Men and Women Candidates for U.S. Senate. *Political Research Quarterly* 46(3): 481–502; and Judith Trent and Teresa Sabourin. 1993. Sex Still Counts: Women's Use of Televised Advertising during the Decade of the 80s. *Journal of Applied Communication Research* 21(1): 21–40.

[27] Bystrom, Banwart, Kaid, and Robertson, *Gender and Candidate Communication*, 2004. The database of television commercials for female and male gubernatorial and U.S. Senate candidates from 1990 through 2002 used in this book has been updated with ads from similar races in 2004, 2006, and 2008 for this chapter. This database now includes 1,786 ads; 918 for women and 868 for men; 870 for Republicans and 916 for Democrats; 1,044 for U.S. Senate candidates, 640 for gubernatorial candidates, and 102 for presidential candidates.

attack their opponents on the issues. However, women candidates are more likely than men candidates to criticize their opponents' personal characteristics and call them names, usually employing an anonymous announcer. This was particularly the case with female U.S. Senate candidates in 2008. Male candidates, on the other hand, are significantly more likely to attack their opponents' group affiliations or associations and background or qualifications.

For example, in her 2012 open-seat U.S. Senate race, Democratic U.S. Representative Tammy Baldwin ran a series of negative ads against her opponent, former Wisconsin Governor Tommy Thompson. In the ads, she consistently uses the label "he's not for you anymore" to describe Thompson, with charges that he made millions of dollars working for Washington, DC, lobbyists and refused to release his taxes. Baldwin went on to win her race against Thompson, becoming the first openly gay woman elected to the U.S. Senate.

Baldwin's ad "No" illustrates this strategy. An anonymous announcer attacks Thompson, with clips of Thompson saying he will not release his taxes interspersed throughout the spot: "What's happened to Tommy Thompson? For years as governor, Tommy released his taxes. But now that he has made millions working for a Washington, DC, lobbying firm, hmm, why won't Tommy Thompson release his tax returns? What is he hiding? Tommy Thompson. He's not for you anymore."

Voters may view attacking the opponent's character rather than issue stances and calling the opponent names as much more personal. Here, female candidates may be taking advantage of voters' stereotypes, which portray women as more caring and compassionate. Female candidates may have more latitude than male candidates to make personal attacks, because they enter the race with the stereotypical advantage of being considered kinder. Of course, defying stereotypical norms also may backfire for women candidates if they are labeled as too aggressive, rather than assertive, by the media. Male candidates, in contrast, may feel more constrained by expectations that they treat women with some degree of chivalry by refraining from attacks on the personal characteristics of their female opponents. Instead, they may lash out significantly more often at their opponent's group affiliations; guilt by association may be a more acceptable and indirect way to question their opponent's character.

Although female and male candidates are increasingly similar in the issues they discuss, image traits they emphasize, and appeal strategies they use in their ads, the differences that did emerge are interesting from a gender perspective. For example, over time, women candidates have been more likely than men to discuss such stereotypically feminine issues as education and health care. However, no consistencies have emerged over time in the issue emphasis of male candidates, who have focused on such topics as crime, welfare, and a decline in morals in various election cycles in their television ads.

As for the images emphasized in their ads, women candidates often portray themselves as successful, action-oriented, aggressive, tough leaders – commonly considered masculine attributes – but also have consistently emphasized their honesty, more commonly considered a feminine quality. In their ads, men often portray themselves as successful, action-oriented, aggressive, tough leaders with experience in politics – all masculine attributes. Among these traits, male candidates have been significantly more likely than women to discuss their experience in politics until the 2008 election, when female candidates were significantly more likely than men to emphasize this trait. Also in 2008, contrary to previous research, male candidates were significantly more likely than women to emphasize their honesty.[28]

The appeal strategies used in female and male candidate ads are closely related to the traits they emphasize and are thus interesting from a gender perspective. Both female and male candidates have been mostly equally likely to employ all the elements of feminine style, characterized by an inductive structure (moving from specific observations to broader generalizations), personal tone, addressing viewers as peers, use of personal experiences, identifying with the experiences of others, and inviting audience participation. The fact that both women and men used elements of feminine style in similar proportions may suggest that this style works best for thirty-second spots on television, regardless of candidate gender. However, male candidates have used statistics – a masculine strategy – significantly more often than female candidates. And female candidates are more likely to make gender an issue in their ads, an indication that at least some women are campaigning as female candidates and not political candidates who happen to be women.

In the 2012 election, several women U.S. Senate candidates made direct appeals to women voters when gender became an issue in such areas as health care and reproductive choice. Missouri's McCaskill ran a

[28] Dianne G. Bystrom and Narren J. Brown. 2011. Videostyle 2008: A Comparison of Female vs. Male Political Candidate Television Ads. In *Communication in the 2008 Election: Digital Natives Elect a President*, ed. Mitchell S. McKinney and Mary C. Banwart, 211–240. New York: Peter Lang.

series of three thirty-second television spots featuring rape victims who criticized Akin for his opposition to allowing sexual assault victims to have access to emergency contraception. In one ad, Diana – who describes herself as a pro-life mother who never has voted for McCaskill but will do so now because of Akin's remarks – says: "In the hospital I was offered emergency contraception. Because of my personal beliefs, I declined. Here's what else I believe: no woman should be denied that choice." In another ad, Rachel says she was raped a decade ago during a home invasion and took emergency contraception at the hospital: "At the worst moment of her life, no woman should be denied that choice. What Todd Akin said was troubling enough, but it's what he believes that's worse."

In the nonverbal content of their television ads, female candidates have been significantly more likely to dress in business as opposed to casual attire and to smile more often than men. Both of these nonverbal characteristics reflect gender-based norms and stereotypical expectations. The choice of business attire reflects the gender-based norms that society imposes on women as they face the challenge of portraying themselves as serious and legitimate candidates. In their everyday life, smiling is regarded as a nonverbal strategy that women use to gain acceptance. Perhaps women are more likely than men to smile in their ads for the same reason – to gain acceptance from viewers in the traditionally male political environment.

Because society's gender stereotypes more often associate women with families and children, it is interesting to note who is pictured in female and male candidate ads. Interestingly, women candidates have distanced themselves from their roles as wives and/or mothers by rarely picturing their families in their ads compared to men candidates, who have included their families in about one-fifth of their ads over time. In 2008, women candidates were significantly more likely than men to picture young children in their ads, but not their own children.[29]

In Massachusetts, Republican incumbent Senator Brown ran a series of ads featuring his family, including his two daughters and wife, Gail Huff. In an ad titled "Gail," Huff says she "wants to set the record straight" against attacks by Warren. "Scott Brown is pro-choice, he supports women's health care, and he supports good jobs for equal pay," Huff says while looking directly into the camera from her living room couch. "Coming from a household of women, we wouldn't have it any other way," Huff adds, now sitting with their two daughters.

[29] Ibid.

In picturing their families or not, both male and female candidates are confronting societal stereotypes. Women candidates may want to show voters that they are more than wives and/or mothers and to dismiss any concerns voters may have over their abilities to serve in political office because of family obligations. Male candidates, in contrast, may want to round out their images beyond business and politics by portraying themselves as loving husbands and/or fathers.

Winning female and male candidates use different strategies than losing female and male candidates. Specifically, female candidates who ultimately won had discussed issues more frequently – taxes, health care, senior citizen issues, and women's issues in particular – and emphasized being an aggressive fighter more often than other candidates had. Male candidates who won had emphasized their leadership and experience more frequently. Women candidates – both winning and losing – used attacks in almost half of their ads. Losing men were the most negative, and winning men – perhaps because they were running in less competitive races in which they did not need to go on the attack to win – were the least negative of all candidates in their campaigns.

Overall, it is notable that female candidates who won tended to be those who emphasized masculine traits and both feminine and masculine issues (although more feminine than masculine ones). Winning candidates, both female and male, used substantial issue discussion in their advertising, but this was particularly true of the ads of winning female candidates. Winning male candidates incorporated a mix of feminine and masculine strategies to ensure their success.

In addition to the content of the television ads, it is interesting to look at the effects these appeals have on potential voters. At first, researchers speculated that masculine strategies (aggressive, career) rather than traditional feminine strategies (nonaggressive, family) worked best for women candidates in their political ads. However, it now seems that women are most effective with voters when balancing stereotypically masculine and feminine traits, such as being tough and caring. Women are more effective when communicating about stereotypically feminine issues such as women's rights, education, and unemployment than such stereotypically masculine issues as crime and illegal immigration.

On the basis of the research, then, women candidates should be advised to emphasize both stereotypically feminine and masculine images and issues in their television commercials. Voters will perceive a woman candidate as more honest, intelligent, and compassionate than a man; just as hard working; and able to forge compromise and obtain consensus.

However, especially in a climate of international terrorism, homeland security, and the war in Iraq, a woman candidate will need to emphasize her ability to lead the nation during a crisis and to make difficult decisions.

Issue emphasis will vary with the context of the campaign. In the 1990 through 2012 elections, taxes, education, jobs, health care, foreign affairs, and senior citizen concerns were the top issues discussed by female and male candidates in their television ads, with women more likely than men to discuss education, health care, and senior citizens. According to survey research, voters rate female candidates more favorably than male candidates on these issues. However, women candidates are considered less able to handle such issues as crime and public safety, national security, and defense. In elections in which war, crime, and terrorism rise to the top among voter concerns, women candidates must work hard to demonstrate their competence on these issues.

WEBSITES OF WOMEN POLITICAL CANDIDATES

In recent years, the Internet has provided political candidates and office-holders with an important means of communicating with voters and constituents and researchers with another way to look at the political communication of female and male politicians. Websites, like television advertising, represent a form of political communication controlled by the politician rather than interpreted by the media.

Recent research shows that female and male politicians present themselves similarly on their websites. For example, in their study of the websites of candidates running in mixed-gender races for seats in the U.S. House of Representatives in 2012, Mary Banwart and Kelly Winfrey found mostly similarities, but some differences, in issues, images, and appeals used by women and men.[30] As for the issues discussed on their websites, both female and male candidates frequently discussed the economy in general, budget deficit, and unemployment. However, the masculine issue of taxes and feminine issue of health care appeared only in the male candidates' top five issues discussed. Conversely, the feminine issues of education and senior citizen concerns were among the top five issues discussed among female candidates but not among the male candidates.

[30] Mary C. Banwart and Kelly L. Winfrey. 2013. Running on the Web: Online Self-Presentation Strategies in Mixed-Gender Races. *Social Science Computer Review* 31(5): 614–624.

After categorizing issues discussed on candidate websites into feminine, masculine, and neutral, Banwart and Winfrey found other interesting gendered results. Both female and male candidates discussed masculine issues most frequently, neutral issues second most frequently, and feminine issues least frequently. However, women candidates discussed the neutral issue of farming and agriculture and the feminine issues of equal pay for women and women's issues in general significantly more often than male candidates. Male candidates, on the other hand, were significantly more likely to discuss the masculine issues of budget deficit and immigration than were female candidates on their websites.

In examining the discussion of leadership traits on the candidates' websites, Banwart and Winfrey found that both women and men frequently mentioned such traits as past performance, their qualifications and experience, and being "of the people." However, male candidates more frequently discussed the masculine trait of being action oriented, whereas female candidates were more likely to discuss the masculine trait of competency. Further examination of traits categorized as feminine, masculine, and neutral revealed that both female and male candidates mentioned masculine traits most frequently, neutral traits second most frequently, and feminine traits least frequently. However, women candidates were significantly more likely to discuss the masculine trait of competency and the feminine traits of being sensitive/understanding and a Washington outsider than the men.

In looking at the campaign strategies employed on candidate websites in 2012, Banwart and Winfrey found that both women and men frequently invited viewer participation, emphasized their accomplishments, shared personal experiences, and used a personal tone. However, female candidates were significantly more likely to use the "voice of the state" challenger strategy and the "above the trenches" incumbent strategy. Male candidates were significantly more likely to employ the "call for change" challenger strategy. Overall, both women and men employed feminine strategies the most frequently and masculine strategies the least frequently. Female candidates were more likely to use incumbent over challenger strategies, while male candidates were more likely to use challenger strategies over incumbent strategies on their websites in 2012.

U.S. Senate candidates Warren of Massachusetts and Fischer of Nebraska employed several strategies more common to female candidates on their websites during their successful campaigns. For example, Warren employed an "above the trenches" incumbent strategy in discussing such feminine issues as education, seniors, and women. Under the "women"

tab, she lists equal pay for equal work and women's health issues, including reproductive health care.

In discussing the neutral issue of agriculture, Fischer employed a
"voice of the state" challenger appeal strategy: "As someone involved in
a family ranch business, I know first-hand the challenges and responsibilities people in agriculture face. Agriculture plays a crucial role in
our Nebraska economy and provides a stable and safe food supply for
our nation and for the world. As a U.S. Senator, I can be a key ally for
Nebraska agriculture."

Overall, female and male candidates discussed mostly the same issues
on their websites as they did in their television ads, suggesting, once
again, that issue emphasis is more related to the context of the particular political campaign than to the sex of the candidates.

Previous research by Banwart and her colleagues on the content of
female and male candidate websites revealed mostly similar findings to
the 2012 study.[31] At the beginning of the twenty-first century, women
were most likely to discuss education, health care, taxes, and senior citizen issues and men to focus on education, the environment, taxes, and
health care. In 2004, Banwart found more frequent discussion, as compared to previous election cycles, of homeland security, unemployment,
and the economy on both female and male candidates' websites. Over
the past twelve election cycles, both female and male candidates also
have attempted to establish similar images on their websites, highlighting performance and success, experience, leadership, and qualifications –
all stereotypically masculine traits.

Candidates also have been more likely to launch attacks on their websites than in their television ads. Again, the greater use of attacks on candidates' websites, as compared to television ads, underscores the difference between these media. As websites are most often accessed by people
already supporting the candidate, it is safer to include attacks. Television
ads, in contrast, have the potential to reach all voters, who may be turned
off by attacks.

As in their political ads, women candidates are most likely to appear
in business attire on their websites; in fact, they were so dressed in more
than 90 percent of the photographs used. In contrast to their televised

---

[31] Mary Christine Banwart. 2006. Webstyles in 2004: The Gendering of Candidates on
Campaign Websites? In *The Internet Election: Perspectives on the Web in Campaign 2004*, ed.
Andrew Paul Williams and John C. Tedesco, 37–56. Lanham, MD: Rowman and Little-
field.

advertising, however, male candidates were also more likely to be seen in business attire as opposed to casual attire on their websites. Women's dominant use of business attire is characteristic of female candidates' self-presentation; that is, women choose such attire to establish a professional appearance that emphasizes their competence and the seriousness of their candidacy to convince voters of their legitimacy. However, on a website – as opposed to television – male candidates also clearly feel the need to appeal to more traditional political expectations by establishing an image of a serious, viable political candidate.

Most of the photographs on candidates' websites have shown the candidate with other people, whether the images were located on the candidates' home pages or in their biography sections. Male candidates have been slightly more likely than female candidates to include pictures of just themselves in their candidate biography sections, while female candidates have been slightly more likely than male candidates to include pictures of themselves with other people, perhaps seeking to illustrate that many are supportive of their campaigns. When others are shown in the photos, female candidates have been more likely than male candidates to have men in their photos, and in many instances, these were men in positions of power and prestige, a strategy undoubtedly designed to lend legitimacy to the female candidate's campaign.

Both female and male candidates have featured women in about 80 percent of their websites and minorities in about 60 percent. Women have been more likely to post photos of senior citizens on their websites compared to men. Male candidates have been more likely than women to include photos of their families on their websites. It seems that some female candidates have chosen not to associate themselves with their families in hopes of not being linked with motherhood and domestic responsibilities, which can diminish their political credibility. For male candidates, however, the presence of family can evoke notions of stability and tradition, suggesting that because they have a family to protect, they will govern in ways that will protect the viewer's family as well.

One advantage that websites have over television ads is the potential for interaction with Internet users, allowing the candidates to appear more personal as well as to raise money and recruit volunteers. Both female and male candidates have taken advantage of the opportunity for interactivity, for example, by including more links from their home page to their biography, issues, contribution page, "get involved" page, and news coverage. Increasingly, both female and male candidates are posting their television ads and other campaign videos on their websites.

Male candidates have been more likely to link to a calendar of events section, which requires more frequent updates and attention than a well-established biography page, contribution page, or even their issues pages. So male candidates either are more aware of the need to have their websites current and up to date or they may simply have the financial ability to pay someone to do the updating.

Overall, the websites of candidates running in recent U.S. Senate, U.S. House, and gubernatorial mixed-gender races were largely similar. Notably, few gender differences emerged. Thus, it appears that the strategies used in political candidate website design are in response to expectations for the medium rather than candidates' sex. The ability to present an unmediated message to potential voters makes the campaign website an appealing venue for female candidates in particular.

CONCLUSION

An examination of how female and male candidates are presented in their campaign news coverage, political advertising, and websites perhaps suggests more questions than answers. Interpreting the results of more than thirty years of research examining the campaign communication of women running for governor and the U.S. Congress is further complicated by studies of the rarer bids of female presidential and vice presidential candidates. In addition, researchers are just starting to examine the impact of the recent emergence of new media – such as online news sites, commercial websites, blogs, social networking services such as Facebook and Twitter, and the popular video-sharing website YouTube – on mainstream media coverage and candidate communication. Nonetheless, several recurring trends help guide our expectations for the future role of gendered campaign communication.

Candidates do not have complete control of how the news media decide to cover their campaigns. In the 1980s and 1990s, especially, female candidates suffered from gendered media coverage that often afforded them less coverage, which focused on their appearance rather than the issues and questioned their ability to win. However, in more recent campaign cycles, female candidates for governor and U.S. Senate have achieved sufficient status as candidates to be given equal and sometimes greater coverage in newspapers than their male opponents.

However, some areas of news coverage remain troublesome for female candidates. The tendency of the media to emphasize candidate sex, appearance, marital status, and masculine issues in news coverage still haunts female candidates. Candidate sex is still mentioned more frequently for women, reporters still comment more often on a female candidate's dress or appearance, and journalists still refer to a female candidate's marital status more frequently. The mostly negative and often sexist coverage of Clinton and Palin in the 2008 presidential race shows that women seeking national executive office face considerable obstacles in their media coverage.

Some of the most negative and sexist comments about Clinton and Palin in 2008 and Bachmann in 2011 first appeared in the new media and then spilled over into the mainstream media in the coverage of their campaigns. The online universe of political commentary operates outside of traditional media editorial boundaries and is sometimes incisive but often offensive and unsubstantiated. Common themes that originated in the new media about Clinton in her 2008 presidential campaign portrayed her as a psychotic, power-hungry stalker or castrator and questioned her sexuality. New media commentary on Palin often exploited her "feminized" sexuality, comparing her to a Barbie doll and Photoshopping her head onto a bikini-clad woman with an automatic weapon. In 2011, almost half of the comments about Bachmann in the blogosphere were negative, with comments questioning her intellect and sanity but praising her beauty.

Although neither male nor female candidates can directly control news coverage, they can have some influence on it. For example, by focusing on a mixture of masculine and feminine issues, a female candidate can achieve a balance that diminishes the likelihood that the media will leave her out of a discussion of masculine issues. Female candidates also can use their controlled communication media – television ads and websites – to influence their news coverage. For the past three decades, the news media have increased their coverage of candidate television advertising. And, in recent campaign cycles, the news media have expanded their coverage of candidates' online campaign presence. So, women candidates can influence their news coverage through high-quality television ads, attractive and interactive websites, and an active presence on Twitter and Facebook that will attract media attention.

Television commercials and websites also provide female candidates with tremendous opportunities to present themselves directly to voters without interpretation by the news media. Television advertising is still the dominant form of candidate communication for most major-level races in which female candidates must compete with male opponents. Female candidates are successfully establishing their own competitive styles of political advertising. For example, women have overcome the stereotypical admonition that they must avoid attacks. Even as challengers, they have been able to adopt strategies typical of incumbents to give themselves authority. Female candidates who win also seem to have been successful at achieving a television videostyle that is overall positive, emphasizes personal traits of toughness and strength, and capitalizes on the importance of feminine issues such as education and health care while also discussing masculine issues such as the economy and national security. Winning female candidates also top their male opponents by keeping their attire businesslike and their smiles bright.

One interesting development in candidate campaign communication in the 2012 election cycle was the launch of a cable television station by former Hawaii Republican Governor Linda Lingle in her open-seat race against Democratic U.S. Representative Mazie Hirono for the U.S. Senate. Digital cable channel 110, which was displayed as LL2012 in channel guides, was designed to provide timely information about Lingle's "positions on important issues affecting Hawaii and the nation, as well as a library of video messages, interactive polling opportunities and live coverage of key events on the campaign trail," according to a release from her campaign. According to her campaign, the channel had 70,000 viewers – each watching an average of three and one half minutes, or the equivalent of seven thirty-second ads – when it was launched in July 2012. Although Lingle lost the race to Hirono, it will be interesting to see if other female and male candidates launch their own television stations in future elections to provide information to voters.

When it comes to self-presentation in the newest campaign medium, the Internet, research shows fewer differences between male and female candidates. The campaign websites of both women and men are characterized by significant amounts of issue information. Interestingly, the most recent research on campaign websites shows that both female and male candidates are more likely to discuss masculine issues and emphasize masculine traits while employing feminine appeal strategies.

The Internet may be the best venue for female candidates wanting an equal competition with male candidates, especially in situations in which resources are limited. A female candidate can do much more for much less through a website than through television advertising. Female candidates should develop sophisticated websites that provide more specialized messages to specific groups, use innovative types of interactivity, and generate a more personalized presence with voters – for example, through audio-visual presentations by the candidate and by providing opportunities for citizens to tune in for personal chats and question-and-answer sessions with the candidate or campaign representatives. Websites also can be used to respond to rumors and attacks generated by the new media.

Despite continuing stereotypes held by voters and the media, women candidates can manage campaign communication tools in ways that improve their chances of success. Women candidates who present themselves successfully in their television ads and on their websites may be able to capitalize on these controlled messages to influence their media coverage for a synergistic communication effort.

10 Women's Election to Office in the Fifty States

Opportunities and Challenges

During presidential election years, all eyes are focused on the top of the ticket. Congressional races attract attention, too, especially in years in which control of Congress could shift. In contrast, state elections are typically carried out with far less fanfare and attention from voters and the media. However, state elections deserve their turn in the spotlight.

State governments are critical to American politics and public policy. The fifty states are often at the forefront of policy innovations, earning them status as "laboratories" for testing out new ideas. For example, the national Family and Medical Leave Act (FMLA) was influenced by state policies, and today some state family leave and maternity leave policies are more generous than the national policy.[1] Meanwhile, a state's experiences can provide warning to Congress and other states about policy directions that should be avoided.

Voters can influence policy choices through state elections. Who runs, wins, and serves matters because state policies are consequential, affecting people's daily lives. The decisions that states make today can have effects over the long run, putting a state on a particular trajectory and foreclosing alternatives. Governors and state legislative leaders can also be agenda setters and opinion leaders in their states. Moreover, today's state legislators and statewide officials are tomorrow's candidates for governor, Congress, and president.

State policy choices are very much in the news today, and the choices are wide ranging. Most states face difficult decisions as they continue struggling to recover economically. How much should be spent on preschool education versus health care? Child care versus job training?

[1] Anya E. Bernstein. 2001. *The Moderation Dilemma: Legislative Coalitions and the Politics of Family and Medical Leave*. Pittsburgh, PA: University of Pittsburgh Press.

What about higher education spending? Meanwhile, the year 2011 saw a record number of abortion restrictions enacted, reflecting the dominance of Republicans in the state legislatures. State-level pro-life restrictions continued to win favor in 2012, and some of the bills, such as those requiring a woman to have a vaginal ultrasound prior to an abortion, made national news (and late-night comedy shows).[2] Same-sex marriage was voted on in many state legislative chambers, and states also debated provisions of President Barack Obama's Affordable Care Act and whether to "opt in" and broaden Medicaid coverage to include more low-income Americans.

The U.S. Justice Department, Democrats, and civil rights groups battled with states and with the Republican Party over new voter identification laws that threatened to reduce turnout of young voters, older voters, and racial minorities. Many state legislatures debated immigration bills addressing law enforcement and access to driver's licenses. The U.S. Supreme Court decision to uphold a central piece of an Arizona immigration law, which critics call racial profiling, ensured that state debates would continue.

States are important actors in many policy areas that have a disproportionate effect on and are of disproportionate interest to women, including abortion and reproductive rights, education, and social welfare policy. Research has found that women legislators are much more likely than their male counterparts to feel an obligation to represent women as a group and to work on legislation designed to help women, children, and families. Gender differences in backgrounds and life experiences can lead to different perspectives on issues, different policy positions, and different policy priorities. Moreover, the states are especially important to understanding women's representation and the status of women candidates. There are 98 women serving in Congress, but 1,769 women serve in state legislatures.[3] And while a woman has yet to reach the Oval Office, five women serve as the governors of their states. Because many statewide officials and members of Congress have prior service as state

---

[2] Guttmacher Institute. 2013. 2012 Saw Second-Highest Number of Abortion Restrictions Ever. http://www.guttmacher.org/media/inthenews/2013/01/02/index.html. Accessed January 19, 2013.

[3] All data on women officeholders and candidates in this chapter are from the Center for American Women and Politics (CAWP), Eagleton Institute of Politics, Rutgers University. The author is grateful to Gilda Morales and Christabel Cruz for their assistance. My focus on even-year elections captures the vast majority of states' elections. However, four states – Alabama, Mississippi, New Jersey, and Virginia – hold their regular elections for state legislature in off years.

legislators, women's ability to gain state legislative office has implications for women's presence in higher-level offices.

In the pages that follow, I describe the barriers and opportunities women face in seeking state legislative and statewide executive office and discuss differences across states in women's officeholding. I use the 2010 and 2012 elections to assess the status of women in the states. We will see that party is a key factor in understanding women's candidacies and women's representation. We will also see that although women are making gains in the states in some respects, women's progress has stalled in recent years.

WOMEN'S PATHWAYS TO THE STATE LEGISLATURES: THE CAWP RECRUITMENT STUDIES

For more than a century, women have been seeking and holding state legislative office. The first three women to win seats in a state legislature did so in Colorado in 1894. Despite this long history and women's status as the majority of the electorate, fewer than one in four state legislators is female: in 2013, women are only 24.1 percent of state legislators, and their presence in the legislatures has been flagging in recent years. The stagnation in recent years in women's state legislative officeholding teaches us that gains for women are far from inevitable and that the passage of time will not necessarily lead to equal representation for women in politics.[4] Of course, women's representation has increased over time; today's situation in which nearly one quarter of state legislators are women is a far cry from the level in 1971 when women were fewer than 5 percent of state legislators. But what the future holds for women's officeholding is unclear.

How have women reached state legislative office in the past? And how can more women do so in the future? One fruitful approach is to study the backgrounds and election histories of those who have successfully reached office in order to learn from their experiences. The most comprehensive studies ever conducted on pathways to the legislatures come from the Center for American Women and Politics (CAWP). The 1981 and 2008 CAWP Recruitment Studies surveyed all female state legislators

---

[4] Kira Sanbonmatsu, Susan J. Carroll, and Debbie Walsh. 2009. *Poised to Run: Women's Pathways to the State Legislatures*. New Brunswick, NJ: Center for American Women and Politics, Eagleton Institute of Politics, Rutgers University; and Susan J. Carroll and Kira Sanbonmatsu. 2013. *More Women Can Run: Gender and Pathways to the State Legislatures*. New York: Oxford University Press.

268 Kira Sanbonmatsu

Figure 10.1: Women's state legislative representation has stalled since the late 1990s.

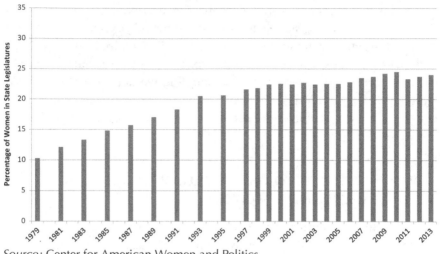

Source: Center for American Women and Politics.

and their male counterparts.[5] This approach provides unprecedented insights into the ways that gender intersects with pathways to office and suggests strategies for increasing women's representation.

A central conclusion of the 2008 CAWP Recruitment Study is that women need not have planned to run for office from a young age in order to reach the legislature. In fact, nearly twice as many women state representatives said that they were recruited to run as said that they ran because it was their idea: 53 percent said they first sought office because someone suggested it, whereas 26 percent said that seeking office was entirely their idea. The remainder of women state representatives (22 percent) said that it was a combination: that they had thought about it and that someone had suggested it to them.

In contrast, nearly half of their male counterparts said that seeking office the first time was their idea (43 percent of male state representatives); far fewer of them (28 percent) said they ran because someone else suggested it, with the remainder (29 percent) stating that it was a combination of their idea and the suggestion of someone else. Similar gender differences were evident among state senators.

---

[5] See Sanbonmatsu, Carroll, and Walsh, 2009, and Carroll and Sanbonmatsu, 2013, for more details and a complete discussion of the methodology. See also Gary F. Moncrief, Peverill Squire, and Malcolm Edwin Jewell. 2001. *Who Runs for the Legislature?* Upper Saddle River, NJ: Prentice Hall.

Thus, receiving encouragement to run for office plays a much more powerful role in women's routes to state legislatures than for their male counterparts. This implies that women's state legislative representation depends on the strength of the recruitment mechanisms that encourage women's candidacies. As Susan J. Carroll has argued, "there is no invisible hand at work to insure that more women will seek and be elected to office with each subsequent election."[6]

One barrier to increasing women's representation is thought to be the "social eligibility pool" – the pool of individuals with the informal credentials for holding office, such as a career in business or law.[7] It has been argued that these gendered career differences make it more difficult for women to run for office than men, although this problem is expected to solve itself as women continue to make educational and occupational gains in fields that usually precede a career in politics. But CAWP's research shows that women and men state legislators traditionally come from somewhat different occupations, and this continues today. Between 1981 and 2008, pathways to the legislature have converged to some extent for men and women; for example, more women legislators come from law and business now than in the past. But gender differences in occupational background persist. Because women are more likely than men to come from the fields of health and education, those interested in increasing the presence of women state legislators can look to female-dominated fields as one source of potential female candidates.

Because nearly half of women state representatives did not have prior elective experience before entering the legislature, CAWP's research provides further support for the notion that there are multiple pathways to officeholding. While some legislators have prior elective service, not all do. The authors of the study conclude:

> Recognizing that women legislators continue to emerge from a range of occupations and vary in age, education, and political experience, we conclude that the pool of women eligible to run is both wider than commonly perceived and more than sufficient for women to achieve parity in state legislatures.

Thus, the good news is that there are more than enough women who could potentially pursue state legislative seats, meaning that equality for women in state legislative officeholding is attainable.

---

[6] Susan J. Carroll. 2004. Women in State Government: Historical Overview and Current Trends. *Book of the States 2004*. Lexington, KY: Council of State Governments, 396.

[7] R. Darcy, Susan Welch, and Janet Clark. 1994. *Women, Elections, and Representation*, 2nd ed. Lincoln: University of Nebraska Press.

LESSONS LEARNED: THE 2010 AND 2012 STATE LEGISLATIVE ELECTIONS

A close look at recent elections illustrates some of the challenges that remain for women's state legislative representation. The 2010 and 2012 elections were rich with opportunities for newcomers to win office. Electoral volatility and heightened competition between the Democratic and Republican Parties in recent years has created significant turnover in the legislatures. And the 2012 cycle included the results of state legislative redistricting – a process that occurs every ten years to ensure that population changes do not lead to imbalances in the numbers of people residing within each legislative district. States used population data from the 2010 Census to guide them in redrawing state legislative district lines. Elections that occur after redistricting usually lead to enhanced open-seat opportunities and a higher number of electorally vulnerable incumbents, decreasing predictability. In fact, according to the National Conference of State Legislatures (NCSL), redistricting years are known to see 30 percent of seats change hands; in 2010, 29 percent of state legislative seats had turned over, and even prior to the 2012 general election, NCSL estimated that 2012 could bring the highest level of turnover in state legislative seats in fifty years.[8]

How did women fare in 2010 and 2012 in light of these electoral opportunities? The quick answer: not particularly well. In 2009, women constituted 24.3 percent of all state legislators; after the 2010 and 2012 election cycles and the redistricting process, women's representation stayed about the same with women comprising 24.1 percent of legislators in 2013. Therefore, the existence of enhanced electoral opportunities and high turnover was insufficient for women to gain as a share of all state legislators. Why? What can we learn from the 2010 and 2012 state legislative elections?

Several important features stand out if we look closely at CAWP's data on women state legislative candidates. First, Table 10.1 demonstrates that incumbency mattered in 2010 and 2012 in the state legislative elections, consistent with past state legislative elections as well as congressional elections (see Richard Fox, Chapter 7, this volume). Studies show that women who run for the legislatures fare about the same as similarly

---

[8] Karl Kurtz. 2012. A majority of state legislators may have two years or less of experience in 2013. http://ncsl.typepad.com/the_thicket/2012/05/a-majority-of-state-legislators-may-have-two-years-or-less-of-experience-in-2013.html. Accessed January 7, 2013.

TABLE 10.1: Success rates of women state legislative candidates, vary across election type, party, and year of election

	2002	2004	2006	2008	2010	2012
Incumbents						
Democrats	91.7% (725)	96.5% (678)	98.7% (775)	97.7% (809)	80.7% (892)	83.3% (791)
Republicans	95.0% (421)	93.2% (444)	87.7% (423)	92.1% (353)	98.6% (351)	84.0% (487)
Challengers						
Democrats	12.6% (373)	14.3% (391)	17.2% (437)	11.6% (406)	1.9% (323)	16.4% (402)
Republicans	19.1% (262)	6.8% (263)	3.8% (262)	6.7% (240)	25.0% (348)	6.4% (203)
Open Seats						
Democrats	46.2% (346)	45.3% (274)	56.2% (356)	57.6% (323)	41.5% (395)	51.3% (448)
Republicans	55.2% (210)	56.8% (155)	40.9% (164)	47.0% (185)	65.0% (214)	50.8% (242)

Source: CAWP 2012, "Women Candidates for State Legislatures: Election Results 1992–2012." Cell entries are percentage of women candidates who won their races with *N* in parentheses.

situated men once incumbency is taken into account. The odds of winning a race depend much more on the type of race than on gender because incumbents – regardless of gender – are strongly favored over challengers. Newcomers are much more likely to gain office if there is an open-seat race without an incumbent. However, party affiliation matters as well; most legislative seats are likely to favor one party over the other, and if a seat is sufficiently safe for one of the major political parties, the other party might not even field a candidate.

Although the incumbency advantage benefits both men and women, incumbency disproportionately affects groups of relative newcomers – including women – because most incumbents are men. Incumbency can therefore be considered an institutional constraint on women's representation (see Richard Fox, Chapter 7, this volume). Because most incumbent legislators are men, women are more likely to increase their presence in office by running for open seats rather than as challengers trying to unseat incumbents.

The second aspect of elections apparent in 2010 and 2012 is the importance of the interaction of gender with political party. Democratic women candidates greatly outnumber Republican women candidates (see Table 10.1). In 2010, for example, 1,610 Democratic women ran in the general election, whereas only 913 Republican women did so. Because most women candidates run as incumbents, it is not surprising that the party gap among women has persisted with each election cycle.

Despite the strong advantage that women candidates have as incumbents compared with challengers or open-seat candidates, the incumbency advantage can be reduced depending on how the parties fare nationally. While Table 10.1 confirms the incumbency advantage, it also shows that changes in the major parties' fortunes have serious consequences for the overall level of women's representation because of the party gap among women. The 2010 election featured a strong national Republican tide and high turnover compared to earlier years. Republicans benefitted from the rise of Tea Party enthusiasts and backlash against President Barack Obama's 2008 election and policy agenda, and many of the 2008 Democratic gains in the state legislatures were erased.[9]

For both Democratic and Republican women, 2010 women candidates running as incumbents were most likely to win their races compared with open-seat and challenger candidates. But Republican women incumbents fared better than Democratic women incumbents, consistent with the national conditions that favored the Republican Party. In 2010, 80.7 percent of Democratic women and 98.6 percent of Republican women won their races when they ran as incumbents, 1.9 percent of Democratic women and 25.0 percent of Republican women won their races as challengers, and 41.5 percent of Democratic and 65.0 percent of Republican women open-seat candidates won.

In 2012, the gender imbalance between the two parties continued; 1,641 Democratic women ran compared with only 932 Republican women. Unlike the 2010 election, Democratic women and Republican women who ran as incumbents fared similarly (see Table 10.1). The success rate for open-seat candidates was also similar for women of the two parties. Meanwhile, Democratic women who ran as challengers were more likely to win than Republican women who ran as challengers.

Thus, because Democratic women are a majority of women state legislators, a bad election year for Democrats is likely to mean a bad year for women state legislators (see Figure 10.2). In this case, the raw number of Democratic women holding office declined from 1,267 in 2009 to 1,060 in 2011. In contrast, the raw number of Republican women ticked upward after the 2010 election, reversing a slow decline that had been occurring since 1997 (see Figure 10.2). Republican women gained state legislative seats: they held 516 seats in 2009 but 672 in 2011. The 2010 losses suffered by the Democratic Party help explain why women's 2011

[9] Karen Hansen. 2010. Red Tide: A GOP Wave Washed Over State Legislatures on Election Day. *State Legislatures*. December 14–17; Theda Skocpol and Vanessa Williamson. 2012. *The Tea Party and the Remaking of Republican Conservatism*. New York: Oxford University Press.

Figure 10.2: Democratic women state legislators outnumber Republican women state legislators.

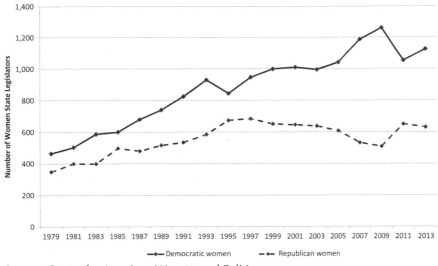

Source: Center for American Women and Politics.

representation represented a slight decline from the previous year – despite a record high of 2,537 women candidates running for the legislature in 2010.

Although Republican women's numbers did increase between 2010 and 2011, it is imperative to acknowledge that recent elections have mainly been missed opportunities for Republican women in light of their party's dramatic gains and the fact that the Republican Party largely controlled the state legislative redistricting process in the states. In 2010, the Republican Party gained 721 seats and claimed majorities in 22 additional legislative chambers.[10] Yet, as a percentage of Republican state legislators, women simply did not share equally in the dramatic gains of their party.[11]

The flagging level of women's representation overall – evident in Figure 10.1 – is largely driven by the fact that Republican women state legislators are not gaining as a proportion of all Republican legislators. Figure 10.3 shows that growth in officeholding is occurring for Democratic women, while Republican women have faced a leveling off in

[10] NCSL. 2010. Republicans make historic gains. http://www.ncsl.org/legislatures-elections/elections/statevote-2010-archive.aspx. Accessed January 5, 2013.

[11] Carroll and Sanbonmatsu, 2013.

Figure 10.3: Democratic women, but not Republican women, are a growing share of their party's state legislators.

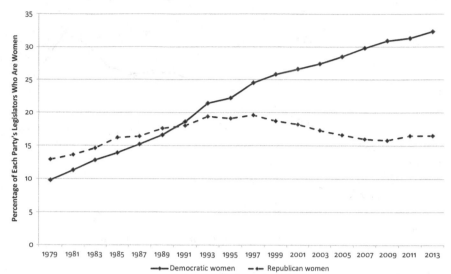

Source: Center for American Women and Politics, Council of State Governments, and National Conference of State Legislatures.

their share of Republican state legislative seats since the mid 1990s (see Figure 10.3). This party difference puts a spotlight on internal Republican Party politics, suggesting that insufficient recruitment is occurring on the Republican side of the aisle.[12]

The 2008 CAWP Recruitment Study also found that most legislators reach office with party support and that among those who cited recruitment as important for their first candidacy, the largest group of recruiters cited was party leaders and elected officials. Meanwhile, many legislators cite recruitment as the single most important reason they sought their current seat. Given that parties are more commonly credited with recruitment than are organizations and that women are more likely to reach the legislature as a result of recruitment than are men, both parties could be reaching out more to encourage women to seek state legislative office.

The third important lesson from the 2010 and 2012 elections, which is related to party, is the encouraging news that the presence of women of

---

[12] See also Laurel Elder. 2012. The Partisan Gap Among Women State Legislators. *Journal of Women, Politics & Policy* 33: 65–86. She finds that the strength of the Republican Party in a state's electorate is negatively associated with the presence of Republican women among Republican legislators.

color as state legislators continues to trend upward (see Wendy Smooth, Chapter 6, this volume). In 2013, women of color are 20.5 percent of all women legislators, up slightly from 19.5 percent in 2009. Most minority women state legislators are Democrats ($N = 341$), with fewer than two dozen identifying as Republican ($N = 21$). Women of color constitute 30.3 percent of all Democratic women legislators in 2013 – a sizable proportion. Because most women of color are elected from majority-minority legislative districts, the parties could play a leading role in encouraging more women of color to pursue electoral opportunities beyond these districts in order to expand their numbers.[13]

The fourth lesson about 2010 and 2012 is that women remain much less likely than men to run for the state legislatures. For example, there were more than 10,000 candidates competing for more than 6,000 state legislative seats in 2012, and only about 2,400 women ran in the general election for those seats.[14] While many women took advantage of the 2012 election's open-seat opportunities, exceeding the number of women who ran as open-seat candidates in the 2002 redistricting cycle, the number of women open-seat candidates in 2012 was lower than the number in 1992 (see Table 10.1).

The scarcity of women running in open-seat state legislative contests is clear from term-limit studies. Fifteen states have laws that place limits on the number of terms that individuals can serve in their legislatures. Many expected that term limits would open doors for women and yield a dramatic increase in women officeholders through the creation of open seats. However, women have not necessarily taken advantage of these openings. And incumbents who are termed out include both women and men, meaning that women who might be interested in seeking reelection are prevented from doing so because of term limits.

The gender gap in political ambition is another important factor in understanding the underrepresentation of women candidates. Women potential candidates in the social eligibility pool, with the right backgrounds and occupations for launching a candidacy, are much less likely than men to even consider running for office. Socialization processes

---

[13] Carol Hardy-Fanta, Pei-te Lien, Dianne M. Pinderhughes, and Christine M. Sierra. 2006. Gender, Race, and Descriptive Representation in the United States: Findings from the Gender and Multicultural Leadership Project. *Journal of Women Politics & Policy* 28: 7–41; Carroll and Sanbonmatsu, 2013.

[14] Tim Storey. 2012. Expect Turnover – But Not a Wave – In State Legislative Races. www.centerforpolitics.org/crystalball/articles/expect-turnover-but-not-a-wave-in-state-legislative-races/. Accessed January 9, 2013.

remain gendered, leading men to be more likely than women to consider themselves qualified for public office.[15]

The outsize role of candidate recruitment for women makes the roles of parties, interest groups, and political action committees (PACs) that much more important to understanding women's presence in the state legislatures. And gender-specific efforts are underway to encourage more women to seek office and provide them with campaign training. For example, The 2012 Project created state coalitions across the country in order to identify and encourage new women candidates. Many organizations hold training programs, and some, such as CAWP's Ready to Run™ and Emerge America, are specifically designed to help women enter politics.[16] Such programs may be especially important for women of color, who typically have fewer role models in their states compared with white women.

STATE VARIATION: DIFFERENCES ACROSS STATES IN WOMEN'S STATE LEGISLATIVE OFFICEHOLDING

Among the most intriguing aspects of women's state legislative experiences are the vast differences across the fifty states. And these differences in women's relationship to politics by state stretch back through U.S. history. For example, the first women to win seats as state representatives did so in Colorado in the 1890s, long before the national fight for suffrage was won. Utah is known for having the first woman state senator. The first woman of color to be elected to a state legislature – Cora Belle Reynolds Anderson, a Native American woman – held office in Michigan in the 1920s.

States continue to build unique histories with regard to women in politics. As more women run for office, there are more opportunities for women potential candidates, voters, parties, donors, interest groups, and the media to become used to women candidates and officeholders. But some states are dramatically outpacing others. As Table 10.2

[15] Jennifer L. Lawless and Richard L. Fox. 2010. *It Still Takes a Candidate: Why Women Don't Run for Office*. Revised Edition. New York: Cambridge University Press. See also Richard Fox, Chapter 7, this volume.
[16] http://www.cawp.rutgers.edu/education_training/2012Project/about2012.php. Accessed September 3, 2013; Valerie Hennings. 2011. *Civic Selves: Gender, Candidate Training Programs, and Envisioning Political Participation*. Ph.D. dissertation. University of Wisconsin, Madison; Kira Sanbonmatsu, forthcoming. Electing Women of Color: The Role of Campaign Trainings. *Journal of Women, Politics, & Policy*.

TABLE 10.2: Women's representation varies across states

Over 30%	25%–30%	20–24%	15–19%	Under 15%
Colorado	Washington	Idaho	Michigan	Alabama
Vermont	New Jersey	Iowa	Kentucky	Oklahoma
Arizona	Nevada	Kansas	Pennsylvania	South Carolina
Hawaii	Alaska (tied)	Ohio	Tennessee	Louisiana
Minnesota	Connecticut (tied)	South Dakota	Virginia	
New Hampshire	Maine	Georgia	Arkansas (tied)	
Illinois	Oregon	North Carolina	North Dakota (tied)	
Maryland	New Mexico	New York	Wyoming	
	Rhode Island	Missouri	West Virginia	
	Montana	Indiana	Utah	
	Delaware	Nebraska (tied)	Mississippi	
	Massachusetts	Texas (tied)		
	California (tied)			
	Florida (tied)			
	Wisconsin (tied)			

Source: Center for American Women and Politics. States are listed from high to low in each column for the percentage of women in state legislatures in 2013. States marked "tied" have the same percentage of women.

demonstrates, the national statistic that women are 24.1 percent of state legislators belies tremendous variation subnationally. In some states, women are a substantial share of the legislature and comprise more than 30 percent of legislators; in fact, in two states – Colorado and Vermont – women's representation exceeds 40 percent. In contrast, in other states, such as Louisiana, South Carolina, and Oklahoma, women are not even 15 percent of the legislators (see Table 10.2).

One implication is that the challenges and opportunities that women face in politics seem to depend on place. Running for the legislature as a woman candidate is a novelty in some states but commonplace in others. These differences across states have implications for the costs and benefits that women potential candidates weigh as they consider a state legislative bid, as well as the likelihood that parties and interest groups will recruit women candidates.[17]

To some extent, this cross-state pattern can be explained systematically. For example, women tend to be more likely to seek and hold office in states in which the public is more liberal in outlook.[18] More liberal

---

[17] Kira Sanbonmatsu. 2006. *Where Women Run: Gender and Party in the American States*. Ann Arbor: University of Michigan Press.

[18] Kira Sanbonmatsu. 2006. State Elections: Where Do Women Run? Where Do Women Win? In *Gender and Elections: Shaping the Future of Gender and American Politics*, ed. Susan

states are more accepting of women in nontraditional roles, with implications for voters', party leaders', and women's attitudes. In states such as Massachusetts, where the public is fairly liberal, the viability of women state legislative candidates is not an issue, whereas in other states, such as Alabama, voters, parties, the media, and interest groups are much less familiar with women candidates.

Being a woman may be perceived as an electoral disadvantage in some states – particularly in places where women have not held office in large numbers.[19] But in other states, being a woman candidate may be an advantage, increasing the likelihood that women will be recruited to run for office. And while some stereotypes disadvantage women, other stereotypes give women an edge. For example, voters perceive women as more honest and compassionate and better on education and women's issues, although voters perceive men as better leaders and better able to handle issues such as crime.[20]

States in the South typically lag behind other states. For example, the bottom ten of CAWP's fifty-state-ranking is filled with Southern states. Traditional gender roles, conservative attitudes, and a more closed political system have hampered women's election to office. But region is not the only factor. Legislative professionalism also seems to matter. Some state legislatures are similar to the U.S. Congress in that service resembles a year-round, full-time job. For example, Pennsylvania legislators earn about $82,000 annually and serve year-round; similarly, California legislators earn more than $95,000 annually. In contrast, New Hampshire legislators earn just $100 per year. Legislators in the legislatures that meet part time with little or no compensation often pride themselves on being citizen-legislators.[21]

Carroll and Richard Fox. New York: Cambridge University Press, 189–214. See also Barbara Norrander and Clyde Wilcox. 1998. The Geography of Gender Power: Women in State Legislatures. In *Women and Elective Office: Past, Present, and Future*, ed. Sue Thomas and Clyde Wilcox. New York: Oxford University Press, 103–117; Kevin Arceneaux. 2001. The "Gender Gap" in State Legislative Representation: New Data to Tackle an Old Question. *Political Research Quarterly* 54: 143–160.

[19] Kira Sanbonmatsu. 2006. Do Parties Know that "Women Win"? Party Leader Beliefs about Women's Electoral Chances. *Politics & Gender* 2: 431–450.

[20] Leonie Huddy and Nayda Terkildsen. 1993. Gender Stereotypes and the Perception of Male and Female Candidates. *American Journal of Political Science* 37: 119–147; Kira Sanbonmatsu. 2002. Gender Stereotypes and Vote Choice. *American Journal of Political Science* 46: 20–34.

[21] The categories of professionalism are taken from NCSL. Full- and Part-Time Legislatures. http://www.ncsl.org/legislatures-elections/legislatures/full-and-part-time-legislatures .aspx. Accessed January 8, 2013.

Among the states with the very highest state legislative representation of women, none has a full-time, professional legislature. Thus, women seem less likely to be successful in states with more professional legislatures, perhaps because the desirability of the office increases competition and may put women – relative newcomers in electoral politics – at a disadvantage. At the same time, many of the states with the lowest levels of women's representation have the most citizen-styled legislatures, indicating that "hybrid" states with a moderate level of professionalism are best for women. Among the top ten states for women state legislators, the most common type of legislature is a hybrid of professional and citizen.

Studies also show that states with multimember rather than single-member districts have higher levels of women's representation. All congressional districts are single member, and single-member districts are the norm for state legislatures, meaning that only one legislator is elected per district. But in some states, more than one legislator is elected from each district. Arizona, Maryland, New Hampshire, Vermont, and Washington, which are among the states with the highest proportion of women legislators, all have multimember districts.[22] Women may be more likely to run if they are part of a team of candidates. Alternatively, voters may seek gender balance when they have the opportunity to elect more than one legislator to represent them.

Finally, the pattern of women's officeholding can be explained by state differences in the role of political parties. Parties actively seek out candidates for the legislature, encouraging some to seriously consider running and promising them resources while discouraging others from throwing their hats into the ring. States with stronger party organizations tend to have fewer women candidates and fewer women serving in the legislature, making the parties' recruitment and gatekeeping practices central to understanding the cross-state variation in women's officeholding. The idea that there is an "old boys network" that favors male candidates is not uncommon in some states. When party leaders look for new candidates, they tend to look for candidates like themselves and people they know personally, such as their business associates or golf partners.[23] Despite dramatic changes in gender roles, social networks remain segregated by gender.

[22] Peverill Squire and Gary F. Moncrief. 2010. *State Legislatures Today: Politics Under the Domes*. Boston: Longman Publishers.
[23] Sanbonmatsu, 2006, *Where Women Run*. David Niven. 1998. Party Elites and Women Candidates: The Shape of Bias. *Women and Politics* 19(2): 57–80.

In some states, concerns about the viability of women candidates can lessen the chances that women will be recruited. Women may not be selected for key state legislative races if party leaders, intent on winning, believe women are disadvantaged.[24] Elsewhere, party leaders may have no concerns about voter reaction to women candidates, and women may very well be drafted to run for the legislature. Party leader doubts about women candidates are typically unwarranted, with voters more open minded than party leaders. A Pennsylvania woman state legislator commented, "I think voters are more used to women than the party leaders are."[25]

STATEWIDE EXECUTIVE OFFICE ELECTIONS

Governors are typically more visible and better known to voters than are state legislators. Beyond governors, there is a vast array of other statewide executive elective officeholders including lieutenant governors, secretaries of state, state treasurers, and attorneys general. In fact, there are a total of 320 statewide elective executive positions. Running for the governor's mansion is much less common for women than running for other positions such as state legislator, and studies show that voters may be more comfortable with women in legislative positions than in executive ones.[26] Gubernatorial candidates must persuade supporters, parties, and voters that they have the requisite leadership skills and can command authority because power rests with one individual. Running for statewide office also tends to be more competitive and more expensive compared with state legislative races.

Although the first women who served as governors did so in the 1920s, their officeholding experiences were unusual. Nellie Tayloe Ross served as governor of Wyoming, winning a special election to replace her deceased husband. Miriam "Ma" Ferguson of Texas served as governor of her state, serving as a surrogate for her husband, who could not run for another term. It was not until 1974 that a woman won a gubernatorial election in her own right. In U.S. history, only thirty-five women from

[24] Sanbonmatsu 2006. *Where Women Run.*
[25] http://www.philly.com/philly/hp/news_update/20120728_Pennsylvania_lags_in_number_of_female_legislators_1.html. Accessed September 3, 2013.
[26] Leonie Huddy and Nayda Terkildsen. 1993. The Consequences of Gender Stereotypes for Women Candidates at Different Levels and Types of Office. *Political Research Quarterly* 46: 503–25; Kelly Dittmar. 2012. *Campaigns as Gendered Institutions: Stereotypes and Strategy in Statewide Races.* Ph. D. dissertation. Rutgers University.

twenty-six states have ever served as governor, and only twenty-three of these women were elected in their own right. The record for women serving as governors simultaneously is nine, which occurred in 2004 and 2007.

Women have had more success winning the office of lieutenant governor. Lieutenant governors are elected on statewide ballots in forty-three states. In the 1990s, balancing the gubernatorial ticket by gender seemed to be an attractive electoral strategy, especially for the Republican Party, which tends to fare better with men voters than with women.[27] But this strategy has apparently declined in popularity. A high of nineteen women served as lieutenant governors in 2000, but only eleven do so in 2013.

Because of the importance of state politics and policies, state executive officeholders are themselves important decision makers. Beyond the governor and lieutenant governor, most states also have a secretary of state and state treasurer, with other positions including such offices as auditor, comptroller, chief agriculture official, and chief education official. Not only are these positions challenging to achieve because of the widespread support needed from across the state, but research shows that statewide offices are themselves gendered. Women are more likely to seek offices consistent with voters' gender stereotypes; they are more likely to run for "feminine offices" and less likely to seek "masculine offices."[28] For example, because education is a policy area in which voters typically see women politicians as more competent than men, the position of state superintendent of education could be considered a feminine office. Party leaders may be particularly interested in recruiting women for feminine offices, or perhaps women are more likely to put themselves forward to run for these positions.

THE 2010 AND 2012 STATEWIDE ELECTIONS: SLOW AND UNEVEN PROGRESS

A closer look at recent elections shows that progress for women running statewide has been slow over time and uneven across states. As Figure 10.4 shows, similar to the trend for state legislative officeholding, recent elections have seen little year-to-year change in the proportion of

---

[27] Richard L. Fox and Zoe M. Oxley. 2005. Does Running with a Woman Help? Evidence from U.S. Gubernatorial Elections. *Politics & Gender* 1: 525–546.

[28] Richard L. Fox and Zoe M. Oxley. 2003. Gender Stereotyping in State Executive Elections: Candidate Selection and Success. *Journal of Politics* 65: 833–850.

Figure 10.4: The proportion of women serving in statewide positions has declined since 2001.

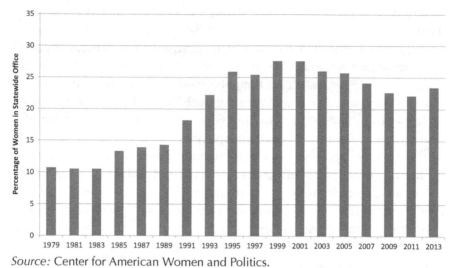

Source: Center for American Women and Politics.

statewide officials who are women; in fact, since 2001, the trend is one of decline. Women are just 23.4 percent of all statewide elective executives, and just 10 percent of governors are women in 2013. The dearth of women governors has implications for the presence of women presidential candidates, because major party presidential nominees are usually either governors or U.S. senators, and governors seem to be advantaged over senators in presidential elections.[29] Perhaps the best known female former governor is Sarah Palin of Alaska – the first Republican woman to have served as a vice presidential candidate.

What can be learned from the 2010 and 2012 statewide elections? In 2010, thirty-seven states had gubernatorial races, including twenty-three open-seat contests. Ten women won party nominations for governor, tying the 2002 record for women gubernatorial candidates. While one of the most high-profile races for governor occurred in California, featuring EBay executive Meg Whitman, a Republican, and resulted in a loss, other women made history that year. New Mexico, Oklahoma, and South Carolina all elected their first women governors, all Republicans. And two of those states represent firsts for women of color: Susana Martinez of New Mexico, who is Latina, and Nikki Haley of South Carolina, who is Asian

---

[29] Nate Silver. June 16, 2011. The Governors' Advantage in Presidential Races Is Bigger Than You Thought. *New York Times.* http://fivethirtyeight.blogs.nytimes.com/2011/06/15/the-governors-advantage-in-presidential-races-is-bigger-than-you-thought/.

American, are the first women of color ever to win gubernatorial office. An additional eighty-three women candidates ran for statewide offices other than governor in the 2010 general election – most of whom were Democrats (fifty-one Democrats compared with thirty-one Republicans).

Fewer statewide executive elections occur during presidential election years, meaning that 2010 saw many more statewide contests than did 2012.[30] In 2012, only four women were party nominees across the eleven gubernatorial seats up for election, including five open-seat contests. The one woman vying for an open seat, Maggie Hassan, a Democrat from New Hampshire, won her race. Hassan's victory contributed to one of the most compelling 2012 election stories. New Hampshire has long been a national leader for women's state legislative representation. But as a result of the 2012 election, New Hampshire had not only a woman governor but also two women U.S. Senators, and both of the state's U.S. House members are women. Governor Hassan observed: "There are lots of opportunities for women to pitch in, prove their competence and learn a lot about governing and the political process. We've had a very deep bench of women."[31]

Perhaps not surprisingly, those states in which women have been more successful gaining state legislative office are also the states in which women have been more successful gaining statewide office. Good examples are Arizona and New Mexico, which have often been at the forefront of both women's state legislative and statewide officeholding. Research has shown that women are more likely to enter gubernatorial primaries in states with more women state legislators and states with more favorable climates, such as a history of women's officeholding and high levels of women's educational attainment and labor force participation.[32]

A comprehensive study of the 2010 gubernatorial campaigns that featured women candidates looked "inside" the campaigns to shed light on the challenges that women face in statewide races.[33] This study found that gender can directly and indirectly shape the campaign strategies of both men and women in mixed-gender contests. Different strategies are perceived to be more effective for men and women candidates, creating campaign challenges that affect all candidates, but particularly women.

---

[30] A few states hold some statewide contests in odd-numbered years.

[31] Katharine Q. Seelye, January 2, 2013, From Congress to Halls of State, In New Hampshire, Women Rule, *New York Times*, p. A1, A13.

[32] Jason Harold Windett. 2011. State Effects and the Emergence and Success of Female Gubernatorial Candidates. *State Politics and Policy Quarterly* 11: 460–482.

[33] Dittmar, 2012.

TEXT BOX 10.1: Women making history, state by state

The 2012 election shattered a record, thanks to events in a small New England state: for the first time in U.S. history, women would make up a state's entire congressional delegation. Moreover, the state would be led by a female governor, meaning women filled all of the top offices. The history-making state was New Hampshire. Maggie Hassan won her bid for governor in 2012 and two women – Ann McLane Kuster and Carol Shea-Porter – won seats in the U.S. House of Representatives. Kuster and Shea-Porter joined sitting U.S. Senators Kelly Ayotte and Jeanne Shaheen.

It wasn't the first time that the progress of New Hampshire women in politics had attracted national attention. The state is well known for the high proportion of women serving in its legislature. Over the past three decades, New Hampshire has ranked among the nation's top five states for women's representation half the time.[34] Currently, New Hampshire ranks fifth, with women constituting nearly one-third of the legislature. The long history of women's officeholding in New Hampshire has given the state a "deep bench of women," according to Governor Hassan.[35] New Hampshire also lacks "a dominant old-boy network," according to Congresswoman Kuster, making for a more friendly environment for women candidates.[36] Several features of New Hampshire make this case unusual. First, state legislators only earn $100 per year, making legislative service more of a voluntary than professional activity. Second, New Hampshire's small population gives the state only two seats in the U.S. House of Representatives, making the feat of an all-female congressional delegation easier to attain compared to larger states with larger delegations. Still, the accomplishments of women in the Granite State are significant and can serve as a model for the rest of the nation.

A national survey of campaign consultants revealed that the success of self-presentation strategies, including professional dress and use of family in campaigns, and many issues and traits depend on whether the candidate is a woman or a man. Overall, it seems to be tougher for women candidates to demonstrate that they are prepared for high office.

The good news is that many women candidates have successfully overcome gender stereotypes and reached office. And this study found that the double binds that women candidates face as they pursue high office, including the way the candidate's family is portrayed during

---

[34] Center for American Women and Politics.
[35] Seelye, 2013, A13.
[36] Ibid.

the campaign, are changing. While women continue to confront "gendered terrain," the 2010 elections also provided a number of examples of women seeking to transform campaign norms and examples of women candidates using their status as women and as mothers to their advantage.[37]

Recent elections also confirm the continued importance of party in statewide officeholding. Interestingly, and unlike the party imbalance among women state legislators and members of Congress, an equal number of Democratic and Republican women hold statewide elective executive office in 2013. On the one hand, this speaks well of Republican women's accomplishments. On the other hand, though, Republican women could be even better represented. After all, among the thirty Republicans serving as governors in 2013, just four are women.[38] The picture is even worse for Democratic women, because only one of the nineteen Democratic governors is a woman. In the 2012 elections, forty-three women ran for statewide elective office, the vast majority of whom were Democrats. Democratic women also comprised a much larger share of Democratic candidates for these offices – 38.0 percent – than did Republican women (16.7 percent) among Republican candidates.

One factor slowing growth in the proportion of women in statewide elective executive offices is the challenge faced by women of color. Women of color are only 12 of the nation's 320 statewide positions, or 3.4 percent, which is far below their proportion of the population. Despite the growth in the number of minority women state legislators, they remain a largely untapped pool of statewide candidates.

CONCLUSION

Women continue to make progress in the states. Each election cycle brings a new first or record for women in at least some respects. While the percentages of women holding state legislative and statewide elective executive positions are not at historic highs, women did make some progress in recent elections. Two women of color have won election to the office of governor, and more women of color are serving in state legislatures than ever before. In New Hampshire, women hold all of the congressional seats and a woman is governor. New Hampshire is unusual.

---

[37] Dittmar, 2012, 15.
[38] http://www.nga.org/cms/home/governors/elections/col2-content/past-election-information/2012-general-election-results.html. Accessed September 3, 2013.

Yet other states have strong histories of women's officeholding, and women's state legislative representation exceeds 30 percent in some places. And the 2010 elections set a record for the number of women competing for state legislative office.

At the same time, recent trends in the level of women's officeholding bode poorly for the future. The dearth of women in state legislative and statewide positions and the lack of growth in women's representation over the course of the past decade have implications for the size of the pool of women poised to launch congressional, statewide, and presidential bids. The problems we are seeing for women's officeholding in the states are much more pronounced on the Republican side than on the Democratic side. Women's share of Democratic state legislative seats continues to trend upward. But Republican women, despite the recent successes of their party, have not kept up.

Numbers matter. Women's voices are likely to be missing from legislative leadership teams and legislative committees without a substantial proportion of women in the legislature. Given the tremendous diversity among women as a group, including party diversity, more women need to be elected in the states in order to ensure that all women's voices are heard.[39] Concerted efforts by parties, groups, and informal networks to increase women's representation could increase women's officeholding, given the importance of recruitment for women's candidacies. Recruitment is especially needed to enhance Republican women's officeholding, as well as to spur the election of more women of color from both parties to statewide positions.

One issue that warrants more attention in the future is the escalating cost of campaigns. State legislative research on women's campaign finance situation is limited, resulting in mixed findings.[40] However, CAWP's research found that women state legislators are much more likely

---

[39] See Tracy L. Osborn, 2012, on the role of party in state legislative behavior. *How Women Represent Women: Political Parties, Gender, and Representation in the State Legislatures.* New York: Oxford University Press.

[40] Brian Werner. 1997. Financing the Campaigns of Women Candidates and their Opponents: Evidence from Three States, 1982–1990. *Women & Politics* 19: 81–97; Hogan, Robert E. 2007. The Effects of Candidate Gender on Campaign Spending in State Legislative Elections. *Social Science Quarterly* 88: 1092–1105; Timothy Werner and Kenneth R. Mayer. 2007. Public Election Funding, Competition, and Candidate Gender. *PS: Political Science and Politics* 40: 661–667; Joel A. Thompson, Gary F. Moncrief, and Keith E. Hamm. 1998. Gender, Candidate Attributes, and Campaign Contributions. In *Campaign Finance in State Legislative Elections*, ed. Joel A. Thompson and Gary F. Moncrief. Washington, DC: Congressional Quarterly, 117–138.

than their male counterparts to see gender inequality in fundraising. As spending on state elections rises and the spending of outside groups has increased with the *Citizens United* decision, these trends may hinder women's progress in state politics.[41]

Women should find encouragement in public opinion polls showing support for a higher proportion of women in office than currently exists; the public would like to see more women in office and believes that women are better able to handle some issues than men, creating favorable opportunities for women candidates.[42] Because there are more than enough women who can seek state legislative and statewide office, there is no time like the present for more women to seek office and play a larger role in state policy debates.

---

[41] See Lawless and Fox, 2010, on a gender gap in perceptions about fundraising among socially eligible Americans.

[42] Kira Sanbonmatsu and Kathleen Dolan. 2009. Gender Stereotypes and Attitudes Toward Gender Balance in Government. *American Politics Research*. 37: 409–428; Kathleen Dolan. 2010. The Impact of Gender Stereotyped Evaluations on Support for Women Candidates. *Political Behavior* 32: 69–88.

Index